al-Ahkam as-Sultaniyyah
The Laws of Islamic Governance

by
Abu'l-Hasan 'Ali ibn Muhammad ibn Habib al-Basri
al-Baghdadi al-Mawardi (d. 450 AH)

Translated by
Dr Asadullah Yate PhD

S. T. Shareef.

Ta-Ha Publishers Ltd.
1 Wynne Road
London SW9 0BB
United Kingdom

Published by:
Ta-Ha Publishers Ltd.
1 Wynne Road
London SW9 0BB

Translated by: Dr Asadullah Yate
General Editor: Afsar Siddiqui
Edited by: ᶜAbdassamad Clarke
Cover Design by: Yahya Cattanach

British Library Cataloguing in Publication Data
Yate, Asadullah
Al-Ahkam as-Sultaniyyah
I. Title

ISBN 1 897940 41 6

Typeset by: ᶜAbdassamad Clarke.
Printed and bound by: Deluxe Printers, London.

Contents

Foreword

Al-Ahkam as-Sultaniyyah of 'Ali ibn Muhammad al-Mawardi is an important handbook written in the fifth century A.H. covering all the various aspects of the deen of Islam which are the concern and responsibility of the Khalifah, his amirs, his wazirs (ministers) and deputies. The rights and duties of these persons are expounded in detail – both as a reminder to persons already active in such capacities and as a guide to those who are new to such offices.

This work affords insights into aspects of the deen that have all but vanished in the twentieth century of the Christian Era – matters, for example, concerning the collection and distribution of zakah, the payment of jizyah, the management of markets, the inspection of weights and measures and the overseeing of the minting of gold and silver, the organisation of the army, its provisioning, the distribution of booty, the management of the frontier Ribats, the management of natural resources, penal law and the appointment of judges empowered to deal not only with marriages and inheritance but with all aspects of Islamic law, including the regulation of fiscal, financial and mercantile matters mentioned above.

Each chapter and section of the work is amply illustrated by quotations from the Qur'an, the hadith and the sunnah of the Prophet, may the peace and blessings of Allah be upon him, and further testimony and support is given by examples of legal and political precedent from the lives of leading figures in the history of Islam. This work will provide a refreshing antidote to the teaching of modernists who, perceiving the deen of Islam to be threatened, insist on a radical rewriting of its parameters – rather than a return to the sources – as the only way forward.

It should be noted, however, that the work (written in the first half of the fifth century A.H.) depicts a stage in the development of Islam which, even at this early date, is manifesting a strong tendency towards empire with all its connotations of central government and extended, at times complicated, bureaucracy: to take but two examples, the divine order to, **"command the good and forbid the evil"** (Qur'an 3: 104), which at the time of the Prophet, may the peace and blessings of Allah be upon him, was understood as a responsibility of each and every man, has now become institutionalised into the concept of *hisbah* and the obligation upon all to maintain law and order has now become the domain of the "forces of law and order," i.e. the state police.

Words such as Dar al-Islam, Dar al-Harb, bait al-mal, mushrik, kafir and the like which have no satisfactory equivalents in English, and which are quickly gaining currency amongst English-speaking Muslims globally, are used throughout the translation. For in depth definitions of their meanings, recourse should be had to the writings of Shaykh 'Abdal Qadir al-Murabit and to the works of translation undertaken under his guidance, especially, for example, his *Root Islamic Education* and the translations of Aisha at-Tarjumana (Imam Malik's *Muwatta* and Qadi 'Iyad's *ash-Shifa*). A simple glossary of terms is, however, appended to this work.

Dr Asadullah Yate

"And if you rule between people then rule with justice"
(The Noble Qur'an, Surah al-Ma'idah: 42)

Introduction

In the name of Allah, the Merciful, the Compassionate, and may the peace and blessings of Allah be on Muhammad ﷺ and on his family and companions.

The Shaykh the Imam Abu'l-Hasan al-Mawardi says:

Praise belongs to Allah who has clarified the features of the deen for us, bestowed on us the gift of the clear Book, laid down the laws, and differentiated between the halal and the haram for us. Whatever He has imposed as law on this world he has stipulated for the benefit of people and by it has made firm the foundations of the Truth; He has entrusted to those in authority the best outcome regarding what has already been predetermined and has made the best judgement regarding the management of affairs: so to Him belongs all praise with respect to what He has predetermined and arranged and may His peace and blessings be on His Messenger, His Prophet Muhammad, the Prophet who has executed His order and who has fulfilled His rights, and also on his family and his companions.

As the laws of governance are more applicable to those in authority but because these latter, being occupied with politics and management, are prevented from examining these laws as they are mixed with all the other laws, I have devoted a special book to them. Thus in response to the person to whom my obedience is due in this affair, I have made known to him the madhhabs of the fuqaha' so that he sees both that his rights are respected and that his duties are fulfilled and that he honours the dictates of justice in their execution and aspires to equity in establishing his claims and

7

in the fulfilment of others' claims. I ask Allah, the Sublime, that He may grant the best possible aid and I desire of Him that He accord success and guidance by Himself and He is enough and sufficient for me.

Allah, may His power be radiant, has delegated a leader to the Ummah who stands in as a successor to prophethood, and has encompassed the affair of the nation by him; He has handed over the affair of political management to him so that management of affairs may proceed from the legitimate deen and so that speech may be contained in a unanimous opinion and is adopted by all the people. Imamate is thus a principle on which the foundations of the nation are established and by which the public interest of the Ummah is maintained: by it the good ordering of matters of public interest ensures the stability of affairs in general and by it other particular or specialised administrations arise. It is therefore necessary to first present the rules governing Imamate before any other rule of governance and to mention what pertains in particular to an examination of these rules before any other examination of the deen so that all further rules of administration may be classified accordingly in their corresponding or analogous sections.

This book of the laws of governance and the various administrations relative to the deen is comprised of twenty chapters:

1. The contract of Imamate; 2. The appointment of wazirs; 3. The establishment of amirate in a country; 4. The amirate of jihad; 5. Wars waged in the public interest within Dar al-Islam; 6. The administration of the judiciary; 7. The court of redress for grievances, injustices and misdeeds; 8. The niqabah-judiciary for those of noble lineage; 9. The imamate of the prayers; 10. The administration of the Hajj; 11. The administration of the zakah; 12. The division of booty and plunder; 13. The imposition of the jizyah and kharaj taxes; 14. Differences in judicial practice in different regions; 15. The reviving of abandoned or "dead" land and water resources; 16. Reserves (*hima*) and places of communal use; 17. Laws governing grants of land and conces-

sions; 18. The establishment of the diwan and its rules; 19. The laws governing crime and wrongdoing; 20. The laws governing public order (*hisbah*).

Chapter 1

The Contract of Imamate

Imamate is prescribed to succeed prophethood as a means of protecting the deen and of managing the affairs of this world. There is a consensus of opinion that the person who discharges the responsibilities of this position must take on the contract of Imamate of the Ummah – although Asam, exceptionally, differs in this matter. There is a difference of opinion, however, as to its obligation, that is, as whether it is obligatory for rational reasons or because it is prescribed in the shari'ah. One group of fuqaha says that it is obligatory for rational reasons because of the natural inclination of men of sound mind to submit to the authority of a leader who thereby prevents mutual injustice and who decides between men in cases of dispute and quarrel – for without governance, disorder and barbaric behaviour would arise amongst the wanton and lawless. As the pre-Islamic poet, al-Afwah al-Awdi has said in his poem:

There is no benefit to a leaderless people when disorder reigns, and they will never have a leader if the ignorant amongst them leads.

Another group says that it is obligatory because of the shari'ah rather than for rational reasons: the Imam carries out the affairs of the shari'ah and it is rationally conceivable that he undertake this Imamate as a form of worship without the option of being able to refuse it; thus the intellect is not instrumental in rendering it obligatory.

The intellect obliges each person of sane mind to avoid mutual injustices and the breaking of social ties, and to fulfil the exigences of justice by dealing equitably with people and by maintaining social contacts: this he organises by means of his own intellect and not someone else's intellect. It is the Law, however, which has delegated affairs to those who wield authority over them in matters of the deen – Allah, may He be exalted, has said: **"O you who believe, obey Allah and obey the Messenger and those in authority amongst you"** (Qur'an 4: 62). Thus He has imposed on us obedience to those in authority, that is those who have the command over us. Hisham ibn 'Urwah has related from Abu Salih from Abu Hurairah that the Messenger of Allah, may Allah bless him and grant him peace, said: "After me governors will rule over you and those who are upright will rule you by their uprightness and those who are corrupt will rule you by their corruptness: listen to them and obey them in everything which is compatible with truth – if they are correct in their dealings then it will be to your benefit and theirs, and if they act incorrectly then that will still be to your benefit (in the next world) but will be held against them."

*

* *

Having established the obligation of Imamate it must then be known that it is incumbent in a social and collective way, like the jihad and the acquisition of knowledge – that is if one person who is competent in the matter takes it up, the obligation is removed from the rest of the community; if no one takes it up, two parties may be distinguished as responsible for making this choice from among the people: the first, those who are worthy of choosing an Imam for the Ummah, and the second, those who themselves are worthy of the office of Imamate. No pressure is to be applied, and no sense of negligence is to be ascribed, to anyone else outside of these two parties regarding the choosing of an Imam. Once these two parties have been distinguished from amongst the Ummah with respect to the election of the Imam, it is necessary to assess each of the two parties according to the conditions which are binding in this matter.

There are three conditions regarding those eligible to make the choice: **1.** That they be just and fulfil all the conditions implied in this quality; **2.** That they possess a knowledge by which they may comprehend who has a right to the Imamate and that they fulfil all the conditions implied by this knowledge; **3.** That they possess the insight and wisdom which will lead them to choose the person who is most fitting for the Imamate and who is the most upright and knowledgeable with respect to the management of the offices of administration. Those living in the country of the Imam do not possess any advantages over those living in other countries: it is rather that someone resident in the country of the Imam contracts to elect the Imam by custom not by any legal imposition of the shari'ah; moreover such residents will come to know of the death of the Imam before people from other countries and usually the person who is most fitting for the succession is to be found in the country of the Imam.

There are seven conditions regarding those suited to the Imamate: **1.** Justice together with all its conditions; **2.** Knowledge which equips them for ijtihad in unforeseen matters and for arriving at relevant judgements; **3.** Good health in their faculties of hearing, sight and speech such that they may arrive at a sound assessment of whatever they perceive; **4.** Sound in limb, free of any deficiency which might prevent them from normal movement; **5.** A judgement capable of organising the people and managing the offices of administration; **6.** Courage and bravery enabling them to defend the territory of Islam and to mount jihad against the enemy; **7.** Of the family of the Quraysh, because of the text (of a prophetic hadith) on the matter and by virtue of consensus. No credibility should be given to the opinion of Dirar who is alone in saying that the post is open to all: Abu Bakr as-Siddiq, may Allah be pleased with him, used the testimony of the Prophet, may the peace and blessings of Allah be upon him, against the Ansar on the occasion of Saqifah when the latter defended the succession of Sa'd ibn 'Ubadah to whom they had given allegiance, in his saying, "The Imams are of the Quraysh." As a result of this the Ansar renounced their exclusive claim to this Imamate and renounced the claim to share in the rights of the Quraysh explicit in their saying, "From among us an Imam and from among you an Imam" – submitting thereby to this narration and affirming its content and accepting the following reply of Abu Bakr, "From us the amirs and from you the wazirs." The Prophet, may the peace and blessings be upon him, said: "Give precedence to the Quraysh and do not put others before them." There is not the least doubt or controversy attached to this impeccable text.

Imamate comes into being in two ways: the first of these is by the election of those of power and influence, and the second is by the delegation of the previous Imam.

As for its formation by the election of the people of power, the 'ulama, according to the different madhhabs, have different opinions as to the number of persons needed in the formation of the Imamate. One group says that it can only be conferred by way of the majority of those of power and influence in each country, such that acceptance is general and submission to the Imamate is by a consensus; this madhhab is rejected by the oath of allegiance to Abu Bakr, may Allah be pleased with him, that is to a succession arrived at by way of the election of only those who were present: they made the oath of allegiance to him and did not expect any other person from outside to present himself for this election. Another group say that the minimum number of persons that should gather for the formation of the Imamate is five or that it should be formed by one of them with the agreement of four others. They take two matters as their proof: the first that the oath of allegiance to Abu Bakr, may Allah be pleased with him, was made by five persons together and that the people followed them in this matter. These persons were 'Umar ibn al-Khattab, Abu 'Ubaidah ibn al-Jarrah, Usayd ibn Hudayr, Bashir ibn Sa'd and Salim the freed-slave of Abu Hudhayfah, may Allah be pleased with them. The second proof is that 'Umar set up a council of six persons so that one of them should take on the Imamate with the acceptance of the other five – and this is the opinion of most of the fuqaha and the mutakallimun from amongst the people of Basra. Others from amongst the 'ulama of Kufa say the Imamate comes into being by way of three persons, one of them taking charge by virtue of the acceptance of the other two such that there is one who decides the matter together with two witnesses, in the same way as the contract of marriage is made valid by the man in charge (the wali) and two witnesses. Another group says that it comes about by way of a single person as 'Abbas said to 'Ali, may the pleasure of Allah be upon them both, "Reach out your hand so that I may make allegiance to you and that the people say that the uncle of the Messenger of Allah, may the peace and blessings of Allah be upon him, has given allegiance to his paternal nephew and so that there will not be two persons disputing your succession." They also say that it is ruling which when given, even by one person, has to be carried out.

When the people of power and influence have gathered together to make the choice they should examine the state of those suitable for the Imamate from amongst them in accordance with the conditions stipulated for this matter and they should then present the most excellent among them for the oath of allegiance, that is the one who best fulfils the conditions from amongst these persons and the one whom the people would most readily accept obedience to and to whom they would not hesitate in making the oath of allegiance. Thus if it becomes clear to them which person from amongst the community their ijtihad is leading them to choose, they should offer the Imamate to him: if he accepts, they should make the oath of allegiance to him and the Imamate thus comes into being by their act of allegiance and it is then incumbent upon the whole of the Ummah to enter into this allegiance and to accept obedience to him. If, however, he abstains from accepting the Imamate and does not respond to it, he is not coerced into it as it is a contract based on willing choice, there being no compulsion or force in the matter. They should leave him and turn to someone else from amongst those who merit this office.

If two people fulfil equally the conditions of Imamate, the most advanced in years is the preferred choice although superiority in years, assuming the age of puberty has been reached, does not constitute a condition and it is permissible for allegiance to be given to the youngest of the two. If one of them is more knowledgeable and the other more courageous then attention should be paid to the situation at the time of making the choice: if there is a greater need for the quality of courage because of expansion of the border fortresses or the spread of injustice and tyranny, then the more courageous person would have the most right to the Imamate; if, however, there was a greater need for excellence in knowledge to ensure the tranquillity of the masses or because of the existence of the people of innovation then the one with more knowledge is more eligible.

If a choice is made of one of them and they both dispute with each other, some of the fuqaha say that this leads to their censure and disqualification and that someone other than these two should be considered. The majority of the fuqaha, however, are of the opinion that their disputing with each other is not a cause for censure or disqualification and that seeking after the Imamate is not a blamable quality as the people involved in the council have contested each other's right by their very involvement while no one who has sought involvement has been rejected nor has anyone who desires it been excluded.

The fuqaha differ when deciding in the case of a dispute between the two of persons of equal stature. One group says that lots should be drawn and the winner should become the Imam. Others say that the people involved in the election should choose between whichever of the two they wish without drawing lots. If it seems to the electors that one of the two is the more excellent and they make the oath of allegiance to him for the Imamate but then someone more excellent than him appears then this first Imamate stands and it is not permitted to abandon it for someone who is more excellent than him; if they begin by giving allegiance to the one who is surpassed in excellence when the one who surpasses him in excellence is available then they should examine the situation: if there is an excuse for this, such as the fact that the more excellent was temporarily absent or ill or because the one surpassed is more shown more obedience by the people and is dearer to their hearts, then the allegiance to the one surpassed stands and his Imamate is valid. If, however, they give allegiance to him without any such excuse, then there is a difference of opinion as to whether this oath of allegiance stands and whether the Imamate is valid: one group, among them al-Jahiz, is of the opinion that the oath of allegiance to him does not stand because if people choose the best of two things it is not permitted to abandon this for something else other than the best, like, for example, making a new judgement with respect to the rules of the shari'ah. Most of the fuqaha and mutakallimun, however, say that his Imamate is valid and the existence of the one who is more excellent does not disqualify the Imamate of the one surpassed in excellence as long as he is not deficient regarding the conditions of the Imamate – just as in the case of the administration of judgeship it is permitted to follow the one surpassed in excellence even though the more excellent person is available since a greater degree of excellence is only an extra dimension of choice and is not considered as one of the necessary conditions.

If one person alone fulfils, at a given time, the conditions of Imamate and there is no other person of similar merit, then the Imamate comes into being in him and it is not permitted to renounce him for someone else. However, the people of knowledge differ as to whether his Imamate is established with certainty and whether his authority stands if there is no contractual agreement and no election. Some of the fuqaha of Iraq are of the opinion that his authority is established and that his authority stands and so they consider that the obedience of the Ummah to him is obligatory: this they say is the case even if those capable of election have not agreed to it because the aim of election is to distinguish the person of authority and in this case he is distinguished by his own qualities. The majority of the fuqaha and the mutakallimun, however, are of the opinion that his Imamate does not stand except by approval and election: it is necessary for the electors to agree to his Imamate and that once agreed, it comes into effect because Imamate is a contractual agreement and it is not brought into being except by the contracting partner; it is thus similar to the case of judgeship: if there is only one person suitable for the post he nevertheless does not become the judge until he is given authority. Some however, go further than those who are of this opinion saying that he does become the judge if he is the only person possessed of qualities of excellence, just as he would become the Imam if he were the only one to have his qualities of excellence. Some, however, say that he does not become the judge when he alone is qualified, even though someone may become an Imam when he alone is qualified, arguing that the two instances must be distinguished: judgeship is a specially delegated office but it is permitted to remove the person from office even though the person retains the prerequisite qualities; his authority is only established following a directive from the person in authority over him. Imamate, however, is one of those general rights which are shared between Allah, may He be exalted, and men and it is not permitted to remove a person who has taken up the post if he fulfils its requirements: so someone who alone merits the post does not need a formal contractual agreement in order to establish him in authority

If two Imamates are established in two countries none of the two is valid as it is not permitted for there to be two imams at one time, even though one group, who are an exception, do permit it.

The fuqaha differ as to which of them is to be the Imam. One group say that it is the one whose Imamate was established in the country in which his predecessor died as the people of this country are more connected to and more entitled to confirming this Imamate; they also say that it is incumbent on the rest of the Ummah in all the other territories to affirm the agreement of the first people and to submit alongside those who have already made the oath of allegiance so that the affair does not become unnecessarily complicated through differences of opinion and the manifestation of heretical sects. Others, however, have said that each of the two should reject the Imamate for himself and offer it to the other thereby seeking peace, preventing discord and civil strife: in this way the people responsible for arranging the contract of Imamate may elect one of them or someone other than these two. Others have said that lots should be drawn between them both in order to prevent dispute and to put an end to any argument – the one to whom the lot falls having the greatest claim to the Imamate.

The correct opinion in this matter and that which the competent fuqaha hold to is that the Imamate belongs to the one who first received the oath of allegiance and the contractual agreement: this resembles the case in which there are two guardians marrying off a woman for if two of them marry her off the marriage is only actually contracted by the first of the two. Thus it is clear who is the first to receive the Imamate, it remains with him and it is incumbent upon the second of the two to submit the affair to the first and to make the oath of allegiance to him. If however, the Imamate was established for both of them at the same time, neither of them preceding the other, then both contracts of Imamate are annulled and the contract is renewed with one of them or with someone other than these two. If the oath of allegiance to one of them does take place before that of another but there is some ambiguity in this first transaction, the affair of both of them is delayed in order to have an investigation. If they both dispute the matter and each claims to be the first, neither of their claims are entertained and no oath is taken as it has nothing to do with the claim of each in the matter but rather to do with the claim belonging to all the Muslims such that it does not depend on a judgement based on an oath or a refusal to take an oath; likewise if the dispute comes to an end and one of them offers the Imamate to the other, that of the latter still does not stand unless there is proof that he was the first. If one affirms that the other preceded him then the one who makes this affirmation thereby relinquishes the Imamate but it is not, however, established for the other as his affirmation is not binding in respect to a right of the Muslims. If the one making the affirmation of the other's precedence does so with another witness, his bearing witness is accepted as long as he makes mention of his doubt or misgiving regarding the matter at the time of his claim; his testimony is not accepted if this doubt is not mentioned as there would be a contradiction between his two statements.

If the matter in doubt between the two persists after an investigation and no proof is forthcoming regarding the precedence of one of them, lots are not drawn between them for two reasons: the first of these is that Imamate is a contractual agreement and lots have no place in contracts; the second is that sharing is not permitted in the case of Imamate and that the drawing of lots is not permitted where a division of something is not admissible, as in the case of women, whereas it is permitted wherever a division into shares is possible, as in the case of wealth.

Persistence of this doubt annuls the contracts of Imamate for both persons and those involved in election should renew the contract of Imamate with one of the two. Some say that if they want to disregard these two in favour of someone else, this is permitted as both the others have effectively been excluded from the Imamate; others, however, say that it is not permitted as the Imamate must be excluded from other than these two persons by the oaths of allegiance made to both of them and because the existence of doubt does not prevent the confirmation of the Imamate in one of them.

There is a consensus of opinion that the Imamate of the first contract is permitted and agreement as to its validity is for two reasons: the Muslims base their practice on these two and deny neither of them. The first of these is that Abu Bakr, may Allah be pleased with him, entrusted 'Umar with it and this was confirmed by the Muslims. The second is that 'Umar, may Allah be pleased with him, entrusted the matter of Imamate to a council, consisting of the most prominent members of the community, and this was then accepted by the community which was convinced of the validity of this way of contracting the Imamate and of the fact that the rest of the Companions had been excluded from it. 'Ali replied to 'Abbas, may Allah be pleased with them both, after the latter criticised him for participating in the council: "It is one of the mighty affairs of Islam and I did not think I should be excluded from it." Thus the contract of Imamate was fulfilled by a consensus agreement.

If the Imam wants to entrust the Imamate to a successor he should strive to arrive at a clear decision as to who has the greatest claim to it and who best fulfils its conditions. If, in his effort to decide, someone becomes clear to him, then this choice should be examined: if it is neither his son nor father, he may, on his own, make the contract of allegiance to him and may delegate authority to him without taking council with any of the electors. There is a difference of opinion, however, as to whether or not there must be some sign of acceptance on their part of the contracting and execution of his act of allegiance. Some of the 'ulama of the people of Basra maintain that the electors' acceptance of his transfer of allegiance must exist before it is binding on the Ummah as it is a right which belongs to the electors and the transfer of Imamate is not binding on the Ummah except with the acceptance of those amongst them involved in the election. The valid position is that this transfer of allegiance stands and that their acceptance of it is not taken into consideration as the act of allegiance to 'Umar, may Allah be pleased with him, was not dependent upon the acceptance of the companions and as the Imam has more right over the Imamate than them – his choice of another for the Imamate takes precedence and his word in the matter is executed. If the successor is his son or father there are three differences of opinion as to whether he is permitted to carry out the transfer of Imamate alone. The first of these is that it is not permitted until he has sought counsel of the electors and they consider that he is worthy of this post: if this does happen his act of allegiance to a successor is validated as this seeking of council is like an assessment of his integrity and has the same value as a testimony and the appointment conferred on him over the Ummah has the same value as a legal judgement. It is not permitted that he bear witness in favour of his father or son or that he decide in their favour because of the suspicion that he will naturally show partiality towards them. According to the second, however, he may entrust the Imamate to his son or father as he is the Imam of the Ummah and the executor of affairs both in their favour or against them: thus the status of this office takes precedence over that of family ties and no cause for suspicion may be entertained and no possibility of opposition to him in this matter is accepted; it is treated in the same way as his entrusting of the Imamate to any person other than his son or father. As we have already discussed above, there are two aspects as to whether or not the acceptance of the electors – made after the valid assigning of the Imamate – is considered with regard to making this Imamate binding on the Ummah. The third opinion is that it is permitted for him, acting alone, to make the contract of allegiance with his father but not with his son as he will be naturally more inclined to favour the son than the father; for this reason everything he acquires is usually stored up for the son rather than the father. As for transfer of the Imamate to his brother or to other relations amongst his kith and kin, the ruling as to whether he may act alone in this is the same as if he were transferring it to totally unrelated persons.

*

* *

If the Imam, in accordance with the relevant conditions, entrusts the succession of khilafah to someone to whom it is proper to entrust it, this agreement still depends on the acceptance of the person entrusted. There is a difference of opinion as to the time of his acceptance: some say that it is the period, after the death of the Imam, required by the person charged with the Imamate to examine the situation; others say, with more justification, that it is the time between the reigning Imam's entrusting of someone and the former's death such that the Imamate may be transferred from him by prior acceptance.

The Imam who is still in office may not dismiss his successor as long as his state does not change although it is permitted him to dismiss any other of his delegates standing in for him: these latter he delegates for his own benefit and thus is permitted to dismiss them whereas the person he has appointed as his successor is appointed on behalf of the Muslims and so he cannot dismiss him – just as the electors cannot dismiss someone they have made the contract of allegiance to as long as his condition has not changed. If the Imam entrusts a second person, after the first, the second is invalidated and the contract of allegiance to the first stands. If the first withdraws, the contract of allegiance to the second is not valid unless the process is begun again. If the successor tenders his resignation, his office is not annulled by his resignation until he is excused, because of some necessary reason, by the Imam. The matter is then to be examined – if someone else is found, his resignation is permitted and he is relieved of the office by their mutual agreement based on the tendering of the resignation and the exemption. If no one else is found, neither his tendering of resignation nor the exemption is permitted and the office is necessarily still binding both on the Imam still in office and the one entrusted with his succession.

The conditions of Imamate are taken into consideration with respect to the person charged with succession at the time this charge is made. If he is a minor or corrupt at the time of the agreement as to his succession, but of age and of just character at the time the reigning Imam dies, his khilafah is not valid until his contract of allegiance is renewed by the electors. If the reigning Imam delegates the office to someone who is absent and it is not known whether he is living, his being entrusted with the office is not valid. If it is known that he is alive then the office is dependent upon his appearance. If the one who has appointed a successor dies and the successor is absent at the time, the people of election should summon him. If he remains absent for a long time and the Muslims suffer from the resulting delay in examining their affairs, the people of election should appoint a representative to stand in for him and they make the contract of allegiance with him as a representative rather than as the successor proper. If the absent successor appears, the one appointed to represent the succession should withdraw and his handling of and jurisdiction over affairs prior to the appearance of the successor is validated but annulled thereafter.

If the successor wishes to appoint someone else to his responsibility as successor before the death of the reigning Khalifah, this is not permitted as the khilafah is not established in him until after the death of the one who has appointed him as the successor. So if he says, "I have made him my successor if the khilafah falls to me," it is not permitted as he is not yet in the state of being Khalifah and so it is not valid that he delegate someone with the khilafah. If the Khalifah resigns from the office of his own accord, then succession is transferred to his delegated successor and his resignation has the same effect as his death. If the Khalifah delegates two persons and does not give preference to either of the two, this is permitted: the electors, as a council, then choose one of them after his death – as 'Umar, may Allah be pleased with him, placed the khilafah amongst six persons.

Ibn Ishaq relates from az-Zuhri from Ibn 'Abbas saying, "I came across 'Umar one day in a state of distress: he was saying, 'I do not know what to do in this matter. I get up to settle the matter then I sit down.' I said to him: 'Have you considered 'Ali?' He replied, 'He is surely suitable for it but he is a man with a sense of jest and I consider that if he took charge of your affairs he would not lead you on the path of truth that you are familiar with.' I said: 'And where do you stand with 'Uthman?' He replied, 'If I were to designate him he would have (his family of) Banu Abu Mu'ayt lords of the people and the Arabs would not turn to him but to strike off his neck. By Allah, if I were to choose him he would do this and when he had done it they would react accordingly.' I then said: 'And Talhah?' He replied, 'He is proud: Allah would not entrust the affair of the Ummah of Muhammad to him, may the peace and blessings of Allah be upon him, considering what He knows of his pride.' I then said, 'And what of az-Zubayr?' He replied, 'Surely he is a brave man but he asks about the saa' and mudd measures in the Baqi' market – is this man to be entrusted with the affairs of the Muslims?' I then said, 'Sa'd ibn Abi Waqqas?' He said, 'He is not the one – he is a warrior well able to defend his squadron but as for being in authority, no!' I said, 'What about 'Abd ar-Rahman ibn 'Awf?' He replied, 'Yes, you have mentioned the best of men, but he is weak. By Allah, O Ibn 'Abbas, only the strong person without violence, the one who is gentle without being weak, the one who is economical but without being miserly and the one who is generous without being wasteful is worthy of this affair.'" Ibn 'Abbas continued saying, "When Abu Lu'lu'ah wounded him and the doctor had given up hope of saving him, they asked him to designate a successor and he instituted the Imamate by appointing a council of six of them saying 'This affair belongs to 'Ali and with him az-Zubayr, and to 'Uthman and with him 'Abd ar-Rahman ibn Awf, and to Talhah and with him Sa'd ibn Abi Waqqas.' So when the council met after the death of 'Umar, may Allah be pleased with him, 'Abd ar-Rahman said, 'Make the affair a matter between three of you.' Then az-Zubayr said, 'I have handed over my part in the matter to 'Ali,' and Talhah said, 'I have handed my part over to 'Uthman,' and Sa'd said, 'I have handed my part to 'Abd ar-Rahman' and so the council was composed of these three from among the six as the other three had left it. Then 'Abd ar-Rahman said, 'Which of you will renounce this affair so that we may entrust him – and Allah will be a witness over him – to maintain the good of the Ummah?' No-one replied however. Then 'Abd ar-Rahman said, 'Do you consider it my responsibility? – Then I will step down and Allah is my witness that I will not be lacking in giving advice.' So they agreed and 'Abd ar-Rahman said, 'This I have done!' Thus the council was reduced to three after the six and then to two after the three: 'Ali and 'Uthman. Then 'Abd ar-Rahman went to see what people thought of the matter. When night had fallen he summoned al-Miswar ibn Makhrama and, taking him with him, he went and made each of the two pledge that if one of them received the oath of allegiance they would act according to the Book of Allah and the sunnah of His Prophet, and if he entrusted another (with the khilafah) they would obey and submit. Then he gave allegiance to 'Uthman."

So this council in which the people worthy of Imamate participated, and as a result of which a consensus was agreed upon, formed the basis for the creation of this Imamate: it was achieved by the agreement and the act of allegiance of a number of persons from amongst whom the Imam was designated by the election of the people of influence and power. It is of no importance that this council consists of two persons or more as long as the number is restricted. The matter is then conclusive – such that the Imamate may not be assigned to anyone else after this. However, if the Imamate has been assigned through election to someone, it is permitted for this person to confer it on someone else.

If the reigning Imam has appointed the people of election as a council to choose from a specific number of persons they should not choose one of them while the one who has given authorization for the choice of a successor is still alive, unless he gives permission since he has more claim to this Imamate and it is not permitted that anyone have a share in this. If they fear that disorder will ensue after his death they should seek his permission and make the election if permission is granted. If he loses his faculty of discernment then the case must be examined: if he loses his sense of responsibility and lacks the capacity for judgement, then his state is judged to be the same as that after his death namely that election becomes permitted. If however, he has the faculty of discrimination and sound judgement, they are not allowed to elect someone without his permission.

Ibn Ishaq has related about 'Umar, may Allah be pleased with him, that on arriving wounded at his house and hearing a loud noise he said: "What are people doing?" When he was told that they wanted to see him he gave them permission and they said, "O Amir of the believers, pledge that 'Uthman will succeed you in authority over us," to which he replied, "How is it that he loves wealth and land?" and they left his house. Then he heard a further commotion from them and he said: "What is the matter with the people?" When he was told that they wished to see him he gave permission and they said: "Make 'Ali ibn Abi Talib your successor over us." He replied, "Then will he take you to the path which is the Truth?" 'Abdallah ibn 'Umar said: "Then I leaned over him and said: 'O Amir of the believers: What prevents you from appointing him?'" He replied: "O son, I bear the Imamate both in life and death."

It is permitted for the Khalifah to stipulate the people of election just as it is permitted for him to stipulate those from amongst whom one will be chosen: thus it is valid only to choose someone from amongst those stipulated just as it is only valid to appoint the one to whom succession has been assigned as these two matters are amongst the rights of his khilafah.

It is permitted for the Khalifah to designate succession to two persons or more and to lay down an order of succession amongst them by saying, "The Khalifah after me is such and such a person, and if he dies then the Khalifah after his death will be such and such, and if he dies then the Khalifah after him will be such and such a person." Thus the khilafah will be transferred to the three persons in the order he has designated. The Messenger of Allah, may the peace and blessings of Allah be upon him, designated Zayd ibn Harithah as vice commander over the army of (the battle of) Mu'tah saying, "If he is struck down then Ja'far ibn Abi Talib, and if he is struck then 'Abdallah ibn ar-Rawahah, and if he is struck then the Muslims should agree on another man." So it was that Zayd went forward and was killed, and then Ja'far took the banner and went forward and was killed; then 'Abdallah ibn ar-Rawahah took the banner, advanced and was killed and so the Muslims chose Khalid ibn al-Walid after him. If the Prophet, may the peace and blessings of Allah be upon him, did this with regard to amirate, the like is permitted regarding the khilafah. If it is argued that it is a contract of authority with a particular character and condition, and that contracts of authority are not based on such specific conditions and characteristics, then it must be replied that it is a general matter of public interest which should be addressed with more largesse than in the case of private contracts between individuals.

This was acted upon during two dynasties (the Umayyads and the Abbasids) and none from amongst the 'ulama of the age have rejected it. Sulayman ibn 'Abd al-Malik pledged succession to 'Umar ibn 'Abd al-'Aziz and then after him to Yazid ibn 'Abd al-Malik. Even though Sulayman's judgement was not accepted as a proof, his acceptance by those amongst the 'ulama of the Followers (who had known the Companions and) who were his contemporaries and among those, **"who do not fear the censure of those who censure"** (Qur'an 5: 55), in matters regarding the truth constitutes a proof. Moreover ar-Rashid, may Allah be pleased with him, designated three of his sons in turn: al-Amin, then al-Ma'mun and then al-Mu'tamin after consulting some of the most excellent 'ulama of his time. When the Khalifah designates succession to three persons, stipulating also the order of succession, and subsequently dies while the three are still alive then the khilafah goes to the first after his death; if the first dies during the life of the Khalifah the khilafah goes to the second after him; if the first and the second die during the life of the Khalifah then the khilafah goes to the third after him as he has pledged the khilafah to each of the three. If the Khalifah dies while the three to whom he has designated succession are still alive and the khilafah falls to the first of them and he wishes to pledge succession to someone other than the two whom the previous Khalifah had chosen for succession, then there are some fuqaha who forbid it basing their judgement on the order of succession stipulated (by the previous Khalifah) – except if they forgo their right to it voluntarily.

As-Safah pledged succession to al-Mansur, may Allah be pleased with them both, and then to Isa ibn Musa second in line after him; then al-Mansur wanted to give preference to al-Mahdi over Isa and wanted the latter to renounce his right of succession and to refrain from making any claim to it; numerous fuqaha of the time, however, did not consider he was justified in depriving him against his will of his inheritance of the succession but rather to seek to induce him with gentleness to step down of his own free will.

What is most evident within the school of ash-Shafi'i, may Allah have mercy on him, and amongst the majority of the fuqaha is that it is permitted for the one who becomes Khalifah from amongst the designated successors to designate the next successor from amongst whomever he pleases and to remove any right of succession from those following after him in line since this line of succession is restricted to those who have a claim to the khilafah after the death of the one who has named them. Thus if the khilafah falls to one of them, in accordance with the designated order, it is this person who is most entitled to designate succession as he pleases since overall authority for the execution of the responsibilities of this office became his when the khilafah fell to him: thus his right is the strongest and his capacity to pledge succession takes precedence. This differs from what the Messenger of Allah did in his designation of the order of commanders over the army of Mu'tah: in effect the Messenger of Allah, may the peace and blessing of Allah was still alive at a time before the direction of affairs had been transferred to another, whereas in this case it occurred after the transfer of command to someone else following the death of the Khalifah. The judgement concerning the two contracts of succession are therefore different. As for al-Mansur wanting Isa ibn Musa to renounce the right of succession voluntarily, this was because he wanted to reinforce family cohesion at a time when the dynasty had only just begun and the right of succession only recently established: a widespread sense of equality combined with a debilitating resentment characterised his inner circle. What he did was thus an act of political expediency, even though he was permitted legally to do as he wished.

Thus in accordance with this reasoning, if the first of the three persons assigned the succession dies after having taken up the khilafah without stipulating another, the second becomes the Khalifah after him by virtue of the pledge of the original Khalifah and he takes precedence over the third in accordance with the order of succession; if this second person dies before assigning succession to anyone, the third becomes the Khalifah after him as the validity of the pledge of the Khalifah who originally designated succession ensures that his decision stands for all three as long as a different assignment of succession has not been made after him. Thus assignment of succession in the case of the first of the three is certain but is dependent in the case of the second and the third: it is not permitted to annul the first and thus it is a matter of certainty but it is permitted, according to this madhhab, to annul the second and the third as their case is relative.

If the first of the three dies after succeeding to the khilafah without having pledged succession to anyone else it is not permitted for the electors to choose someone other than the second in line; likewise if the second were to die after the khilafah had fallen to him, it is not permitted for them to choose other than the third in line. It is, however, permitted for the second to assign it to other than the third as the decision to stipulate succession is final and recourse to an election is only made when this decision is lacking.

If, however, the Khalifah assigning succession says, "I pledge the succession to such and such a person, and if he dies after taking up the khilafah the Khalifah after him will be such and such a person," then the second khilafah will be invalid and the contract of succession will not be binding as his succession is not direct but conditional upon the khilafah of the first in line who might die before taking up the khilafah. Thus this pledge of succession to the second is not definite and so is annulled; it is permitted for the first in line to pledge it to another after he has succeeded to the khilafah and if he dies without assigning succession the electors may choose other than the second in line.

If the khilafah is established in either the person who was assigned succession or in the person elected to it, it is binding upon the whole of the Ummah to recognise that it has been established in a person worthy of this office by reason of the qualities he possesses: it is not, however, necessary for them to know him in person or by name; this is only incumbent on the electors by whom his claim to khilafah stands and by whose oath of allegiance the khilafah is formed.

Sulayman ibn Jarir says, however, that it is incumbent on everyone to know the Imam in person and by name just as knowledge of Allah and his Messenger is incumbent on them. But the majority of the people consider that knowledge of the Imam is only necessary for the nation as a whole rather than as individuals and it is not incumbent upon each and every person to know him in person or by name except if he is needed in specific circumstances: the general public at large must likewise have an awareness of the judges by whom the laws are upheld and of the fuqaha who make fatwas regarding the halal and haram, but individuals have no need to know them except when they have recourse to them in special circumstances. If everyone in the Ummah had to know the Imam in person and by name, it would necessitate emigration: even those living in the most outlying regions would have to move; this would result in whole regions being abandoned and would be contrary to common practice and cause great harm.

Given that every individual must know him in the manner we have detailed above, it is incumbent upon the whole of the Ummah to hand over all matters of public interest to him without any remonstrance or opposition on their part, so that he might carry out the social responsibilities entrusted to him and the ordering of works.

He is called the Khalifah (successor) as he stands in for the Messenger of Allah at the head of his Ummah and so it is permitted for someone to say, "O, Khalifah of the Messenger of Allah!" or for someone to say, "Khalifah," on its own. There is a difference of opinion as to whether it is permitted to say, "O Khalifah of Allah!" Some have permitted this based on the fact that he fulfils Allah's rights over His creation and because of His saying: **"And He it is who has made you the khulafa of the earth and has raised some of you over others by degrees"** (Qur'an 6: 165). The majority of the 'ulama, however, do not permit this and treat those who do say this as corrupt, arguing that the Khalifah succeeds someone who is absent or dead and Allah is not absent and does not die. When Abu Bakr as-Siddiq was addressed, "O Khalifah of Allah," he replied, "I am not the Khalifah of Allah but rather the Khalifah of the Messenger of Allah, may the peace and blessings of Allah be upon him."

The Ten Points.

There are ten matters regarding affairs of a public nature which are binding on him:

1. He must guard the deen as it was established in its original form and about

27

which the first generations of the Ummah are agreed; if an innovator appears, or someone of dubious character deviates from this deen he should make clear to him the legal proof of his error, explain the right way to him and take the appropriate measures regarding his liability and his punishment such that the deen is protected from blemish and the Ummah is prevented from going astray;

2. He must execute the legal judgements between two contestants and bring to an end any dispute between two litigants so that equity prevails, the tyrant does not transgress and the weak are not oppressed;

3. He must protect the territory of Islam and defend the sanctuaries so that people may earn their sustenance and journey safe from any threat to their persons or belongings;

4. He must establish the hadd-punishments in order to protect what Allah, may He be exalted, has made inviolable from being violated and prevent the rights of His slaves from being abused;

5. He must fortify the border posts against attack and defend them with force against an enemy which might appear unexpectedly and violate what is sacred or shed the blood of Muslims or dhimmis protected by a pact;

6. He must make jihad against those who resist Islam after having been called to it until they submit or accept to live as a protected dhimmi-community – so that Allah's rights, may He be exalted, **"be made uppermost above all [other] religion"** (Qur'an 9: 33);

7. He must collect the fay and zakah taxes from those on whom the shari'ah and legal judgement has made it an obligation to pay, and this without fear or oppression;

8. He must apportion the stipends and whatever is due from the bait al-mal without wastefulness or meanness and make payments punctually, neither before their time nor after it;

9. He must ensure the employment of trustworthy persons and the appointment of worthy counsellors capable of undertaking those tasks delegated to them and of safeguarding monies made over to them;

10. He must personally take over the surveillance of affairs and the scrutiny of circumstances such that he may execute the policy of the Ummah and defend the nation without over-reliance on delegation of authority – by means of which he might devote himself to pleasure-seeking or worship – for even the trustworthy may deceive and counsellors behave dishonestly: Allah, may

He be exalted, has said, **"O Dawud, surely I have made you a Khalifah on the earth so decide equitably between people and do not follow passions lest you be led astray from the way of Allah"** (Qur'an 38: 26). So Allah does confine the matter to delegating duties to someone who does not participate directly in the affairs himself; nor does He grant him an excuse to follow his passions as He has described this as a going astray. Although it is a duty incumbent on Dawud from the point of view of the deen and the office of Khalifah, it is nevertheless a duty of every subject to manage his affairs properly: The Prophet said, may the peace and blessings of Allah be upon him: "Each of you is a shepherd and each of you is responsible for his flock." The poet expressed this when he described the leader and the person who arranges affairs:

Entrust your affair, and your achievement is Allah's, to one who is open handed and skilled in war, someone not excessive in the ease of life which might have been his, someone who does not fade or submit when adversity strikes: he continues to draw out his portion of the milk of time, conquering one day and conquered another, such that his strength and magnanimity last even in difficulty, firm in judgement neither grandiose nor full of humiliation.

Muhammad ibn Yazdad, a minister of al-Ma'mun, said to the latter:

Whoever is a guardian of this world, it is not fitting that he sleep while all the people are asleep; and how can there be rest for the eyes of the one who must address the two difficulties of his affair: resolving and contracting (the affairs of others).

So if the Imam fulfils the rights of the Ummah, as we have described above, he will have executed the claim of Allah, may He be exalted, regarding their rights and their duties: in which case they have a duty to obey and support him as long as his state does not change. Two changes in a person's state will exclude him from the Imamate: the first of these is a lack of decency and the second is a physical deficiency.

As for a lack of decency, that is a moral deviation, it is of two kinds: the first of them resulting from lust, the second from his holding dubious opinions. As for the first it is connected to physical action: he commits forbidden acts, pursues evil, is ruled by his lust and is subject to his passions; this counts as a moral deviation which excludes him from taking up the Imamate or from carrying on with it. Thus if such behaviour befalls someone who has become the Imam, he is disqualified. If he recovers his decency he may not return to the Imamate except by way of a new contract; some of the mutakallimun, however, have said that he may return to the Imamate on his return to probity – without a renewal of his contract and without the oath of allegiance – because of his overall authority in governance and the difficulty involved in renewing his oath of allegiance.

The second aspect is connected to his creed and his dubious manner of interpreting contrary to the truth. The 'ulama differ in this. One group among them are of the opinion that this excludes him from contracting the Imamate or continuing in office: he is thus to be excluded from office as soon as such belief manifests since the judgement of kufr (disbelief) upon him stands irrespective of whether it is arrived at based on his interpretation or not; in effect, his state of moral deviation remains whether judged on his manner of interpretation or not. Many of the 'ulama of Basrah have said that it does not prevent someone from taking up the Imamate and remaining in office, just it would not prevent him from judgeship or giving testimony.

There are three kinds of physical defects: a deficiency in the senses, a deficiency in his members, a deficiency in his mobility.

As for a deficiency in his senses, it is also divided into three parts: that which excludes him from Imamate, that which does not and that about which there is a difference of opinion. As for what excludes him from it, it may be either a loss of the intellect or loss of sight.

As for a loss of intellect, it is of two kinds. The first of these is that which occurs temporarily and which is expected to disappear, like fainting: this neither excludes someone from contracting or continuing the Imamate as it is a well-known illness and is quick to pass. The Messenger, himself, fainted, may the peace and blessings of Allah be upon him, during his illness. The second kind is that which is chronic and which one does not expect to pass, like madness and mental disorder. This is of two kinds: **A.** that which carries on continually, unaccompanied by any respite: this would both exclude a person from contracting and continuing the Imamate; thus if it occurs, and it has been verified and certified, the Imamate is annulled; **B.** that which is accompanied by periods of lucidity in which he returns to health, in which case it is investigated: **i.** if the period of mental disorder is longer than the period of lucidity it is regarded as continuous and it excludes him from contracting and continuing Imamate, and this takes effect as soon as it occurs; **ii.** if, however, the period of lucidity is greater than the time of mental disorder he is excluded from making the contract of Imamate. There is a difference of opinion, however, as to whether he is excluded from continuing the Imamate: some say that he is prevented from continuing the Imamate just as he is prevented from commencing it; if it occurs, the Imamate is annulled for otherwise this deficiency in his judgement would entail a deficiency in execution of office. Others, however, say that he is not prevented from continuing the Imamate even though he is excluded from contracting the office in the beginning – as his perfect health is taken into consideration before the Imamate is contracted while his total deficiency is considered before deposing him from it.

As for the loss of sight, it excludes him from becoming Imam and continuing in it. If Imamate is contracted, it is annulled forthwith because this loss annuls his capacity for judgeship and for giving testimony: it is thus all the more fitting that it should also invalidate Imamate. As for dim-sightedness such that one cannot see when night falls, it does not entail exclusion from Imamate for it is an illness that one hopes, by leading a calm life, will pass. As for weakness of sight, if he can recognise people when he sees them, he is not excluded from Imamate, but if he can perceive people but cannot recognise them he is excluded from becoming or remaining the Imam.

As for the second kind, regarding the senses which are without influence in the validity of Imamate if lost, it consists of two things: the first of these is injury to nasal cartilage such that the sense of smell is lost. The second is a loss of taste and the capacity to distinguishes between flavours. Neither are of influence on the contract of Imamate as they are of influence with respect to pleasure but not of influence in judgement and action.

As for the third division, regarding those senses about which there is a difference of opinion, this comprises two matter, deafness and dumbness. They both exclude anyone from initiating the contract of Imamate as their lack denotes an imperfection of attributes. There is a difference of opinion as to whether someone may be deposed because of this. One group argues that the Imam is deposed for these two things just as he would be deposed for loss of sight because of their effect on his capacity for organisation and action. Others say that he is not deposed from the Imamate as indication and gesture may be used instead and that only his total deficiency results in his being deposed. Yet others say that if he is capable of writing well, he should not step down on account of these two things but that if he is not good at writing, he should, as writing is clearly understood whereas indication is subject to conjecture. The first of these schools is more valid.

As for a speech impediment and his being hard of hearing such that he can hear only when people speak loudly, they do not exclude him from Imamate. They differ, however, as whether he may take up Imamate when afflicted by these two defects. Some say that they prevent his becoming the Imam as they detract from his state of perfection, although others say that it does not, as the Prophet Musa, may peace be on him, was not prevented from prophethood by having a speech impediment: it is thus all the more fitting that it should not exclude a person from Imamate.

✳

✳ ✳

As for loss of limb, this is divided into four sections:

1. This section concerns what does not invalidate Imamate at the time of contract or while in office: it refers to those limbs whose loss does not effect judgement, action or movement and does not cause disfigurement. Likewise the cutting off of the penis and the testicles does not stop the contract of Imamate nor its continuance after the contract as the loss of these two members only has an effect on reproduction and not on judgement or one's capacity to function in worldly matters: it is thus on a par with impotence. Allah, may He be exalted has described Yahya ibn Zakaria in this way but while praising him saying of him: **"A chief, and chaste (hasour), a prophet from amongst those of right action"** (Qur'an 3: 39). As for the meaning of "chaste," there are two opinions: one of them is that it refers to the impotent person who cannot have sexual intercourse with women, and this has been said by Ibn Mas'ud and Ibn 'Abbas. The second is that it refers to someone who does not have a penis large enough to penetrate women or that it is like a date-stone, and this has been said by Sa'id ibn al-Musayyab. As this does not exclude a man from Prophethood it is all the more fitting that it should not exclude him from Imamate. Likewise when both ears have been cut off: this is of no effect in judgement nor action and is a minor deformity which can be covered up so as not to be seen;

2. This concerns what does stop the contract of Imamate and the continuance of it: it refers to that which prevents one from acting, like the loss of both hands, or from moving like the loss of both legs. Neither the contract of Imamate nor the continuance of it is valid in this case because of the incapacity of the person to act or move as is incumbent on him with respect to his duties towards the Ummah;

3. This concerns that which excludes someone from becoming the Imam while there is a difference of opinion as to whether it excludes someone from remaining as Imam. It refers to a partial loss of action or a partial loss of mobility, like the loss of one hand or one leg. In this case is not valid for someone to become the Imam because of his incapacity to undertake a complete range of actions. If such a deficiency occurs after the contract of Imamate, there are two schools of thought amongst the fuqaha as to whether he should step down: the first, that he should, as the incapacity which excludes him from initiating the Imamate would also stop him from carrying on with it; the second, that he should not, because even though he is excluded from initiating this contract, the perfection of a man's health being taken into consideration at this point, it is a man's total deficiency which must be considered when deposing him;

4. This concerns what does exclude someone from continuing the Imamate. There is a difference of opinion as to what prevents someone from initiating the contract. This refers to blemishes and disfigurements which do not affect action or mobility, like having the nose cut off or one of the eyes gouged out; such defects would not oblige him to step down from the Imamate after having undertaken it because they in no way effect the fulfilment of the duties of Imamate. As for preventing him from initiating the contract, there are two schools amongst the fuqaha: the first is that these deformities do not stop one from making the contract as they are not subject to the conditions considered in this matter, none of the rights and duties of Imamate being affected thereby. The second is that it does exclude someone from the contract of Imamate and that indeed this contract is conditional upon his being free of such deformities: the governor of the nation should be free from blemish lest he be reproached and belittled for it and lest respect for him be diminished with the result that his people are less disposed to obey him. Whatever leads to this will also lead to a deficiency regarding the rights of the Ummah.

*

* *

As for deficiencies in his capacity to act, it is of two kinds: control or coercion by others.

"Control" here describes the situation when someone from his retinue gains authority over him and rules autocratically over affairs without appearing to commit any act of disobedience and without any manifest sign of opposition. This does not exclude him from Imamate and it does not impair the validity of his governance, but the actions of the person who has taken over his affairs should be investigated: if they are in accordance with the judgements of the deen and according to the requirements of justice, he may be allowed to remain in order that the Imamate may continue to function and its rulings be executed, lest the affairs of the deen be interrupted and the Ummah is corrupted. If however, his actions are outside the rule of the deen and the requirements of justice, he may not tolerate his actions and he must seek the help of another in order to overcome him and put an end to his dominance.

The "coercion" referred to here means that the Imam has become the captive of an overpowering enemy force from which he cannot free himself: this prevents the contract of Imamate being concluded with him because he is incapable of examining the affairs of the Muslims. It is of no consequence whether the enemy is a mushrik or a rebel Muslim. The Ummah may choose another than him from amongst those who have power to act by themselves. If he is made captive after having become the Imam, it is up to the whole Ummah to save him as the office of Imamate obliges that he be saved; he remains the Imam as long as there is hope he will be released – either by force or by ransom. If there is no hope for him, consideration must be made of whether his captors are mushrikun or rebel Muslims.

If he is a captive of the mushrikun, he is excluded from the Imamate as there is no hope of his release and the electors should make the oath of allegiance to someone else. If he assigns the Imamate to another at the time of capture, the matter is investigated: if it occurred after there was no hope of his release, his pledge is annulled as it was made after his exclusion from Imamate and was thus invalid. If he made the pledge before all hope was lost of his release, that is at a time when there was still some hope of his release, then his pledge is valid as he was still the Imam: the Imamate of his heir is thus established when there is no longer hope of his release, his Imamate having come to an end. If he is freed from captivity after having nominated a successor, his release is investigated: if it occurred after all hope was lost, he may not return to office because he was excluded from Imamate the moment this was lost and the transfer of Imamate to his heir ensued; if he was released before loss of hope, he retains his Imamate and his successor is established even though he does not become the Imam.

If he is made captive by rebel Muslims and there is hope of his release, he retains his Imamate; if there is no hope of his release, then the rebels will necessarily be in one of two situations: either they have set up an Imam for themselves or they have not. If there is chaos and they have no Imam, the captive Imam in their hands retains his Imamate since their oath of allegiance to him is binding and their obedience to him is obligatory: his relationship to them is the same as that of someone placed under a restriction (by a subordinate) to people of probity. The people of election must appoint someone to stand in for him if he cannot act himself; if he is able to do this, he is more entitled to choose someone to take his place than them. If the captive renounces office himself or he dies, the person appointed to take his place does not become the Imam as he was only representing someone who was still in office but this authority ceases when the office ceases.

If the rebels have set up an Imam for themselves, have given the oath of allegiance and have pledged obedience to him, the captive Imam, in their hands, is excluded from the Imamate when all hope of his release has been lost as they have occupied a territory whose rule is contrary to that of the community and they have abandoned obedience: those who remain loyal no longer expect assistance from them, the captive Imam no longer has any power, and so it is up to the people of election in the territory where just rule still reigns to assign the Imamate to the person they agree upon. If the captive is freed or escapes, he may not return to the Imamate as he has been excluded from it.

Having described the rules of Imamate and its general duty to take care of the interests of religion and the organisation of the Ummah, we would continue by saying that if this Imamate is duly established, the administrative authority of his deputies which issues from the Imam is of four types:

1. Those officials who have general authority over all provinces in general: these are the wazirs as they are representatives in all matters, without specialisation;

2. Those with general authority but only with regard to particular provinces: these are the amirs of the regions and cities as their power of investigation regarding the particular tasks they are charged with is general;

3. Those whose administration is particular with respect to the provinces in general: these are the supreme judge, for example, the commander of the armies, the defender of the outposts, the collector of the kharaj taxes and the collector of the zakah taxes, as each of these is restricted to a particular responsibility but in all provinces;

4. Those who have a particular authority with regard to particular provinces: they are the judge of a city or region, for example, or the collector of kharaj tax of these places or the collector of their zakah tax, the defender of their outposts or the commander of their army as each of these has a particular responsibility for a particular province.

Each of these administrations is established and its authority validated according to certain conditions. We shall describe them in their corresponding chapters and sections by the will of Allah and success from Him.

Chapter 2
The Appointment of Wazirs

Wazirate (ministry) is of two types: ministry of delegation and ministry of execution.

The ministry of delegation is where the Imam appoints a minister to whom he delegates authority for the organisation of affairs in accordance with his judgement such that he effects them properly by his own efforts. The permissibility of this ministry cannot be denied: Allah, may He be exalted says, speaking of his Prophet Musa, on whom be peace and blessings: **"And appoint for me a wazir from my people, Harun, my brother, and consolidate my strength by him and make him a partner in my affair"** (Qur'an 20: 29-32). If this is permissible with respect to prophethood then it is all the more permissible regarding Imamate; moreover the Imam cannot deal directly with all the organisation of the Ummah which has been entrusted to him except by appointing representatives. Representation by a minister, cooperating with the Imam in the organisation of affairs, is also a more efficient way of executing such affairs than doing it alone: this minister will protect him from (the weaknesses of) his self and the Imam will thus be less likely to make mistakes and will be prevented from committing errors.

The same conditions of Imamate apply when entrusting someone with this ministry, except that of lineage: the wazir, having to sanction judgements and execute decisions arrived at by ijtihad, must necessarily be of the mujtahidun. One further condition, besides those of Imamate, is required: that he be capable in the two matters with which he has been entrusted, namely of war and kharaj, and that he have a profound experience of these two things given that he must deal directly with them in person at times and appoint representatives at others: he will not find capable representatives unless he himself is one of them just as he will not be able to deal directly with them if he is inferior to them. This condition is the pivot of wazirate and on it its good administration depends.

It has been related that al-Ma'mun, may Allah be pleased with him, wrote regarding the choice of wazir saying: "I am looking for a man for my affairs who has all of the qualities of goodness, who is modest in his behaviour and resolute in his ways, a man who has been refined by manners and strengthened by experience, a man who if entrusted with secrets acts accordingly and if entrusted with important matters moves to execute them, a man whose forbearance causes him to be silent and whom knowledge causes to speak, a man for whom the moment is enough and for whom a glance is sufficient, a man who has the intrepidity of amirs and the perseverance of the wise, the humility of the 'ulama and the understanding of the fuqaha; if people treat him well, he is grateful and if put to the test by their mistreatment, he is patient; he does not sell the portion of today only to be deprived the next; a man who captures the hearts of men by the sharpness of his tongue and the beauty of his eloquence."

A poet has combined these qualities and concentrated them when describing one of the ministers of the Abbasid state:

His insight and thought are both sound when people are confused by affairs; he is the most judicious of his age when counsellor and counselled have wearied: his is a breast which finds expansion in cares when others have become constricted with cares.

If these qualities are perfected in someone in charge of organisation – and few are those who achieve this perfection – then the benefit resulting from his authority is general and everything connected with his judgement and organisation is complete; if, however, they are deficient, then this benefit is restricted accordingly and is limited in proportion to these qualities.

Although such a condition is not absolutely required by the deen, it is a condition of good administration which is inseparable from those of the deen because on it depend the interests of the Ummah and the upholding of religion.

If the conditions of this ministry are fully met in someone who is capable of the task, the validity of his appointment will depend on the verbal expression on the part of the Khalifah who is creating this wazirate: this is because it is an administration which has to have a contract and this legal agreement is not correct unless by way of an unequivocal statement. If jurisdiction and permission are granted to someone, the appointment is nevertheless not legally complete – even if it comes about in this way customarily – unless the contract of wazirate is concluded by means of a clear statement according both a general competence and the right of representation. If only general competence, without representation, is accorded, such a nomination is reserved for designating a successor and wazirate is not contracted thereby; if it is restricted to representation only it will be unclear whether representation is general as well as particular or whether it confers executory as well as delegatory powers in affairs and so likewise wazirate is not contracted; if both aspects are involved then it is duly contracted and completed.

When both aspects are present, two possibilities present themselves. The first of them, and this belongs rather to the rules of contractual agreements, is that the Sultan says, "I have entrusted you with whatever is being carried out in my name,"– with this the wazirate is contracted, as he has accorded him both a general and a representative authority. If, however, he says, "Represent me in my affairs!" wazirate may possibly be contracted, as his statement comprises both aspects of general authority and delegation, but it is also possible that it is not contracted, as it may be regarded merely as a permission which must necessarily be preceded by a contract, and permission alone does not validate contractual agreements, according to the rules of contractual agreements. If, however, he had said, "I make you a representative in my affairs," wazirate is contracted as he has modified the simple permission into a statement of contractual agreement. If he says, "Look to what is mine," it is not contracted because it may refer to an investigation of his affairs, to their execution or to taking over responsibility for them: a contract is not concluded by an ambiguous statement until something is added which removes this ambiguity.

However, general contractual agreements concluded by the khulafa and kings of the Ummah are subject to less rigorous conditions than contracts of a private or individual nature on two accounts: **1.** It is their habit to make do with little speech, rather than a lot, and this becomes a particular custom of theirs; moreover speech sometimes becomes burdensome for them and thus they limit themselves to gesture, although there is no legal basis for this in the shari'ah in the case of healthy persons who are able to speak: thus their custom excludes them from the shari'ah. **2.** Because they deal so rarely with contractual agreements, one must consider the circumstances compelling them to speak with such conciseness and the purpose thereof rather than any other possible interpretation – and this is one aspect. The second aspect, and this is the more likely given the customary practice of the post, is that he says, "I appoint you as wazir and rely on your representation,"– this wazirate is thereby duly established as both general authority is granted him by his saying, "I appoint you as wazir," (as the authority of this ministry is general), and representation is granted by his words, "and rely on your representation." In this way it is clearly established as a ministry of delegatory and not executory function. If he says, "I have delegated my ministry to you," it is possible for this ministry to be established as he has mentioned "delegation" and as such it is not an executive ministry; it is also possible, however, that it is not established, as delegatory powers are already implicit in the nature of this ministry and a contract should in any case precede the granting of such powers. The first of these two possibilities is more likely to be the correct interpretation.

If he says, "We have delegated the wazirate to you," this is valid as those in authority use the plural form when speaking of themselves, enhancing their importance by this addition and also omit possessive pronouns: thus his saying, "We have delegated to you," stands in place of, "I have delegated to you," and his saying "the ministry" stands in place of "my ministry"; this is the most elevated and most concise way of expressing the meaning, "I have contracted hereby the ministry of delegation." If people other than kings call themselves by this plural form and omit possessive pronouns, it will not express the singular or the possessive pronoun as they will be breaking the norms of agreed practice.

If the ruler says, "I have entrusted you with my ministry," or, "We have entrusted you with the ministry," he does not become a delegatory minister by these words until the ruler explains why he is entitled to delegation as Allah, may He be exalted, speaks of his Prophet Musa, may the blessings of Allah be upon him, saying, **"And appoint for me a wazir from my people, Harun, my brother, and consolidate my strength by him and make him a partner in my affair"** (Qur'an 20: 29-32). Thus Musa does not restrict himself to speaking of wazirate alone but rather refers also to a consolidation of his strength and an association with him in his affair.

The word "wazirate" has three possible derivations: the first, that it is derived from *wizr*, meaning heavy burden, as he takes up the heavy burdens of the king; the second, that it is derived from *wazar*, meaning refuge – occurring in Allah's words, may He be exalted: **"No, indeed, there is no refuge"** (Qur'an 75: 11), – as the king takes refuge in his judgement and his aid; the third, that it is derived from *azr*, meaning the back, as the king gains strength in his minister just as the body is strengthened by the back. Whichever of these derivations one adopts, however, none of them would indicate an absolute authority over affairs.

✳

✳   ✳

This then is how the wazirate of delegation comes into being. Exercise of this authority however, despite the general nature of this authority, is subject to two conditions by means of which Imamate and wazirate are differentiated. The first is peculiar to the wazir: he should keep the Imam informed of any governmental arrangements he makes, of any administrative actions he carries out and any appointments he makes lest, in acting alone, he usurp the Imam himself. The second is particular to the Imam: he should inspect the actions of the wazir and his management of affairs, so that he may endorse what is correct and curtail what is incorrect, as government of the Ummah is entrusted to him and is dependent upon his efforts.

It is permitted for this minister both to sit in judgement on his own and to appoint judges just as it is permitted for the Imam as he fulfils the conditions for judgeship; he is also permitted to investigate grievances and to appoint another as deputy as he fulfils the conditions for this office; he is permitted to take charge of the jihad in person or to entrust another with the task as he fulfils the conditions for waging such a war; he is permitted to execute those matters of governance he has decided on or to appoint a deputy to carry them out as he fulfils the conditions of sound judgement and the capacity to govern; everything, in fact, which is valid for the Imam is also valid for the minister except for three things: **1.** the designation of succession as it is up to the Imam to designate whomever he sees fit but not the minister; **2.** it is the Imam's prerogative to ask of the Ummah that he be allowed to resign from the Imamate but it is not the prerogative of the minister; **3.** it is the prerogative of the Imam that he may discharge whomever the minister has appointed but the minister may not dismiss anyone the Imam has entrusted with office.

Apart from these three things, his powers of delegation necessarily ensure that his actions are sanctioned and that his authority is validated. If the Imam is opposed to something he has carried out – and it concerns a judgement which has been properly executed or a property which has been assigned to its rightful owner – then the Imam is not permitted to undo what the minister has carried out after the latter's considered decision in the matter or to seek a return of property which the minister has duly handed over after reaching a judgement concerning it. If, however, it concerns the appointment of a governor, the preparing of an army or the waging of war it is permitted for the Imam to oppose him in this by dismissing the person appointed, to change the military arrangements as he wishes and to organise the war in a better way, since it is the prerogative of the Imam to change his own plans so it is all the more fitting that he may change those of his minister.

If the Imam entrusts someone with a task while the minister entrusts another with the same task, one must investigate who first entrusted him with the task: if it was the Imam, then his appointment carries more weight and no authority is invested in the person appointed by the minister; if however, the minister was the first to make the appointment there are two possibilities: if the Imam was aware of this appointment, then the Imam must annul this previous appointment as he has entrusted it to another, and confirm the appointment of the second; if however, the Imam did not know of this appointment by the minister, the latter's appointment carries more weight and the authority of the first-appointed, rather than the second, is validated, as ignorance of appointment of the first does not merit his dismissal.

One of the companions of ash-Shafi'i has said, may Allah be pleased with him, that the person appointed first by the minister is not dismissed even if the Imam was aware of this appointment when appointing another – unless the Imam dismisses him expressly: in effect he may only be dismissed by an express statement, not merely by the appointment of someone else. According to this opinion, if authority may be shared, the appointments of both remain valid and the authority is shared; if authority may not be shared, the appointment of each is dependent upon the dismissal of one of them and the confirmation of the other. If it was the Imam who granted this authority, he may dismiss and confirm whichever of them he wishes; if it was the minister, he may dismiss the particular person he appointed but not the person appointed by the Imam.

As for the wazirate of execution, its rule is weaker and its conditions are fewer as its authority is restricted to the judgement and direction of the Imam: the wazir is a mediator between him and his subjects, carrying out his commands, executing his instructions, enacting what he decides and announcing any governmental appointments or military preparations of the armies; he also informs him about anything of importance which happens and any new developments which come to his notice, so that he may act in accordance with the Imam's command. He is thus appointed for the execution of affairs but not to organise them – indeed he is not appointed for this purpose. If he shares in making judgements, the name "wazir" is more fitting while if he does not, then the name "mediator" or "ambassador" is more applicable.

No appointment is necessary for this wazirate: one must only ensure that permission has been granted. Neither the quality of being a freeman nor in possession of knowledge is considered in potential candidates as he does not exercise authority by himself or have the power to appoint others – for which it would be required he be a freeman, and he may not take decisions – for which he would have to have knowledge. Rather, his authority is restricted to two things: the first, to transmitting things to the Khalifah and the second, to transmitting things from the Khalifah to others.

Seven qualities are demanded of the wazir: **1.** Trustworthiness, such that he does not misuse whatever he has been entrusted with and does not deceive regarding whatever he is consulted about; **2.** Truthfulness, such that his report of what he has carried out is believed and his word is acted upon regarding what he transmits; **3.** Lack of greed, lest he accept bribes in return for influence and lest he allow himself to be cheated and become careless; **4.** Lack of enmity or hate between him and the people, for enmity prevents equitable transactions between people and excludes mutual sympathy; **5.** A retentive memory, such that he can transmit things to and from the Khalifah and be able to bear witness for him and against him in such matters; **6.** Acuteness and astuteness, such that affairs do not confuse him and he slips up or that affairs muddle him and he makes mistakes: determined action is of no use when affairs are confused and resoluteness is of no use when mistakes are being made. This quality is expressed by the minister of al-Ma'mun, Muhammad ibn Yazdad when he said:

A man's sound judgement is the spirit of his speech: if he makes a mistake of judgement, it will mean his death; if the heart of a man no longer watches over his expression, his apparent wakefulness in the two worlds will merely be lethargy.

7. Lack of craving and desire, as such passions will divert him from truth to falsehood and he will no longer discriminate between those who speak the truth and those of falsehood: such passions deceive the intellect and lead it away from what is correct. It is for this reason that the Prophet has said, may the peace and blessings of Allah be upon him, "Your love of something makes you blind and deaf." A poet has said:

For us, when the clamourings of desire lessen, and the listener gives ear to the speaker, and the people wrestle with their intellects, we reach a judgement which is just and decisive; we do not give a right to falsehood, and we do not pronounce on falsehood without truth; we fear that our discernment and intelligence will become foolish and then we will bear the burden of time along with the ass.

If this minister participates in making judgements, he needs to have an eighth quality and that is that he be worldly wise and have an experience which will allow him to arrive at correct judgements and to organise efficiently, for from experience comes an understanding of the way things will turn out. If he does not participate in decision-making, he does not need this quality even though he might acquire it through much practice.

It is not permitted for a woman to undertake this office even if she has sufficient experience in such matters as a saying of the Prophet, may the peace and blessings of Allah be upon him, indicates that the exercise of such authority has not been granted women: "A people who entrust their affairs to a woman will not be successful;" moreover, application of judgement and resoluteness of determination are diminished in women, and they would have to deal directly and openly with people, something which is prohibited to them.

An executory wazir may be of the people of dhimmah, although not a delegatory wazir; the difference between these two ministries varies according to their different functions in four ways: **1.** A minister of delegation may himself make legal judgements and have jurisdiction over acts of injustice whereas a minister of execution may not; **2.** The minister of delegation may proceed independently with the appointment of officers whereas the latter may not; **3.** The former may dispatch armies and conduct wars but not the latter; **4.** The former may dispose of treasury monies, taking what he has a right to take to make necessary payments, but not the former.

There are no other matters besides these four which would prevent a dhimmi from being an executory minister, except if they display arrogant behaviour as they are forbidden from being arrogant.

Because of these four differences between the two, four further conditions are required of the two ministries: **1.** The status of a freeman is required for the wazir of delegation but not for the executory wazir; **2.** That he be a Muslim is required of the former but not the latter; **3.** That the former have knowledge of the laws of the shari'ah but not the latter; **4.** That knowledge of the two matters of war and kharaj tax are required in the former but not the latter.

Thus the above two ministries differ in four ways regarding the conditions of appointment just as they differ in four aspects regarding their realm of jurisdiction; they are, however, the same regarding their rights and conditions in other than these aspects.

It is permitted for the Khalifah to appoint two executory ministers acting together or separately, but he may not appoint two delegatory ministers to work together because of the general nature of their powers of authority: likewise two Imams may not be appointed because they might dispute with each other in the arrangement or cancellation of matters and in the appointing or dismissal of officers. Allah, may He be exalted, has said, **"If there were a god other than Allah in the heavens and the earth they would both have been corrupted"** (Qur'an 21: 22).

If he appoints two ministers of delegation, their appointment must necessarily be one of three kinds:

1. The Khalifah delegates general authority to each of them both, in which case it would not be valid because of the evidence and reasoning we have mentioned above. Such appointments should be investigated: if they were both made at the same time, both are invalidated; if one of them preceded the other, the appointment of the first is valid and the second invalid. The difference between the invalidity of an appointment and a dismissal is that the former prevents the execution of what he has already authorised whereas dismissal does not;

2. The Khalifah ensures they both share jurisdiction and does not give it to one of them alone: this is valid and the ministry is then shared between them such that they may execute what they jointly agree upon but not what they differ about – this being dependent on the judgement of the Khalifah and outside the jurisdiction of these two ministers. This ministry is restricted with respect to the ministry of delegation proper in two aspects: their execution of something together is dependent on their mutual agreement whereas their authority ceases over what they differ about.

If they agree after having differed then the matter is investigated: if it is based on a judgement the justice of which they have both agreed upon after having disagreed about it, then it comes under their jurisdiction and their joint execution of it is valid: this is because a previous difference does not preclude a subsequent agreement. If, however, one of them follows his colleague in the matter, while both retain their contrary opinions, it is excluded from their joint jurisdiction as it is invalid for a wazir to carry out something which he does not judge to be correct.

3. In this case the Khalifah does not share jurisdiction between them but rather accords to each an authority for matters over which the other has no sway; this may occur in one of two ways: either he grants to each a specific task over which he has general jurisdiction – giving to one, for example, the ministry of eastern territories and to the other, that of the western territories – or he grants each special jurisdiction in a region where both have general authority – by appointing one of them, for example, minister for war and the other for kharaj tax. Appointment is valid in both the above ways although neither of them is a plenipotentiary minister but rather both are functionaries responsible for two different tasks; ministry of delegation should be concerned with what is general, and thus these two ministers should be able to execute all tasks and exercise full jurisdiction: in fact the appointment of each is restricted to each person's particular task and neither can oppose the other's jurisdiction or particular responsibility.

The Khalifah may appoint two ministers, a delegatory minister and an executory minister, such that the first is completely free to act as he wishes and the second is restricted to executing the commands of the Khalifah; moreover the executory minister may not reappoint someone who has been dismissed nor dismiss someone who has been appointed. The delegatory minister may, however, do both of these, but he may not dismiss someone appointed by the Khalifah. The executory minister may not sign on his own behalf nor on behalf of the Khalifah, except on his orders, whereas the minister of delegation may write orders using his own signature to his own agents and those of the Khalifah and they must accept his signatures. He may not, however, sign on behalf of the Khalifah except on his orders, both in general and particular matters.

If the Khalifah dismisses the executory minister none of the officials are thereby dismissed. If he dismisses the minister of delegation, executory agents are dismissed while delegatory agents are not as the former are representatives and the latter are functionaries.

A plenipotentiary minister may appoint someone to stand in for him but an executory minister may not, as this substitution would represent an appointment and this is valid coming from the former but not from the latter. If, however, the Khalifah orders the plenipotentiary minister not to appoint a substitute then he should not appoint a substitute. If he does allow the executory minister to appoint a substitute, this is permitted as each of the two ministers are subject to the command or interdiction of the Khalifah, even though at the time of appointment each assumes different jurisdictions.

If the Khalifah grants the direction of the provinces to their governors but gives jurisdiction to those who have seized power over them, (as is the case amongst our people today), the ruler of each province may appoint ministers and the relationship of these ministers to the ruler is the same as that of the Khalifah's ministers to the Khalifah – that is with regard to the validity of the two types of ministry and the rulings regarding the two types of jurisdiction.

Chapter 3
Establishing Amirate in the Provinces

If the Khalifah appoints an amir over a province or a town, his amirate may be one of two kinds, either general or particular. As for the general, it is of two kinds: either that freely contracted by the Khalifah with the person chosen specifically for the task, or that contracted at times of conquest in compelling circumstances.

As for amirate which has been specifically and freely assigned, it comprises a clearly defined task and a clearly determined jurisdiction: the Khalifah delegates the amirate of a country or province to the person appointed for this task and accords the right of governance over all its people together with jurisdiction over the customary acts of his office: he thus assumes a general responsibility for a particular territory and for specific and clearly defined tasks, and his corresponding jurisdiction covers seven matters:

1. The ordering of the armies, assigning them to various territories and apportioning their provisions, unless the Khalifah has fixed the amount of provision in which case the amir has only to ensure its payment to them; **2.** Application of the law and the appointment of judges and magistrates; **3.** Collection of the kharaj and zakah taxes, appointment of collectors, and distribution of what is collected to those entitled to it; **4.** Protection of the deen, defence of what is inviolable and the guarding of the deen from modification and deviation; **5.** Establishment of the hadd-punishments both with respect to Allah's rights and those of people; **6.** Imamate of the Friday gatherings and prayer assembly, he himself acting as Imam or his substitute; **7.** Facilitating the passage of hajjis from his territory or those of other territories such that he affords them protection. If this province is a border territory adjacent to the enemy, an eighth matter becomes obligatory, that is jihad against the neighbouring enemy, and distribution of the booty amongst the fighters after a fifth has been taken for those entitled to it.

The conditions considered in this amirate are the same as those applicable in the wazirate of delegation as the only difference between the two is that there is specific authority in the former but a general one in the latter, there being no difference in the conditions applicable to specific or general authorities.

Examination must now be made of the contractual agreement in this amirate. If it is the Khalifah who has designated the amir, the wazir of delegation has the right to subject him to his control and surveillance but not to dismiss him or transfer him from one province to another. If the wazir of delegation was alone in appointing him then there are two possibilities: the first is that he appoints him with the permission of the Khalifah, in which case he may not dismiss him or transfer him without the Khalifah's permission and command; moreover if the Khalifah dismisses the minister it does not entail the dismissal of the amir. The second is that he appoints him himself, in which case he stands in for the minister and the latter may himself dismiss him or replace him with someone else in accordance with his considered judgement of what is the better and more correct procedure. If the wazir does not stipulate which kind of appointment this amir is subject to and does not tell him explicitly whether it is from the Khalifah or from himself, the appointment is treated as being from himself and he himself may dismiss the amir. If the wazir is dismissed, so too is this amir unless the Khalifah reaffirms his amirate, in which case it would be a renewal of his authority and a reappointment although the same oral statement of contract, necessary at the outset of the agreement, is not required again: it is enough that the Khalifah says, "I confirm your authority of governance," whereas at the beginning of the contractual agreement he must say, "I accord you the amirate of such and such a region and its people with jurisdiction over everything connected with it," that is, stating the nature of the appointment in detail rather than in a general way so there is no room for doubt.

If it is the Khalifah who establishes this amirate, the wazir cannot be excluded from subjecting it to his control and surveillance. Moreover if he appoints a new minister, it does not entail the dismissal of the amir because if, emanating from the Sultan, there is an appointment of a general nature combined with that of a particular nature, the general one is customarily concerned with the surveillance and investigation of the particular, and the particular is concerned with the task proper and its execution. This amir may appoint an executory minister on his own initiative, with or without the Khalifah's permission, but he may not appoint a plenipotentiary minister except if the Khalifah permits and commands him to do this, as the former is assigned to a specific task while the latter is independent.

If this amir wishes, without specific reason, to increase the provisions of his army, he is not permitted to do so as it would be an unjustified waste; if, however, he increases them in response to a specific incident, the reason must be examined: if it is something of a temporary nature such that the increase will not have to be fixed at this level, like a rise in prices, an unexpected incident or the cost of a war, the amir may pay for this increase from the treasury and does not need to consult the Khalifah, as this figures as part of the administrative duties with which he is entrusted. If, however, the reason for the increase is the mounting cost of an ongoing campaign in which the combatants have proved themselves steadfast and victorious, he should submit this proposed increase to the Khalifah and should not proceed with it on his own. He may give provision to those of the combatants' children who have reached puberty and assign a stipend over to them without any instructions, but he may not fix the salary of a newly recruited army except on orders.

If there is an excess of wealth from the kharaj tax after provision has been made for the army, it should be handed over to the Khalifah to be deposited in the treasury and used in the public interest; if, however, there is an excess of wealth from the zakah tax after payment to those entitled to it has been made, it is not necessary for it to be handed over to the Khalifah: rather the revenue officer should distribute it to those living nearest to his district who are entitled to it. If the kharaj tax is not enough to provide for the army, he should ask the Khalifah to make up the amount; if the zakah is not enough to meet the needs of those entitled to it he may not ask the Khalifah to make up the amount, as the provisioning of the army is a binding communal duty, while those having a right to the zakah funds are only entitled to actually receive them if they exist.

If the appointment of the amir was made by the Khalifah, he is not deposed at the death of the Khalifah; if, however, it was at the hand of a minister, he is deposed at the death of this minister because an appointment made by the Khalifah is made in the name of all the Muslims, whereas the appointment made by a minister is merely in his name. A minister is deposed at the death of the Khalifah while an amir is not, as the ministry represents the Khalifah while the amirate is established in the name of the Muslims as a whole.

This then is the status of the first of the two kinds of general amirate, namely the amirate for which a suitable amir is freely chosen by the Khalifah.

We shall now discuss the status of "special" amirate, before dealing with the other kind of "general" amirate, because they both entail a contract made by choice; we shall then explain the second kind of amirate, namely that of conquest and occupation contracted under duress, so that we might contrast the nature of this latter together with that based on free choice and thereby demonstrate the difference between them with regard to their respective conditions, duties and rights.

Special amirate refers to that in which the amir is restricted to organisation of the army, establishment of public order, defence of the territory and protection of what is inviolable; it is not, however, up to him to undertake responsibility for the judiciary and the rulings of jurisprudence, or for the kharaj and zakah.

As for the establishment of hadd-punishments or the resolving of issues which require that a considered choice be made because of differing opinions of the fuqaha, or other issues which require the production of proof because of disputing litigants, then he is under no obligation to intervene, as these matters are outside the scope of the particularity of his amirate. If, however, they do not require that a choice be made or evidence be provided – or indeed if they require both these things but a judge resolves the issue after making ijtihad or establishes a proof – such matters will necessarily be concerned either with the rights of Allah, may He be exalted, or with those of man. If it concerns the latter, like the punishment for slander, or retaliation for a killing or loss of some part of the body, this is considered according to the demands of the plaintiff: if he turns to the magistrate, then the magistrate has more right to resolve the matter as such a claim is among those rights the fulfilment of which is the responsibility of the magistrate. If the plaintiff looks to fulfilment of the punishment or retaliation from this type of amir, then the latter is more entitled to deal with it, as it is not a judgement but rather an assistance in the fulfilment of a right, and the person who has the power to assist is the amir rather than the magistrate.

If this punishment is purely one of the rights of Allah, may He be exalted, like the punishment for fornication either by lashing or by stoning, then the amir has more right to see it is carried out than the magistrate, as it counts as a public order law and the defence and protection of the deen: such concerns for the public interest are entrusted to the amirs who are delegated specifically to look into them – rather than the magistrates who are concerned with resolving contention between litigants. Such matters are therefore part of the duties of amirate and may not be excluded from it except by an explicit textual statement; likewise they are excluded from the duties of the judiciary and may not be included in it except by an explicit textual statement.

As for his jurisdiction in grievances and complaints, the following must be considered:

1. If it concerns a matter covered by legal rulings and sanctioned by judges and magistrates, the amir may see to its fulfilment by way of an assistance to the person affirming the claim against the person who is denying it, and by removing the disputed object from the false claimant (who is delaying handing it over) in order to render it to its rightful owner; this he may do as he has a responsibility to prevent injustices and oppression and to deal with compassion and equity between people;

2. If, however, the injustices are such that rulings and judgements must be had from the judiciary, this amir is excluded from getting involved, as such decisions are not part of his contract of amirate and he must refer them to the magistrate of his city. If the latter pronounces judgement in favour of one of the parties but is incapable of carrying it out, it is the amir who should execute it. If there is no magistrate in his city, he should transfer the matter to the nearest magistrate as long as the two litigants will have no difficulty in travelling there; if there is difficulty, he does not oblige them to travel there but rather consults the Khalifah concerning the object of their dispute and carries out his ruling in the matter.

Assisting the hajjis within his territory is also one of the tasks of his amirate, as it constitutes one of the acts of assistance for which he is responsible.

Some say that leading the prayers on Fridays and the Eid days is the responsibility of the judiciary rather than that of the amir, and this is the most convincing opinion for the followers of ash-Shafi'i, although it has also been said that the amirs are more entitled to it, and this is the most convincing view for the Hanafis.

If the territorial authority of this type of amir lies adjacent to a border he may not initiate a jihad except with the Khalifah's permission, although he must wage war on them and repulse them if they initiate the attack, without the Khalifah's permission, as this forms part of his duty to protect and defend what is inviolable. The same conditions which are considered when appointing a wazir of delegation are taken into consideration for this type of amirate – with the addition of two conditions, namely being a Muslim and having the status of a freeman, as this amir is responsible for matters of the deen and it is not correct for these to be dealt with by a kafir or a slave. Knowledge and legal understanding, however, are not taken into consideration, although if present, are considered an extra advantage.

Thus the conditions of general amirate are the same as those of the delegatory wazirate, as they both share a general jurisdiction even though they differ in the particularity of their tasks. As for the conditions required for the special amirate, they are the same as those of the general amirate except for one condition, namely knowledge, as judgements must be made within the jurisdiction of general amirate but not within that of the special amirate. Neither of these two types of amir need inform the Khalifah regarding any normal affair he undertakes within his own particular amirate, except if he chooses to and as a show of obedience. If something unusual happens, they should both refer the matter to the scrutiny of the Imam and then act upon it in accordance with his order. If, however, they both fear an aggravation of the problem, if they refer it to him, they both take necessary measures to repulse any violation of public order until the permission of the Khalifah reaches them concerning the matter: in effect it is the judgement of the Khalifah who is in a position to oversee the generality of affairs which takes precedence in new situations.

As for the amirate of conquest, contracted in compelling circumstances, this occurs when an amir takes possession of a country by force and the Khalifah entrusts him with this amirate and grants him authority to order and direct it: thus the amir, while acting despotically in his ordering and directing of the amirate by virtue of his conquest, is nevertheless accorded legal sanction by the Khalifah's religious duty to transform an irregular situation into a correct one, that is a forbidden one to one which is legally permitted. Even though such practice departs, in its laws and conditions, from what is customary regarding normal appointments, it nevertheless protects the laws of the shari'ah and upholds the rulings of the deen which may not be allowed to degenerate into disorder or be weakened by corruption. Thus this is permitted in cases of conquest and compelling circumstances, but not in the case of a fitting candidate freely chosen for the appointment – because of the difference which exists between the possibility (to act freely) and incapacity.

There are seven laws of the shari'ah which must be upheld with respect to the appointment of an amir of conquest: both the Khalifah in authority and the amir who has seized authority share the responsibility for imposing these laws, although the latter bears a heavier responsibility:

1. Protection of the office of Imamate, which is the successor of Prophethood, and the organisation of religious affairs, so that this obligatory institution of the shari'ah is maintained and all rights and duties issuing from it are preserved;

2. A manifest obedience to the deen which negates all possibility of rebellious or fractious behaviour on the part of the amir;

3. Unanimity in friendship and mutual help such that the authority of the Muslims may be above all other peoples;

4. Contracts issuing from governmental authority which are connected to the deen should be concluded, and the rulings and judgements pertaining to them should be executed; they should also not be invalidated by mere imperfections in such contracts, or annulled by mistakes in the obligations ensuing from such contracts;

5. The receipt of money for something due in accordance with the shari'ah must be paid in such a way that the person acquits himself of what is owing and the person receiving it acts licitly;

6. The hadd-punishments should be executed correctly and should be applied to those who deserve them as the body of the believer is inviolable except from the rights of Allah and His punishments;

7. The amir must be scrupulous in protecting the deen from the things prohibited by Allah, must command the obligations of the deen if it is being obeyed and call to its obedience if it is being disobeyed.

By means of these seven fundamental laws of the shari'ah, the rights and duties of Imamate and the rulings governing the Ummah are maintained: it is for the sake of these laws that the appointment of the amir who has seized power is obligatory. Moreover if he fulfils the conditions of a freely-chosen amir, allegiance to his appointment becomes obligatory as a way of encouraging his obedience and preventing any schism or opposition on his part. Permission duly granted enables him to establish the religious rights and duties and the laws governing the Ummah. The procedure is the same for whomever he appoints as a minister or representative as the procedure adopted by the Khalifah when appointing a minister or representative. He may appoint a wazir of delegation and an executory minister.

Even if the conditions for a freely chosen appointment are not met in the amir who seizes power, the Khalifah may nevertheless openly announce his appointment as a way of encouraging his obedience and pre-empting any opposition or rebellious behaviour on his part; any activity on his part regarding laws and rights, however, is dependent on the Khalifah appointing a representative for him in these matters, that is someone who meets the required conditions: the fulfilment of the conditions in the person assigned to him as a representative will thus make up for any lack in the conditions in the amir; nominal authority is thus granted to the conquering amir while executive power is with the representative.

Such a procedure is permitted, even though it deviates from the principles, for two reasons: **1.** Necessity annuls conditions which are otherwise required when there is a possibility of their fulfilment; **2.** If it is feared that matters of general interest will be harmed, conditions may be less rigorous than those relative to a particular or individual interest.

Given that the amirate of conquest has been validly established, it differs in four respects from the amirate established under normal conditions:

1. The amirate of occupation is established in and constituted by the person in charge, while the latter depends only on the free choice of the person who institutes it;

2. The former extends to those countries which the amir has conquered, and the latter is restricted to those countries stipulated in the agreement contracted by the person who institutes it;

3. The former comprises both normal and abnormal juridical matters, while the latter is restricted to what is known and established in matters of jurisdiction but not to the unusual;

4. The wazirate of delegation is valid in the former, while it is not in the latter. This is because of the difference in matters of jurisdiction between the amir and his minister: the jurisdiction of the minister is limited to what is normal, while the one who seizes power has jurisdiction in unusual matters as well; in the latter case, where the situation has been regularised, the amir of conquest may only deal with normal matters and it would not be valid for him to have a wazir with the same capacity as his own, because of the equivocal situation in which the wazir and the amir who appointed him would then find themselves.

Chapter 4
The Amirate of Jihad

The amirate of jihad is particularly concerned with fighting the mushrikun and it is of two kinds:

A. That which is restricted to the administration of the army and the direction of war, in which case the conditions pertaining to special amirate are applicable;

B. That in which all laws regarding the division of booty and the negotiation of the peace treaties are delegated to the amir, in which case the conditions pertaining to general amirate are applicable. Of all the authorities of governance this is the most important with respect to its laws, and the most comprehensive with regard to its sections and departments.

This type of amirate, when special, is subject to the same rulings as the general, and so we have confined ourselves to a description of the latter for the sake of brevity.

There are six sections regarding the rulings connected to a general amirate:

1. The mobilisation of the army, pertaining to which there are seven matters:

First, kindness should be shown to those travelling, such that the weakest of them is capable of keeping up and the strength of the strongest is maintained: the pace must not be so great that the weak perish and the strong use up every ounce of their strength, for the Prophet, may the peace and blessings of Allah be upon him, has said, "This deen is enduring, so press on with kindness, for surely whoever is unable to proceed on his journey, his camel that bears him foundering, travels across the earth no more and his mount will not survive: the worst kind of journeying is that in which the beast is made to exert itself to the very utmost." It is also related of the Prophet, may the peace and blessings of Allah be upon him, "The person mounted on a weak beast is the amir of the caravan," meaning that people have to travel at the pace of the owner of the weak animal;

Second, the horses and other mounts used in the jihad should be examined: no big and heavy horses should be amongst those used in the jihad, nor any spare and small ones, nor those broken with old age, frail and thin, or those with broken limbs or emaciated, as they will be incapable of the task required of them and might even perish. Other mounts and beasts of burden should be examined: those mounts incapable of travel are excluded, and beasts of burden are not allowed to carry more than they can bear. Allah, may He be exalted, has said, **"And prepare for them what you are able of force and war horses"** (Qur'an 8: 60). The Messenger of Allah has said, may the peace and blessings of Allah be upon him, "Train horses for war, for surely their mounts are power for you, and their bellies are a treasure for you;"

Third, overseeing the combatants who are of two kinds: regulars and volunteers. As for the former, they are registered in the Diwan and participate in the fay-booty and the jihad; their stipend is taken from the treasury and allocated from the booty according to their wealth and need. As for the latter, they are not registered in the Diwan: they are those from the desert areas, the Arabs and other inhabitants of the towns and villages who have left for battle in accordance with Allah's instructions, may He be exalted, to people, **"Go out [to battle] light and heavy and fight with your wealth and your selves in the way of Allah"** (Qur'an 9: 41). As for the words of Allah **"light and heavy"**, there are four interpretations: the first that they refer to young men and old men, and this has been related by al-Hasan and 'Ikrimah; the second, to the wealthy and the poor, and this is related by Abu Salih; the third, mounted soldiers and infantry, and this Abu 'Umar has said; the fourth, those with a family and those without, and this is al-Farra's opinion. These volunteers are granted an amount from the zakah rather than the fay, that is from the portion accorded to those who fight in the way of Allah and mentioned in the Qur'anic ayat about zakah. It is not permitted to pay them from the fay, but rather from the zakah – just as the regulars, registered in the Diwan, are not given of the zakah, but are entitled to the fay: each group receives a sum from a source in which the other is not permitted to share. Abu Hanifah, however, has permitted each of the two kinds of wealth to be spent on each of the two groups according to need; but Allah has made a distinction between the two groups, and it is not permitted to treat as one what has been differentiated;

Fourth, leaders and lieutenants are assigned to both groups so as to be kept informed by them of their state and to ensure that they are well-disposed towards them if he calls for them, as the Messenger of Allah, may the peace and blessings of Allah be upon him, did this in his raiding parties and Allah, may He be exalted, said, **"We have made you into peoples and tribes so that you should get to know each other"** (Qur'an 49: 13). There are three interpretations: the first, that **"peoples"** are those most closely related and **"tribes"** are those most distant, and this is Mujahid's opinion; the second, that **"peoples"** refer to the Arabs of Qahtan and **"tribes"** to the Arabs of 'Adnan; the third, that the former are the clans of non-Arabs and the latter the clans of Arabs;

Fifth, a rallying-cry is given to each group to distinguish those belonging together and to rally them as allies. It is related by 'Urwah ibn az-Zubayr from his father that the Messenger of Allah, may the peace and blessings of Allah be upon him, made the rallying-cry of the Muhajirun, "O Bani 'Abd ar-Rahman," that of the Khazraj, "O Bani 'Abdallah," and that of the Aws, "O Bani 'Ubaidullah," and he called its horsemen, "the horsemen of Allah";

Sixth, he should inspect the army and the serving troops and dismiss those who might cause the mujahidin to desert, those who might spread false rumours about the Muslims or act as spies against them for the mushrikun: the Messenger of Allah, may the peace and blessings of Allah be upon him, rejected 'Abdallah ibn Abi Saluk on one of his raiding parties because he was instigating defection from the Muslims and Allah, may He be exalted, says, **"And fight them until there is no more strife or dissent and until the deen is all for Allah"** (Qur'an 8: 39) – in other words until you no longer cause strife and dissent amongst each other;

Seventh, he should not show partiality, conspire with or aid those who are of the same race or who share his opinions or madhhab, to the detriment of those unrelated to him or who oppose his views and madhhab, lest peoples' differing circumstances result in a split in the unity of the community and a preoccupation with divisions and discord: the Messenger, may the peace and blessings of Allah be upon him, turned a blind eye to the hypocrites, who are the enemies of the deen, and judged them according to their outward appearance such that his fighting force was strengthened by them, the numbers of adherents multiplied and his strength was perfected. He entrusted the judgement of their hearts' hidden hypocrisy to the Knower of the Unseen and to the One who punishes what the hearts conceal. Allah, may He be exalted, says, **"And do not dispute with each other lest you fail and your prosperity departs from you"** (Qur'an 8: 46). There are two interpretations of this: the first, that what is meant by **"prosperity"** is dominion, this being the opinion of Abu 'Ubaid, and the second, that it refers to power, and the word here in Arabic – *reeh* (lit.: wind) – is used because of the sense of power it conveys.

2. This section deals with the direction of war. The mushrikun of Dar al-Harb (the arena of battle) are of two types:

First, those whom the call of Islam has reached, but they have refused it and have taken up arms. The amir of the army has the option of fighting them in one of two ways, that is in accordance with what he judges to be in the best interests of the Muslims and most harmful to the mushrikun: the first, to harry them from their houses and to inflict damage on them day and night, by fighting and burning, or else to declare war and combat them in ranks;

Second, those whom the invitation to Islam has not reached, although such persons are few nowadays since Allah has made manifest the call of his Messenger – unless there are people to the east and extreme east, or to the west, of whom we have no knowledge, beyond the Turks and Romans we are fighting: it is forbidden us to initiate an attack on the mushrikun while they are unawares or at night, that is, it is forbidden to kill them, use fire against them or begin an attack before explaining the invitation to Islam to them, informing them of the miracles of the Prophet and making plain the proofs so as to encourage acceptance on their part; if they still refuse to accept after this, war is waged against them and they are treated as those whom the call has reached. Allah, may He be exalted, says, **"Call to the way of your Lord with wisdom and kindly admonition and converse with them by what is better in argument"** (Qur'an 16: 125), – which means calling to the *deen* of your Lord with **wisdom**, about which there are two interpretations: the first, that **wisdom** refers to prophethood and the second, that it refers to the Qur'an, and al-Kalbi is of this view. For **"kindly admonition"** there are also two interpretations: the first, that it refers to the Qur'an on account of its quiet, restrained speech, and this is again al-Kalbi's view, and the second, that it refers to the commands and interdictions therein. As for, **"and converse with them by what is better in argument,"** it means, "explain the truth to them and make clear the proofs to them!"

If the amir initiates the attack against them before calling them to Islam or warning them by means of cogent proofs, and kills them by surprise or at night, blood money must be paid; according to the most correct judgement of the Shafi'is, it is equal to the blood money paid to Muslims, although according to other it is equal to the blood money paid to the kuffar, because of the difference of their beliefs. Abu Hanifah, however, says that no blood money is liable for killing them and their blood is shed with impunity.

If the ranks are ranged against each other in war, one of the combatant Muslims may advance between the two ranks in order to identify himself and proclaim in what manner he himself may be distinguished from the rest of the army: to this purpose he may ride a piebald horse if the horses of the others are black or brown. Abu Hanifah, however, forbids any such identification or the riding of a piebald horse, although there is no reason for his prohibition: 'Abd ibn 'Awnallah relates from 'Umayr from Abu Ishaq that the Messenger of Allah, may the peace and blessings of Allah be upon him, said at Badr, "Make a mark for yourselves, for the angels have also done so."

It is permitted for someone to sally forth in single combat in response to a challenge: Ubayy ibn Khalaf called the Messenger of Allah, may the peace and blessings of Allah be upon him, to single combat on the day of Uhud to which the former responded and killed him. The first battle witnessed by the Messenger of Allah, may the peace and blessings of Allah be upon him, was that of Badr: three nobles of the Quraysh, 'Utbah ibn Rabi'ah, his son al-Walid, and his brother Shaybah, sallied forth and they called out a challenge, to which three of the Ansar, Awf and Mas'ud, the two sons of Afra, and 'Abdallah ibn Rawahah responded. The challengers declared however: "Let those who can match our standing sally out to us, for we do not recognise you." Thus three of the Banu Hashim came out to confront them: 'Ali ibn Abi Talib came out to face al-Walid and killed him; and Hamzah ibn 'Abd al-Muttalib confronted 'Utbah and killed him; 'Ubaidah ibn al-Harith faced Shaybah and both delivered blows severing each other's limbs: Shaybah died there and then, while 'Ubaidah was carried away alive with his leg torn off, but later he died at as-Safra. Ka'b ibn Malik said of him:

O eye of abundance, do not withhold your tears with just a trickle, do not let them diminish for a warrior whose death has crushed us; a noble of the martyrs' field, a noble in lineage. 'Ubaidah has departed this evening, he who came to us in the morning to do us good and not evil he it was who warded off the enemy fighters, warding off the army with his mutilated limb.

Then Hind, the daughter of 'Utbah, made a vow at the battle of Uhud to reward Wahshi if he killed Hamzah in revenge for the killing of her father; when he killed him, she split open his belly and chewed off his liver, may Allah be pleased with him, and recited these lines:

We have punished you for the day of Badr, and one battle after the other brings madness and affliction. I could not resign myself to the loss of 'Utbah, neither of my brother, or his uncle and my first-born. O Wahshi, you have cured my self and fulfilled my vow. You have cured the desire for revenge in my breast. So all my life I owe thanks to Wahshi until my bones are gathered in my grave.

This then was the single combat on the day of Badr which the Prophet, may the peace and blessings of Allah be upon him, permitted his closest relatives from amongst the Banu Hashim and the Banu 'Abd al-Muttalib, despite the strongest of attachment to them and his fear for them. He himself fought Ubayy in single combat on the day of Uhud and he gave permission for 'Ali, may Allah be pleased with him, to do the same at the battle of the Trench, when the matter was more difficult and his affection and concern for him greater. 'Amr ibn 'Abd Wudd had made a challenge the first day which no one had taken up; this he renewed on the second day, but again no one took it up; when he challenged them on the third day and saw how they retired and avoided him, he said: "O Muhammad, do you not claim that those slain from amongst you are in the Garden, alive and provided for, with their Lord, and those of us who are slain are being punished? Yet none of you concerns himself with receiving the generosity of his Lord or despatching an enemy to the Fire!" Then he began to recite:

I have approached their company to cry out whether there is a combatant, but I have come to a halt as the brave have become cowards, although I am ready for battle. I am like this: always hastening towards the struggle. Surely courage and generosity in a man are the best of qualities.

'Ali ibn Abi Talib then got up and sought the permission of the Messenger of Allah, may the peace and blessings of Allah be upon him, to take up the challenge, which the latter granted saying: "Go out O 'Ali with the protection and refuge of Allah!" Then he sallied forth saying:

Hear the good news, a man who is not incapable in combat has come to you to respond to your voice: one who has resolve and insight, anticipating the everlasting happiness of success in the morning. Surely I hope to bring upon you a wailing funeral by a grand stroke whose remembrance will shine in the memories of battles.

So they engaged each other in battle and a cloud of dust arose obscuring them from view; when it cleared around them, 'Ali could be seen wiping his sword with the garment of the man he had killed. This is related by Muhammad ibn Ishaq in his *Book of Battles.*

These two accounts thus prove the permissibility of sallying forth to single combat despite exposing oneself to danger. But if it is the Muslim warrior who wants to make the first challenge, Abu Hanifah forbids it, arguing that a provocative challenge and the initiation of violence is a transgression. Ash-Shafi'i, however, permits it saying it is a manifestation of the strength of Allah's deen, may He be exalted, and an act of solidarity with His Messenger. The Messenger, himself, may the peace and blessings of Allah be upon him, recommended the like of it, encouraged it and chose the person who should take up and respond to the provocation – while he himself prepared for action. Muhammad ibn Ishaq relates that the Messenger of Allah, may the peace and blessings of Allah be upon him, appeared wearing breastplates on the day of Uhud, seized his sword and brandished it saying, "Who will take this sword by its right?" Then 'Umar ibn al-Khattab, may Allah be pleased with him, stood up saying, "I will take it by its right." But the Prophet turned from him and brandished it a second time, saying, "Who will take it by its right?" Then az-Zubayr ibn al-'Awwam stood up saying, "I will take it by its right." But the Prophet again turned away from him and these two men were aggrieved by this. Then he showed it a third time saying, "Who will take this sword by its right?" and Abu Dujana Simak ibn Kharasha stood up and asked, "And what is its right, O Messenger of Allah?" He replied, "That you strike the enemy until he writhes!" Taking it from him, he made a show of a red kerchief by which the people knew that he would show prowess in combat. He then went out to battle saying:

I am the one who took it, in service to him, when he said: "Who will take it by its right?" I, amongst creation, have accepted it by his justice and authenticity in view of the all-Powerful, the Merciful, Whose overflowing generosity of provision reaches all people both of the west and the east.

Then he began to swagger between the two serried ranks and the Prophet, may the peace and blessings of Allah be upon him, said, "Surely Allah would find such behaviour reprehensible except in these circumstances." Then he went into battle: he initiated the fight, showed great zeal and caused great carnage, saying:

My friend made me give a promise, when we were in the palm grove at the foot of the mountain, that never would come the day I would be in the last ranks. I have taken the sword of Allah and of His Messenger.

Having established with the above mentioned proofs that single combat, both for the one who provokes it and also for the one who is provoked, is permitted, it should be added that it is conditional upon two things: **1.** That the champion be vigorous and brave and aware that he will not fail in withstanding the enemy – if not, it is forbidden; **2.** That he is not an army leader whose loss would have a detrimental effect: in effect the loss of an army chief might lead to defeat. The Messenger of Allah established single combat, trusting in the support of Allah, may He be praised, and that He would keep His promise – but this is not permitted to another.

The amir may, when urging his army to jihad, incite someone willing to die for Allah if he knows his death in battle will have one of two effects: either that it will incite the Muslims to fight to avenge him, or that it will cause the mushrikun to lose heart on account of his audacity against them for the sake of Allah.

Muhammad ibn Ishaq reports that the Messenger of Allah, may the peace and blessings of Allah be upon him, came out of the palm-frond shelter on the day of Badr after urging the people to the jihad and promising each man whatever booty he seized. Then he said, "By the One in Whose hand is my self, no man will fight them today and be killed – steadfast, God-fearing, facing the enemy and without turning his back – but that Allah will take him to the Garden." Then 'Umayr ibn Humam of the Banu Salima said, while still holding some dates he was eating, "Goodness! Nothing remains between me and the Garden except those people killing me." Then he threw away the dates he was holding in his hand, took hold of his sword and fought them until he was killed, may Allah have mercy on him, reciting:

Forward to Allah without any provision for the journey but fear of Him, actions for the Next World, and patience for Allah in jihad. Every provision can be depleted other than fear of Him, right action and correctness.

A Muslim may put to death any mushrik combatant he seizes, whether or not he is involved in the fighting. There is a difference of opinion regarding the killing of old persons and monks inhabiting cells and monasteries. One view concerning them is that they are not to be killed unless they fight, as they are covered, like women and children, by treaty; another, is that they are killed even if they are not fighting, because it may be that their opinions will cause more harm to the Muslims than fighting. Durayd ibn as-Simma, who was more than one hundred years old, was killed during the battle of Hawazin at Hunayn while the Prophet, may the peace and blessings of Allah be upon him, was watching and he did not oppose his killing. As he was being killed, Durayd recited:

I gave them my orders at the bend in the sand-dune, but it was only the next morning that they discerned the right path. When they disobeyed I was with them, but I see now that they were in error and I was not guided.

It is not permitted to kill women and children in battle, nor elsewhere, as long as they are not fighting because of the prohibition of the Messenger of Allah, may the peace and blessings of Allah be upon him, against killing them. The Prophet, may the peace and blessings of Allah be upon him, forbade the killing of those employed as servants and mamlouks, that is young slaves. If women and children fight, then they are fought and killed, but only face to face, not from behind while fleeing. If they use their women and children as shields in battle, then one must avoid killing them and aim only at killing the men; if, however, it is impossible to kill them except by killing the women and children, then it is permitted. If they are shielding themselves with Muslim captives, and it is not possible to kill them except by killing these captives, it is not permitted to kill them. If desisting from attacking them leads to the Muslims being encircled, then the latter must attempt to free themselves as best they can, but while taking care not to kill any Muslim deliberately by their hands. If one is killed, then the killer must pay blood-money and make expiation if he knew that he was a Muslim; he becomes liable for the expiation alone if he did not know.

It is permitted to cut their horses from under them if they are fighting on them, although one of the fuqaha has forbidden injuring them. Handhalah ibn ar-Rahib cut down the horse of Abu Sufyan ibn Harb on the day of Uhud and mounted it to kill Abu Sufyan; when Ibn Sha'ub saw him he sallied forth to challenge Handhalah saying:

I will surely defend my companion and myself with a blow as brilliant as the rays of the sun.

Then he struck Handhalah, killed him, and thereby saved Abu Sufyan, who escaped saying:

From the morning to the approach of sunset, my young mare was always as far away from them as a scolded dog. I will fight them, urging on to violence, calling (my ancestor) Ghalib, and repulse them from

about me with my horse's solid support – and if I had wished, my met-
tled horse would have saved me and I would not bear any favour to
Ibn Sha'ub.

News of this reached Ibn Sha'ub's ears, and he replied to this ingratitude by
saying:

Without my defence and my help in battle, O Ibn Harb, you would
have met an invincible enemy in that gully, and were it not for the
repeated charges of my mare in that gully, hyenas and packs of dogs
would be growling over his limbs.

As for a Muslim wanting to hamstring his own horse, it is related that
Ja'far ibn Abi Talib, may Allah be pleased with him, rushed forth on the day
of Mu'tah on his russet horse right into the middle of the fight, then dis-
mounted, hamstrung his mount and fought until he was killed, may Allah be
pleased with him. He was the first of the Muslims to hamstring his horse in
Islam, but no other Muslims should hamstring their horses as they constitute
a force which Allah has commanded us to have at the ready in the jihad
against His enemy: **"And prepare what you can of force and of fighting
horses so that you may strike fear into the enemies of Allah and your
enemies"** (Qur'an 8: 60). Moreover, Ja'far only hamstrung his horse after he
had been surrounded and it is conceivable that he did this so the mushrikun
would not be able to use it to reinforce themselves against the Muslims: in
such circumstances, the hamstringing becomes legitimate, as would be the
hamstringing of the enemies' horses, for Ja'far was too respectful of the deen
to have done something prohibited by the law. When his army returned, the
Messenger of Allah, may the peace and blessings of Allah be upon him, and
the Muslims went out to meet them, and the people started to throw earth at
them shouting: "O you who flee, why have you fled while fighting in the
way of Allah?" and the Messenger of Allah responded: "They are not people
of flight but rather people who, Allah willing, will return to fight."

3. The third section about the rules of this type of amirate concerns what
is incumbent upon the amir of the army with respect to his organisation of
the combatants, and this is composed of ten things:

First, he should protect them from surprise attacks which would enable
the enemy to become victorious; that is, he should investigate likely places
of ambush and surround their encampments by a guard, such that they them-

selves and their baggage are safe and they can repose in times of peace and feel safe from attack from the rear in times of fighting;

Second, he should choose a site for their encampments which is best suited for fighting their enemy, that is the flattest place, the one containing the most pasturage and water and the most protected from the flanks and from the sides, such that it affords the most support for the defence of their encampment and the strongest position for the offensive;

Third, he should prepare whatever provisions and forage are necessary for the army: these should be distributed to them when needed so that they feel assured and will not need to search for it – such that their numbers are greater for fighting and they are more capable of withstanding the enemy;

Fourth, he should have knowledge of the enemy and understand their movements; he should investigate their circumstances and be able to interpret them, such that he escapes their stratagems and it enables him to launch surprise attacks on them;

Fifth, he is responsible for arranging the army into battle lines and should be able to rely, in all respects, on those he deems capable of a particular task; he should also make sure that there are no gaps in the ranks and should protect every flank under threat from the enemy by affording any assistance required;

Sixth, he should strengthen their resolve by convincing them of victory and by evoking ways and manners of divine assistance in order to diminish the adversary in their eyes and make them more audacious – for audaciousness facilitates victory. Allah, may He be exalted, says, **"Remember when Allah made them appear to you as few in number. If he had shown you them as many, you would have lost heart and disputed with each other in the matter"** (Qur'an 8: 45);

Seventh, he should promise Allah's reward to those among them who are steadfast and indomitable, if they are people of the next world, and of a part and particular portion of the booty, if they are people of this world. Allah, may He be exalted, says, **"And whoever wants the reward of this world, We will give it to him, and whoever wants the reward of the next world, We will give it to him"** (Qur'an 3: 146); The reward of this world is booty and the reward of the next is the Garden. Allah thus encourages them both by mentioning two matters such that each of the two parties will vie to be the best;

Eighth, he should consult those of sound judgement concerning problematic matters and have recourse to the people of resolve in cases of difficulty, so as to be safe from mistakes and free of error, and thereby be more likely to be amongst the victorious. Allah has said to His Messenger, **"And consult them in the matter, and if you have come to a decision, then place your trust in Allah"** (Qur'an 3: 153);

The commentators differ in four ways regarding this command to His Prophet, may the peace and blessings of Allah be upon him, to consult others – given the fact that Allah afforded him success and assisted him (in every way). The first of these is that He commanded him to seek their advice regarding war, so as to arrive at the right judgement and act accordingly, and this is al-Hasan's view, who also said, "Never do a people consult with each other but that they are guided to the most correct way in their affairs." According to the second, He commanded him to seek their advice in order to draw them closer to him and out of deference to them, and this is Qatada's opinion. Thirdly, according to ad-Dahak, He commanded him to consult them because He was aware of the excellence in it and of the benefit it could bring. Fourthly, Sufyan is of the view that He commanded him to consult them in order to establish a sunnah for the Muslims, such that the Muminun would follow this practice, but that, in fact, the Prophet had no need to consult them;

Ninth, he should see that his army implements what Allah, may He be exalted, has imposed as obligations with respect to rights and duties, and whatever He has commanded regarding the hadd-punishments, such that there is no violation of the deen among the troops, nor any infringement of a right or duty: in effect, those making jihad for the deen are the persons most duty-bound to uphold its laws and to discriminate between the halal and haram. Harith ibn Nabhan has related from Abban ibn 'Uthman that the Prophet, may the peace and blessings of Allah be upon him, said, "Forbid your army from wreaking havoc for no army wreaks havoc, but that Allah casts fear into their hearts; forbid your army from purloining the booty, for surely no army defrauds but that Allah will have them conquered by common foot-soldiers; forbid your army from fornication, for surely no army fornicates but that Allah brings the plague on them." And Abu'd-Darda said, "O people act correctly before the raid, for surely you fight by your good actions";

Tenth, he should not allow any of the army to busy themselves with trade or agriculture, because this would distract them from persevering against the enemy and carrying out the jihad properly. It has been narrated from the

Prophet, may the peace and blessings of Allah be upon him, that he said, "I have been sent to deal forcibly (with the kuffar) and mercifully (with the Muslims). I have not been sent as a trader or a farmer: surely the worst people of this Ummah, apart from those who are niggardly in their practice of the deen, are traders and farmers." One of the Prophets of Allah went on a raiding party, saying: "No man who has begun a building but not completed it, no man who has married a woman but has not consummated the marriage, and no man who has sown and has not yet harvested, will go on the raiding party with me."

4. The fourth section concerning the rules of this type of amirate is about the rights and duties of jihad which are incumbent on the mujahidin. They are of two types: their obligation to Allah, may He be exalted, and their obligation to the amir.

A. As for what is incumbent on them with respect to Allah's right, there are four things:

i. They must be steadfast in the face of the enemy when the two forces meet, and not retreat before an army which is twice as large or less. At the beginning of Islam, Allah, may He be exalted, obliged every Muslim to fight ten of the mushrikun, saying, **"O Prophet urge the Muminun to the fight: if there are twenty from among you who are steadfast, they will overcome two hundred and if there are a hundred of you, they will overcome a thousand of the kuffar, because they are a people who do not reflect"**. (Qur'an 8: 66)

Then Allah, may his power and splendour be manifest, reduced this ratio for them when Islam had gained power and its adherents had increased in number, obliging every Muslim, when encountering the enemy, to fight no more than two of them: **"Now Allah has alleviated the situation for you, being aware that there are weak persons among you: so if there are a hundred steadfast persons among you, they will overcome two hundred and if there are a thousand from among you, they will overcome two thousand by the permission of Allah, and Allah is with the steadfast"** (Qur'an 8: 67). It is forbidden for any Muslim to turn his back on two enemy fighters except in one of two situations: when for tactical reasons he retires to rest or for strategic reasons he returns to renew the battle, or when he turns away to join forces with another group to continue the fight. In effect, Allah says, may He be exalted, **"And whoever turns their backs to them on that day, except as a manoeuvre in battle or in order to join forces with another group, then they will incur the anger of Allah"** (Qur'an 8: 16).

It does not matter whether the group they are joining forces with is far or near, for 'Umar, may Allah be pleased with him, said about those fighting at the battle of Qadisiyyah, when they turned round towards him [in Madinah]: "I, myself, count as a rallying force for every Muslim."

If the enemy are more than double in number, the Muslims may turn their backs on them if they do not find the wherewithal to resist them – that is, without them needing the justification of engaging in tactical manoeuvres or intending to join forces with another group. This is the madhhab of ash-Shafi'i. His followers, however, differ regarding those who are not capable of withstanding a force twice their number, but who are also threatened by death if they flee: some say that they may not turn their back in retreat even if it means death because of the text on this matter; others, however, say that they may retreat as long as they intend to engage in manoeuvres for battle or to join forces with another group, in order to escape death. There is no real difference of opinion in this matter, however, as anyone incapable of resisting the enemy would not be incapable of having this intention.

Abu Hanifah, however, says that such a detailed distinction is not valid as the relevant text is abrogated: a Muslim should fight as much as he is able, and take flight when he can give battle no longer and fears he will be killed.

ii. He should give battle with the intention of supporting the deen of Allah, may He be exalted, and of destroying any other deen which is in opposition to it: **"so as to render it victorious over all [other] deen even if the mushrikun detest it"** (Qur'an 9: 33). Having such a conviction, he will be rewarded with the recompense promised by Allah, he will be in a state of obedience to His commands, he will be supporting His deen, and it will allow him to seek His aid over his enemies to facilitate any encounters with the enemy: he will thus become more firmly established and more capable of inflicting injury, not intending by his jihad simply to benefit from the booty; if this is not the case, he will become someone seeking merely to enrich himself, rather than being one of the mujahidin. The Messenger of Allah, may the peace and blessings of Allah be upon him, when he gathered together the forty-four men captured at Badr, after a like number of the Quraysh nobles had been killed, consulted his Companions about it. 'Umar said,

"O Messenger of Allah, kill the enemies of Allah, the kafir leaders, and the chiefs of deviation, for surely they have called you a liar and expelled you"; Abu Bakr said, "They are of your clan and family – forgive them and Allah will spare them the Fire for your sake." The Messenger of Allah, may the peace and blessings of Allah be upon him, entered Madinah a day before the entry of the captives: there, some people were saying what 'Umar had said and others were saying what Abu Bakr had said. Then the Messenger of Allah, may the peace and blessings of Allah be upon him, went out to his Companions and said: "What do you say of these two men? Their likeness is the likeness of two of their brothers before them: Nuh said: **'Lord, do not leave any of the Kuffar on the earth'** (Qur'an 71: 27), and Musa said: **'Our Lord, destroy their goods and harden their hearts'** (Qur'an 10: 88). 'Isa said: **'If You torment them, they are surely Your slaves, and if You forgive them, then surely You are the Mighty, the Wise'** (Qur'an 5: 118). Ibrahim said, **'Whoever follows me then surely he is with me, and whoever disobeys me then surely You are forgiving, merciful'** (Qur'an 14: 39). Truly Allah hardens the hearts of some men so much that they become harder than stone. He softens the hearts of some men until they are softer than milk. If there are poor amongst you, then none of these captives should be discharged from you except on payment of a ransom or having his neck cut." He ransomed each captive for four thousand dirhams.

Among the captives was al-'Abbas ibn 'Abd al-Muttalib, a corpulent man, who had been made captive by Abu'l-Yasar, a squat man. The Prophet asked, may the peace and blessings of Allah be upon him, "How did you capture al-'Abbas, O Abu'l-Yasar?" to which he replied, "O Messenger of Allah, a man whom I had never seen helped me and whose appearance was such and such." Then the Messenger of Allah replied, may the peace and blessings of Allah be upon him, "A noble angel has surely helped you against him." He then said to al-'Abbas "Pay the ransom for yourself, for your two nephews, 'Aqil ibn Abi Talib and Nawfal ibn al-Harith, and your confederate, 'Utbah ibn 'Umar." Then he said, "O Messenger of Allah, I was a Muslim, but my people forced me (not to declare it openly)." Then the Messenger of Allah, may the peace and blessings of Allah be upon him, said, "Was I aware of your Islam? But if it is as you say, then surely Allah, may He be praised, will reward you." Al-'Abbas paid the ransom for himself with a hundred ounces, and paid the ransom for each of his nephews and his confederate with forty ounces. It is regarding al-'Abbas that the words of Allah were revealed, **"O Prophet, say to those captives in your hands: 'If Allah knows of any**

good in your hearts, He will give you better than that which has been taken from you and He will forgive you and Allah is the Forgiving, the Merciful'" (Qur'an. 8: 71).

When the Messenger of Allah, may the peace and blessings of Allah be upon him, took ransoms for the captives of Badr for the poor from amongst the Muhajirun and their needs, Allah, may He be exalted, reproached his Prophet for what he did, saying, **"It is not for a Prophet to have captives until he has made slaughter in the land"** – that is, has put people to death – **"you desire the transient lure of this world"** – that is, the money of the ransom – **"and Allah desires the next world"** – that is, action which leads to the reward of the next world – **"and Allah is the Mighty, the Wise"** – that is, Mighty in that He comes to your aid, and Wise with respect to what He desires for you – **"If there had not been a written decree which had gone before from Allah an awful torment would have struck you on account of what you took"** – that is, the money of the ransom taken from the captives (Qur'an 8: 69). There are three interpretations of these ayat: first, that if there had not been a written decree which had gone before from Allah about the people of Badr, saying that He would not torment them, a painful torment would have afflicted them for taking ransoms for the captives of Badr, and this is the opinion of al-Mujahid; second, that if the decree from Allah had not gone before, making the booty lawful, a painful torment would have afflicted them because of their haste in taking it from the people of Badr, and this is the opinion of Ibn 'Abbas, may Allah be pleased with him; third, that if a written decree had not preceded from Allah, saying that He would not punish anyone for an action made in ignorance, a painful torment would have afflicted them because of what they took, and this is the opinion of Ibn Ishaq.

After the revelation of this ayah, the Messenger of Allah, may the peace and blessings of Allah be upon him, said, "If Allah had punished us as stated in this ayah, no one other than you, O 'Umar, would have been saved."

iii. Each combatant should fulfil the trust (accorded him by Allah) regarding the booty which has come to him, and that none of them should take anything from it until it has been shared amongst all those entitled to the booty: that is, those who participated in the battle and were of assistance against the enemy, as each has a claim to it. Allah, may He be exalted, says, **"And it is not for a Prophet to act deceitfully; whoever acts deceitfully will bring his deceit with him on the day of raising up"** (Qur'an 3: 155). There are three interpretations to this: first, that a prophet should not deceive his companions or defraud them of their booty, and this is the opinion of Ibn 'Abbas; second, that the Prophet should not be deceived or defrauded regarding the booty his Companions have taken, and this is according to al-Hasan and Qatada; third, that the Prophet should not hide from his companions, either through fear or envy, what he has been entrusted to deliver to them from Allah, and this is the opinion of Muhammad ibn Ishaq.

iv. He should not show preferential treatment towards a relative from amongst the mushrikun, or show partiality towards a friend, when having to uphold the deen of Allah (against them), for surely Allah's right is more binding, and upholding His deen is more incumbent. Allah, may He be exalted, says, **"O you who believe, do not take My enemy and your enemy as your friends, meeting them with kindness, when they have denied what has come to you of the Truth"** (Qur'an 60: 1). This ayah was revealed concerning Hatib ibn Abi Biltaa who wrote a letter, expedited by way of Sara, the client of the Banu 'Abd al-Muttalib, to the people of Makkah – just as the Prophet, may the peace and blessings of Allah be upon him, was making ready to attack them – informing them of his expedition against them. Allah, however, apprised His Prophet of this, and so the latter sent 'Ali and az-Zubayr after her, and they were able to extricate the message from a tress of her hair. Then the Prophet called for Hatib and asked, "What made you do what you did?" He said, "By Allah, O Messenger of Allah, I believe in Allah and His Messenger. I have not become a kafir and I have not changed (my deen), but I am a man who does not have any roots amongst your people, nor any relatives, whereas I have a family with those (Quraysh) and so I informed them of the expedition." The Prophet, may the peace and blessings of Allah be upon him, pardoned him.

B. As for the duties of the fighters towards the amir, there are four:

i. They must obey him and submit to his authority over them as this has been duly established, and obedience is obligatory wherever authority has been duly established. Allah, may He be exalted, says, **"O you who believe, obey Allah and obey the Messenger and those in command amongst you"** (Qur'an 4: 62). There are two interpretations regarding **"those in command"** – the first, that it refers to the amirs, and this is the opinion of Ibn 'Abbas, may Allah be pleased with him, and the second, that it refers to the 'ulama, and this is the opinion of Jabir ibn 'Abdallah and al-Hasan and 'Ata. Abu Salih has related from Abu Hurairah, who said: The Messenger of Allah, may the peace and blessings of Allah be upon him, said, "Whoever obeys me, obeys Allah and whoever obeys my amir, obeys me and whoever disobeys me, disobeys Allah and whoever disobeys my amir, disobeys me";

ii. They should hand affairs over to his judgement and entrust matters to his direction, so that any discord in their opinions will not destroy their unity of purpose and split the unity of their community. He, may He be exalted, says, **"If they had referred the news to the Messenger or to those in command from amongst them, those amongst them who are able to think out the matter would have known it"** (Qur'an 4: 85). The fact of handing over the matter to his authority is thus established as a means of his attaining this knowledge and resolving the affair. If, however, some correct course of action appears to them which is not known to him, they should explain it to him and advise him: this is why it is recommended for him to consult so as to arrive at the correct solution;

iii. They should make haste to follow his instructions and respect his prohibitions and admonitions, because these two matters are among the obligatory aspects of obedience to him. If, however, they do not carry out what he commands and they proceed towards what he has prohibited, he should chastise them in accordance with their circumstances, but without brutality. Allah, may He be exalted, says, **"You have shown gentleness to them, by a mercy from your Lord; if you had been rough and hard of heart they would have scattered from round about you"** (Qur'an 3: 153). Sa'id ibn al-Musayyab has related that the Prophet, may the peace and blessings of Allah be upon him, said, "What is best in your deen is that which is the easiest";

iv. They should not dispute with him concerning articles of booty after he has apportioned it: they should accept that he has shared it out fairly amongst them, for Allah has made the high and the low classes equal in this respect, and has treated the strong and the weak in the same way. 'Umar ibn Shu'ayb has related from his father, who related it from his grandfather: "In the year of Hunayn people pursued the Messenger of Allah, may the peace and blessings of Allah be upon him, saying that he should share out their portion of the spoils: they forced him to seek refuge against a tree and his cloak was snatched from him. Then he said, 'O people, give me back my cloak. By Allah, if you had as many cattle as the number of trees in Tihama I would have apportioned them to you, and you would not have found me mean, cowardly or a liar.' Then he took a hair from the hump of his camel and held it up saying: 'O people, by Allah, of your spoils I have nothing, not even this hair. I only had a fifth and even that has been handed over to you. Bring needle and thread for on the day of raising-up those who purloin from the booty will have shame, fire and dishonour.' Then a man from the Ansar came with a skein of camel hair saying, 'O Messenger of Allah, I took this skein to make a saddle-cloth for one of my camels who has caught cold.' Then he replied: 'As for my portion of it, it is for you.' Then he said, 'If you say this, then I have no need of it,' and he threw the skein down in front of him.

5. This section regarding the laws of this type of amirate concerns the steadfastness of the amir in the face of the enemy – that is, for as long as they fight, even if this becomes long and drawn out – and his not turning his back on them as long as strength is in him. Allah, may He be exalted, says, **"O you who believe, be steadfast, vie with each other in endurance, prepare yourselves for war and have fear of Allah so that you might be successful"** (Qur'an 3: 200). There are three interpretations of this: first, that you be steadfast in your obedience to Allah and vie with each other against the enemies of Allah and make ready for war in the way of Allah, and this is the opinion of al-Hasan; second, that you be steadfast in your deen, vie with each other in awaiting the promise He has made you and make ready for war against My enemy and yours, and this is according to Muhammad ibn Ka'b; third, that you be steadfast in the jihad and vie with each other against the enemy and make ready for war by constant manning of the frontier posts, and this is the opinion of Zayd ibn Aslam. Moreover as continual perseverance in fighting is among the duties of jihad, it is binding until one of four things occurs:

First, they (the enemy) become Muslims, in which case they receive the same rights as us, become responsible for the same obligations as us and they are allowed to retain any land and property they possess. The Messenger of Allah, may the peace and blessings of Allah be upon him, said, "I have been commanded to fight people until they say, 'No god but Allah.' If they say this, then their blood and their property are safe from me – except when there exists another legitimate reason." Their country becomes part of the Territory of Islam when they become Muslims and the law of Islam then applies to them. If a group of them become Muslims during battle – be they small or great in number – any land or wealth belonging to them in the battle-zone remains theirs. If the amir conquers the battle zone he cannot take the wealth of those who have accepted Islam.

Abu Hanifah, however, says booty is taken in the form of immovable properties of land and houses, but not movable wealth or chattels. This is at variance with the sunnah: in the blockade of the Banu Quraydhah, the two Jews Tha'labah and Asid, sons of Shaba, became Muslims and their Islam protected their wealth.

Their Islam also entails Islam for any minors amongst their children and any still in the womb. Abu Hanifah, however, says that if a kafir becomes a Muslim in the Territory of Islam, it does not entail Islam for his children who are still minors, whereas if he becomes a Muslim in Dar al-Harb (the war zone), it entails Islam for his children who are minors, but not for the foetus, for his wife and the foetus are treated as fay.

If a Muslim enters Dar al-Harb and buys land and goods therein, he is not dispossessed of these if the Muslims conquer it, as the purchaser still has more claim over them. Abu Hanifah, however, is of the opinion that any land he possesses is treated as fay;

The **second** thing that might occur is that Allah gives victory over them but they remain mushrikun, in which case their women and children are taken prisoner, and their wealth is taken as booty, and those who are not made captive are put to death. As for the captives, the amir has the choice of taking the most beneficial action of four possibilities: the first, to put them to death by cutting their necks; the second, to enslave them and apply the laws of slavery regarding their sale or manumission; the third, to ransom them in exchange for goods or prisoners; and fourth, to show favour to them and pardon them. Allah, may He be exalted, says, **"When you encounter those who deny [the Truth] then strike [their] necks"** (Qur'an 47: 4). There are two ways of understanding this: the first, that it refers to the striking of their necks while in fetters after having taken control of them; the second, that it refers to fighting them with weapons and stratagem in order to arrive at striking their necks in battle. Then He says: **"Then when you have weakened them, make the fetters tight"** (Qur'an 47: 4), and what is meant by **"weaken them"** is wounding them, and **"make the fetter tight"** the taking of prisoners. **"Then either grace or ransom"** (Qur'an 47: 4). Regarding **"grace"** there are two opinions: the first, that it means pardon and setting free, just as the Messenger of Allah, may the peace and blessings of Allah be upon him, pardoned Thumamah ibn Uthal after having made him captive; the second, that it means manumission after being enslaved, and this is the opinion of Muqatil. As for **"ransom"**: there are two opinions as to its meaning in this case: the first, that it refers to the purchase of the prisoner with wealth, or in return for the setting free of another prisoner, just as the Messenger bought back the prisoners of Badr for money, while on another battlefield he bought back one of his men for two enemy captives; the second, that it refers to the sale, and this is the opinion of Muqatil. **"Until the war lays down its burdens"** (Qur'an 47: 4). There are two interpretations of this: the first, that it refers to the submission of the burdens of kufr to Islam and the second, to a heavy load, meaning the weapons and instruments of war. If it is taken as meaning the laying down of weapons, it refers either to the Muslims laying down their arms after the victory, or to the mushrikun abandoning their arms after their defeat. There will be a further explanation of these four rules in the section dealing with booty below.

The **third** possibility is that the enemy make a payment in return for peace and reconciliation. It is permitted to accept this payment and reconciliation with them in two ways:

i. Payment is made immediately and is not treated as ongoing tribute. This payment is treated as booty as it has been taken as a result of riding out on horses and camels; it is shared amongst those entitled to the booty and it represents a guarantee that those paying it will no longer be fought during this jihad; it does, however, not prevent a jihad being carried out against them in the future;

ii. They make a payment every year in which case it constitutes an ongoing tribute by which their security is established. What is taken from them in the first year is treated as booty and is shared amongst those entitled to booty; whatever is taken in the following years is shared amongst the people entitled to the fay. It is not permitted to resume the jihad against them as long as they make the payments, because the peace is being maintained by the regularity of these payments. If one of them enters Dar al-Islam, this contract of reconciliation guarantees safety for himself and his wealth. If they refuse to make payment, however, the reconciliation ceases, their security is no longer guaranteed and war must be waged on them – like any other persons from the enemy camp. Abu Hanifah, however, says that their refusal to make the jizyah payment and that of reconciliation does not invalidate their guarantee of security, as this tax constitutes an ongoing claim against them but the contract is not broken by their nonpayment – just as in the case of contracts of debt.

As for presents which the enemy offer before hostilities, their acceptance does not mean any arrangement has been made and it is permitted to make war on them after the offer – as any such arrangement was not the result of a contract;

The **fourth** possibility is that the enemy request a guarantee of safety and a truce. It is permitted to make a truce of peace for a specific period with them if victory over them and taking payment from them is too difficult to obtain – as long as the Imam has given him permission to undertake this or has delegated full authority to him. The Messenger of Allah, may the peace and blessings of Allah be upon him, made a ten-year truce with the Quraysh in the year of Hudaybiyyah. It should be as short as possible and not exceed ten years; if a truce is made with them for more than this, the period in excess of this is invalidated. Their security is guaranteed until the period comes to an end, and jihad is not waged against them as long as they respect the agreement; if, however, they break it, then hostilities begin again and war is made against them without warning. The Quraysh broke the treaty of Hudaybiyyah and so the Messenger of Allah, may the peace and blessings of Allah be upon him, set out on a campaign against them in the year of the Victory and conquered Makkah – as a result of the peace treaty, according to Shafi'i, but by an act of war, according to Abu Hanifah.

It is not permitted to kill any of their hostages in our hands if they break the agreement. During the time of Mu'awiyyah, the people of Rum (the Byzantines) broke their agreement while he was holding some of them hostage, but all the Muslims desisted from killing any of them and let them go saying, "fulfilment of a promise after treachery is better than responding with treachery." The Prophet, may the peace and blessings of Allah be upon him, also said, "Fulfil the trust of those who place their trust in you, and do not betray the one who betrays you." Just as it is not permitted to kill hostages, it is not permitted to free them if war is not being waged against them; when, however, war is being waged against them the hostages must be freed, in which case one has to distinguish between them: if they are men, they are conveyed to a safe place, and if they are women and children, they must be taken to their families as they are dependants and do not act by themselves.

It is permitted for them to stipulate in the contract of truce that those of their men who have become Muslims are to be handed over: this is done if the safety of his life can be guaranteed, but he is not handed over if this is not the case. The handing over of those of their women who have become Muslims cannot be stipulated as they have become inviolate with respect to non-Muslims; if this stipulation has been made, they are nevertheless not to be handed over. Their dowries are returned, however, to their husbands if they are divorced.

If there is no necessity for a truce, this is not permitted although it is permitted to make a peace treaty with them for four months or less – but no more – because of what Allah, may He be exalted, says, **"So travel in the earth for four months"** (Qur'an 9: 2).

As for a particular guarantee of security, it may be granted by any Muslim, man or woman, free or a slave – because of the saying of the Prophet, may the peace and blessing of Allah be upon him, "The blood of each and every Muslim is of equal worth, and they are as one hand over all non-Muslims, and the least of the Muslims (referring to slaves) can extend his protection to non-Muslims." Abu Hanifah, however, says that it is not correct for a slave to grant security, except if he has been given permission to fight.

6. This section concerning the rules of this type of amirate is about the action to be taken in assailing and fighting the enemy. The amir of the army may use ballistas and catapults when besieging the enemy, for the Messenger of Allah, may the peace and blessings of Allah be upon him, set up a catapult against the inhabitants of Ta'if. He may also destroy their homes, make night raids against them and cause fires. If, moreover, he reckons that by cutting their date-palms and their trees down it will serve to weaken them, such that they are overcome by force or are compelled to make a peace agreement, then he should do so; he should not, however, act in this way if he does not see any such benefit in it.

The Messenger of Allah, may the peace and blessings of Allah be upon him, cut down the vines of the people of Ta'if and this was a reason for their becoming Muslims. He also ordered the cutting down of the type of date-palm known as the yellow date-palm, whose date-stone can be seen through its flesh, and its flesh was dearer to them than a slave. When these palms of theirs were cut down, they were aggrieved, saying, "All the palms have either been cut down or burned down." The Jew Sammak declaimed the following verses as they were being cut down:

Have we not inherited the Wise Book from the time of Musa and we
have not strayed from it? And you people, shepherds of thin sheep on
the plain of Tihama and al-Ahnaf, you regard your shepherding as a
glory for you, as you have done in every age passing over you. O those

of you present! stop this injustice and these words of incitement. It may well be that the nights and the vicissitudes of time will bring down the just and upright person because of the killing and expulsion of the Nadir tribe and the destruction of the date-palms before they have even been harvested.

Then Hassan ibn Thabit replied with the following:

They have been given the Book and have abandoned it: they are blind to the Tawrah and are a people doomed. "You have denied the Qur'an which came to you as an affirmation of what the one who warns said," so the fire engulfing al-Buwayra (inhabited by Banu Nadir) was an insignificant thing for the nobles of Bani Lu'ayy (ascendants of the Quraysh).

When the Messenger of Allah, may the peace and blessings of Allah be upon him, did this to them, the Muslims felt ill at ease in their breasts and said, "O Messenger of Allah! Will we be rewarded for what we have cut and reproached for what we have left?" And then Allah revealed the following, **"Whatever of the date palms (*lina*) you cut down or left standing on their roots, it was by the permission of Allah and so as to bring loss to the corrupt ones"** (Qur'an 59: 5). As to the word *lina*, there are four interpretations: first, that it refers to any kind of date-palm, and this is according to Muqatil; second, that it refers to the best quality date-palms, according to Sufyan; third, that it refers to the offshoots as they are more supple than the date-palm itself; and fourth, that it refers to all trees because of their suppleness when alive.

It is also permitted to block off the supply of water to them, or to prevent them from using it, even if there are women and children amongst them, as it is one of the most potent means of weakening them and gaining victory over them, either by force or through a treaty. If a thirsty person amongst them requests a drink, the amir may either give him to drink or refuse him, just as he has the option of killing him or letting him live.

Anyone who kills one of them should hide him from the sight of others, but he is not obliged to bury him. The Messenger of Allah, may the peace and blessings of Allah be upon him, commanded that those killed at Badr should be thrown into an old well. It is not permitted to burn any of them, be they dead or alive, for it is reported that the Messenger of Allah, may the peace and blessings of Allah be upon him, said, "Do not torment the slaves of Allah with the torture of Allah." Abu Bakr, may Allah be pleased with him, did burn a group of the people who refused to pay the zakah, but it could well have been his own decision before news (of the Prophet's precedent) had reached him. Those Muslims who are killed as shaheeds are wrapped and buried in the clothes they were killed in; they are not given a ghusl and the prayer is not said over them. The Messenger of Allah, may the peace and blessings of Allah be upon him, said of the shaheeds of Uhud, "Wrap them up along with their wounds for they will be raised on the Day of Raising Up and the veins on their necks will be flowing with blood, their colour will be the colour of blood and their breath the scent of Musk." This he did as an honour to them, carrying this out in accordance with the promise of life accorded to them: Allah, may He be exalted, says, **"And certainly do not reckon that those who are killed in the way of Allah are dead, but rather they are alive and being given provision, with their Lord"** (Qur'an 3: 163). There are two interpretations of this: the first, that they are alive in the Garden after the raising-up but they are not alive in this world; the second, that they are alive after death, and this is the opinion of the majority, who base their judgement on the literal text, thus making a distinction between these dead persons and those who are not described with the attribute of life.

Armies in enemy territory should not be prevented from consuming any food they need or taking any fodder for their animals; moreover they are not liable to pay it back. They are not, however, to take any more than their sustenance and fodder in the way of clothing and mounts; if they do take something out of necessity then whatever they take to wear, mount or use should be reclaimed from them so as to return these things to the stores of booty – if they still exist – and reckoned against them when calculating their share thereof – if already used up.

It is not permitted for any of them to have intercourse with a girl from amongst the captives until after she has been allotted to him in his share, in which case he may have intercourse with her only after the waiting period (*istibra*) of one month. If, however, he does have intercourse with her before the sharing of the booty, he is punished at the discretion of the amir; he is not, however, given the hadd-punishment (of lashes or stoning) as he has a legal share in her, although it is incumbent upon him to pay the equivalent bride-price for her which is then added to the booty. If he has made her pregnant, her child becomes his and she has the status of Umm Walad for him when he possesses her (legally). If, however, he has intercourse with a woman who is not one of the captives, he is given the hadd-punishment, as intercourse with her is fornication, in which case her child is not attached to him if she has become pregnant.

If this type of amirate has been created for a single raiding party, the amir is not to make any other raids, irrespective of whether he has taken booty in it or not. If however, it has been formulated in a general way, continuing year after year, then it is incumbent upon him to renew the raiding whenever he is able, and he should not hesitate from this as long as there are no obstacles – except for rest periods. The least amount of time which may pass without his mounting a jihad is a year. Moreover the amir granted authority of amirate over mujahidin should make sure that they observe the laws relative to them and should apply the hadd-punishments to them, irrespective of whether they are regulars or volunteers. He is not, however, to enforce those laws which pertain to others as long as he is travelling towards his frontier fortification; when, however, he is installed in the frontier post to which he has been assigned, he may oversee the enforcement of the law among all its inhabitants, be they fighters or subjects. If his amirate is one with a particular (restricted) mandate, he should rule them in accordance with this particular mandate.

Chapter 5
Command of Wars Waged for the Public Good

There are three kinds of jihad other than that against the mushrikun: fighting renegades, rebels or bandits:

A. This section concerns those persons who reject after having been legally acknowledged as Muslims, irrespective of whether they were born into the natural behavioural pattern of Islam or they became Muslims after a state of kufr: both of these groups are treated as renegades. If they do abandon Islam for any other deen – be it for that of the Jews or the Christians which is accepted of them, or that of the heretics or pagans which is not – it is not accepted of those who renege, since their previous recognition of the Truth necessarily entails that the corresponding laws of this Truth be adhered to. The Messenger of Allah, may the peace and blessings of Allah be upon him, said: "Whoever changes his deen, then kill him." If they are subject to the death sentence, having reneged on the deen of Truth for some other deen, one of two possibilities exists:

i. Either they are dispersed as individuals and do not have a territory which distinguishes them from the Muslims, in which case there is no need for us to fight them in order to subject them to our control: rather the reason for their rejection of the truth should be investigated. If they express doubt in some aspect of the deen, it should be explained to them using proofs and reasons until the truth becomes clear for them and they turn away from the falsehood in which they had engaged. If they do turn away, their renunciation of rejection is accepted and they return within the pale of Islam as before. Malik, however, says: "I do not accept the tawbah of someone who reneges [on his Islam] to a heresy which he has to keep hidden – unless he does it of his own accord – although I accept the tawbah of others who have reneged." After their tawbah, it is incumbent on them to make up what they have not done of the prayer and the fasting during their time as renegades, because they had acknowledged the obligation of these things before they reneged. Abu Hanifah says, however, that they are not liable to make them up, just as in the case of someone who becomes Muslim after being a kafir.

The Hajj of someone in Islam, that is prior to his reneging, is not invalidated thereby and he does not have to perform it again after making tawbah. Abu Hanifah, however, says that it is invalidated through his reneging and that he does have to make it up after tawbah.

Whoever sticks to his reneging and does not make tawbah then must be put to death, be it a man or a woman. Abu Hanifah, however, says: "I would not have a woman killed for rejection," – but the Messenger of Allah, may the peace and blessings of Allah be upon him, had a woman known as Umm Ruman killed for her having reneged.

It is not permitted to confirm a renegade in his state of reneging by exacting the jizyah tax or by means of an agreement, nor is the meat slaughtered at his hand to be eaten, and nor is a woman from under his protection to be married.

The fuqaha differ regarding such persons being put to death as to whether this should be carried out immediately or be delayed for three days: according to the first of these opinions, they should be killed immediately as this is a right belonging to Allah, may He be exalted, and it may not be delayed; according to the second, they are given a respite of three days in the hope that they acknowledge their error and make tawbah. 'Ali, may Allah be pleased with him, accorded a respite of three days for tawbah to al-Mustawrid al-Ijli and then killed him.

The execution is carried out by the sword, although Ibn Surayj from amongst the companions of ash-Shafi'i says that he is beaten with a wooden club until he dies, arguing that this method of killing is slower than the sword – which eliminates the person irrevocably – and allows time for tawbah to be made.

After execution, the body is not given a ghusl and the prayer is not done over it; it is, however, covered with earth in a grave although it is not buried in any of the Muslim cemeteries, because the act of reneging excludes the person from Islam, nor in the cemeteries of the mushrikun because his previous inviolate status within the pale of Islam differentiates him from them. His wealth is deposited as fay in the bait al-mal of the Muslims and distributed amongst those entitled to the fay as no Muslim or kafir (from his relatives) may inherit from him. Abu Hanifah, however, says that inheritance may proceed from him with respect to what he has earned before his act of reneging, and whatever he has earned after it is treated as fay; Abu Yusuf says that inheritance may proceed from him with respect to both what he has earned before reneging and after it.

If the renegade leaves for Dar al-Harb, his wealth in Dar al-Islam is confiscated; if he returns to Islam, it is returned to him but if he dies in a state of denial, it becomes fay. Abu Hanifah, however, says: "If he goes to Dar al-Harb, my judgement of this is the same as if he had died and I apportion his wealth amongst those who may inherit from him; if he returns to Dar al-Islam, then whatever of his wealth still remains with them is returned to him, but I do not consider them liable to pay back what they have consumed of it."

This is the judgement regarding renegades when not located in a particular area but dispersed amongst the Muslims.

ii. The second possibility is that these renegades gather together and withdraw into an area away from the Muslims and become inaccessible – in which case they must be fought because of their reneging but only after having expounded Islam to them and made clear its proofs. The rules governing combat – which is only initiated after having warned them and given them the possibility of offering an excuse – are the same as those against the people of Dar al-Harb, namely, that the attack may be made by surprise or at night, as well as in open battle-ranks, and either from the front or from behind. Those who are taken prisoner may be executed if they do recognise their wrongdoing, although it is not permitted to enslave them according to ash-Shafi'i, may Allah have mercy on him. Their children are not enslaved after they have been conquered – irrespective of whether they are born within Islam or after the act of reneging, although some say those born after the act of reneging may be enslaved. Abu Hanifah says that women who have reneged may be enslaved if they are found in Dar al-Harb.

If their wealth is captured in booty, it is not distributed amongst those who have captured it; rather, the wealth of those killed becomes fay and that of those who survive is confiscated. If they accept Islam it is returned to them, but if they die in a state of reneging it becomes fay. If it is unclear who is the owner of the captured wealth, it becomes fay as long as there is no longer any hope of finding the owner. As for whatever is used or destroyed by the Muslims during the war against them, it does not have to be restored to the renegades if they accept Islam, whereas the latter must replace any property of the Muslims which they have used or destroyed in circumstances other than in the heat of battle. However there is a difference of opinion regarding restitution of what they have destroyed in the heat of battle: according to the first, they are responsible for restoring the value (of the property destroyed) as their act of disobedience during their state of reneging does not relieve them of a debt for which under normal circumstances they would be held responsible; according to the second, they are not responsible for their destruction of wealth or persons. At the time of Abu Bakr, may Allah be pleased with him, the renegades caused death and destruction of property and it was known who had done it. 'Umar declared, may Allah be pleased with him: "They must pay the blood-money for those of us they have killed, but we will not pay the blood-money for their dead." But Abu Bakr said: "They should not pay the blood-money for our dead, nor should we pay the blood-money for their dead," and this policy was adopted after his death. Tulayhah accepted Islam after being made captive, and after himself having killed and made captives, and 'Umar, may Allah be pleased with him, left him in peace after his acceptance of Islam and did not demand blood-money or compensation for property. One of the renegades, Abu Shajara ibn 'Abd al-'Uzza came to 'Umar ibn al-Khattab while he was sharing out the zakah and said: "Give me some for I am in need," to which 'Umar replied: "Who are you?" and he replied: "Abu Shajara." Then 'Umar said: "O enemy of Allah was it not you who said:

> *I have quenched my spear in Khalid's battalion and surely I harbour the hope of living to the full after it?"*

Then he started to hit him over the head with his stick, until the other turned round to return to his people, saying:

> *Abu Hafs has been parsimonious in his giving to us; the one who seeks will normally be given silver. He has hit me so much I have become ill. Fear has come upon me without my gaining my desire: I took fright at Abu Hafs and his guards, for the old man beats sometimes in a state of madness.*

But 'Umar did not exact any more than a discretionary punishment for his act of overreaching pride after having accepted Islam.

The rules governing territory occupied by renegades differs from those of Dar al-Islam and Dar al-Harb

As for how it differs from Dar al-Harb, then it is in four ways: first, a treaty guaranteeing peace in their lands may not be concluded, while it is permitted with those with whom one is at war; second, an accord by means of payment – which would have the effect of confirming them in their state of reneging – is not permitted, while it is with those with whom one is at war; third, it is not permitted to enslave them or make their women captives while it is permitted in the case of those one is at war with; fourth, the combatants cannot take possession of the booty they seize, while they can in the case of those with whom they are at war.

Abu Hanifah, however, says, may Allah be pleased with him, that by their act of reneging their land is treated like that of Dar al-Harb: one can enslave them, take booty and their land becomes fay – in fact they can be treated like the idol worshippers amongst the Arabs in his opinion.

Their territories differ from those of Dar al-Islam in four ways: first, there is an obligation to fight them, be it facing them or from behind, as in the case of the mushrikun; second, their blood may be spilt, both while they are captive or while defending themselves; third, their wealth becomes fay for all the Muslims; fourth, any marriages between them are invalidated at the end of the 'iddah period, even if both partners took part in the act of reneging. Abu Hanifah says, however, that the marriage is invalidated if one of the partners reneges, but not if both of them do so.

If someone is accused of reneging and denies it, his word is accepted without an oath. If proof of his act of reneging is furnished and he denies this proof, he is not accepted as a Muslim until he declares the two shahadahs.

If a people refuse to pay the zakah to a just Imam, and deny that it is an obligation for them, they are treated in the same way as renegades because of this denial. If they refuse to pay, but nevertheless recognise that payment is obligatory, they are treated like rebel Muslims and are fought for their refusal to pay. Abu Hanifah, however, may Allah have mercy on him, says that they are not fought. Abu Bakr, however, may Allah be pleased with him, did fight those who refused to pay, but who still held to their Islam until they declared, "By Allah, it was not because we reneged after having believed, but rather out of avarice for our property." 'Umar, may Allah be pleased with him, then said: "Why do you fight them when the Messenger of Allah, may the peace and blessings of Allah be upon him, said: 'I have been commanded to fight the people until they say, "no god but Allah," and if they say this, then their blood and their children are safe from me except if they violate the obligations implied in this declaration?'" Abu Bakr then said: "That is one of the obligations contained in it – how would you consider the matter if they requested not to have to do the prayer? What would you think if they requested not to have to perform the fast? What would you think if they requested not to perform the Hajj? – none of the pillars would remain standing! By Allah if they were to refuse me a saddle or tether-rope which was due the Messenger of Allah, may the blessings of Allah be upon him, I would fight them for it." 'Umar, may Allah be pleased with him, said: "Allah expanded my breast to the knowledge with which He had expanded the breast of Abu Bakr, may Allah be pleased with him."

Their leader, Harithah ibn Suraqah, declared their Islam in his verse saying:

Give us to drink before the fire of dawn: it may be that our death is near without our knowing it. We have obeyed the Messenger of Allah as long as he was amongst us. O how strange, what is the matter with Abu Bakr's rule? Surely what they are demanding of you and what you are refusing is as sweet as a date for them or even sweeter. We will defend you as long as there is a drop of nobility to inspire greatness in us in this time of difficulty.

B. Concerning the fight against the rebels:

If a party of the Muslims rebels, and contradicts the view of the community with a separate teaching they have innovated, then as long as they do not make a show of deviating from obedience to the Imam, and do not occupy a particular territory nor isolate themselves in it, and as long as they are dispersed individuals susceptible to the power of authority and the rule of law, then they are left alone, war is not waged against them, and legal obligations and punishments are applied either in their favour or against them. Some of the Khawarij opposed 'Ali ibn Abi Talib's view, may Allah be pleased with him: one of them spoke to him while he was on the mimbar, saying, "There is no judgement but that which belongs to Allah," (meaning that he should not consent to arbitration between him and Mu'awiyyah), to which 'Ali replied: "Words of truth by which a lie is intended. Three things are, however, incumbent on us: we must not prevent you from entering the mosques of Allah to remember the name of Allah therein, we must not initiate any fight against you, and we must not withhold the fay from you as long as your hands are united with ours."

If they make a show of their belief and intermingle with people of just belief, the Imam should expose their corrupt beliefs and innovative falsehoods in order that they return to true belief and rejoin the community. The Imam may reprimand and make discretionary punishments against those who vaunt their corruption, but may not impose the death penalty or the hadd-punishments. It is related that the Prophet, may the peace and blessings of Allah be upon him, said: "The blood of a Muslim is not to be shed except in three circumstances: rejection after belief, adultery after being a Muhsan, or killing someone other than in retaliation."

If this rebellious group separate from the people of justice, take up occupation in a territory and have no intercourse with the community, war is not waged against them as long as they do not refuse any obligation or cease to be obedient and continue to obey and carry out their obligations. A group of the Khawarij at Nahrawan separated from 'Ali, may peace be upon him; he appointed a governor over them and they submitted to him for a while; 'Ali maintained peace with them until they killed the governor. He then sent word to them that they should hand over the person who had done the killing, but they refused, saying: "All of us killed him," to which he replied: "All of you should surrender and I will kill some of you." He then went to them and killed most of them.

If this group of rebellious persons refuse to obey the Imam, or to fulfil the obligations incumbent on them, and if they collect taxes and execute the laws independently, then as long as they do not set up an Imam or leader for themselves the wealth collected in taxes is treated as an illegal usurpation and they remain responsible for its repayment, and all judgements they have executed are annulled and have no legal validity. If, however, such action is taken after the setting up of an Imam for themselves, such that wealth is collected and judgements are carried out on his orders, then neither are his judgements annulled nor are the taxes which have been collected invalidated. In both cases these rebels are fought in order to bring an end to the schism and to bring them to obedience. Allah, may He be exalted, says: **"If two groups of believers fight each other, then make peace between them; and if one of them acts unjustly towards the other, then fight the one acting unjustly until they return to the command of Allah; if they return, then make peace between them with justice and deal equitably, for surely Allah loves those who are equitable"** (Qur'an 49: 9). As for His words, **"and if one of them acts unjustly towards the other,"** there are two interpretations: first, that it refers to those who commit an act of armed hostility; and second, that they deviate from the agreement. As for His words, **"then fight the one acting unjustly,"** this means fighting with the sword in order to put down the insurrection and to prevent any opposition. As for His words, may He be exalted, **"until they return to the command of Allah,"** there are two interpretations: the first, according to Sa'id ibn Jubayr, is that they return to the peace agreement to which Allah has commanded, and the second, that they return to the Book of Allah and the sunnah of His Messenger with respect to their obligations and rights, and this is the opinion of Qatada. As for, **"if they return,"** it refers to their ceasing to act unjustly. As for, **"then make peace between them with justice,"** there are two interpretations: first, that it means "with truth (*bi'l-haqq*)"; and the second, "with the Book of Allah," may He be exalted. If the Imam appoints an amir to fight the rebels who refuse to submit, he must first warn them and give them an opportunity to offer their excuses; only if they persist in rebellious action may he fight them openly, but he may not attack them by surprise or during the night.

There are eight differences between fighting these rebels and fighting the mushrikun or renegades:

First, the aim of the amir in fighting them is to dissuade them but not to kill them, whereas he may have the intention of killing the mushrikun or renegades.

Second, he should fight them face to face and desist from attacking from behind, whereas he may fight the other two groups both from behind and from the front.

Third, he should not finish off their wounded, whereas he may finish off the wounded from the other two groups. 'Ali, blessings be upon him, ordered his herald on the Day of the Camel to cry out: "Those fleeing should not be pursued, nor the wounded finished off."

Fourth, he should not kill the prisoners, while this may be done in the case of the others. He must take into consideration, however, the character of those captured: those he is sure will not fight again are set free; if not, they are detained until the war ends, and then set free. It is not permitted to detain them after this. Al-Hajjaj set free a captive from amongst the supporters of Qatari ibn al-Fuja'ah because they knew each other, and Qatari told him to return to fight the enemy of Allah, al-Hajjaj. He replied, "What! The one who enchains a hand then frees it and the one who enslaves a neck then lets it go?" Then he began to recite:

Shall I go and fight the power of al-Hajjaj by this hand which confirms that it is his client? That would be to act like a mean person whose treachery is attested to by this most vile of actions. What should I say if I were to meet him face to face in single combat, him whose actions bear witness in his favour – could I attest to his injustice towards me? No! for then I would merit punishment more than the one who is subject to the injustice of his masters, and people would say that the benefits sown in me have produced dates palms of a bitter kind.

Fifth, he should not seize booty from them, nor should he enslave their women and children. It is related that the Messenger of Allah, may the peace and blessings of Allah be upon him, said: "Everything in Dar al-Islam is protected while everything in Dar ash-Shirk is open to seizure."

Sixth, he should not seek the help of the mushrikun – whether allies or dhimmis – whereas he may when fighting the other two groups.

Seventh, he should not conclude any temporary treaties or agreements in return for a tribute: no treaties made with them are binding. If he is too weak to fight them, he must wait until he has the strength to do so. Any agreement based on a payment of wealth is annulled: as for any payment already made, if it is a result of their fay or from their zakah, it is not returned to them: the zakah is distributed amongst those entitled to it and the fay is given to those who have a claim to it. If however, it is purely of their own wealth and property, he may not keep it from them and he must return it to them.

Eighth, he may not set up ballistas against them, burn down their houses, or cut down their date palms and trees, as they are in Dar al-Islam and everything in it is protected, even if its people are acting rebelliously. If, however, the people of justice are surrounded and fear that they will be annihilated, they may defend themselves in any way they are able, by killing their enemy or by setting up ballistas against them, for if a Muslim is under the threat of death, he may defend his life by killing the person who is threatening it, as long as there is no other way of defence. It is not permitted to profit by their animals nor their arms, nor to make use of them when fighting them: they should not be touched, neither during the fighting nor after it. Abu Hanifah, however, says, may Allah be pleased with him, that it is permitted to use their animals and arms to help them to fight them as long as the war is being waged. The Prophet of Allah, may the peace and blessings of Allah be upon him, has said, however, "A Muslim's property is not lawful for anyone else unless he freely consents to it."

When the war comes to an end and the people of justice have property belonging to them in their possession, it should be returned to them. Anything lost or destroyed outside of the fighting is the responsibility of the person who lost or destroyed it. There is no obligation of restitution for anything destroyed during the heat of the battle, be it people or property. Anything of the people of justice, be it persons or property, destroyed by the rebels outside of the heat of battle, then restitution is the responsibility of the latter. As for what they have destroyed in the heat of battle, there are two opinions as to whether there is an obligation of restitution on them: the first, that it is considered lost and there is no responsibility of restitution; and the second, that they are responsible for it, since an act of disobedience does not invalidate a right and does not annul a debt – just as a murder with intent entails a requital, and blood money is exacted when it is unintentional.

A ghusl is made for the rebels who are killed and the prayer is said over them. Abu Hanifah, however, says that the prayer is not said over them as a punishment for them – although there is no punishment of a dead person in this world, as the Prophet, may the peace and blessings of Allah be upon him, said: "There is an obligation on my Ummah to wash its dead and to pray over them." As for the people of justice who are killed in battle, there are two opinions as to washing them and praying over them: the first, that no ghusl is made and the prayer is not said over them as a mark of respect and honour for them, as in the case of shaheeds fighting against the mushrikun; the second, that ghusl is given to them and the prayer is said over them even though they have been killed unjustly. The Muslims performed the prayer over 'Umar and 'Uthman, may Allah be pleased with them, and later they performed the prayer over 'Ali, blessings be on him, even though they were killed unjustly by rebels.

The one who rebels does not inherit from the just person he has killed, nor *vice-versa*, since the Prophet, may the peace and blessings of Allah, be upon him, said: "The one who kills does not inherit." Abu Hanifah, however, says: "I allow the just person to inherit from the rebel, as he affirms the truth, but not the person who rebels from the just, as he denies the truth." Abu Yusuf says: "I allow each to inherit from the other, as each is killing the other according to his own understanding of the situation."

If traders pass (through their territory) and the 'ushr tax (the 'tenth') is exacted of them by the tax collectors of the rebels, but then the rebels are conquered, the tenth part is again taken from them: that already taken from them does not acquit them as they passed rebel territory voluntarily – unlike in the case of zakah which is taken from residents whether they like it or not.

If the rebels, before their subjugation, have been sentenced to hadd-punishments, there are two opinions as to whether the hadd-punishments are executed after their subjugation.

C. Concerning the fight against those who persist in disobeying, both those who keep on fighting and bandits:

If a group of the corrupt join together to use arms, cut off the highways (i.e. in brigandage), steal property, kill people and prevent the free passage of persons, they are treated as "those who make war," about whom Allah, may He be exalted says: **"Surely the recompense of those who make war on Allah and His Messenger and who strive in the land to work corruption is that they are killed or crucified, or their hands and their feet are cut off from them on alternate sides or they are exiled from the land"** (Qur'an 5: 37). The fuqaha differ in three ways as to the judgement concerning this ayah:

The first, that the Imam, or whoever is charged by him to fight them, has the option of killing them without first crucifying them, or killing them and crucifying them, or cutting their hands and feet off alternately, or exiling them from the country, and this is the opinion of Sa'id ibn al-Musayyab, Mujahid, 'Ata and Ibrahim an-Nakha'i;

The second, that those among them capable of judgement and organisation should be killed and are not spared, those of violence and strength should have their hands and feet cut off alternately, and those who are capable neither of judgement nor strength should suffer a discretionary punishment and should be detained, and this is the opinion of Malik ibn Anas and a group of the fuqaha of Madinah, who assess the situation according to their differences in character and not according to their different actions;

The third, that punishment should be according to their different actions and not according to their different characters: those who have killed and stolen property are killed and crucified, those who have killed but have not stolen property are killed but are not crucified, those who have taken wealth and have not killed have one of their hands and one of their feet cut off alternately and those who have fomented the affair and intimidated travellers but have not killed and have not taken wealth are given discretionary punishments but not put to death, and this is the opinion of Ibn 'Abbas and al-Hasan, Qatada, as-Suddi, and it is also the madhhab of ash-Shafi'i, may Allah be pleased with him. Abu Hanifah says that if they have killed and seized wealth, the Imam has the option of either killing them and then crucifying them, or of cutting off their hands and feet alternately and then killing them. The judgement concerning those with them who used intimidation and encouraged the affair is the same.

As for Allah's words, **"or they are exiled from the land"**, there are four interpretations: the first, that it means sending them away from the territories of Islam to those of the idolaters, and this is the opinion of Malik ibn Anas, al-Hasan, Qatada and az-Zuhri; the second, that it refers to their expulsion from one town to another, and this is the opinion of 'Umar ibn 'Abd al-'Aziz, may Allah have mercy on him, and Sa'id ibn Jubayr; the third, that it refers to detention and this is the opinion of Abu Hanifah and Malik (*sic*); the fourth, that they are to be sent for in order to apply the hadd-punishments and then to exile them, and this is the opinion of Ibn 'Abbas and ash-Shafi'i.

As for His words, may He be exalted: **"except those who turn in tawbah [to their Lord] before you gain the upper hand over them"** (Qur'an 5: 34), there are six opinions according to the various interpretations: the first, that it refers to the corrupt amongst the kuffar who are waging war and who turn to their Lord, away from their idolatry, by accepting Islam; the tawbah of Muslims, however, does not remove hadd-punishments or divine obligations from them, and this is the opinion of Ibn 'Abbas, al-Hasan, Mujahid and Qatada, may Allah be pleased with them; the second, that it refers to Muslims amongst the warring party who turn in tawbah under a guarantee of safety on the part of the Imam before they are brought to submission; the tawbah of those which is made without this guarantee of safety from the Imam, however, is of no consequence in removing the hadd-punishment or his obligations from him, and this is the opinion of 'Ali ibn Abi Talib, may Allah ennoble his face, and ash-Shafi'i; the third, that it refers to the Muslims who turn in tawbah after their settling in Dar al-Harb and who then return (to the right way) before they are overcome, and this is the opinion of 'Urwah ibn az-Zubayr, may Allah be pleased with him; the fourth, that it refers to those in Dar al-Islam in a fortified refuge and who turn in tawbah before they are overwhelmed: punishments are not applied to them, although if they are not in a fortified refuge such punishments remain in force, and this is the opinion of Ibn 'Umar, Rabi'ah and al-Hakam ibn Utayba, may Allah be pleased with them; the fifth, that their tawbah before being overwhelmed – even if they are not in a fortress – annuls any application of the hadd-punishments of Allah, may He be glorified, although all obligations towards their fellow men remain in force, and this is the opinion of ash-Shafi'i; the sixth, that tawbah made before being overwhelmed annuls all hadd-punishments and obligations from them except those concerning the spilling of blood, and this is the opinion of Malik ibn Anas.

This is the judgement concerning this ayah and the differences of opinion of those concerned with its interpretation. To continue, we would say that if they persist in their insubordination, they are in general fought just as those who rebel are fought, although there are five differences between the two: the first, that one may fight them both face to face and from behind in order to obtain fulfilment of their obligations, whereas it is not permitted to pursue rebels who turn in flight; the second, that it is permitted to deliberately set out to kill one of them who has himself killed someone, whereas one may not deliberately set out to kill a rebel; the third, that they are held responsible for any destruction of persons or property, both during the war and outside of it, which is not the case regarding rebels; the fourth, that one may detain those who are made captive in order to clarify their situation – but not those who rebel; the fifth, that kharaj or zakah collected by them are treated as having been taken by force or pillaged, and the claim of those entitled to the kharaj or zakah stands: it thus remains a debt to be exacted from them.

If the person charged with fighting them has been given only a limited mandate in combating them, he is not to exact the hadd-punishments on them after having brought them to submission, nor is he to execute any claim over them; rather he is to bring them to the Imam who may order that the hadd-punishments be carried out on them, and that redress for any claim be made against them. If, however, his mandate regarding the fight against them, the execution of the hadd-punishments against them, and the fulfilment of any claims against them, is of a general kind, such matters must be carried out by a man of knowledge and justice. If this is the case, he may clarify the circumstances of such persons in one of two ways: either by their own admission given voluntarily without beating or constraint, or on the evidence of persons of just character when they deny the accusations. If the crimes of any of them become known by either of these two ways, then the following points are considered:

First, those who have killed and stolen property are put to death and then crucified. Malik says that such persons are crucified while still alive and then are pierced with lances until they die. This killing is irrevocable and it is not permitted to pardon such persons; if someone, by way of retaliation, has the right to pardon a person, his pardon is annulled. The crucifixion lasts for three days, no longer, and then the corpse is taken down;

Second, someone who has killed but has not stolen any property is put to death but is not crucified, and the ghusl is made and the prayer is recited over him. Malik says that the person who says the prayer over him must be someone other than the person who has pronounced the death sentence on him;

Third, someone who has stolen property but not killed any one has his foot cut off on one side and his hand on the other: the cutting off of his right hand for theft, and the cutting off of his left leg for the public nature of his crimes;

Fourth, someone who has inflicted wounds but not killed anyone and has stolen property must suffer the act of retaliation if there is a corresponding retaliation for the wound in question. As for the irrevocable nature of the act of retaliation in the case of wounds there are two points of view: the first of these is that it is irrevocable and pardon is not permissible, just as in the case of a killing; the second, that it becomes obligatory if demanded by the one who has the right of retaliation but is dropped if he offers a pardon. If the nature of the wound is such that there is no act of retaliation, then payment of the blood-money becomes obligatory if demanded, while its payment is waived if a pardon is forthcoming;

Fifth, anyone who has intimidated others or encouraged the affair, but who did not take part in any killing, wounding or stealing property, is given a discretionary corporal punishment and chastised. It is also permitted to imprison him, as this is one of the two methods of inflicting discretionary punishment. It is not, however, permitted to go so far as cutting off any limbs or putting such persons to death. Abu Hanifah, however, permits them to be treated in the same way as those who perpetrated such actions directly themselves.

If they turn in tawbah from their crimes after they have been brought to submission, their wrongdoing is removed from them, but they are not excused the consequences of their actions: thus they are held to account for hadd-punishments and any financial obligations. If they turn in tawbah before they are overwhelmed their wrongdoing is removed along with the hadd-punishments due to Allah, may He be exalted – although any claims outstanding on the part of their fellow men are not removed.

If one of these brigands has killed someone, then the person charged with the retaliation has the right to exact it or offer a pardon; if they turn in tawbah, the absolute necessity to put the person to death is removed. If among those who turn in tawbah are persons who have stolen property, the necessity for amputation is removed, but not the obligation to repay a debt, unless it is waived.

The same law is applied to brigands and highwaymen waging war in towns as those in deserts and on caravans and is not considered with less severity – rather their audacity in perpetrating their activity in towns will perhaps increase the severity of the punishment. Abu Hanifah, however, says that the judgement applies to them in particular, that is with respect to the countryside, where no help is to be found; as for the settled towns or those areas around which help is to be found, the same punishment as that inflicted on brigands is not meted out.

If they claim to have turned in tawbah before they are overwhelmed and this claim is not accompanied by indications supporting the truth of their tawbah, their claim is not accepted – as it would entail the annulling of a hadd-punishment which has already become obligatory. If, however, their claim is accompanied by corresponding signs of tawbah, there are two opinions as to the acceptance of this tawbah without witnesses: the first, that it is accepted as the hadd-punishments may be annulled in cases of doubt; the second, that it is not accepted, except with the testimony of a just person who bears witness to their tawbah before they were brought to submission, because the hadd-punishment has been duly pronounced and any doubt in the matter must be related to the act and not something which comes after it.

Chapter 6
The Administration of the Judiciary

No one may take up office as judge unless he has fulfilled all the conditions necessary for this appointment; once appointed his judgements must be executed. These conditions are seven in number:

First, he must be a man, that is, having the two qualities of puberty and maleness. Anyone who has not attained puberty is not held responsible for his acts and no judgement is made against him on the basis of his speech: it is, therefore, all the more fitting that he does not pass judgement on others in this state. A woman may not take up office as she is not suited to administrative office even though judgements may be made on the basis of her statements. Abu Hanifah, however, says that a woman may make judgements concerning matters about which she is able to make testimony, but that she may not whenever her testimony is unacceptable. Ibn Jarir at-Tabari differs from the consensus in that he permits her to make judgements in all cases. However a view which rejects both the consensus and Allah's words cannot be considered: **"Men are guardians over women by virtue of His having given more to them than the latter"** (Qur'an 4: 38), that is, more intellect and powers of discernment. Thus it is not permitted for them to rule men;

Second, there is a consensus of opinion that it is not enough that his intellect be merely such that his basic powers of perception render him responsible for his actions, but that he is also competent in his faculty of discrimination, of sagacious understanding, removed from any lapses of intellect and from moments of inattentiveness, and that he is able to arrive at an elucidation of any problem by his perspicacity, and capable of reaching decisions in cases of complexity;

Third, he must be a free man, as the deficiency implicit in a slave's inability to rule his own affairs precludes him from being given authority over others; moreover as slavehood precludes the acceptance of testimony, it is all the more fitting that it preclude the passing of judgement or investment with authority. The same applies to those who have not attained to complete freedom, like mudabbars (slaves to be freed on their master's death), mukatabs (slaves with a written contract to purchase their freedom), and those in partial slavery. Slavery, however, does not preclude him from giving fatwas, just as it does not preclude him from narrating hadith, as there is no execution of authority in either of these. If he is freed, he may make judgements – even though this means he is a freed slave of another – as genealogy is not taken into consideration in judicial authority.

Fourth, he must be a Muslim because it is a condition of legal testimony, and because of the words of Allah, **"Allah will never give the kafirun a way over the Muminun"** (Qur'an 4: 140). It is not permitted to appoint a kafir in judgement over Muslims or kuffar. Abu Hanifah says that he may be appointed to judge between people of his own deen. However, even though such appointments are made by the authorities, they are to establish him as a leader and head amongst his people rather than to offices of arbitration and the judiciary. Moreover his judgement over them is binding by virtue of their obligation towards him, and not by any obligatory characteristic of his judgement. The Imam does not have to accept his word regarding his judgement between them. If they refuse to accept him as their judge, they are not to be coerced, and the judgement of Islam is then carried out in preference;

Fifth, he must be of just character, a quality requisite in all kinds of authority. Justice consists in being true in speech, manifest in his fulfilment of a trust, free of all forbidden acts, careful to guard himself against wrong actions, free of all doubt, equitable both when content and when angry, chivalrous and vigorous both in his deen and his worldly affairs. When such qualities are perfected in him, this quality of justice – by which his testimony is permitted and his judicial authority is acceptable – may be said to be present. If, however, he is lacking in any of these qualities, his testimony is not accepted, his words are not accepted and his decisions are not executed;

Sixth, he must be sound of hearing and sight in order that he may properly attend to people's rights and claims: thus he is capable of discriminating between litigant and defendant, and of differentiating between the one who affirms and the one who denies; he can distinguish truth from falsehood in the affair, and can recognise the truthful person from the liar. His authority is annulled if he is blind, although Malik permits the appointment of such a person, just as he permits his testimony. If he is deaf, the same distinctions are made as in the case of Imamate. As for soundness of limb, it is not taken into consideration, even though it is in the case of Imamate: he may make judgements sitting and when he can no longer move, although absence of any physical defect is preferred in those in authority;

Seventh, he must have knowledge of the laws of the shari'ah and his knowledge must extend to a comprehension of its principles and to the execution of legal decisions based on these principles. The principles from which the laws of the shari'ah are based are four in number: first, he should have knowledge of the Book of Allah, may He be exalted, in such a way as to enable him to attain a proper knowledge of the various kinds of laws contained within the Book, be they of the abrogating or abrogated type, clear or equivocal, general or particular, undetermined or precise; second, he must have knowledge of the authentic sunnah of the Messenger of Allah, may the peace and blessings of Allah be upon him, that is his sayings or deeds, and the way in which they have been transmitted – in multiple chains of transmission or isolated ones, a knowledge of whether such transmissions are sound or false, and whether they may be applied only to specific circumstances or in all cases; third, he must have a knowledge of the interpretations arrived at by the first generations – both regarding what they have agreed upon and what they differ about – in order that he can follow the consensus and strive to apply his own intellectual judgement in cases of difference; fourth, he must have a knowledge of analogy enabling him to refer matters about which the law is silent to clearly formulated principles accepted by all, such that he knows how to deal with new situations and is able to differentiate the true from the false.

If his knowledge embraces these four principles of the laws of the shari'ah, he is entitled to make ijtihad in the deen, he can make fatwas and judgements, and others may seek fatwas and judgements of him. If, however, he is deficient in these or in some of them, he is not of the people of ijtihad and he may not make fatwas or judgements. Should he nevertheless be appointed to the judiciary and rightly or wrongly, he makes judgements, his appointment is annulled and his judgements are rejected, even if they corresponded to the truth and were correct. Moreover, a wrong action has been committed both by the person who sat in judgement and by the person who handed the responsibility for arbitration and passing judgement over to him. Abu Hanifah, however, permits the appointment to the judiciary of someone who is not among those of ijtihad as long as he consults others in his arbitration and judging. The majority of the fuqaha, however, are of the opinion that his authority is void and that his judgements are to be rejected, as he must imitate the legal judgements (*furu'*) of others: this is fitting for all those who merely follow what others have judged to be legally binding, but it is not fitting for those responsible for deciding what is binding in the law. The Messenger of Allah, may the peace and blessings of Allah be upon him, put Mu'adh to the test when he sent him to the Yemen as a governor saying: "By what will you judge?" He replied: "By the Book of Allah." He then asked: "And what if you do not find the answer in it?" He replied: "Then by the sunnah of the Messenger of Allah." He then asked "And what if you do not find it there?" He replied: "Then I will strive to come to a decision with my intellect." Then the Messenger of Allah said: "I give praise to Allah that He has made the messenger of the Messenger of Allah agree with what the Messenger approves of."

The appointment of someone who does not accept hadith known as "isolated" hadith is not permitted, as he is abandoning a principle about which the Companions were in agreement and on which most of the laws of the shari'ah are based: he would be on a par with those who do not accept the validity of the ijma'; such an appointment to the judiciary is not permitted, as he rejects something based on a primary text.

As for those who reject analogy they are of two kinds: **i.** those who reject it and follow the literal meaning of a text. They use the sayings of those who have preceded them concerning matters about which there is no text, rejecting ijtihad and avoiding any reflection or deduction. It is not permitted to appoint such persons to the judiciary because of their restricted access to legal processes; **ii.** those who reject analogy but make ijtihad in legal matters by adhering to the most apparent meaning of a text and to what is implied in the words, like the Dhahiris. The followers of ash-Shafi'i differ in two ways as to whether it is permissible to appoint such persons to the judiciary: some say that it is not permissible for the above-mentioned reason, while others permit it, since they do take the most clear and manifest of the meanings into account even though they avoid any hidden analogy.

Even if the conditions necessary for appointment to the judiciary which we have described above have been met, it is not permitted to appoint someone until it is known, either by a prior knowledge or by way of examination and interrogation, that these qualities are contained in him. The Messenger of Allah appointed 'Ali, may Allah be pleased with him, over the judiciary of the Yemen, but did not subject him to an examination because of his previous knowledge of him, although he did give him advice, warning him of the character of the judiciary: "If two contending parties present themselves before you, do not give judgement to one of them before hearing what the other has to say." 'Ali, may Allah ennoble his face, said: "After this, no matter of the law was difficult for me to resolve." However, the Prophet, may the peace and blessings of Allah be upon him, sent Mu'adh to a part of the Yemen and questioned him beforehand.

*

*   *

It is permitted for someone belonging to the school of ash-Shafi'i, may Allah have mercy on him, to appoint to the judiciary someone belonging to the school of Abu Hanifah, as the Qadi must strive to come to decisions based on his own judgement: it is not necessary that he follow someone from his own school in his assessment of the details of the case and the appropriate judgements. Thus if he is of the school of ash-Shafi'i, it is not necessary that he adhere in his judgements to the sayings of ash-Shafi'i, unless his own ijtihad leads him there. Thus if his ijtihad leads him to adopt an opinion of Abu Hanifah, he should act on it and apply it.

Some of the fuqaha, however, have forbidden someone belonging to one school from making judgements based on another, such that a Shafi'ite is forbidden from making judgements based on the sayings of Abu Hanifah, and it is forbidden for a Hanafi to judge according to the madhhab of ash-Shafi'i, even if his ijtihad leads him to it. This is because of the suspicion of partiality which might arise regarding his decisions and judgements: if he judges according to one madhhab and does not go beyond it, there is less likelihood of any suspicion, and it will be more satisfactory for the litigants. Although this practice is required for the smooth management of law, it is not an obligation imposed by the laws of the shari'ah: indeed the following of a school is forbidden in such cases and ijtihad must be used instead.

If a judge comes to a judgement and the same case comes up later, he should again make ijtihad and pronounce a judgement in accordance with what his ijtihad leads him to, even if it conflicts with the judgement he made before. 'Umar, may Allah be pleased with him, pronounced in favour of a sharing of the mustaraka inheritance one year, but he left it out another year.

When someone said to him: "What is this! You judged otherwise last year," he replied: "That was in accordance with what we decided then, and this is what we have decided now."

If the person responsible for the appointment, be he Hanafi or Shafi'ite, stipulates that the person he appoints to the judiciary should only judge by the madhhab of ash-Shafi'i or of Abu Hanifah, there are two possibilities:

A. If he stipulates this in a general way, in all judgements, then this is an invalid condition, irrespective of whether it is in accordance with the madhhab of the person responsible for the appointment or in conflict with it. As for the validity of the appointment, if this stipulation was not formulated as a separate condition, but rather included in an order or prohibition – whereby the person responsible says, by way of a command: "I have appointed you as the Qadi – judge according to the madhhab of ash-Shafi'i, may Allah have mercy on him," or, by way of a prohibition, "do not judge according to the madhhab of Abu Hanifah," – then the appointment is valid and the condition is invalid, irrespective of whether it contains an order or a prohibition. It is permitted for him to judge in accordance with what his own ijtihad leads him to, irrespective of whether it is in accordance with this condition or not. The stipulation of the person responsible for the appointment renders it defective if he is aware that he is stipulating something which is not permitted, although it does not if he is ignorant of this – although this ignorance in effect annuls the validity of the person appointing and the person appointed. If it is stipulated as a condition of the contract of appointment, and he says: "I have appointed you as judge on condition that you only make judgements in accordance with the madhhab of ash-Shafi'i, or the opinion of Abu Hanifah," then this appointment is invalid as its contract is based on a condition which is null and void. The people of Iraq, however, say that the appointment is valid and the condition is invalid.

B. When the condition is particular to a specific judgement, it is necessarily either an order or a prohibition:

i. If it is an order, and he says "Exact vengeance (i.e. the death penalty) for the slave's murder of a free man, vengeance on a Muslim for the murder of a kafir and obtain requital for a killing with other than the sword," then his command accompanied by this condition is void. If this condition is stipulated in the contract of appointment, the latter is annulled; if not, the contract is valid and the person appointed should judge in accordance with the result of his ijtihad.

ii. If it is a prohibition, it is of two kinds: the first, that he forbids him to judge in the case of a Muslim killing a kafir, or a free man who murders a slave, or to judge as to whether or not there is to be retaliation – and this is permitted, since the person responsible for the appointment is limiting his appointment relative to his capacity, and in effect this is outside his field of examination; the second, that he does not prohibit him from judging as such, but rather from taking decisions in matters of requital. Our fellow jurists (i.e. Shafi'ites) differ regarding this prohibition as to whether it necessarily prevents him from investigating such cases: some say he is excluded from judging in such matters, being outside his authority, and he is unable to decide both that requital should be exacted, or that it be dropped; others, however, say that it does not necessarily exclude him from such cases, that he is entitled to command that his judgement be carried out, and that his investigation is validated as long as the contrary has not been stipulated at his appointment; in this way, he judges in such matters in accordance with the results of his ijtihad.

The appointment of a judge is contracted in the same way as appointments to other positions of authority, namely, either orally by way of a declaration to someone present, or by a message or a written letter to someone absent; in the case of a letter, however, it must also be accompanied by circumstances which confirm (the validity of) the appointment and (the authority of) those appointing him. The expressions by which the contract of appointment is concluded are of two kinds: by way of a manifest declaration, or by an indication. A manifest declaration may take the form of four expressions: "I have appointed you," "I have given you authority," "I have made you my substitute," and, "I have named you as my representative." If he uses one of these four expressions, the appointment to the judiciary or any other office, is concluded; no additional words are needed, unless as an expression of corroboration – but they cannot express a condition. As for expressions which indicate, they are seven in number, according to some of our companions: "I rely on you," "I put my confidence in you," "I hand it over to you," "I have made it over to you," "I have delegated you," "I have recommended you," and "I find my support in you." As these expressions contain ambiguity, they are too weak to effect appointments in the same way as manifest declarations, that is, unless accompanied in the contract by something else which removes the ambiguity, thereby transforming its status to that of a contract based on an open declaration like his saying: "Look to what I have entrusted you with," or, "Make decisions regarding those matters concerning which I have placed my reliance on you," – thus the appointment is concluded by the addition of these words to the preceding indicative expression.

Its completion is dependent, however, on the acceptance of the appointed person: if his appointment is oral, his acceptance is given immediately by verbal expression; if it is written or by letter, acceptance may be delayed, just as it is permitted to be delayed when verbal. There is a difference of opinion as to whether his beginning to investigate cases constitutes acceptance. Some permit it, considering it to be on a par with verbal acceptance, while others reject it as long as there is no verbal expression, saying that his beginning to investigate only constitutes a detail of the contract of appointment, but does not mean that the contract of appointment has been concluded.

The completion of an appointment concluded by means of the four above-mentioned verbal expressions of investiture is guaranteed by four conditions: first, the person being appointed must know that the person making the appointment is empowered to do this; if he does not know this, his appointment is invalid. If he learns of this incapacity after the appointment, the appointment should be made again and he must not rely on what has happened before; second, the appointed person must know how the person carrying out the appointment is entitled to assume this power, must know what qualities permit him to assume it, must be aware of the fact that he has assumed such a responsibility and that he is entitled to appoint someone in his place – although this condition only applies to the acceptance of the appointed person and the legitimacy of his legal investigations, not to the contract of appointment itself, in contrast to the preceding condition. It is not, however, demanded that this knowledge be possessed in person by the interested party, but that it is generally well-known and the subject of discussion between people; third, mention should be made of what the appointment entails, namely judicial authority, the governance of a country, or the collection of the kharaj tax, since these are conditions required in every appointment: the task should be described in detail so that the purpose of this responsibility is clear. If this is not known the contract is null and void; fourth, mention should be made of the area over which authority has been given, so as to know the province in which authority may be exercised. An appointment without this knowledge is not correct.

If the contract is concluded and the handing over of authority takes place according to the above-mentioned conditions, it is necessary to comply with one further condition, namely, that he make his appointment known to those affected by his jurisdiction so that they may show obedience to him and submit to his rule; this condition pertains to the necessity of their obedience and is not a condition in the execution of any order.

If the appointment and the obligation of obedience is concluded correctly in accordance with what we have described, it is correct to regard the appointed person and the one carrying out the appointment as having engaged in a contract of reciprocal responsibility; it is not, however, binding on either of them to stay together on this basis, and the appointed person may withdraw from the arrangement if he wishes and *vice-versa*, although it is better if each only does this with a specific excuse, as the interests of the Muslims are involved. If a man is dismissed or resigns, this must be made known, just as any appointment must be made known so that the execution of a judgement is not obstructed, and a plaintiff does not erroneously seek redress from someone who is no longer qualified to judge. If a judgement is made after someone no longer holds his post and this person is aware of it, then the judgement is not carried out; if, however, he does not know of his dismissal, there are two ways of understanding how the execution of his judgement may be made, just as there are two ways of understanding the contracts made by an agent or a deputy.

The jurisdiction of a Qadi is necessarily either of a general or a specific nature. If it is of a general nature and he is free to act in the capacity assigned to him, then his examination will extend to the following ten cases:

First, he decides in disputes and brings to an end differences and discord by making peace to the mutual satisfaction of both parties, either by considering possible solutions to the affair, or by enforcing an irrevocable judgement based on what is obligatory in the situation;

Second, he ensures that those delaying their obligations towards others fulfil them to the benefit of those entitled to them – after having ascertained that they are due, either by testimony or by evidence; there is a difference of opinion as to whether he may pass judgement on the basis of his own personal knowledge of the case. Malik and ash-Shafi'i, may Allah be pleased with them, both permit it, that is, according to the most correct of ash-Shafi'i's two opinions in this matter, as he has forbidden it in his other opinion. Abu Hanifah, may Allah have mercy on him, permits him to make a judgement based on knowledge acquired during his jurisdiction but not before;

Third, he has guardianship over those who are forbidden to dispose freely of their wealth by reason of their insanity or their being under-age and imposes restrictions on those he considers should be restrained because of their foolishness or their bankruptcy, in order to protect their wealth from those who might lay claim to it, and to validate the laws of contract pertaining to this wealth;

Fourth, he examines waqf-properties to see that the fundamental capital is maintained, that any business based on it grows, and that its profit is received and duly spent on what it is meant for; if there already exists someone responsible for inspecting the waqf, the position of this person is respected, but if there is not, then he should take on this responsibility: he does not have to deal with the specific details of the waqf if his appointment is of a general nature; it may be, however, that he carries out matters of a general nature even if his appointment is of a specific nature;

Fifth, he sees that wills are executed according to the wishes of the testator, as long as it is in accordance with the shari'ah and is not prohibited. Execution of wills is brought about by allowing possession to take place – in the case of beneficiaries who have been identified by name, and by identifying beneficiaries by way of ijtihad and facilitating their taking possession – in the case of those who are simply described by certain qualities. If there is an executor of the will, he should be respected, but if not, he himself should take responsibility;

Sixth, he is to effect the marriage of single women, whether widowed or divorced, if they have no legal guardian and are demanded in marriage. Abu Hanifah, however, does not consider it a responsibility of his jurisdiction, as he permits such women to make a marriage contract themselves;

Seventh, he applies the hudud to those deserving such punishments: if it concerns one of the rights of Allah, may He be exalted, he is to carry out the punishment acting on his own – without any plaintiff – as long as proof has been established either by confession or by the testimony of others. If it concerns one of the rights of people, then it is subject to the petition of a plaintiff. According to Abu Hanifah, however, he is not to apply the hadd-punishments in either case unless there is a specific demand;

Eighth, he oversees matters of public benefit within his zone of jurisdiction by preventing any criminal activities on highways or squares, and by evicting from buildings and houses anyone who is not entitled to be there; he may proceed on his own in examining such cases, even if no plaintiff is present. Abu Hanifah says that he may not examine the case unless a plaintiff has recourse to him. These are part of the rights of Allah, however, and it is of no consequence if there is a demand for intervention or not: for this reason it is more fitting that the judge proceeds alone;

Ninth, he carefully examines any witnesses or persons entrusted in the judicial process; he chooses his representatives – establishing and relying on them if they prove to be correct and upright, and removing them and replacing them if they demonstrate a deficiency and betrayal of trust. If someone is not up to his task, the person who appointed him should choose the best of two options: either he should substitute him with someone who is stronger and more suitable, or else attach someone to him who, by keeping him company, renders him more efficient and more decisive;

Tenth, when judging between the strong and the weak, he should treat both equally: he must decide equitably between the lord and the lorded-over, and not follow his whim by giving short measure to someone entitled to something, or by favouring someone who withholds the right of another. Allah, may He be exalted, says: **"O Dawud, surely We have established you as a khalifah on the earth, so judge between people with the truth and do not follow your whim lest it lead you from the way of Allah; those who turn from the way of Allah will have a painful torment because they forget the Day of Reckoning"** (Qur'an 38: 25).

'Umar ibn al-Khattab, may Allah be pleased with him, listed all the conditions of the judiciary and the rules of appointment in his instructions to Abu Musa al-Ash'ari saying: "The task of the judiciary is an undisputed obligation and a sunnah to be followed. Seek to comprehend when people have recourse to you, for it is of no use to speak of a right if it is not put into effect. See that your face, your justice and your sitting are the same between people, such that the lord does not hope for your partiality nor the weak despair of your justice. It is up to the plaintiff to supply evidence, and it is up to the defendant to swear on oath. Agreement based on compromise is permitted between Muslims, except an agreement which permits what is forbidden or forbids what is permitted. There is nothing to prevent you from returning to the truth if you made a judgement yesterday, but which you then amend after reflection leads you to change your opinion: the truth is eternal and reassessment of one's judgement is better than remaining in falsehood. Comprehension is demanded concerning matters which stick in the breast, but which are not in the Book of Allah or the sunnah of His Prophet: be aware of comparable and similar situations, and only draw analogies in various matters by using examples of equal status. Anyone who makes a claim based on an absent document or proof, accord him a respite: if he brings proof within the allotted time, then his claim is recognised; if not, then judgement is made against him. This is the best way of eliminating doubt and of illuminating any obscurity. The Muslims may act as honourable witnesses to each other, except those who have been given lashes as a hadd-punishment, or who are known to have given false witness, or who are suspect with regard to their relationships or family bonds. Surely Allah is protected from oaths and can repulse any proofs. Avoid anxiety, trouble or grumbling about the plaintiff for when truth is established where it should be, Allah will grant a great reward to the one responsible and grant him a good remembrance by it. And peace be on you."

It might be noted that these instructions are deficient in two ways: firstly, the absence of the word "appointment", by which the handing over of authority is concluded, and secondly, the consideration of the apparent probity of the witnesses, rather than the actual probity established after investigation and examination. One can, however, reply that there are two aspects to be noted regarding the absence of the expression "appointment": first, that the word has been used previously, and that these instructions are concerned only with recommendations and rules to be followed; second, that the expressions used in these instructions encompass the meaning of appointment, like his saying, "Seek to comprehend when people have recourse to you," and his saying, "If he brings proof, then his claim is recognised; if not, then judgement is made against him." Thus the obvious import of these instructions, together with the circumstances in which they were given, render the use of the actual word "appointment" unnecessary.

As for considering the apparent probity of the witnesses, there are two aspects to the matter: first, that it perhaps reflects an opinion held by 'Umar ibn al-Khattab, who mentions it to communicate his own belief, but not as an absolute command; second, it may mean that after examination and interrogation they are considered persons of probity as long as no cause for reproach manifests – except those who have been given lashes as a hadd-punishment.

This type of Qadi, even though he has general jurisdiction, may not exact the kharaj tax as its use is dependent upon the judgement of others, namely the commanders of the armies. As for the zakah taxes, if they are the responsibility of a particular inspector, then they lie outside the realm of his authority. If no inspector has been assigned to this task, some say that it then comes under his general responsibility: he should collect it from those who must pay it and distribute it to those who have a claim to it, as it concerns a right of Allah, may He be exalted, regarding those whom He has designated by name. Others, however, say that it does not come under his jurisdiction, and that it is forbidden for him to get involved in it, as these taxes are to do with financial rights which are left to the ijtihad of the Imams to deal with. This is the same judgement with respect to the imamate of the Friday and the Eid prayers.

If, however, his jurisdiction is restricted, his competence is conferred for a specific matter, and his power of investigation is contained within certain limits: like those who make judgements in some of the cases we have mentioned above, or who judge in cases of avowal without proof, or in the cases of debts (but not marriages), or to establish the nisab (the lowest amount on which zakah is payable). Such jurisdictions are valid, but it is not correct for the person thus appointed to go beyond these limits, as it is a matter of delegation. Thus it may be valid both in a general or a specific way, as in the case of agency.

It may be that the Qadi can investigate in a general way but is restricted as to the action he takes. Thus he may have jurisdiction over all cases in one half of a town or in a particular quarter, in which case he executes all judgements either in the half or the quarter of the town for which he has been appointed, and he may investigate both residents and recently-arrived persons – for the latter are treated as residents – unless his jurisdiction has been restricted to examining cases involving residents and not foreigners or recently arrived persons, in which case his influence does not extend to them. If he has been appointed for the whole town, but on the understanding that he give judgements in just one half of it, or in a particular quarter, or a particular house, he may exercise his judgement in every place, as it is not possible to restrict him to the places assigned to him if his jurisdiction is of a general kind. If this has been stipulated as a condition in the contract of appointment, the latter is annulled and his judgement becomes unacceptable in both the place assigned to him and elsewhere. If he is appointed to judge between those who come to him in his home or to his mosque, then this is valid: it is thus not permitted for him to make judgements outside his home or his mosque, as this condition restricts his judgement to those who enter his home or his mosque – and they, and only they, are determined by the fact that they arrive at his home or mosque. Abu 'Abdallah az-Zubayri said: "The amirs here with us in Basra have for a long time appointed a Qadi at the Jami' mosque – whom they call the Qadi of the mosque – to make judgements in cases involving two hundred dirhams or twenty dinars or any lesser amount, and to fix the standard expenditure (of a husband on his wife for example) and he does not go beyond the place assigned to him, nor beyond the amounts wherein his jurisdiction lies."

If two qadis are appointed to the same region, three possibilities exist: the first, is that one part of the region is assigned to one of them, and the other part to the other; this is correct and each restricts his jurisdiction to the particular part assigned to him; the second, is that a particular kind of legal judgement is assigned to one, and another kind to the other, like the matter of debts to one, and marriages to the other; this is permitted and each restricts himself to an investigation of the particular judgement in question over the region as a whole; the third, is that each is assigned jurisdiction over all cases throughout the country. Our (Shafi'ite) scholars differ as to its permissibility. One group forbid it lest it lead to discord when each party tries to draw the other to the judge of their choice. The jurisdiction of each is annulled if it is made at the same time, while that of the first is valid if the time of appointment is different. Another group, however, permit it, and they are in the majority, arguing that it is a question of delegation, as in the case of agency. When each party seeks their own judge, it is the plaintiff who decides rather than the defendant. If they are in agreement, one should have recourse to the judge nearest the two claimants; if each party appears to have an equal claim to a different judge, lots are drawn, according to some, while they are prevented from seeking redress until they agree on one of the judges, according to others.

*

* *

The jurisdiction of the Qadi may be restricted to a particular case between two litigants, in which case he may not investigate any further cases involving these two persons and a third party. His jurisdiction over the case between them remains in effect as long as the dispute exists between them, and it comes to an end when he pronounces a final judgement. If another dispute between them occurs, he is not empowered to investigate between them unless he has renewed permission.

If he is not appointed to a particular type of litigation, but rather his appointment is restricted to particular days and it is said, for example, "I appoint you to investigate adversaries only on Saturday," his investigation is permitted regarding the opposing parties – whatever the case in question – although his jurisdiction comes to a close at sunset that day. If it is said to him, "I give you jurisdiction every Saturday," this is also permitted, as long as his investigation is restricted to those days only: at the end of (the first) Saturday, however, his jurisdiction does not come to an end – by virtue of his practice on the subsequent Saturdays – but rather he is prohibited from investigating on all other days. If he says – without actually naming someone – "Whoever has jurisdiction between the litigants on Saturday, he is my representative," then this is not permitted, as it is not known who the person invested with authority will be, and it may well be that the person with jurisdiction is not among those of ijtihad; if he says, "Whoever among the people of ijtihad has jurisdiction that day is my representative," this is also not permitted, because the person involved is not known and because the designation of the mujtahid is dependent upon the opinion of someone other than him, namely the litigants; if he says, "Whoever among the teachers of the Shafi'ite school, or from among the muftis of the Hanafi school," it is also not permitted; likewise if he names a number of persons saying, "Whoever has jurisdiction that day from among such and such a person or such and such a person, then he is my representative," this is not permitted, irrespective of whether he names a large or a small number, as the person invested is not known; if, however, he says, "I hand over jurisdiction to such and such a person and to such and such, and to such and such," this is permitted irrespective of whether the number named is small or great, as all of them are appointed: thus if one of them has jurisdiction, he alone occupies the post and the others no longer have jurisdiction as he has not appointed them to have jurisdiction all together but rather appointed one of them; if he does appoint them to have jurisdiction together, this is not valid if their number is great; as to whether it is permitted if they are few in number, there are two aspects to the matter – corresponding to the difference of opinion amongst the scholars of our school regarding the simultaneous jurisdiction of two judges.

As for someone who seeks appointment to the judiciary, if he is not someone from amongst the people of ijtihad, his seeking is forbidden, and he becomes disqualified by his seeking; if, however, he is from amongst its people and has the qualities necessary for the post, his demand may take place in the following circumstances:

First, the judiciary is in the hands of someone who is not entitled to it, either because of a deficiency in his knowledge, or because he is manifestly unjust. Thus he seeks the post of judge in order to get rid of someone who is not entitled to it, and to place it in the hands of someone more entitled to it. This is acceptable, as it implies the removal of something evil; but then the following is kept in mind: if his intention is primarily to get rid of someone who is not entitled to the post his act is rewarded (by Allah), but if it is primarily so that he can take charge of the post, it is simply permitted;

Second, the judiciary is occupied by someone who is entitled to it and who is qualified for it, and the person seeking the post wants to remove him from it either because of some enmity between them, or to obtain the benefit of the post for himself. Seeking the post in this way is forbidden, and he is disqualified from it by his seeking it;

Third, there is no one overseeing the judiciary and the post is empty: in this case the circumstances of his claim are investigated – if it is based on his need of the stipend of the judiciary to which he would be entitled from the bait al-mal, then his demand is permitted. If it is based on his desire to establish truth and his fear that the post would be taken by someone unworthy of it, then his claim is recommended. If, by his claim, he wants glory and position, there is a difference of opinion as to the degree to which it is disliked – although they agree that it is permitted. One group say that it is disliked, as seeking glory and position in this world is disliked; Allah, may He be exalted, says: **"That later abode: We make it for those who do not wish for high position in the earth nor for corruption; and the final reward is for those who have fear of the Divine"** (Qur'an 28: 83). Another group are of the opinion that his claim is not disliked, as seeking a position which is permitted is not disliked. The Prophet of Allah, Yusuf, on whom be peace, desired authority from Fir'awn to be his representative, saying: **"Place me over the treasures of the earth, surely I am a knowledgeable guardian"** (Qur'an 12: 55). There are two interpretations of this seeking of authority and of his saying that he is entitled to it with his words, **"surely I am a knowledgeable guardian"**: the first, that it means, "I am a guardian of what you have placed me over, and wise regarding the authority you have invested in me," and this is the opinion of 'Abd ar-Rahman ibn Zayd; the second, that it means he is "guardian of the accounts and knowledgable regarding languages," and this is the opinion of Ishaq ibn Sufyan. These words go beyond the normal terms used to establish the probity of one's character and to praise one's self, because there was a specific reason for them: this is why there is a difference of opinion as to the permissibility of an unjust person conferring the judiciary on someone. Some are of the opinion that it is permissible if the appointed person acts justly regarding what he has been charged with – as Yusuf, on whom be peace, took up the task on the authority of Fir'awn in order to prevent, by his own justice, the injustice of the latter. Another group, however, are of the opinion that it is forbidden, and that exposure to such a position is to be avoided because of the implications of receiving responsibility from tyrants and of helping them, arguing that in effect legitimacy is conferred on them when their orders are obeyed. They account for the appointment of Yusuf, on whom be peace, by Fir'awn in two ways: firstly, the Fir'awn of Yusuf was right-acting, whereas the Fir'awn of Musa was tyrannical; secondly, he had jurisdiction over his goods and wealth, and not over his lands.

As for making a payment of money when seeking an appointment as judge, it is considered – in the same way as other forbidden actions – as an illegitimate bribe and both the donor and the receiver disqualify themselves thereby from the judiciary. Thabit has related from Anas that the Messenger of Allah, may the peace and blessings of Allah be upon him, cursed the one who gave a bribe, the one who received it, and the one who served as intermediary.

Anyone who takes up a post as a judge must not accept a gift from a litigant, nor from anyone working with him in the judiciary, even if he is not a litigant as he might have to seek the protection of the judge subsequently. It has been related that the Prophet, may the peace and blessings of Allah be upon him, said: "Gifts given by amirs are fetters." If the Qadi accepts them and immediately gives the equivalent in return, they become his; if, however, he is not quick to return the equivalent, the bait al-mal has the most right to them if it is not possible to return them to the donor as the bait al-mal has priority over him.

The Qadi should not keep litigants waiting if they have brought their dispute to him, except when there is a valid excuse. It is also not permitted for him to shut his door except during times of rest. He is not allowed to judge in favour of one of his parents, nor of his children, because of the suspicion of favouritism involved, although he may judge against them, as this suspicion then no longer exists. Likewise he may not bear testimony for them, but he may against them, just as he may bear testimony for his enemy, but not against them; he may judge in favour of his enemy, but not against him: the reasons for his judgement are manifest while those for his testimony are hidden, so he is beyond suspicion regarding the judgement he gives, while he is exposed to suspicion regarding the testimony.

If the Qadi dies, his deputies are removed from office, but if an Imam dies, his judges are not removed from office. If the people of a region agree to appoint a Qadi over themselves where there is no Qadi, this appointment is invalid if the Imam of the time exists; if not, it is valid and he may execute his judgements over them. If a new Imam appears after he has taken over the judiciary, he should not continue in office without the permission of the former, although any previous judgements are not invalidated.

Chapter 7
Judicial Redress

Judicial investigation of wrongs or abuses is concerned with leading those who have committed wrongs to just behaviour by instilling fear in them, and with dissuading litigants from undue obstinacy in their disputes by instilling a feeling of respect. Thus among the qualities demanded of the judicial investigator is that he be of imposing stature, that he ensures action follows his words, that he commands great respect, is manifestly correct in his keeping within moral bounds, restrained in his appetites, and possessed of great scrupulousness: he needs to have the strength of the law-enforcement officers, and the firmness of the qadis in their judicial tasks and to combine the qualities of these two types of person, so that by the majesty of his bearing he is able to execute any command with respect to both parties. If he is among those who have control over the generality of affairs, like ministers and amirs, he does not need to have a specific appointment to this office, since the general nature of his authority gives him jurisdiction in this; if, however, he is not of those to whom general jurisdiction has been delegated, he does need to be appointed and entrusted with this specific task, as long, that is, as all the above-mentioned qualities are to be found in him. Such a task should be assigned, in the case of general jurisdiction over cases of redress and abuse, to those who may be chosen as hereditary successors, or ministers authorised by delegation, or amirs of provinces; if, however, this office is restricted to carrying out whatever the qadis are incapable of carrying out and to the execution of whatever their power does not permit them to execute, then a person below this rank in influence and importance may be chosen, as long he is blameless regarding his respect for the truth, and greed does not fill him with such longing that he accepts bribes. The Messenger of Allah, may the peace and blessings of Allah be upon him, investigated the dispute about irrigation between az-Zubayr ibn al-'Awwam, may Allah be pleased with him, and a man from the Ansar. He came personally and said to az-Zubayr: "You water, O Zubayr, and then the Ansari," to which the latter said: "Surely he is the son of your maternal aunt, O Messenger of Allah." The Prophet became angry at his words and said: "O Zubayr, cause it to flow over his stomach until the water reaches the ankles." He told him to have it flow over his stomach as a reprimand for his audacity. There is a difference of opinion regarding why he ordered him to have the water flow up to the ankles, that is, whether it was to affirm a right in the form of a judgement between them, or whether to merely affirm that it was permitted – but delivered as a reprimand to the two parties.

No one sought redress for a wrong from any of the four khulafa as they were at the very beginning of the affair when the deen have just appeared among them – among men who willingly allowed themselves to be guided to the truth and who desisted from wrong action by mere admonition; any disputes occurring between them were confined to dubious matters, which judicial judgement then explained to them; if a brutish bedouin committed an injustice, admonition alone sufficed to make him renounce it, and rough treatment made him act correctly. The khulafa of the first generations restricted themselves to settling disputes between them by way of judicial decisions, that is by applying the yardstick of Truth to these disputes, aware as they were of the peoples complete acceptance of the necessity of this Truth.

'Ali, however, at a time when his Imamate was weakening as a result of people's interference and their headstrong and excessively individualistic political action, found himself obliged to make great efforts to arrive at solutions to obscure points of law. He was the first to pursue this path and he achieved mastery in it, although he did not end up by devoting his attention solely to cases of redress and abuse, as he was able to do without such cases: thus in the matter which came to be known as the Mimbariyyah case (as he was questioned about it on the mimbar), he replied, "The eighth part (of the inheritance) has become the ninth part;" or in the case where a young girl pinched another she was carrying on her back, with the result that the latter fell and broke her neck, he judged that the blood price be divided in three parts; or when he decided regarding a baby claimed by two women.

After him, however, such cases became more frequent – so much so that people would openly act unjustly towards each other and try to get the better of each other; admonition and exhortation were not sufficient to prevent them from mutual hostilities and recriminations. There was thus a need for a judiciary – which combined the power of authority with the fairness of the legal system – to investigate cases of wrong doing and abuse in order to prevent people from taking advantage of each other, and to see that justice was done for those taken advantage of. The first to assigning a specific day for the investigation of claims by those who had suffered wrong actions – without actually taking part directly himself – was 'Abd al-Malik ibn Marwan. If the latter had to deal with some problem, or if he needed an executory judgement, he would hand it over to his Qadi Abu Idris al-Awdi; the litigants would accept his judgements out of fear of 'Abd al-Malik ibn Marwan who was aware of the circumstances and reasons for the decision. Thus Abu Idris was actually conducting the cases and 'Abd al-Malik was giving the orders.

Thereafter the injustice of officers and the oppressive conduct of the haughty increased to such a point that only the most powerful authority and most strict of commands could restrain them. 'Umar ibn 'Abd al-'Aziz, may Allah have mercy on him, was the first person to undertake judicial investigation of wrong actions and abuse: he would reject all such wrongdoing and would maintain respect for just and fair practices, or re-establish such practices if necessary; he reinstated goods seized unlawfully by the Bani Umayyah to their owners with such force and roughness that it was said, "We fear the consequences of such repression for you," to which he replied, "I am at pains to guard my actions before Allah and fear Him every day on account of them – but my fear for the Day of Raising Up, from which there is no protection, is still greater." Later, several of the Abbasid khulafa sat in judgement, the first of these being al-Mahdi, then al-Hadi, ar-Rashid, al-Ma'mun and finally al-Muhtadi, with the result that goods and property were returned to their rightful owners.

The kings of Persia had considered this to be amongst the fundamental practises of sovereignty and the rules of justice: correct behaviour and equity amongst the general population could only be established by observing such practices.

During the Jahiliyyah, at a time when those claiming leadership multiplied, when those behaving like chiefs became widespread, when people tried to get the better of each other, and when they acted unjustly towards each other, such that no authority was able to resolve this state of affairs, the Quraysh made an oath to do away with these abuses and to see that justice was given to those suffering at the hands of the wrongdoers. The reason for this, according to Zubayr ibn Bakkar, was that a Yemeni man from the Banu Zubayd came to Makkah to perform the 'Umrah with merchandise, and a man from the Banu Sahm, said to be al-'As ibn Wa'il, bought it from him; the latter refused to acknowledge what he owed the other, who in turn demanded his money or return of the goods. When he still refused his demand, he got up on the wall surrounding the Ka'bah and declaimed the following at the top of his voice:

O Banu Qusayy, help someone who has been unjustly deprived of his goods in the middle of Makkah, far from his home and his people, his hair dishevelled, in the state of pilgrimage, still within the sanctity of the station of Ibrahim and the surrounding wall and the Black Stone; is the wealth of someone on 'Umrah to be respected by the Banu Sahm or is it to be left as lost?

Then Qays ibn Shaybah as-Sulami sold the merchandise to Ubayy ibn Khalaf who, without recognising the debt, made off with the money paid. Qays sought, unsuccessfully, the protection of a man from the Bani Jumu'ah and then said:

O Banu Qusayy, what is this in the sacred limits where the inviolability of the House and the rules of hospitality should be? I have been wronged and no-one protects me from the one who has done me wrong!

'Abbas ibn Mirdas as-Sulami then replied to him in the following manner:

If your neighbour's protection is to no avail and you have drunk draughts from the cup of humiliation, come to the houses (of your family) and keep close to their people; such a man will not suffer any outrage or violent behaviour: whoever gains safety within the confines of the House will find Ibn Harb and the true man Abbas. My people are the Quraysh, of perfect character, glory and resolution, as long as they live and govern; they provide water for the pilgrims but that is a minor success, for glory is acquired little by little

Abu Sufyan and al-'Abbas then rose to give him back his due and the clans of the Quraysh gathered in the house of 'Abdallah ibn Jud'an to bear oath that they would see that justice was done in any case of wrongdoing in Makkah, that they would prevent anyone from committing any injustice, and that they would ensure that the right of the person wronged was fulfilled. The Messenger of Allah, may the peace and blessing of Allah be upon him, (at the age of 25 years, before his prophethood), was with them that day when they took the Oath of the Fudul as it was known. Recalling the incident, he said, may the peace and blessing of Allah be upon him "I was a witness to the Oath of the Fudul in the house of 'Abdallah ibn Jud'an: I would honour it if I were called to, and I would not wish for the most excellent of camels in its place." He thus recounted an incident whose significance has only intensified with the advent of Islam. One of the Qurayshis recited the following concerning the oath:

> *If you were to ask, then know that Taym ibn Murrah, Hashim and Zuhra al-Khayr took an oath together in the house of Ibn Jud'an, to respond to any call as long as the turtle dove coos on a branch in the valley of Kitman.*

Although this was an act in the time of the Jahiliyyah which they were called upon to do by the administration of the time, it has become a rule of the shari'ah and a prophetic act by virtue of the presence and affirmation of the Messenger of Allah, may the peace and blessing of Allah be upon him.

✳

✳ ✳

When the person charged with investigating cases of wrongdoing takes up office, he should appoint a specific day on which he can investigate the claims of the litigants so that he may devote the remaining days to his responsibility for administration and organisation – except if he is one of the officers responsible solely for incidents of wrongdoing, in which case he is charged with investigation every day. He should be of pleasant demeanour and have good companions. The courtroom where his investigations are carried out should be composed of five categories of personnel: they indispensable for without them the investigations cannot proceed:

First, guards and officers, to bring the powerful before him, and to put the audacious in their place;

Second, qadis and judges, so that he may make enquiries as to the rights and claims established by them, and so that he may know what happens between litigants at their tribunals;

Third, fuqaha, so that he may have recourse to them in difficult cases, and may ask them about doubtful or problematic points;

Fourth, scribes, in order that they may record what happens between litigants, and what rights or claims against them are decided upon;

Fifth, witnesses, so that they may attest to any right he recognises, or any judgement he orders to be carried out.

If the court investigating wrongdoing is composed of all of these five above-mentioned categories, the person responsible may begin to carry out his investigations. There are ten areas covered by his investigation into wrong-doing:

1. He investigates any abuse of power by rulers towards their subjects, and brings them to account for the injustice of their actions; this is a necessary part of investigation and is not dependent upon a petition from a plaintiff; thus he examines the behaviour of governors and enquires after their state in order to strengthen their case if they are equitable, to restrain them if they go beyond the limits, and to replace them if they are unjust. It is reported that 'Umar ibn 'Abd al-'Aziz gave a khutbah, which was his first, to the people at the beginning of his khilafah, in which he said, "I recommend to you that you have taqwa of Allah, as He does not accept other than this and does not make welcome other than its people. There are certain governors who do not give what is true and right, its due such that justice may be bought from them, and they spread falsehoods about them in order that ransoms be given to them. By Allah, if I had not revived a sunnah which had died, or caused to die a false practice which had come into being, I would not have cared to live for a moment. When you put your hereafter in order, your dunya will be in order. A man who is separated from Adam by nothing but death, is already submerged in death."

2. Extortions made by agent-collectors when exacting the taxes on wealth and property – in this case he should have recourse to the laws of justice contained in the diwans of the imams: he should ensure that the people are treated accordingly, that the agents apply the directives accordingly, and that they investigate any overestimations – if these amounts have been paid to the treasury, they should be returned, and if the agents themselves have taken them, he makes them return the money to their owners.

It is recounted that one day, while al-Muhtadi was holding an audience for the repression of abuses, various petitions regarding the coins known as *Khusroes* were made to him; when he enquired about them, Sulayman ibn Wahb replied: "'Umar ibn al-Khattab, may Allah be pleased with him, had imposed on the inhabitants of as-Sawad, and of the areas around it to the east and west which he had conquered, payment by instalments of the kharaj tax in silver and gold; the dirhams and the dinars were minted with the weight of Khusroes and of Caesar, and the people of these regions would pay the money they had, according to the number required, without considering the disparity in weight between the various coins. Then the people became corrupt and those who had to pay the kharaj would give *Tabari* coins, which were four daniq, and would keep the *wafi* money of full weight, which had the weight of a mithqal. When Ziyad became governor of Iraq, he exacted payment in *wafis* and imposed payment in Khusroes. The agents of the Bani Umayyah continued the practice until 'Abd al-Malik began his rule. The latter examined the difference between the two weights, and assessed the weight of the dirham at five and a half mithqals, leaving the mithqal as it was. Later, al-Hajjaj began to demand payment in Khusroes, something which was annulled by 'Umar ibn 'Abd al-'Aziz but which was reinstated by those after him, until the time of al-Mansur. When, however, as-Sawad was destroyed, al-Mansur put an end to payment in silver of the kharaj due on the wheat and the barley, and transformed it into a proportional tax in kind. These two grains are the most common in as-Sawad, and he left the few other grain-crops, dates and fruit-trees to be assessed in accordance with the kharaj, which is still now exacted in Khusroes and provisions." Al-Muhtadi then said, "May Allah guard me from imposing an unjust measure on the people, be it from long ago or the recent past – relieve the people of it!" Hasan ibn Makhlad said that this abolishment of the Amir al-Mumineen's represented an annual loss of 12 million dirhams to the treasury. Al-Muhtadi replied that he, "would establish what was right and remove an injustice, even if it were to the detriment of the treasury."

3. Registration of the diwan-officials, since they occupy positions of trust: in this way the wealth of the Muslims may be correctly administered, both in its collection and in its distribution. Thus he has to investigate the nature of what has been entrusted to them, and if there is any excess or deficiency with respect to any incoming or outgoing funds, then he applies the corresponding laws and takes the necessary measures regarding all irregularities.

It is narrated that al-Mansur (the Abbasid Khalifah), may Allah be pleased with him, on learning that a group of his scribes had made falsifications and alterations in the diwan ordered them to be brought before him and punished; one of them uttered the following lines as he was being whipped:

O Amir of the Believers! may Allah prolong your life in prosperity and power. We seek protection in your forgiveness, for if you grant us protection, it is by virtue of your being able to afford safety to the whole world. As for us, we are merely scribes who have made mistakes so forgive us for the sake of the noble recording angels.

Thereupon he commanded them to be released, and he bestowed gifts on the young man and treated him in a most generous way, as he had manifested his sense of trust and shown his nobility.

For these three types of abuse it is not necessary for the one investigating to wait for someone to lodge a complaint.

4. Claims of deficiency, delay or negligence towards those receiving provision. In these cases, he should refer back to his diwan in order to establish the obligation and justice of any payment, and to see whether it continues to be paid to them; he should examine if officials have made short-payments in the past or have prevented payment: if the officials in charge have taken the funds, he should recover the sum from them, if not, he meets the loss from the treasury.

One of the army commanders wrote to al-Ma'mun, saying that the army had mutinied and engaged in pillage; the latter wrote to him saying "If you had been just they would not have mutinied, and if you had given them their full due, they would not have pillaged;" he then relieved him of the command and awarded them the provisions owing them.

5. Restitution of things seized by force; these may be divided into two types:

A. The first of these are those seized by the authorities, that is those taken by unjust governors, such as property taken from its owner either out of greed or out of hostility towards its owner. As soon as the person responsible for putting a stop to abuses comes to learn of this during his investigation, he should order its restitution without waiting for anyone to lodge a complaint with him. If, however, he does not learn of anything in his investigation, his taking action is dependent on the owner lodging a complaint. In the case of a claim, he may consult the diwan in question: if he finds that mention is made of a property which has been seized from its owner, he acts accordingly and orders its restitution without needing any (further) proof in the matter, his finding mention of it in the diwan being sufficient. Thus it is related that 'Umar ibn 'Abd al-'Aziz, may Allah have mercy on him, went out one day to the prayer and found himself confronted by a man who had journeyed from the Yemen to make a claim and who recited the following:

You have called a confused person to your door who has suffered an injustice and who has come to you from a far-off country.

The Khalifah asked him: "What is your complaint?" He replied: "al-Walid ibn 'Abd al-Malik has taken my lands from me." The Khalifah then said: "Muzahim! give me the register of confiscated lands whose title is still being settled." He then found the following: "Abdallah al-Walid ibn 'Abd al-Malik has confiscated the lands of such and such a person." He then said: "Delete this from the register and record that his land has been restored to him, and that double the amount which he draws from it be given to the claimant."

B. The second kind of property seized by force is that taken by powerful individuals and who dispose of it with violence and coercion, as if they were the owners. Its restitution is dependent on a complaint on behalf of their true owners, but they may only be recovered from those who have seized them in one of four circumstances: **i.** either by way of an admission and confirmation by the one who took it; **ii.** on the basis of information possessed by the person responsible for setting right the abuse, in which case he may give judgement in accordance with what he knows; **iii.** by means of witnesses who testify to the improper seizure or to the victim's right to ownership; **iv.** the corroboration of accounts, which exclude all possibility of collusion by the witnesses: as witnesses may testify to the ownership of goods, the person responsible for setting aright the abuse, has all the more cause to base his judgement on a concordance of statements.

6. The surveillance of Waqf-institutions. They are either of a general or of a particular kind:

A. As for the general, he should begin by examining these waqfs even if there has been no complaint against them – in order that he might have them run in the manner appropriate to them, and so that they are administered in accordance with the conditions stipulated by the waqf donors. This, however, he may only do if he knows of them from one of three sources: **i.** from the diwan-registers of the authorities responsible for the enforcing of judgements; **ii.** from the diwans of the Sultan which contain descriptions of standard practices or mention of such institutions by name; **iii.** from ancient manuscripts on the subject which appear to be correct, even if there is no mention of witnesses – lack of litigation concerning these waqf would mean that there was no need for witnesses. The scope of such decision-making is thus larger than in the waqf-cases of a particular kind.

B. As for waqfs of a particular kind, his inspection of them is dependent upon receipt of a complaint from interested parties who have differences of opinion – given that these waqfs have been set up for the benefit of specific parties. In the case of a dispute, he should proceed according to the law before a judge in any establishment of rights; he may not have recourse to the diwan of the Sultan, nor to any proof afforded by ancient manuscripts lacking any attestation by just witnesses.

7. The execution of those judgements which qadis have suspended because of their own weakness and incapacity in applying them to the party against whom judgement has been made – because of the latter's strength and power, or because of the superiority of his position and standing. As the person responsible for redressing the abuse is stronger and more capable of executing an order, he should carry out the judgement against the person in question either by taking away what he possesses, or by coercing him into giving up what he owes.

8. The inspection of whatever the muhtasib-inspectors have been unable to undertake in matters of public good: thus concerning the open practice of something illicit which they are too weak to prevent, transgressions committed on public highways which they cannot stop, or violation of rights which they do not have the means to put an end to, he applies Allah's judgement, may He be exalted, to them, and orders that they be forced to respect this judgement.

9. He sees that the public acts of worship are respected, like the jumu'ah prayer, the 'Eids, the Hajj, and the jihad, and that there is no deficiency or omission regarding any aspect of them, for the rights and obligations of Allah, may He be exalted, have priority concerning their fulfilment and execution.

10. Arbitration between two disputing parties and judgement between two litigants, although he is not to depart from the demands of the law and its consequences in his investigation, and he may not pronounce judgement between them by other than that by which judges and qadis judge. Many a time judgement in cases of abuse causes ambiguity for those responsible for their investigation, and so they in turn transgress in their judgements and go beyond the appropriate limits.

There are ten differences between the authority of someone responsible for suppressing abuses and that of a judge:

First, the inspector of abuses enjoys a greater degree of respect and power than that of the judge, that is regarding his capacity to prevent the mutual recriminations of the two litigating parties, and to restrain any violent or excessive behaviour on behalf of either of them.

Second, he is permitted to abandon the restricting ambit of obligatory judgements in order to act with greater freedom of movement in the realm of the permissible: thus he has wider scope and more liberty in his pronouncements;

Third, as he is able to use a greater degree of intimidation and is able to uncover the truth by means of relevant facts and appropriate evidential testimony – which would be difficult for judges to do – he makes manifest what is right and at distinguishes between truth and falsehood;

Fourth, he punishes those who openly commit injustices, and reprimands, with criticism and censure, those whose hostility is manifest;

Fifth, he is able to delay judgement when the matter involving the litigants is unresolved because of the ambiguity of their case and the uncertainty regarding their rights; this, in order to make an examination of their details and circumstances. In short, a judge may not do this if one of the litigants asks for a definitive judgement, while the person responsible for suppressing abuses may do so;

Sixth, he is able to refer litigants to the arbitration of trusted persons – if the former become very troublesome – in order that they may resolve the differences to the satisfaction of both parties. The Qadi, however, is not able to do this unless the litigants agree;

Seventh, he may place the litigants under surveillance if there are clear indications that their mutual denials are inconsistent, and he can authorise the obligation of surety or bail with respect to matters where such guarantees are allowed, in order to compel the litigants to a mutual sense of justice, and to make them avoid all mutual denials and mutual denigration;

Eighth, he may hear testimonies from good and honest persons in circumstances where qadis would not be able to hear them without breaching established practice in the case of upright citizens;

Ninth, he may have the witnesses swear on oath when he is in doubt as to whether they are making their testimonies of their own accord; he may also demand that there be a number of them, so as to avoid any possibility of doubt and to remove any uncertainty he may feel. This is not, however, permitted for a judge (who forms his decision on the basis of two witnesses, except, that is, in the case of fornication);

Tenth, he is permitted to initiate the summoning of the witnesses and to ask them what they know of the dispute between the litigants, whereas the custom amongst judges is to charge the plaintiff with producing witnesses – whom he does not hear until after questioning the plaintiff.

These are the ten differences between these two offices, in the case of disputes and quarrels – they being equal in cases other than these two. We shall explain in detail the exact distinction between the two offices, if Allah, may He be exalted, wills.

✳

✳ ✳

Such being the situation as described above, any claim or complaint taken to the magistrate in charge of grievances will necessarily be one of three kinds: either one accompanied by corroborating evidence, or by evidence which weakens it, or by neither of these two:

1. If there is corroborating evidence, it will be of six types, their degree of corroboration varying accordingly:

First, one in which the claim is accompanied by a written list of the just witnesses present. Two aspects are special about the investigation of grievances in this particular claim: the first, that the investigator initiates the calling of witnesses for their testimonies and second, that he reprimands anyone who refuses to testify, in accordance with his standing and the circumstances surrounding his situation. When the witnesses are present, then if the magistrate in charge is of elevated standing, like the Khalifah, or a delegated wazir, or the amir of a province, he takes account of the circumstances of the conflicting parties in accordance with what political astuteness requires, that it either by sitting personally in judgement between the two, if they are of high social rank or by referring the case to his Qadi – who attends to the case if they are of middle rank, but does not attend if they are of inferior status.

It is narrated that al-Ma'mun, may Allah be pleased with him, used to personally sit in the court for grievances on Sundays; one day he rose to leave a sitting when a woman in rags confronted him, saying:

O flower of the just to whom even uprightness itself is guided, O Imam by whom the whole land has been illuminated! A widow takes her complaint to you, O support of the realm, against whom, without means of defence, a lion has made an attack: he has seized lands from her after she was rendered incapable and had become separated from her family and children.

Al-Ma'mun lowered his eyes a moment and then raised his head saying:

Before less than what you have spoken of, patience and fortitude themselves would have weakened; my heart is sickened by your sadness and affliction. Now is the time for the midday prayer, so depart and bring your adversary on the day I shall promise to you: the court sits on Saturday, and if I sit on that day I will see that you receive justice; if not, then at the Sunday sitting.

She then departed and attended on Sunday in the first row. Al-Ma'mun then asked her: "Against whom do you lodge a complaint?" She replied: "The one standing by your side, al-'Abbas, the son of the Amir of the Believers." Al-Ma'mun then told his Qadi, Yahya ibn Aktham, (while others say that it was his wazir Ahmad ibn Abi Khalid), to hold a sitting with both of them and to investigate the case – which he did in the presence of al-Ma'mun. When the woman raised her voice and one of the attendants reprimanded her, al-Ma'mun said: "Leave her, for surely it is the truth which is making her speak, and falsehood which is causing him to be silent," and he ordered that her land be restored to her. Al-Ma'mun's action in having the investigation take place in his presence, but without taking it up in person was indicative of good administration in two ways: firstly, it concerned a judgement which might have been in favour of or against his son: one may not pronounce judgement in favour of one's son, although one may pass judgement against him; secondly, the litigant was a woman with respect to whom al-Ma'mun was too highly placed to respond; moreover his son, by virtue of his rank, found himself in a position in which no one other than the caliph could enforce the law. Thus al-Ma'mun referred the investigation, in his son's presence, to someone who was able to converse with the woman and so resolve the claim and elucidate the pertinent facts – but it was al-Ma'mun himself, may Allah be pleased with him, who issued the executory judgement and enforced the law;

Second, in support of the claim, there is an accompanying written statement from a trustworthy, yet absent, witness. In this case, there are four methods employed by the magistrate responsible for the suppression of abuses: **i.** putting pressure on the defendant: it often happens that the latter is quick to confess under pressure, which precludes the need to listen to the evidence of the witnesses; **ii.** an order compelling the witnesses to attend, if their place of residence is known and this does not present any serious difficulties; **iii.** an order placing the defendant under surveillance for three days: he then takes a considered decision as to whether to increase this period in accordance with the strength of the what transpires and what evidence is verifiable; **iv.** investigation of the claim: if it concerns a debt which is owed, he obliges the person in question to furnish a guarantee; if it is a question of a specific object, like a building, then the latter is placed under guardianship but without actual possession being taken from the person who claims ownership; any profit accruing from this building is handed over to a trustworthy person, who then returns it to the litigant whose rightful ownership is established.

If the wait is prolonged and there is no hope that the witnesses will appear, the magistrate responsible for claims may interrogate the defendant while renewing his pressure, in order to discover how it came into his possession. Malik ibn Anas, may Allah be pleased with him, is of the opinion that the defendant may be interrogated as to the cause of his coming into possession of the thing in question, whereas ash-Shafi'i and Abu Hanifah are not; but the magistrate in charge may use any permitted means and he is not obliged to keep to the means which have been declared obligatory. If the defendant replies in such a way as to put an end to the dispute, then he executes the matter accordingly; if not, he decides between the two parties in accordance with the law.

Third, in support of the claim, there is an accompanying statement, signed by witnesses who are present, but who are not considered trustworthy by the judge: what is particular to the investigation of claims and complaints is that the magistrate in charge orders the witnesses to attend and checks who they are. He will necessarily find them to be of three types: either they are people of standing and honesty, in which case their testimony is all the more credible; or they are mean and low, and their credibility is decreased, and the pressure he puts them under is intensified; or they are of average standing, in which case, after investigating who they are, he may have them take an oath, if he thinks fit, before or after they give testimony.

As for hearing these two types of witnesses, he finds himself in one of three positions: either he hears them himself and he pronounces judgement accordingly; or he sends them to the Qadi who is charged with hearing them and to report what they say to him: only then may the Qadi make a decision, since the Qadi may not pronounce judgement except on the testimony of those whose trustworthiness is established in the magistrate's eyes; or he refers the hearing of these persons to honourable witnesses, and if they are charged with returning a report of their statements to him, they do not have to investigate who they are; if, however, he sends testimonies collected by him back to them, together with affirmation of their correctness, then they will have to investigate these persons, so as to establish whether these testimonies are acceptable – so that, in turn, these honourable witnesses may attest, based on their own knowledge, that these testimonies are true, and then judgement may be pronounced accordingly.

Fourth, the claim is supported by an accompanying written statement in which there is the testimony of just witnesses who are now dead, but whose correctness is manifestly clear. The investigation of claims and grievances is then characterised by three things: **i.** putting pressure on the defendant by coercing him into telling the truth and into affirming what is just; **ii.** interrogation concerning how he came into possession (of the thing), as the truth may become apparent from his reply; **iii.** enquiry into the situation from the neighbours of the property, and the neighbours of those who dispute the claim, so as to reveal the truth and to arrive at a recognition of the rights of the claimant.

If he does not achieve results by any of these methods, he refers the matter to an arbitrator of substance and authority, who knows the two parties and is aware of the object of their dispute, in order that he may coerce them by dint of insistence and perseverance over time into recognising the truth of one of the parties over the other, or into coming to an arrangement: if the matter is resolved in one of these two ways, then so be it; if not, a final judgement is made according to the conditions required by that of the judge.

Fifth, in support of his case, the claimant possesses something written by the defendant which is relevant to the claim. Investigation of the grievance in this case consists of questioning the defendant about the document saying: "Is this your writing?" If he accepts that it is his, he is questioned as to the veracity of its contents; if he accepts its veracity, it is treated as an admission and he is judged accordingly. There are, however, judges who will pronounce judgement against him even if he does not accept its veracity, that is, just for acknowledging his own handwriting, even though he might disavow its veracity: they treat this as a piece of legal evidence and consider the matter in the light of customary practice. However, the practice amongst those given to very precise investigations, and the opinion of all the fuqaha amongst them, is that an investigating magistrate may not pronounce judgement merely on the basis of handwriting until the author acknowledges the veracity of what is written: this is because investigation of grievances does not render judgements legal which would otherwise be forbidden in the law. Thus any investigation of grievances has to take into account what he says of his handwriting: for example, "I wrote that for a loan from him, but he did not make the loan to me," or, "So that he might pay me for what I sold him, but he did not pay me," which people do sometimes. In such cases, the investigator of grievances should employ means of applying pressure in accordance with how he appraises the situation, and how the indications corroborate it. After this he refers it to a mediator: if it leads to a solution, so be it; if not, the Qadi pronounces a definitive judgement based on their mutual oaths.

If he does not acknowledge the writing as his, then some magistrates responsible for grievances would compare it with other writings of his: to this purpose they would oblige him to furnish many examples of his writing, so as to prevent any falsehood. If they are alike, they would pronounce judgement against him. This, then, is the opinion of those who consider that an acknowledgement of one's writing is sufficient to decide a judgement; however, those amongst them who are of a more precise nature do not do this in order to pass judgement, but rather to put pressure on the person in question. The probability of there being any similarity is less when he does not acknowledge his writing than when he does; all probability of similitude is lost if the writing is unlike his writing, in which case pressure is then put on the plaintiff, and then (if necessary) the two parties are referred to a mediator. If this leads to a solution, then all well and good; if not, the Qadi makes a definitive decision after taking oaths from them.

Sixth, in support of the claim, relevant accounts are shown – which happens in the case of commercial transactions; such accounts are necessarily of two types: either those of the plaintiff, or of the defendant. If the plaintiff's, their authenticity is more in doubt: in such cases, investigation of irregularities must concern itself with the order of such accounts; if they are in disorder, fraudulent practice may well have taken place, in which case they are rejected, as they indicate the weakness of the claim rather than strengthening it; if, however, they are in good order and well arranged, and the totalling up of the figures is correct, then they should be trusted all the more. Pressure is to be applied in accordance with what these accounts show; then the two parties are referred to a mediator and (if necessary) a final judgement is made.

If, however, the accounts belong to the defendant, their value relative to the claim is all the stronger. They are necessarily either in his own handwriting or in that of his scribe: if they are in his own writing the investigating magistrate must ask him, "Is this your handwriting?"; if he acknowledges it, he is asked, "Do you know what it says?"; if he affirms that he knows, he is asked, "Do you know if they are correct?"; if he affirms that they are correct, then he is treated as having made an avowal of their contents by these three affirmations, and he is legally responsible for what is in them. If he acknowledges that it is his writing, but that he is unaware of its contents, and does not acknowledge that they are exact, then those among the investigating magistrates who do pronounce judgements on the basis of something written, pass judgement against him on the basis of his accounts – even if he does not acknowledge that they are correct; they trust this more than they do the odd loose leaves (of uncompleted transactions), as accounts are only drawn up when monies have actually been received. Those magistrates among them, however, who are particularly conscientious in their attention to detail – and this is the opinion of the fuqaha – do not pass judgement against him on the basis of accounts the contents of which he does not acknowledge their accuracy. However, on the basis of these accounts, more pressure is required against him than in the case of loose leaf accounts – in accordance with the recognised differences between the two types of account mentioned above. Then both parties are referred to a mediator and to the final decision of the judge.

If the writing is attributed to the defendant's scribe, the latter is questioned before his scribe: if he acknowledges the contents he becomes legally responsible; if he does not, then his scribe is questioned; if the latter denies having written it, doubt is increased by his denial and pressure is put on him if he is suspect but not, if he is a trustworthy person; if he acknowledges it, and affirms its exactness, he becomes a witness for the plaintiff against the defendant, if he is an upright man, and judgement is pronounced against the defendant on the basis of his testimony under oath – either as a point of law, or by virtue of the criteria which are applicable in the circumstances. These circumstances have the effect of producing different judgements in the case of complaints and grievances: for each case there is a specific limit to the pressure involved, and this is not to be exceeded, but one must distinguish between the various circumstances and the features of each case.

2. On the other hand, the claim may be made accompanied by elements which weaken it, in which case there are six different aspects to such a claim, and they represent the opposite of those aspects which strengthen the case; the pressure which is to be brought to bear associated with this cases is then transferred from the defendant to the plaintiff:

First, over and against the claim which is made together with a written piece of evidence made by (absent) witnesses is the presence of other just witnesses who give testimony annulling the claim – in four ways: **i.** they testify against him saying that whatever he is claiming has been sold; **ii.** or, that the claimant had affirmed that he had no right to whatever he is claiming; **iii.** or, that his father had avowed that the property had been transferred from his own hands and that the claimant had no right to it; **iv.** or, that the defendant is the rightful owner of the thing being claimed from him. Such testimony annuls the claim, and it is then up to the magistrate to make a discretionary punishment in accordance with his situation.

If the defendant states that the testimony concerning sale was made under duress and intimidation – which happens many a time – the magistrate should examine the contract of sale: if it states therein that it is not made under duress or intimidation doubt as to the defendant's statement is increased; if this is not mentioned the veracity of his claim is strengthened; pressure is brought to bear on both parties in accordance with the situation indicated by the testimonies given by each, and recourse is taken to questioning their neighbours and relations: if it becomes clear that it is necessary to keep to the letter of the contract, one acts accordingly; if not, the execution of the act of sale according to what is recorded by the witnesses of that sale is preferable.

If the plaintiff demands that the defendant take an oath that the sale has been correct and that it has not been made under duress or coercion, the fuqaha differ as to whether this oath-taking is permitted, because of the diversity of the kinds of claim he might be making: Abu Hanifah, may Allah be pleased with him, and a group of the followers of ash-Shafi'i, consider that it is permissible arguing that his claim may be well-founded. Other Shafi'ites oppose this, since his previous affirmation conflicts with his later claim. It is up to the magistrate responsible for claims and grievances to apply the law in accordance with the testimonies of both parties. Likewise, if the claim concerns a debt of money, and the defendant shows written evidence of his having paid the debt, and then the plaintiff claims to have had him witness the act of payment but that payment did not in fact take place, then the defendant is made to take an oath as mentioned above.

Second, in the case where the witnesses to the written evidence which contradicts the plaintiff's demand are just citizens, but absent, there are two possibilities:

i. It contains a rejection of the demand and gives a reason like, "He has no right to these lands as I bought it from him and paid the price to him; this is a document testifying that I am opposing his claim." The defendant thus becomes a plaintiff furnished with a document, the witnesses to which are absent, such that the legal situation remains the same, but he retains possession and the right to dispose of it as well: in which case the indications and circumstances are stronger and clearer for him. If this does not lead to the establishment of the right to the property, the magistrate should bring pressure to bear on the two parties to a degree dictated by the circumstances of each; he should also order the witnesses to appear, if possible, but can stipulate a delay to their appearance, so that he may refer both parties to a mediator. If this leads to an agreement to their mutual satisfaction, then the matter is settled and there is no need to hear the witnesses when they appear; if, however, there is no solution to their dispute, thorough investigations are carried out at both of their neighbours and those of the property; during these investigations, the magistrate considers which of the three possibilities his ijtihad should adopt in the light of the indications and circumstances: either to take the property from the defendant and give it to the plaintiff, until evidence of the sale against the latter is established; or to hand it over to trustworthy person for safekeeping and for him to collect any profit made on it for the benefit of the rightful owner; or he leaves it in the hands of the defendant, but has it sequestered and appoints a man of trust over it to protect any profit issuing from it. The situation of the two parties will be subject to the magistrate deciding upon one of these three possibilities as long as there is any expectation of one of two things: the revealing of the truth by means of the investigation, or the appearance of the witnesses to give evidence. If there is no hope of their coming, then a final judgement is made; if the defendant demands that the plaintiff take an oath he is made to do this for him, and this will lead to a final judgement between the two of them;

ii. The document does not contain the rejection of the demand together with an acknowledgement of the reason for this, but rather reads, "This property belongs to me and the claimant has no right to it." The evidence of the document testifies either to the statement that the claimant has no right to it or, that the property belongs to the defendant, and in this latter case the property stays in the hands of the defendant and it may not be taken from him. As for having it sequestered from him and having any resulting profits kept in trust during the period of investigation and mediation, this depends on the circumstances of each party, and on the ijtihad of the magistrate in charge of grievances who considers the dispute between them until he makes a definitive decision between them;

Third, the witnesses to the document opposed to the claim are present, but they are not upright citizens. Thus the magistrate takes into consideration, with respect to what we have said concerning the plaintiff, the three criteria which may be applied to them, and the fact of his denial, that is, whether or not it contains an acknowledgement of the reason for this denial. He then acts in accordance with what we have explained above, while relying on his ijtihad regarding the circumstances of the case;

Fourth, the witnesses to the document are now dead, but were upright citizens; in this case no judgement based thereon may be made; only pressure may be brought to bear in order to complete the rest of the investigation. Thereafter there follows a definitive judgement in accordance with what the denial contains, whether there is an acknowledgement of the cause or not;

Fifth, the defendant is confronted with the written statement of the plaintiff which appears to establish the falsehood of the demand: the magistrate acts in accordance with what we have explained above concerning handwriting, and any pressure applied must depend on the circumstances;

Sixth, accounts produced on behalf of the claim itself result in the establishment of the falsehood of the claim. The magistrate should then act in accordance with our above explanation concerning accounts: the investigation, pressure, and delay, are dependent on the circumstances; thereafter he comes to a final decision if there is no other hope of resolving the dispute.

3. If the claim lacks any presumptive or circumstantial evidence, for or against, such that there are no accompanying indications supporting or detracting from it, then any investigation of a grievance demands that the circumstances of the litigants be weighed up according to "overwhelming probability." This will be one of three kinds: either this overwhelming probability will favour the plaintiff, or the defendant, or it will result in both having equal probability. What will lead him to an awareness of overwhelming probability with respect to one or other of the two parties is recourse to applying pressure to them both and, preferably to proceed to an investigation of them both; a strong impression of probability on his part, however, is not enough to establish a definitive judgement.

If the circumstantial evidence is in favour of the plaintiff and doubt is cast on the side of the defendant, this may be of three different types;

i. The plaintiff, although lacking proof which might give him the upper hand, is of weak means but of an accommodating character, whereas the defendant is strong and has means: if the plaintiff claims that the latter usurped his house or property, one is more likely to think that a man of his gentleness of character and weakness would not exaggerate in his claim against someone who possesses force and strength;

ii. The plaintiff is well-known for his truthfulness and trustworthiness, and the defendant for his lying and deceit; thus one accepts the truth of the plaintiffs's claim;

iii. Both of them are of like circumstance, but the plaintiff was known to have possessed the thing, whereas it is not known how it came into the hands of the defendant.

In these three cases, two things are to be done: pressure is brought to bear on the defendant because of the doubt surrounding him, that is, he is interrogated as to the reason for his coming into possession of the thing and how he became the rightful owner. Malik ibn Anas, may Allah be pleased with him, considers the judiciary should proceed in this way when there is doubt – and the investigation of grievances has all the more right to follow this procedure.

Many a time, the defendant, because of his high standing, disdains to place himself on the same footing as his adversary before a court, and so he cedes whatever is in his possession of his own accord. Thus it is related that Musa al-Hadi was sitting at a court-hearing for claims and grievances, and 'Umarah ibn Hamzah, who had influence in court, was sitting next to him. Thereupon one of those who were seeking redress claimed that 'Umarah had taken his property from him, and so al-Hadi ordered him to sit with him at the hearing; 'Umarah, however, said, "O Commander of the Believers, if the property is his, then I will not oppose him in this, and if it is mine, then I give it to him: I do not wish to sell my position at the court of the Commander of the Believers."

It can sometimes happen that the magistrate acts graciously when according the victim his right, but maintains at the same time a respect for the defendant, which safeguards his honour from suspicion of using force or preventing a rightful claim. Thus Awn ibn Muhammad relates that the people of Nahr al-Mirghab at Basra began a suit against al-Mahdi about this area through his Qadi 'Ubaidullah ibn al-Hasan al-Anbari, but neither he nor al-Hadi, his successor, handed it over to them. Then ar-Rashid came to power, and they sought redress from him before Ja'far ibn Yahya, who was the magistrate responsible for grievances, but ar-Rashid did not cede it to them either. Then Ja'far ibn Yahya purchased it from ar-Rashid for 20,000 dirhams and gave it to them saying "I am doing this so that you may be aware that the Commander of the Faithful, holding to his right, did not want to cede it to you, and that his servant has purchased it from him and has granted it to you." Ashja as-Sulami then recited:

His generous hand has restored their brackish ground whose people were as isolated from it as the Spica Virginis star. They were sure they had been lost and that they themselves would perish because of this, but Time was guarding it during difficult days. Then he liberated it for them when Time had them between their neck and their breast. Their liberation was not hoped-for from any other; surely the generous is tenacious in the face of every affair.

It is possible that Ja'far ibn Yahya undertook what he did by himself in order to remove ar-Rashid from suspicion of wrongdoing in the affair; it is also possible that ar-Rashid had him do it, so that neither his father nor his brother be accused of an injustice – and the latter is more likely; however, whichever of the two it was, justice was received by those entitled to it, honour was guarded and any meanness prevented.

If the defendant appears to have the more credible case, it will be in the following ways: **i.** the plaintiff is known for his injustice and duplicity and the defendant is known for his equity and trust; **ii.** the plaintiff is of low and contemptible character and the defendant is free of defect and upright – in which case an oath is demanded of the claimant because of his baseness; **iii.** when the thing came into the possession of the defendant, there was a known cause, while the reason for the plaintiff's claim is not known. The more credible case is that of the defendant in these three cases, and suspicion lies on the side of the plaintiff. According to the madhhab of Malik, may Allah have mercy on him, such a demand, if it concerns a specific object which exists, is not heard until the cause which gave rise to this demand is stated; if it concerns a debt, it is not heard until the plaintiff produces evidence of a transaction between him and the defendant. Ash-Shafi'i and Abu Hanifah, however, may Allah be pleased with them, do not consider this to have a bearing on the Qadi's judgement. As the investigation of grievances has been instituted to see that the best action is taken, the magistrate in charge may proceed in accordance with what is simply permitted, instead of effecting what is obligatory: thus he may act in this way when any doubt manifests, or if there is any attempt at wrong action. He employs all possible means of investigation in order to uncover the truth, and he protects the defendant in whatever manner lies within the scope of the law.

If the matter comes to a mutual oath-taking, this being the last stage before a final judgement, a demand which cannot be refused the plaintiff, neither before a Qadi nor a magistrate investigating a grievance – that is, when neither bringing pressure to bear nor admonition have had any effect – and if the plaintiff separates the various claims, wishing to have the defendant take an oath on each of them at different hearings in order to embarrass and humiliate him, the Qadi is not allowed to prevent him from separating them and having the oath taken individually; the magistrate responsible for claims, however, may order the plaintiff to combine all the claims, and require the defendant to make only one oath for all of them, if any attempt to cause embarrassment becomes apparent.

If the two parties enjoy a similar consideration and the evidence of both is of like weight, and neither has any proof through indication or circumstance which is to be preferred, then they should both be exhorted to tell the truth in like manner – and this applies both to judges and magistrates in charge of suppressing abuses. After this exhortation, however, the magistrates alone may resort to bringing pressure to bear on both, given that they are both equally suspect, and then to an investigation the origin of the claim and the transfer of the property: if, as a result of the investigation, something emerges which makes clear which of the two has rightful entitlement, then the magistrate should act on this; if nothing emerges from the investigation to resolve the dispute, then he should refer them to a mediator from amongst the more important of their neighbours and prominent figures of his family; if this results in a solution, all well and good; if not, a decisive judgement must be made between them and this is final, although the magistrate considers beforehand whether he should take the final decision, or leave it to someone whom he nominates in his place.

It often happens that obscure judgements and difficult disputes are referred to magistrates responsible for grievances concerning which others must attend the court to guide him and experts must be called upon to elucidate matters for him; in these cases, he is not to deny them the right of initiating the investigation, and he must not shy away from concluding the affair in accordance with their counsel.

An example of this is narrated by az-Zubayr ibn Bakkar from Ibrahim al-Hizami, from Muhammad ibn Ma'an al-Ghifari, namely that a woman came to 'Umar ibn al-Khattab, saying, "O Amir of the Believers, my husband fasts during the day and stands in prayer during the night; I dislike complaining about him as he is acting in obedience to Allah." He then replied, "What a fine husband is yours!" She then began to repeat what she had said, and he began to repeat his reply, until Ka'b ibn Sur al-Azdi spoke, saying, "O Amir of the faithful, this women is complaining about her husband because he is keeping her from his bed." 'Umar, may Allah be pleased with him, then said, "You decide between the two of them as you have understood her words." Ka'b said, "I need to see her husband – so have him come;" he then said, "Your wife is complaining about you." He asked, "Is it about food or drink?" He replied: "No, it is about neither of them." Then the wife declaimed:

O Qadi full of wisdom and guidance! the mosque distracts my companion from my bed; his worship day and night keeps him from my side and allows him no rest; so I cannot praise him concerning the affairs of women – so make your judgement, O Ka'b, and do not delay!

to which the husband replied:

What has kept me from her bed and from the marriage chamber is that I am a man who has been stupefied by what has been revealed in the surah of "The Bee", and in the seven long surahs, and in the whole of the Qur'an, namely by a mighty fear.

Then Ka'b spoke saying:

Surely she has a right over you, O man; her portion is a quarter for those of intellect: so accord that to her and desist from making excuses

Then he said to him, "Allah has permitted you to take two, three or four wives, so you have three days and their nights in which to worship your Lord and she will have a day and a night." Then 'Umar said to Ka'b, may Allah be pleased with him, "By Allah, I do not know which of your two affairs is the most admirable – your understanding their affair, or your judgement between them! You make leave, I have appointed you over the judiciary of Basra."

This decision of Ka'b and its execution by 'Umar, may Allah be pleased with him, is a judgement whose application is permitted but not obligatory, since the husband is not bound to apportion the nights when he has one single wife, nor to have her in his bed once he has had intercourse with her a single time. This indicates that the magistrate may pronounce judgement based on what is merely permitted and not obligatory.

✳

✳ ✳

As for the instructions regarding the examination of the two parties' petitions which are made by the magistrate responsible for complaints, the recipient of such instructions will necessarily either be competent regarding the matter in hand or incompetent:

A. If he is competent, as in the case where he undersigns an order referring the matter to a Qadi who will examine between them, then his instructions must necessarily either be authorising him to make a judgement, or authorising him to investigate and arrange mediation: **i.** if they authorise him to make a judgement, he may make a judgement between the two parties by virtue of his competence, and these instructions are merely confirmation of his authority: whatever import one might imagine they have is of no consequence; **ii.** if they authorise him to investigate the matter, or to mediate between the litigants but prohibit him from pronouncing judgement, he is not to pass judgement as this prohibition means the curtailment of his authority to judge between these two parties, although he remains in authority at large with respect to cases other than this particular one; this is because just as his authority may be either general or particular, his being relieved of his duties may be either general or particular. Some say that if, in his instructions, the magistrate does not prohibit him from pronouncing judgement between the two parties when ordering him to make an investigation, then the general nature of his authority includes the permissibility of making a judgement as a command to execute part of his duties does not prohibit him from carrying out the rest of them. Others, however, say that it does prohibit him from making a judgement between them, and that he is restricted to the investigation and mediation mentioned in the instructions, because the manifest import of the instructions indicates this. He then investigates, and if the instructions include mediation, then he does not have to announce the result to the magistrate in charge after its completion, whereas he does have to if there is only an instruction to investigate, as this represents an interrogation to which he must make a reply. This is the procedure when instructions are made to a competent authority.

B. When, however, the instructions are given to someone without authority, like a faqih or a witness, then this must necessarily entail either an investigation of the case in question, or mediation, or a judgement:

i. In the first case, the person instructed has to investigate the case and announce to the magistrate whatever can be safely supported by testimony, so that the latter may make his judgement thereupon; if he communicates something which cannot be substantiated by testimony, this is treated only as information, upon which the magistrate is not permitted to make a judgement, although he incorporates this in his examination of any wrongdoings as an indication – which is of use in any application of pressure, or in assessing the merits of the investigation – which might lead to a convincing advantage in favour of one of the two litigants;

ii. If the instructions are for mediation, the person instructed should immediately mediate between them, without heeding any specific stipulations concerning mediation included in the instructions, since mediation does not need to be done by appointment or nomination: the instructions serve only to stipulate the mediator chosen by the magistrate, and to order the two parties to meet before him. If the mediation leads to a resolving of the dispute, he does not have to communicate this to the magistrate, for he himself is a witness to it and will bear testimony to it whenever he is called to do so; if it does not lead to a solution, he is a witness against them to what they have both acknowledged before him, and he will transmit to the magistrate in charge of grievances if the two litigants renew their claim of grievance, although he does not have to communicate this if they do not instigate the dispute again;

iii. If the instructions call for a judgement between them, then this responsibility demands that the import of the instructions be respected so that his investigation may proceed in accordance with its formalities. These instructions may be of two kinds:

The first is where they require the litigant's demand to be acceded to, in which case what must be taken into consideration is the thing – which the litigant claims has been wrongfully taken from him – and the investigation is thus confined to this particular object. If the plaintiff demands either mediation or an investigation of his case, the instructions accord this power to him and the resulting arbitration or investigation is to be restricted to this. There is no difference if the instructions are in the form of a command – for example, "Accord him his demand," or in the form of a statement, such as, "Your judgement in according him his demand is acceptable," as this latter does not, in the first instance, imply an authority which may pass judgements, its force as a command being less. If in his deposition, the plaintiff asks for a judgement between them, then he must name his adversary and specify the object of litigation, so that jurisdiction over it may be correctly exercised; if neither of these two things are done, the jurisdiction of the person receiving the instructions is not validated, as it is not of a general character to which the magistrate in charge may respond, nor can it be treated as having a particular character as it is not yet known if it will be such. If the plaintiff's deposition does, however, name his adversary and state the object of litigation, he should examine the instructions with a view to making a response to the plaintiff's demand: if, in the form of a command, it says, "Reply to his demand and act according to his demand," his authority to make a judgement between them is validated. If it is in the form of a statement about the case and says, "Exercise your judgement regarding the response to this demand," then these instructions, if concerned with matters of social governance, have the effect of an order and it is customary to act upon them. If they are to do with matters specific to the deen, a group of the fuqaha have permitted them, considering them as having the force of custom and authority, while others, however, do not admit their permissibility nor their authority, considering that this meaning is not contained in the form of expression. If the one who has made the deposition had requested instructions be made which would lead to a judgement between them, and they are duly made with a view to responding to this demand, those who consider what is customary practice, validate these instructions; for those, however, who take into account the meaning of the formulation of the expression, it does not imply proper competence, as the plaintiff had requested judicial instructions regarding a judgement and not the judgement itself.

The second type of instructions do not imply a positive response to the plaintiff's demand, in which case the matter is taken up in accordance with the content of these instructions, and it is the content which determines competence: this occurs either to a perfect degree, or to a permissible degree or to a degree which implies neither of the two:

First, complete validity of competence, including both the order to investigate and the order to make a judgement, are comprised in the formulation: "Investigate between the one who has made the deposition and his adversary, and judge between them by the truth and in accordance with the shari'ah;" if it is like this, it is allowed as a judgement can only be made based on the truth required by the shari'ah, and this is mentioned in the instructions in a descriptive and not a conditional way. Instructions which encompass both the matter of investigation and that of a judgement are instructions of a perfect nature, and validate both the appointment and authority of the person concerned;

Second, the instructions are deemed to be permissible, while not perfect, if they include the order to make a judgement but not an investigation, such that the following is mentioned, "Decide between the author of this petition and his adversary," or, "Judge between them." Competence is assured in this case, as the decision and judgement between them can only come about after a prior investigation, thus such an order necessarily implies an investigation as it cannot proceed without it;

Third, they are deemed neither perfect nor admissible when only the words, "Investigate the dispute between them," occur. Competence and authority are not assured by this as, an investigation could result in either mediation or a judgement of a binding character, and they are both equally likely – and this ambiguity precludes any competence. If what is stated is, "Investigate the dispute between them in legality and truth," then some say that competence is assured, since whatever results in legality and truth must be desirable; others, however, say that it is not, since resolving the matter through mediation is also legal and true, although it does not necessarily have to be resorted to. And Allah knows best.

Chapter 8
The Niqabah Tribunal for those of Noble Lineage

This tribunal is set up to protect the people of noble lineage from being sub-jected to the authority of those whose lineage and nobility are not equal to theirs, so that it may be more willingly accepted as authoritative and more ef-fective in the execution of its orders. It is related of the Prophet, may the peace and blessings of Allah be upon him, that he said: "Know your genealogies, and you will bind together your bonds of kinship; there is no blood-relationship if it is broken,, however, close it may be, and there is no break in continuity be-tween relationships if they are joined,, however, distant they may be."

Nomination to this post may be correctly effected in one of three ways: either by the Khalifah who has authority over all affairs; or by the person to whom the Khalifah has handed over administration, like the wazir of delega-tion or the amir of a province; or by a tribunal of general authority which appoints a tribunal of specific authority to stand in its place.

If the person who has this authority wants to appoint a tribunal over de-scendants of Abu Talib (Talibun), or over the descendants of 'Abbas (Abbasids), he should choose from those amongst them whose house is the most illustrious, or who are the most excellent, or who have the best judgement: thus the person in question combines those conditions which confirm his authority and good management such that those under his jurisdiction will readily show their obe-dience to his authority, recognising that their affairs arc in his capable hands.

This type of tribunal is of two kinds: either particular or general. The par-ticular is that in which jurisdiction is restricted solely to the tribunal and does not extend to passing judgements or carrying out hadd-punishments; thus knowledge of the law is not considered as a condition. The naqeeb (tribunal judge) of his family must adhere to twelve legal points in his investigation:

First, he must protect family genealogies from any intrusion by someone who is not of the line, ensure that anyone attempting to abandon the line, who is of it, is held in it: he ensures that no one abandons the line to the same degree as he ensures that no one intrudes upon it, so that the genealogy is maintained in its purity and individual strength;

Second, he distinguishes between the various clans and branches and is aware of the genealogies of each; he does not allow himself to become out of touch as the years pass, he does not mix up one genealogy with another, and he records them in his diwan under the separate genealogies;

Third, he knows whether a boy or a girl is born to such families and he records the fact; he is aware of anyone dying amongst them and he notes this fact – such that should any child be still unregistered, his genealogy is not lost, and no other can claim to be related to the deceased through lack of any mention of the legitimate child;

Fourth, he inflicts discretionary punishments on them according to the nobility of their genealogies and the illustriousness of their family, so as to maintain the respect due to them and to preserve awe of the Messenger of Allah, may the peace and blessings of Allah be upon him, in themselves;

Fifth, He sees that they avoid gain of a low or mean nature, and stops them making demands of an ugly manner, so that none of them is belittled by erring from what is customary, and no-one suffers by finding himself in a humiliating situation;

Sixth, he prevents them from committing wrong actions and stops them from carrying out what is prohibited, so that they are all the more fervent for the deen, of which they themselves are the champions, and so that they will have more repulsion for the evil which they themselves should be active in eliminating – such that no tongue blames them and no man can insult them;

Seventh, he stops them lording themselves over the common people in the name of their nobility, and exceeding the bounds of justice by virtue of their family name: any such behaviour would arouse enmity and hate towards them, and would cause disputes and aversion amongst their victims; rather, he should encourage them to establish a cordial and friendly relationship towards them, so that people more readily incline to them and their hearts are more readily disposed to them;

Eighth, he helps them in the fulfilment of their rights, such that they do not weaken in their resolve to attain them, but he also supports those who would claim rights from them: thus when he helps them, it is in order that they receive justice, and when he supports others against them, it is so that they should act with justice. Such is the sense of justice inherent in the naqeeb's conduct that justice is done to them and they are aided in their own claims for justice;

Ninth, he acts as their representative if they claim the portion reserved for the family of the Prophet after the distribution of the fay and booty – to which they have no individual claim: then he shares it between them in accordance with what Allah has apportioned for them;

Tenth, he prevents unmarried women, who are of superior nobility with respect to other women, from marrying men who are not of sufficient standing: this is in order to protect their genealogy and to honour their inviolability, lest they be married off to those of incompatible degree or insufficient standing;

Eleventh, he corrects those amongst them who are guilty of misdemeanours – but not including those crimes which carry the hadd-punishments – by applying other less severe punishments which do not involve the spilling of blood, while he shows indulgence towards those of high rank who are guilty of offences and pardons them after admonishing them for their mistakes;

Twelfth, he supervises their waqf arrangements such that their capital base is maintained, and their various day to day functionings are developed; if the profit thereof does not come to him, he supervises the profits which others collect, and likewise their distribution, if they are also responsible for distribution; he also differentiates between those who are particularly entitled to such profits, such that no one who is entitled to something is left out, and no one who is not, may intrude.

✽
✽ ✽

The general responsibility which is borne by a general niqabah-tribunal cntails what has been mentioned above, together with five additional duties: **i.** to pronounce judgement in the case of disputes amongst them; **ii.** responsibility for the wealth of their orphans; **iii.** executing the hadd-punishments against those who break the limits; **iv.** to marry off single women for whom no guardian has been appointed or, if appointed, is someone who prevents the marriage; **v.** to impose restraint on those who have become demented or foolish, and to lift it if they come to their senses or act correctly. Tribunal authority is established in a general way with these five responsibilities. A person's tribunal responsibility and his formal contract of authority are validated when it is confirmed that he is knowledgable about the laws, and that he is someone capable of exercising ijtihad – so that his judgements are valid and his judicial decision is carried out.

If this contract of authority comes into force, then it necessarily either excludes the Qadi from investigating his judgements, or affords him the possibility of exercising this right:

A. If his authority is of an absolute generality, then it does not entail that the Qadi is excluded from investigating any matters arising between the nobles, and the appointment of a tribunal authority to investigate their affairs does not mean that the Qadi is excluded from investigating their affairs: each of them may investigate – the naqeeb, by virtue of his special authority to which they are compelled to submit, and the Qadi, by virtue of his general authority to which they are also compelled. Thus when either of them rules in their disputes and litigation, or regarding the marrying of their women, then his ruling is carried out: their authority regarding the judgement over the nobles is the same as when there are two qadis in one town: if one of them makes a ruling between two litigants, then it is carried out, and the other is not allowed to quash it, even if he is able to justify his own ruling by his ijtihad.

If two noble litigants are in dispute, and one of them wishes to have recourse to the naqeeb and the other calls for the judgement of the Qadi, then some say that the litigant who calls for the naqeeb has precedence, by virtue of the particularity of the latter's authority, while others, however, say that they are both of equal standing: they argue that the position is the same as when two litigants are in dispute before two different qadis in a single town – in which case the plaintiff's demand takes precedence over that of the defendant; if, however, they both claim equal cause for litigation, then as above, one either draws lots between them, and acts in accordance with the wish of the one who wins, or else the litigation between them is adjourned until they both agree on one of the two judges.

B. If the authority of the naqeeb specifies that the Qadi be excluded from investigating in the disputes of these noble persons, then the Qadi may not take up the investigation of their affairs, irrespective of whether any of them have appealed for his assistance or not. This situation is different when there are two judges residing in two different parts of the town: when someone from the other quarter seeks his assistance, he is obliged to help him against his adversary – because of the difference between the two cases: the authority of each of the two qadis is bound by their respective locations, and each gives judgement equally to the residents and to those who come to the area, as both are under his jurisdiction; the authority of the naqeeb, however, is defined by genealogy, which does not vary with the various locations. Thus if the two litigants from among the nobles in question accept the judgement of the Qadi, he is not empowered to investigate their dispute, nor to pronounce judgement either for or against them, as he is excluded from this function (in the contract of the naqeeb).

It is the naqeeb who is more qualified to investigate the dispute between two litigants if this matter is between nobles and does not affect the rights of others – otherwise this is not the case.

If there are two (different) parties, one from the Talibun and one an Abbasid, and the former calls for a judgement from his own tribunal judge, and the latter from his, then neither is obliged to accept the judgement of other than his own naqeeb, since the authority of any such judge would not extend to him; if each refuses to accept the naqeeb of the other, two possibilities present themselves: **i.** they both have recourse to the judgement of the Sultan, who exercises general authority over them both if the Qadi has been excluded from investigating their dispute; thus it is the Sultan who is the judge between them, either in person or else through someone who stands in his place to pass judgement; **ii.** or else, and this is preferable, the two naqeebs meet, and each has his own fellow noble present himself before them, and they both hear the complaint – but it is only the naqeeb representing the defendant, and not that of the plaintiff, who pronounces judgement between them, as it is he who is responsible for seeing to the fulfilment of the rights of those who have a claim over his people. If the establishment of a right is dependent upon a testimony which is heard from one of the two parties, or upon an oath made by one of the parties (against the other), it is the naqeeb of the party against whom the testimony is made, and not the one who benefits by it, who hears it and it is the naqeeb of the party who makes an oath, who hears his oath, and not the naqeeb of the party who exacts an oath, so that the judge between them will be the naqeeb of the defendant and not of the plaintiff. If the two naqeebs refuse to meet, no blame is to be attached to them in the first case but there is in the second, and the most blame falls on the tribunal judge of the defendant, by virtue of the fact that it is he who has the capacity to pronounce judgement.

If the Talibun and the Abbasid are content to be judged by one of the two naqeebs, and one of their naqeebs pronounces judgement between them, then it should be examined: first, if the decision is made by the defendant's naqeeb, it is valid and the adversary is bound by it; second, if the decision between them is taken by the plaintiff's naqeeb, then there are two opinions as to whether it is to be carried out or not.

If one of the parties brings witnesses before a judge, who is not empowered to examine their case, in order for him to hear their testimony and to then transmit it in writing to this plaintiff's naqeeb, then the judge is not permitted to hear the testimony – even if he is of the opinion (as are the Malikis) that one may judge *in absentia* – since his judgement may not be executed regarding a plaintiff against whom testimony is being made even if he were present, let alone if he is absent. However, if a Qadi who is of the opinion that one may judge *in absentia* wishes to hear the testimony of a man who is outside his working jurisdiction, in order to transmit whatever is recorded in his presence to the judge of the man's area, then this is permitted. The difference between the two cases is that judgement against the person resident outside his jurisdiction is carried out, if he is present, and for this reason it is permitted to hear any testimony against him;, however, in the case of two noble families, even if one of them is present, any judgement made by the Qadi against him is not to be carried out, and for this reason he may not hear testimony against him.

If a nobleman makes an avowal of a right in favour of another of his lineage, the Qadi involved may give testimony before the naqeeb of the person making the avowal, but he may not impose a judgement thereby, as any judgement against him could not be executed. Likewise, if an avowal is made by a noble before other than the two naqeebs, then this person may bear witness to having heard this avowal before the naqeeb of this noble. Any avowal made by the noble in front of his own naqeeb is valid, and the latter can pronounce judgement against him based on this avowal. If, however, he makes the avowal before the naqeeb of his adversary, then there are two possibilities, as mentioned above, which present themselves: in the first, the naqeeb is merely a witness and in the second, he is empowered to pass judgement – in accordance with the difference between the naqeeb of the plaintiff and that of the defendant, which we have described above.

This is likewise the case regarding the authority of the chiefs of families and tribal heads in the case of those who enjoy special powers over their families or tribes.

Chapter 9
The Imamate of the Prayer

The subject of imamate may be divided into three sections: that of the five daily prayers, of the Friday prayer, and of the recommended prayers.

1. As for the appointment of the imam of the five daily prayers, consideration must be made of the two kinds of mosques in which these prayers are established, namely the sultanate mosques and the people's mosques.

A. The sultanate mosques include mosques where the Friday jumu'ah prayer may be recited, mashhad-sites of gathering (for the Eid prayers), and any other mosques frequented and revered by the people which come under the care of the Sultan; no one may take up the imamate therein except those appointed by the Sultan for this task and those invested with the imamate – so that his subjects do not practise elsewhere that which the Sultan is responsible for organising. The imam appointed by the Sultan has more right to the imamate in these mosques than any other, even if there is another who is more excellent and more knowledgeable than him.

Such an appointment is a preferred act, not a binding or an obligatory one, as opposed to that of the Qadi the and naqeeb judiciary, for two reasons: **i.** if the people accept an imam to pray in front of them, then this is sufficient, and their prayer together is valid; **ii.** doing the five daily prayers in a group is among the optional sunnahs and recommended practices of excellence, and it is not among the *fard* obligations according to all the fuqaha, except for Dawud, who is alone in making this obligatory, without a valid reason.

As it is a highly recommended act, as soon as the Sultan has designated an imam for such a mosque, no other person should take his place if the designated imam is present; if he is absent, and has appointed someone to represent him, then his representative has the most right to the imamate; if he has not appointed someone in his place, the Sultan's permission is asked regarding someone who has already been an imam, if this is possible; if it is difficult to get his permission, the people of the area should agree on who should lead them, so as not to delay doing the prayer in a group. If the next prayer becomes due and the official imam is still absent, it is said that the person they have already agreed upon has the most right to lead this second prayer, and any other prayer after this, until the imam in charge returns; it is also said, however, that someone else should be chosen and that the first (unofficial imam) should accept this, so that his having first been chosen does not appear as an official appointment on behalf of the Sultan; I am of the opinion, however, that in preference to these two absolute opinions, one should take into account the situation regarding the prayer-group in the second prayer: if those who were present for it are the same as those who attended the first, the person accepted for the first has more right to the imamate in the second; if others are present, however, then the first imam chosen is considered as any of the people present, and the choice of imam to lead them is then reviewed.

If the official imam leads the group-prayer, and some people arrive too late to join this prayer, they must not form another group prayer; rather they should pray individually, as otherwise it would appear to be an act of separation and might lead to suspicion of hostility and opposition.

If the Sultan appoints two imams for such a mosque, making each responsible for some of the five prayers, this is permitted – each being restricted to leading the particular prayers assigned to him, such as the appointment of one for the daytime prayers and the other for the night-time; neither of them is then permitted to take on other than what has been assigned to him. If he appoints them to the imamate without designating either for particular prayers, but rather he assigns to each a day other than his colleague's, then each on his own particular day has more right to the imamate than his colleague. If he appoints them both without designating any special time for either, then they are both on an equal footing: the one who arrives first has more right to it. and the other should not lead that prayer with another group of people, as it is not permitted to establish two prayers in a group in the mosques supervised by the Sultan. There is a difference of opinion as to the meaning of priority established by the first-arrival of one of the two imams: according to some, it refers to his arriving first at the mosque itself, while for others it is his arriving first to lead the prayer.

If the two imams arrive at the same time, then neither takes precedence over the other: if they both agree that one of them should take the prayer, then this person has more right to the imamate; if they are in disagreement, then either lots are drawn to decide who should lead, or recourse is made to the choice of the people who are in the mosque.

The authority of this type of official imam includes the appointment of the muadhdhins, unless he has been told that he has been relieved of this duty, since the adhan is one of the sunnahs of the prayer with which he is charged and which is an integral part of his authority. He should choose the muadhdhins in accordance with his estimation of the time of the prayer and the call to prayer: if he is a Shafi'ite, and considers that the prayer should be done at the beginning of its time, that the (opening phrases of) the adhan should be repeated, and that the iqamah should be said singly, he holds his muadhdhins to this practice even though their own opinion may differ. If he is a Hanafi, and considers that the prayers may be delayed to the end of their time, except that is for the maghrib prayer, and considers that the repetition should not be made in the adhan but that it should in the iqamah, then he should hold them to this even though they may be of a different opinion. Then the imam acts in accordance with his judgement and ijtihad regarding the various features of the prayer: thus if Shafi'ite, he considers that the "In the Name of Allah, the Beneficent, the Merciful" and the qunut supplication of the subh-dawn prayer should be read aloud – and neither the Sultan nor those of the prayer-group can deny him this; likewise if he is a Hanafi, and considers that neither the qunut supplication of the subh prayer should be said nor the "In the Name of ..." should be said aloud, then he should act accordingly – and no-one should oppose him in this.

The difference between the prayer and the adhan is that the imam performs the prayer for himself and it is not permitted to oppose his ijtihad in the matter, whereas the muadhdhin calls the adhan for the sake of others, and so it is permitted to oppose his ijtihad in the matter. If the muadhdhin wishes to make the call for himself in accordance with his own ijtihad, he may make a special call in accordance with his own ijtihad in a low voice, not in a high voice, after the main one.

The qualities to be considered in the appointment of this type of imam are five in number: that he be a man, that he is just, able to recite, a faqih, having a sound pronunciation without defect or lisp. If he has not yet reached puberty, or is a slave, or of corrupt behaviour, his imamate is valid but his appointment does not come into effect – since being underage, a slave, or corrupt, prevents someone from this appointment, while it does not stop the imamate. The Messenger of Allah, may the peace and blessings of Allah be upon him, ordered 'Amr ibn Salima, who was underage, to lead the prayer before his people as he was the best at reciting amongst them – and he himself, may the peace and blessings of Allah be upon him, prayed behind one of his freed slaves, saying, "Pray behind anyone, be they good or corrupt."

This type of imam may not be a woman, or a hermaphrodite, or dumb, or someone with a speech defect. If a woman or a hermaphrodite leads the prayer, the prayer of any men and hermaphrodites alike who follow her in the prayer are invalid; if the person leading the prayer is defective in speech or dumb, such that he confuses some words with others, then the prayer of those behind him is rendered invalid, unless they are equally dumb or defective in speech.

The least amount of recitation or fiqh incumbent on this type of imam is that he know by heart the opening surah of the Qur'an and that he know the laws of the prayer, as this is the amount required for the task, although it is preferable that he know by heart the whole of the Qur'an and that he know all the laws. If there is both a faqih who is not a reciter, and a reciter who is not a faqih, then the faqih takes precedence over the reciter as long as he knows the opening surah, since what it is necessary to know of the Qur'an is limited, while the possible incidents which may happen during the prayer are without limit.

It is permitted for this type of imam and his muadhdhins to take a salary for the imamate and the adhan from that portion of the treasury reserved for the public interest, although Abu Hanifah has prohibited this.

B. As for people's private mosques, built by the inhabitants of local streets, or by tribes in their streets or tribal areas, then the Sultan should not oppose them in their choice of imam in their mosques, the imam being the person they find acceptable for the task; moreover, the people cannot remove him from the imamate once they have accepted him, unless his situation changes, and he cannot appoint someone in his place once they have agreed on him, the people of the mosque having more right to this choice. If there is a difference of opinion amongst the people of the mosque as to the choice of an imam, then the opinion of the majority should take effect; if the two parties are of equal number, then the Sultan should choose the one who is the best in the deen, the older person, the best reciter, and the most knowledgeable in fiqh, in order to put a stop to the dispute. Should his choice be restricted to a consideration of those who are disputing, or extend to all of the people of the mosque in general? There are two opinions: the first, that it should be restricted to choosing one of those who are disputing, and not extend to any others, as there is agreement that these latter should be left out of the matter; the second, that he should choose someone from among all the people of the mosque whom he judges to be entitled to the imamate, as a Sultan's choice cannot be restricted.

If a man builds a mosque and does not seek special entitlement to the imamate therein, then he and the others from amongst the neighbours of the mosque are on an equal footing regarding the imamate and the adhan. Abu Hanifah, however, is of the opinion that he is most entitled to the imamate and too the calling of the adhan therein.

When a group of persons gather in a man's house to pray, the owner of the house has more right to lead the prayer, even if he is of a lesser degree in excellence; if the Sultan is present, then according to one opinion, he has more right than the owner by virtue of his general authority over the latter; according to the second, the owner has more right, because of his particular right to dispose as he wishes with his property.

2. As for the imamate of the jumu'ah prayer, the fuqaha differ as to the obligation of appointment to this post: Abu Hanifah and the people of Iraq are of the opinion that it is among the obligatory offices of authority, and that the jumu'ah prayer is not valid unless the Sultan or his representative is present; ash-Shafi'i and the fuqaha of the Hijaz consider that this appointment is a recommended act, and that the presence of the Sultan is not a condition of validity: if those participating establish the prayer according to its rules, then it is considered complete and valid. The imam may be a slave, even if his official appointment cannot take place. There are two opinions as to whether someone underage may leading the prayer.

It is only permitted to establish this prayer in a place containing enough homes and inhabitants to constitute a jumu'ah prayer, and only if these inhabitants do not leave their homes in winter or summer, except out of necessity, irrespective of whether this place be a town or village. Abu Hanifah, however, is of the opinion that the jumu'ah prayer is particular to towns and is not permitted in villages. A settlement is considered to be a town if there is a person in authority who sees that the hudud are established, and a Qadi who executes the judgements.

There is a difference of opinion as to whether the jumu'ah is obligatory on people outside the town: Abu Hanifah considers that it is not, while ash-Shafi'i makes it an obligation if they are able to hear the call to prayer.

The fuqaha differ as to the number required to constitute a jumu'ah: ash-Shafi'i, may Allah be pleased with him, considers that it may only take place when forty men take part in the jumu'ah, without counting women, slaves, or travellers; his followers differ as to whether the imam counts as an extra person or one of them – some of them are of the opinion that it is not valid unless there are forty, excluding the imam, while most of them say that it is permitted when there are forty including the imam; az-Zuhri and Muhammad ibn al-Hasan say that it may take place with twelve men, including the imam, while Abu Hanifah and al-Muzani say that four is enough, including the imam; al-Layth and Abu Yusuf say that it may be held with three, with one of them the imam, while Abu Thawr says that it is two, like the rest of the prayers made in a group; Malik considers that it is not the number itself which determines whether it take place, but rather whether it would be customary for the number of persons in the area in question to build a mosque for their use.

It is not permitted to establish the jumu'ah on a journey, or outside the town, unless the place is connected to the latter. If the town also comprises villages, such that its buildings have become connected to each other because of the number of inhabitants, like Baghdad, then it is permitted to establish the jumu'ah in the old quarters of the town – and this joining of buildings also does not prevent the jumu'ah being established in the (new) areas. If the town is still a whole, in the original site, and the jami' mosque can contain all the inhabitants, such as Makkah, then it is not permitted to pray this prayer other than in one place in the town. If, however, the town is a whole, its buildings forming a continuity, but its jami' mosque cannot contain all its inhabitants because of their great numbers, like in Basra, then the followers of ash-Shafi'i differ as to whether it is permissible, because of the number of inhabitants, to establish the prayer in two different places: some consider that it is permissible, while others have prohibited it, saying that if space is lacking, they will find room in the streets and will therefore not be forced to split up the jumu'ah-prayer into other sites. If the jumu'ah is established in two places of the town, the inhabitants of which have been forbidden (by their teaching) from splitting the jumu'ah prayer, then there are two opinions: the first, is that the valid jumu'ah is that which was established first and that those who pray in the later one should make it up by praying the dhuhr prayer; the second, is that the valid jumu'ah belongs to the larger of the mosques attended by the Sultan, irrespective of whether the prayer there was the first to be established or not, and those who pray in the smaller mosque must make it up by praying the dhuhr prayer.

The person who has been appointed as a jumu'ah imam does not have to lead the five daily prayers, but there is difference of opinion concerning the person appointed as an imam for the five prayers, as to whether he is entitled to lead the jumu'ah prayer: those who consider that the jumu'ah is a unique act in its own right forbid it, while those who treat it as a shortened kind of dhuhr prayer permit it.

If the imam of the jumu'ah considers that it should not be established with less then forty men, while those following the imam consider that the jumu'ah should be established even though they are less than forty men, then it is not permitted for him to lead them, and he is obliged to appoint someone else instead of him from among them. If, however, the imam considers that it should be established with less than forty men, while those following him do not, and they constitute less than this number, then neither the imam nor those following him need perform it, since the latter do not consider it necessary and so the imam has no one to lead in the prayer.

If the Sultan commands the imam of the jumu'ah not to pray with less than forty men, then he should not pray with less than this number, even if he is not of this opinion, as his authority is only valid with this number and he is relieved of this authority below this number; moreover, he may not appoint someone in his place to lead the prayer in front of them, as his authority does not extend to this. If the Sultan commands him to lead the prayer with less than forty men, and he is not of this opinion, then there are two views as to his standing: the first, is that his authority is null and void by virtue of his incapacity in this respect; and the second, is that it is valid and that he may appoint as a substitute for this prayer someone from amongst them whom he considers suitable.

3. There are five kinds of imamate regarding the sunnah prayers: the two Eid prayers, the solar and lunar eclipse prayers, and the rain prayers; for these it is recommended that an imam be appointed, as it is permitted to make these prayers both in a group and singly.

There is a difference of opinion as to the ruling regarding these prayers: some of the followers of ash-Shafi'i consider that they are among the strongly recommended prayers, while others regard them as obligations incumbent on (at least) some of the community. The imam appointed for the five daily prayers, or for the jumu'ah, is not entitled to lead these prayers unless he has been appointed to lead all prayers in general.

The time of the 'Eid prayer occurs between sunrise and the moment the sun passes its zenith, although it is preferable to have the 'Eid of sacrifice (of the Hajj) early and to delay that of the breaking of the fast (of Ramadan). During both nights before the 'Eids, the people should proclaim "Allahu Akbar" after sunset until they begin the 'Eid prayer. The 'Eid of sacrifice is characterised by repeating "Allahu Akbar" after the obligatory prayers, starting after the dhuhr prayer of the day of sacrifice until after the subh prayer on the last day of the three days of tashriq (of the 11th, 12th, and 13th of Dhu'l-Hijjah). Both of the 'Eid prayers are done before the khutbah, while the jumu'ah prayer is done after it, in accordance with the sunnahs of these two prayers.

The two 'Eid prayers are also characterised by extra takbirs; the fuqaha differ as to their number; ash-Shafi'i, may Allah be pleased with him, considers that in the first rak'ah, seven takbirs, besides the opening takbir (takbir al-ihram), are said, while in the second rak'ah there are five, besides the takbir said on standing (takbir al-qiyam), before the recitation of the Qur'an. Malik says that six are added in the first, and five in the second, besides the takbir of standing. Abu Hanifah says that three takbirs are made in the first before the recitation, and four in the second, besides the takbir al-qiyam made before the second recitation. The imam should act, with respect to these additional takbirs, according to his judgement and his ijtihad, and the person who appointed him should not insist he act according to his own judgement – this is in contrast to the question of numbers in the jumu'ah prayer, since the imam acquires a specific authority when the number in the jumu'ah prayer is stipulated for him, which he does not have when the number of takbirs in the 'Eid prayer is stipulated for him, and so in this way they differ from each other.

As for the two eclipse prayers, they are led by the person appointed by the Sultan to do them, or by the one who has a general authority, as this authority would cover these two prayers. It consists of two rak'ahs, each comprising two bowings and two standings, together with an extended recitation of the Qur'an: in the first standing of the first rak'ah there is a silent reading, after the opening surah (the Fatihah), of the surah of "The Cow" or another of similar length; then he bows, saying the subhanas for a time equal to the recitation of a hundred ayahs, and then he straightens up and recites, after the "Fatihah", the surah "Ali 'Imran" or another of similar length; then he bows, saying the subhanas for a period equivalent to eighty ayahs, and then makes two prostrations as in the other prayers; then he does the same in the second rak'ah, reciting in the standing and saying the subhanas in the bowing, for a period equivalent to two thirds of his recitation and subhanas in the first rak'ah; then he makes the khutbah after this. Abu Hanifah, however, says that he should pray two rak'ahs as in the other prayers, and pray both the moon eclipse prayer and that of the sun aloud, arguing that they belong to the night prayers. According to Malik, the prayer for the eclipse of the moon is not the same as the prayer for the eclipse of the sun (the former aloud and the latter silently).

As for the rain-prayer, it is recommended when rainfall is lacking and drought is feared. The person appointed for it should fast for three days before it, during which he should avoid all unjust action and dispute, and make peace between all contesting, litigating and conflicting parties. The time for this prayer is the same as for the 'Eid prayers. If a person is appointed to lead the 'Eid prayer in one year, then he may lead it every year, as long as he has absolute authority and is not divested of this authority. If he is appointed to lead the eclipse or rain-prayers in one year, then he is not to lead them in any other year, even if he enjoys absolute authority – unless he is (again) appointed to lead them – since the prayer of the 'Eid is a recurring event, while the others are occasional. If it begins to rain while they are performing the rain-prayer, they should complete it and give the khutbah after it as an act of gratitude; if it begins to rain before the prayer has been begun, it is not carried out, but those participating should give thanks to Allah, may He be exalted, and there is no khutbah; likewise when the sun or moon appear (before commencing the prayer).

If the rain prayer is confined to a simple supplication without prayer this is acceptable, but Muslim narrates from Anas ibn Malik that an Arab came to the Messenger of Allah, may the peace and blessings of Allah be upon him, saying: "O Messenger of Allah, we have come to you and we have no camel to groan or infant to cry," and then he recited the following:

> *We have come to you and the virgin's breast is bleeding, the mother has abandoned her child who has dropped in a torpor of weakness from hunger; here our people have nothing to eat but the common colocynth and the bitter castor-plant; it is only to you we can flee, for where else can people flee to but to the prophets?*

The Prophet, may the peace and blessings of Allah be upon him, got up dragging his cloak and mounting the mimbar he praised and glorified Allah, saying: "O Allah, pour on us an abundant rain, one which saves us, is profuse, well-distributed and without delay, one which makes the crops grow, which fills the women's breasts, and revives the earth after its death – and this is how you (O people) will be revived (after death)." He had not finished his prayer before the sky opened its torrents and his people came to him crying: "O Messenger of Allah, it is a flood!" He then prayed: "About us and not upon us;" then the clouds withdrew from the town, forming an encircling diadem, and the Prophet smiled so much that his back teeth became apparent, and he said: "May Allah bless Abu Talib; if he were still alive he would be filled with joy – who will recite some of his poetry?" Then 'Ali ibn Abi Talib rose, saying: "O Messenger of Allah, it is as if you wanted to put into effect what he said:

It is an honoured being who seeks rain from the clouds by his face, the protector of orphans and the guardian of widows; it is to them that the unfortunate Hashimis seek refuge, for they find themselves in bounty and overflow when they are with him; you would be lying if you were to say that Muhammad had been wronged and that we would not fight for him with the bow and the spear and would not fall around him, losing both children and women

Then a man of the Kinanah rose and declaimed to the Prophet, may the peace and blessings of Allah be upon, him:

To you belongs praise, praise from the grateful; rain has watered us by virtue of the Prophet; he has made a supplication to Allah, his Creator, turning his gaze to Him at the same time; there was hardly the time to turn up his cloak when we saw the rain fall in fine rivulets from abundant rain-clouds, and so Allah has come to our aid, the people of Mudar. It is just as he said, his uncle Abu Talib, the honoured being with the special mark; it is by him that Allah has sent water from the clouds – and this is the proof of what was foretold before.

The Prophet then said: "If there is a poet who speaks well then it is you."

Wearing black is particular to the imams who lead the prayers in which an invocation is made for the Sultan; it is a customary mark of respect for him nowadays. It is disliked that imams act otherwise – even though it is not stipulated by the shari'ah – so as to guard from any possibility of dissension.

When those who would prevent the prayer in a group have the upper hand, the imam has a valid excuse not to pray aloud. If the one who has the upper hand establishes the prayer, but has incorrect beliefs, he is still to be followed as long as he does not introduce any innovations.

Chapter 10
The Administration of the Hajj

There are two kinds of authority regarding the Hajj: the first, to assist the Hajj pilgrims; the second, to establish the Hajj.

1. The first kind concerns its administration, governance and organisation. The conditions stipulated for the person in charge are that he is obeyed by others, possessed of judgement and courage, respected, and capable of guiding people. Ten obligations are incumbent on him:

First, he should gather people together, both when they are travelling and stopping over, so as to prevent them from dispersing lest they be delayed or exposed to danger;

Second, he organises them, both in travel and at stopping places, by giving each group a position by which each group may recognise itself while travelling, and so that it will know where to gather when stopping, so that there is no dispute over sites and no one loses his way;

Third, he treats them gently, so that the weak among them can manage the journey, and those who are tired or short of supplies do not lose their way. It has been narrated that the Prophet, peace and blessings be upon him, said: "The weak person is the amir of the group," meaning thereby that if someone's mount weakens. then the rest should travel at his speed;

Fourth, he should lead them by the easiest route and the one containing the most pasture, avoiding that which is harsher and rockier;

Fifth, he searches out the water-holes and pastures if they become scarce;

Sixth, he sets up a guard whenever they come to a halt and protects them when travelling, lest they be caught unawares by bandits, or come under the scrutiny of thieves;

Seventh, he keeps them out of the way of those who would bar their path, and repulses those who would stop them from performing the Hajj – by fighting them if he is able, or by payment of money if the Hajj pilgrims consent to it; he may not, however, coerce anyone into paying this protection-money; rather consent must be given freely and with good will – for it is not an obligation to expend money in order to perform the Hajj;

Eighth, he makes peace between disputing parties and acts as a mediator between litigating parties, but he should not get involved in passing judgements out of a desire to help – unless this power has been delegated to him and he is capable of such a task, in which case it is permissible for him to pass judgement between them. If the travellers enter a town in which there is a judge, then both the latter and he may judge between them, and whichever of them passes judgement, then it is to be carried out. If there is a dispute between the Hajjis and the people of the town, then it is only the judge in the latter who may pass judgement;

Ninth, he should not go so far as to impose hadd-punishments when making discretionary punishments, unless he has been given permission to do so and he is also a person of ijtihad. If he comes to a town in which there is someone responsible for exacting the hadd-punishments on the inhabitants, the case should be examined: if the crime demanding the hadd-punishment has been committed before entering the town, then the person in charge of the Hajjis has more right to exact the hadd than the person in charge of the town; if it has been committed in the town, then the person in authority in the town is more entitled;

Tenth, he must take care to see that there is ample time, lest he cause them to miss the Hajj or compel them to undue speed in their travelling because of the shortage of time. Once they have arrived at the miqat points of assembly, he allows them the necessary time to don the ihram dress, and to perform the sunnah acts; if there is enough time, he takes them to Makkah so as to be able to leave with its inhabitants to the miqat assembly-points; if time is short, he does not take them to Malah but rather straight to 'Arafah lest they miss this place – for in doing so they would miss the whole Hajj. The time of standing at 'Arafah, is from just after the sun has passed its zenith on the day of 'Arafah to daybreak on the day of sacrifice (10th of Dhu'l Hijjah). Anyone who is able to stand for just a moment during this period, either during the night or the day, has caught the Hajj; if he fails to make the standing before sunrise on the day of sacrifice, then he has not attained the Hajj, and he has to complete the remaining basic rites and make up for his missing it by sacrificing an animal, and by performing it properly the following year if he is able, or another year if he has a valid excuse.

This Hajj cannot be then treated as an 'Umrah-visit after missing ('Arafah), and the person does not revert to his normal state after missing 'Arafah until he comes out of Hajj-state in the correct way. According to Abu Hanifah, however, he reverts to his normal state by performing an Umrah, while Abu Yusuf says that, after missing ('Arafah), his state of ihram becomes that of an 'Umrah.

When the head of the Hajj-group has led them to Makkah, then those who are not going to return with him are no longer under his authority, and he has no power over them; those, however, who are going to return, remain under his authority and must continue to obey him. After the people have completed their Hajj, he should leave them a few days to clear up their affairs, and he should not urge them to leave in such a way as to inconvenience them unnecessarily. When he sets out with them on the return journey, he should take the road to Madinah, in order to visit the tomb of the Messenger, may the peace and blessings of Allah be upon him, so as to combine the Hajj of the House of Allah, may He be exalted and glorified, with a visit to the tomb of the Messenger of Allah, may the peace and blessings of Allah be upon him – in order to pay due respects and make a homage of obedience: the latter is not one of the obligations of the Hajj, but rather a recommended act of the shari'ah, and a customary practice of the Hajjis.

Nafi' has related from Ibn 'Umar, may Allah be pleased with him, that the Messenger of Allah, may the peace and blessings of Allah be upon him, said: "Whoever visits my tomb, then my intercession will certainly be assured for him." 'Utbah narrates: "I was at the tomb of the Messenger of Allah, may the peace and blessings of Allah be upon him, and an Arab came up to it, greeted him kindly, and said, 'O Messenger of Allah, I have found that Allah says, **"If after committing an injustice to themselves they come to you seeking forgiveness of Allah, and the Messenger seeks forgiveness for them, then they will find Allah oft-turning and merciful"** (Qur'an 4: 67), so I have come to you, turning away from my wrong action, seeking your intercession before my Lord;' then he began to weep, reciting :

O you whose bones are the best of those buried in the plains – and both these plains and hills have taken on their goodness – I sacrifice myself for the tomb where you lie, wherein is all modesty, generosity and nobility.

Then he got on his mount and left." 'Utbah then continued by saying: "I fell asleep, and I saw the Messenger of Allah, may the peace and blessings of

Allah be upon him, and he said to me, 'O 'Utbah, catch up with this Bedouin and tell him that Allah, may He be glorified, has forgiven him.'"

On the return trip, the leader of the group is obliged to guarantee the same rights for them as he did on the outward journey, until he arrives back in their town with them. As soon as they arrive back, his authority over them ceases.

Eleventh, if his authority is to perform the Hajj, then he is on a par with the imam responsible for the prayers. Among the conditions of his authority, besides those shared in common with the imams of the prayers, is that he should be knowledgable of the rites and rules of the Hajj, and of the miqat assembly-points, and of the dates of the rites, and that the period of his authority is for seven days, from the time of the dhuhr prayer on the 7th of Dhu'l-Hijjah to the day of cutting the hair, i.e. the day of the second leaving (the final return from Mina to Makkah) which takes place on 13th day of this month; before or after this period he is merely one of the participants and has no authority.

If he has been given absolute authority for the performance of the Hajj, then he must perform it every year as long as he is not relieved of this task; if he has been given it for one particular year, then this authority does not extend to another year, unless this authority is renewed.

His authority is characterised by – and his powers of investigation are limited to – five actions upon which there is general agreement, and by a sixth about which there is a difference of opinion:

First, he should inform his people as to the time of donning the ihram and their departure for the ritual sites so that they may follow him and model their actions on his;

Second, he must guide them through the various rites in accordance with how they are defined in the shari'ah; as it is he whom they should follow, he should not do any of them before the proper time, or delay them beyond their time – irrespective of whether this order of performance is an obligation, or just something which is desirable;

Third, he should determine the periods of stopping by the length of his stay in each station and his moment of parting, just as the (timing of the) prayer of the believers is determined by the prayer of the imam;

Fourth, those with him should follow him in the pillars of the shari'ah, and say the "amen" after his supplications, so as to follow him in what he says as well as in his actions: in this way the harmony of their prayers will more readily receive acceptance;

Fifth, he should be their imam and gather them together for the prayers of the days when the khutbahs of the Hajj are given, namely on four occasions:

A. At his exposition of the sunnah and recommended aspects of the Hajj after having donned the ihram, although this khutbah is also acceptable if he has not yet put it on: so he prays the dhuhr prayer in Makkah on the 7th of Dhu'l-Hijjah and gives the first of the four khutbahs of the Hajj beginning it with the "Labbayk" (at Your service), if he is in ihram, and "Allahu Akbar", if he is in the normal state; he informs the people that they are to go to Mina the following day, so that they will all leave on time with him, that is on the 8th of the month, and that he will then stop on the side of this hill at the Banu Kinanah, where the Prophet, may the peace and blessings of Allah be upon him, stopped; he then informs them that they will spend the night there and depart the following morning at sunrise, on the 9th, towards 'Arafat – taking the Dabb pathway and returning by way of the two Mazims, following the example of the Prophet, may the peace and blessings of Allah be upon him, so as to come back a different way than the one taken to go there. After overlooking 'Arafat, he goes down to the depression of Batn 'Arafah and stays there until sunset, at which moment he leaves to go to the Ibrahim Mosque, may Allah's blessings be upon him, in the 'Arafat valley.

B. Here he makes the second of the Hajj khutbahs, before the prayer, as for the jumu'ah, because all khutbahs come after the prayer except for the two khutbahs of jumu'ah and the khutbah of 'Arafah: he reminds the people in it of the basic acts and rites of the Hajj which are incumbent on them, and of what things are forbidden to them; after this khutbah, he leads them in the combined prayer of dhuhr and 'asr, said at the time of dhuhr, the travellers among them shortening them, and the residents praying them in full – in accordance with the practice of the Messenger of Allah, may the peace and blessings of Allah be upon him, who shortened them or prayed them in full in this way; after having finished them both, he goes to 'Arafah, which is the obligatory station: The Prophet, may the peace and blessings of Allah be upon him, said. "The Hajj is 'Arafah, so whoever attains 'Arafah has caught the Hajj, and whoever misses it, has missed the Hajj."

The area of 'Arafah lies outside the part of the valley where the mosque is situated – neither the latter nor the former valley are part of 'Arafah – and extends to the mountains opposite; people may stand from as far as 'Arafah itself up to the three mountains, an-Naba, an-Nubaya and an-Naib. The Prophet, may the peace and blessings of Allah be upon him, stood on a point of an-Naib and turned the girth of his mount towards the mihrab, and this is the place where, preferably, the Imam should stand;, however, any place he and the people stand on 'Arafah is acceptable; it is also preferable that he stay on his mount so that the people follow him in this.

After sunset he should go to Muzdalifah, where he delays the Maghrib prayer so as to join it with that of 'isha, leading the people in the prayers, and then spends the night in Muzdalifah itself – this latter place beginning beyond the two Mazims of 'Arafah, which are not part of it, and extending to Qarn Muhassir, which is also not part of it. It is from this place that the people should collect the pebbles for stoning – pebbles of the thickness of one's fingers, like jet-stones. He leaves this place after dawn, although if he leaves before this after midnight, then it is acceptable, as it is not one of the basic rites to spend the night there: one may compensate for not spending the night by making a sacrifice. According to Abu Hanifah, however, it is one of the obligatory acts of the Hajj.

From here he goes to al-Mash'ar al-Haram where he stops at Quzah to make a supplication, although this is not an obligation; then he continues on to Mina where he begins by stoning the Jamrah al-'Aqabah with seven pebbles, before the sun has passed its zenith, and then those who have brought along a sacrificial animal, sacrifice it; then they shave their heads and cut their hair as much as they wish, although it is better to shave. Then the imam goes to Makkah where he does the final tawaf (circumambulation of the Ka'bah), which is a necessary obligation; then he does the sa'y (the running between Safa and Marwa) if he has not already done it before 'Arafah. Doing the sa'y before 'Arafah is acceptable, but making the tawaf before it, is not. Then he returns to Mina, and leads the people in the dhuhr prayer and then he delivers the third Khutbah.

C. The third of the four khutbahs of the Hajj is that in which he reminds the people of the remaining rites they must perform, the ruling regarding the first and second ihlal (returning to normal state), and those things which become permitted for them which were prohibited in the state of ihram, explaining each of the two periods individually. If he is a faqih, then he should also add, "Is there anyone who has a question?" although if he is not, he should not expose himself to questioning. He spends the night at Mina, and then on the next day, the 11th of the month, which is the day of staying (as opposed to the 12th and 13th which are the days of dispersal), he begins, after the sun has just passed its zenith, to make the three stonings, each of seven pebbles, that is a total of twenty-one. He then spends the second night there, and the following day, the first day of dispersal, he again begins the three stonings.

D. Then after the dhuhr prayer, he pronounces the fourth and last of the khutbahs of the Hajj, and he informs the people that they have two days of dispersal in which Allah has allowed them a choice, in His words: **"Remember Allah on specific days: as for those who make haste to finish in two days, then there is no blame on them; while those who delay, then there is no blame on them – as long as they are amongst the people of taqwa"**. (Qur'an 2: 199). He also informs them that those who depart before the sunset of that day have no obligation to pass the night there, or to make the stonings the next day, while those who do stay until the sunset must also stay the night there and make the stonings the next day. But the imam cannot, by virtue of his responsibility, leave on the first day of dispersal; he must remain so as to stay the night there and then leave on the second day of dispersal, that is two days after the day of shaving the head, on the 13th of the month, after the three stonings – as he is the person being followed and may not leave until the rites have all been completed. As soon as the time of the second dispersal has legally begun, his authority comes to an end and he has discharged his responsibility.

Such then are the five tasks connected with his authority. As for the sixth, about which there is disagreement, there are three issues:

i. If one of the Hajjis commits a wrong action which merits a discretionary or hadd-punishment, he may not impose such punishments if this action is not connected with the Hajj; if it is connected, then he can impose a discretionary punishment, either by way of reprimand or corporal punishment. As for imposing the hadd-punishment, there are two opinions: according to one, he may do so, as it is considered to be among the rules of the Hajj; according to the other, he may not do so, as it is not included among the rules of the Hajj;

ii. He is not permitted to pass judgement between two Hajjis if their dispute lies outside the rules of the Hajj. There are two opinions as to whether he may judge between them if their dispute is over one of the rules of the Hajj, for example, if a married couple dispute as to the payment of the kaffarah in compensation for having had sexual intercourse (while in ihram), and as to the amount that must be paid for it: according to the first, he may pronounce judgement, while according to the second, he may not;

iii. There is also a difference of opinion, concerning a Hajji who has to pay a compensatory fidyah (ransom), as to whether or not the imam, while having the right to compel and order him to recognise and meet this obligation, should actively see that he makes the payment – and become, as it were, the plaintiff in a complaint against him. Likewise in the case of someone meriting the hadd-punishment.

The leader of the Hajj-group may make fatwas as long as he is a faqih, even though he is not permitted to pass judgement. He must not, however, say that something which is tolerated is illicit, unless he fears that the ignorant person will take it as a model to be followed. 'Umar ibn al-Khattab disapproved of Talhah ibn Ubaidullah wearing Mudraj cloth (of a red colour) while on Hajj, saying, "I fear that the ignorant will take you as an example." Nor is he to compel the people to perform the rites according to his own madhhab. It is disliked that he lead the Hajj for the people while being in a state of ihlal and not ihram, although the Hajj is valid when done with him in this way – in contrast to the prayer, which would not be valid if he were to lead them in it but not perform the prayer himself.

It is permitted for people to deliberately go ahead or fall behind their imam in the Hajj even if it is disliked for those following (the imam of the prayer) to act differently from the person followed (in the prayer); if they deliberately act differently in the prayer, then it becomes invalid, as there is a direct connection between those behind the imam and the imam himself, while this does not exist between the people's Hajj and that of the imam.

Chapter 11
The Administration of the Zakah

Tax in Islam is known as sadaqah and zakah, and the latter is the same as the former; the names are different but the issue is the same, and a Muslim has no other obligation to pay tax other than this tax on his wealth. The Prophet, may the peace and blessings of Allah be upon him, said: "There is no right to a person's wealth other than the zakah." Zakah becomes an obligation on wealth which is susceptible to growth, either of itself or by the work which is done to it; it is given as a purification, and as an assistance to those entitled to a portion thereof.

Zakatable wealth is of two kinds: manifest and hidden. The first refers to that which cannot be concealed, like crops, fruit and cattle; the second, to that which can be concealed, like gold and silver and merchandise.

The person in charge of tax collection does not concern himself with the zakah of concealed goods and wealth, as their owners are more entitled to pay the zakah thereof, unless they hand it over to him of their own free will, in which case he accepts it and distributes it by way of being of assistance to them. His assessment of the zakah of wealth is restricted to what is manifest.

Those who possess such wealth (manifest wealth) are commanded to hand it over to him. There are, however, two opinions as to the nature of this command, provided that is it is given by a just person. For some, it is an obligation, and they are not permitted to pay it individually, and neither is it accepted if they do; according to others, it is only a recommendation, as a means of making plain people's obedience (to Allah's command), in which case when they pay it individually it is accepted of them. However, in both cases, he must fight them over it if they refuse to pay it, just as Abu Bakr as-Siddiq, may Allah be pleased with him, fought those who refused to pay the zakah – as in effect they become rebels by refusing to obey those in authority. Abu Hanifah, may Allah be content with him, prohibits fighting them if they pay the zakah themselves.

The conditions stipulated for this authority are that the person be free, a Muslim, just, and knowledgable of the rules of zakah if he is one of the delegated agents; if he is merely an executory collector, appointed by the Imam with instructions of how much to collect, then it is permitted that he not be among those knowledgable about this tax. He may also appoint someone who, because he is of the family of the Prophet, peace and blessings of Allah be upon him, may not receive any of the zakah – any remuneration to him must be paid out of that portion of the zakah reserved for the public interest.

The person appointed may be of three types:

A. He is responsible for its collection and distribution, and he must combine both functions, as we shall explain;

B. He is responsible for its collection but is forbidden to distribute it – thus his assessment is restricted to collection only, and he is prohibited from distributing it. If the person who is responsible for both tasks delays its distribution, then he is blameworthy unless he himself has delegated someone else to distribute it in good time;

C. He is appointed in a general manner, such that he is neither commanded to nor forbidden from distributing it, and so he is charged by the generality of the appointment with both tasks, both collection and distribution.

Thus this task comprises both the collection and the distribution. Each task has its own rules, but we shall treat them both together in this chapter for the sake of brevity, beginning with the rules concerning its collection. There are four kinds of zakatable wealth:

1. Animals, that is camels, cows, sheep/goats – and these are all called *mawashi* (Arabic: "creatures that walk"), as they pasture by walking:

i. As for camels, the minimum zakatable amount is five, and from this number up to nine, a lamb or a *jadh'ah* sheep or a *thaniyyah* goat is to be paid; the *jadh'ah* refers to a sheep of at least six months and the *thaniyyah*, to a goat of one year; if the number of camels reaches ten and up to fourteen, then two sheep are payable; from fifteen to nineteen, three sheep, and from twenty to twenty-four, four sheep; from twenty-five onwards, the obligation to pay in sheep changes: from twenty-five to thirty-five, a *bint mikhad* must be paid, that is a young female camel of one year, or if there are none of this kind, an *ibn laboun* male (of two years); from thirty-six to forty-five, an *ibnat laboun* (female camel of two years) which is at least two years; from forty-six to sixty, a *hiqqah*, (a female camel) of at least three years which may be mounted and capable of receiving the stallion; from sixty-one to seventy-five, a *jadh'ah* which has attained four years; from seventy-six to ninety, two female *ibnat laboun* camels of two years; from ninety-one to one hundred and twenty, two *hiqqah* camels of three years.

This information is contained in the texts and about it there is a consensus; the fuqaha differ as to the ruling when there is more than a hundred and twenty: Abu Hanifah says it has to be calculated again using the first set of calculations. Malik says that there is nothing extra to pay until the number reaches a hundred and thirty, for which a three-year old *hiqqah* camel and two two-year old *ibnat laboun* camels. Ash-Shafi'i says if there are more than a hundred and twenty-one, then there is an *ibnat laboun* to be paid on each further forty, and on each further fifty, a *hiqqah*, such that for a hundred and twenty one, three *ibnat labouns;* and on a hundred and thirty, a *hiqqah* and two *ibnat labouns*, and on one hundred and fifty, three *hiqqah;* and on a hundred and sixty, four *ibnat labouns;* and on a hundred and seventy, a *hiqqah* and three *ibnat labouns*, and on a hundred and eighty, two *hiqqah* and two *ibnat labouns*. On a hundred and ninety, there are three *hiqqahs* and an *ibnat laboun*, and if they attain two hundred, then there are one of two payments: either four *hiqqahs* or five *ibnat labouns*; if there is only one of these two types, then this is taken, but if both exist then the collector should take the best of the two – although some say the *hiqqahs,* as they are more useful and cost less to maintain. Above two hundred head, the tax is calculated in like manner: an *ibnat laboun* for every forty, and a *hiqqah* for every fifty.

ii. As for cows, the minimum zakatable amount is thirty head, for which a *tabi'ah* male of at least six months which is able to follow its mother, although if a female *tabi'ah* is given it is acceptable; from forty, a female *musinnah*, that is, having reached a year, and if a male of the same age is offered, it is not to be accepted if there is a female of the same age in the herd; if the whole herd comprises males, then the offer of a male is accepted according to some, and not accepted, according to others.

There is a difference of opinion if there are more than forty cows: Abu Hanifah says, according to one of two narrations from him, a *musinnah* cow and an autumn calf are taken for fifty head, while ash-Shafi'i says there is nothing to pay on them after forty, until sixty head, in which case two *tabi'ah* cows; for each thirty above sixty, a six-month calf is to be paid and for each forty, a one-year old, such that for seventy, a one-year old, and a six-month calf are due; for eighty, two one-year olds; for ninety, three six-month calves; for a hundred, two six-month calves and a one-year old; for a hundred and ten, two one-year olds and a six month calf; for a hundred and twenty, one or the other type, just as one does for a herd of two hundred camels – that is, either four six-month calves or three one-year olds: according to some the agent takes what he finds, or if both exist the most useful; according to others he takes the cows. Thereafter on each thirty head, a *tabi'ah* and on each forty, a *musinnah*.

As for sheep and goats, forty head is the minimum zakatable amount and up to a hundred and twenty, a *jadh'ah* sheep or *thaniyyah* goat is paid, unless all in the flock are young, that is containing animals less than the (six month) *jadh'ahs* or the (two year old) *thaniyyahs*, in which case, according to ash-Shafi'i, a young animal less than a *jadh'ah* or *thaniyyah* is taken, while Malik says only a *jadh'ah* or a *thaniyyah* may be taken. From a hundred and twenty-one to two-hundred head, two sheep; from two to four-hundred, three; from four-hundred and one, four sheep; and then one sheep for each hundred thereafter.

Sheep are included with goats for the purpose of calculation, as are buffaloes with cows, and working camels with racing camels, as they represent two kinds of the same species; camels are not, however, included with cows, nor cows with sheep and goats, because they are different species.

The wealth of someone is calculated altogether for the zakah, even if his various goods are situated in different places. Goods belonging to different persons but which are mixed together are counted as one zakatable amount if they form a nisab and satisfy the conditions of association thereof. Malik, however, says that this association of goods has no significance until one of them reaches a nisab, in which case zakah is taken from the combined goods as a whole. Abu Hanifah says that this association of goods has no significance and that each party is assessed individually.

This zakah on animals becomes an obligation on two conditions:

First, they search out their own sustenance, feeding off pasture-land (*sa'imah* animals), such that their maintenance is of insignificant cost, and their produce in milk and offspring is abundant. If, however, they are put to work or are fed, then zakah is not due on them according to Abu Hanifah and ash-Shafi'i, although Malik considers that zakah must also be paid, as in the case of *sa'imah* animals.

Second, a full year has passed on them such that reproduction has taken place, for the Prophet, may the peace and blessings of Allah be upon him, said: "There is no zakah on goods over which a year has not passed." Newborn animals are only taken into consideration when a year has passed with respect to their mothers – if they are born before the commencement of the current assessment year, and if their mothers constitute a nisab. If the mothers do not form a nisab, then according to Abu Hanifah, zakah is paid if the mothers have been possessed for a year and they constitute a nisab when their newborn are added to their number – although according to ash-Shafi'i, the requirement that they have been possessed for a year may only be taken into consideration from the moment the nisab is reached.

There is no zakah on horses, mules and donkeys; Abu Hanifah, however, considers that a dinar must be paid for each *sa'imah* mare. But the Prophet, may the peace and blessings of Allah be upon him, said: "I have spared you any tax on horses and slaves."

If the person in charge of tax-collection is a delegated agent, then he takes the zakah, in the cases where the fuqaha differ, in accordance with his own judgement and ijtihad, and not according to the ijtihad of the Imam or the ijtihad of the owners of the goods; the Imam may not set the amount which he should take. If he is an executory agent, then he acts in accordance with the ijtihad of the Iman, but not that of the owners, in disputed cases; he may not make his own ijtihad; it is the Imam who must set the amount for him to collect – he is merely the person sent to collect what the Imam has decided upon. As a consequence, this agent may be a slave or a dhimmi, although general responsibility for zakah is not then permitted in this case, since the task involves an authority which cannot be validly established in the case of non-belief or slavehood. If it is a question of a specific zakah, a distinction must be made: if the original amount of the goods and the amount of zakah payable is known, the person charged with the task of collection may be a slave or a dhimmi, as he has no authority as such but rather fulfils the role of a messenger; if, however, neither the original nor the zakatable amount is known, he may not be a dhimmi, as it would mean entrusting him with wealth but not being able to trust what he says about it – although he may be a slave, as the latter's words are accepted (as valid) at law.

If the tax-collector is late in approaching the owners of goods after their zakah has become due, and if it occurs after commencement of collection from other persons, then they should wait, as he can only collect from one group after the other; but if he is late in coming to all of them, and the customary time for payment passes, then they should pay it themselves as the command to pay it to him is dependent upon their being able to do so, and this obligation is annulled when they are unable. The person who undertakes to pay himself, may do so in accordance with his own ijtihad if he is a person capable of ijtihad; if not, then he should seek the advice of a faqih whose judgement he accepts, and he does not have to seek the advice of another; if however, he does seek the advice of two faqihs, and one advises him that he must pay and the other that he is exempt, or one makes an assessment of one amount and the other of a greater amount, then the followers of ash-Shafi'i differ as to what he should do: according to some, he should accept the more demanding of the two, while according to others, he may choose between the two. If the collector arrives after the owner of the goods has paid, according to his own ijtihad or that of the person he consults, and judges that he has an obligation to pay when he has been exempted, or that he must pay more than he has paid, then the ijtihad of the agent should be put into effect as long as there is enough time left; if not, then the ijtihad of the owner of the goods is considered good and is acted upon.

If the zakah agent collects in accordance with his ijtihad, and considers either that someone is obligated or is exempt in accordance with his judgement, and then the owner of the goods makes his own ijtihad, such that he considers he has an obligation to pay what has been exempted him, or that more is due, then the owner of the goods must pay what has been exempted him or must pay the additional amount owing: this is because of what he owes Allah, may He be exalted, as he himself recognises that he still has an obligation towards those categories of persons entitled to the zakah.

2. The second kind of zakatable wealth is the fruit of date-palms and other trees. According to Abu Hanifah, zakah is payable on all fruit-trees, while for ash-Shafi'i, it is only on date-palms and vines, and no zakah is payable on any other fruit-trees.

The zakah of fruits is payable on two conditions: **i.** ripening has commenced and they are good for eating; anyone who harvests them before ripening has begun has no obligation to pay – although it is disliked that someone does this deliberately in order to get out of paying, while it is not disliked if done out of necessity; **ii.** the second condition is that the amount should be of five *wasq*; there is no zakah, according to ash-Shafi'i, if the amount is less than this. A *wasq* is equivalent to sixty *saa'* and a *saa'* is five (Iraqi) pounds and a third. Abu Hanifah considers that it must be paid on both small and large amounts alike.

Abu Hanifah has also prohibited the assessment of fruits on the part of their owners; ash-Shafi'i permits such an assessment for zakah as a way of helping those who are entitled to a portion of it. The Prophet, in effect, appointed agents to assess the fruits, saying to them: "Be exact in your assessment as there is *wasiyyah*, *'ariyyah*, *waati'ah* and *naa'ibah* in this wealth." The *wasiyyah* refers to the inheritance bequeathed by the owner after his death; the *'ariyyah* refers to dates given as a gift during the owner's lifetime; the *waati'ah*, to the dates eaten by travellers on the road (the word *watia* referring to their treading the earth); and the *naa'ibah* to the natural losses incurred during times of natural disasters.

As for the fruit of Basra, its vines are assessed, as is done elsewhere, but not its palms, as they are too numerous and would be too difficult to estimate; moreover, they willingly permit travellers to eat therefrom. The assessment, made by the first generation of Muslims, of the produce of the narrow paths, which was collected on Fridays and Tuesdays, is for the most part given to those entitled to this tax; as compensation for the produce of these narrow paths, they were (later) given the biggest fruits and this tax was imposed on (the owners in) the middle of Basra, and a tenth thereof was taken from them there. This obligation is not imposed on others, and so they find themselves in a quite different situation from other people.

It is not permitted to assess the vines and palms until the fruits are fully formed; thereupon both fresh dates and grapes are assessed, and then also estimated as dried dates and currants; then the owners, if they are trustworthy, are given the choice as to whether they keep the amount estimated, in order that they may deal with them, but remain liable to pay out the equivalent amount of zakah later, or that they keep them in trust but are prevented from dealing with them until the drying is complete, in which case the zakah is taken when It reaches the nisab.

The amount of zakah is a tenth, if they are irrigated with sweet or flowing water, and a twentieth, if irrigated by means of buckets or reservoirs. If both methods are used, then according to some, the one which is used the most is considered, while others say that each is calculated according to the degree employed. If the owner of the fruit and the agent differ as to the manner of irrigation, the owner's word is taken and the agent has him make an oath of affirmation; if, however, he refuses to make the oath, he is still only liable for what he himself acknowledges.

The various kinds of dates are calculated together as a whole, as are the different kinds of vine-fruits, since they are all of one species; the dates and vine-fruits are not, however, combined together, as they are two different species. When the fruits of the palm and the vine have dried into dates or currants, then their zakah is not taken until the drying is complete. If they are of the type that is only taken fresh, a tenth of their sale-price is taken after sale. If those entitled to them need to claim their right when the fruits are fresh, this is permitted, according to one of two opinions – if the division is considered as a singling out of a share, while it is not, according to others – if the division is considered as a sale.

If the fruit perishes after it has been assessed – by means of a natural disaster from the earth or the sky – but before any possibility of payment of the zakah, then the obligation is annulled; if, however, it perishes after a possibility of payment, then it must still be taken.

3. The third category of zakatable goods comprises crops. Abu Hanifah considers it an obligation on all crops, while according to ash-Shafi'i, it is only obligatory on whatever is sown by people to be used as storable food-stuffs; according to him, it is not an obligation on green beans and salad greens, nor on non-comestible items like cotton and linen, nor on what grows in the valleys and mountains which is not planted by man. According to him, it is taken on ten kinds of crops: wheat, barley, rice, maize, Egyptian bean, haricot bean, chickpeas, lentils, millet and julban-wheat. As for *'alas,* a kind of wheat with a double husk, it is include in the latter; zakah is not payable when it is still in the husk, unless the amount reaches ten *wasq*; it is likewise in the case of rice which is still in the husk. As for *sult,* a kind of barley, it is calculated with the latter. *Jawars* is a kind of millet, and is also included along with the latter. Apart from these, there are different species which cannot be included with each other. As for Malik, he includes barley with wheat, and he combines lentils and bean-like plants in a group called the *qutniyyah.*

The zakah on crops becomes due when they acquire their strength and vigour; it is only taken after threshing and winnowing, and when each reaches five *wasq*, while for any amount less than this no zakah is payable – although Abu Hanifah considers it obligatory on any amount, both small and large.

When the owner cuts his crops as if they are fresh or green vegetables, he is not liable to zakah, although it is disliked (*makruh*) for him to do this as a means of escaping payment, while it is not disliked if he does it out of necessity.

If a dhimmi owns some 'ushr land (land on which the 'tenth' of crops is paid as zakah) and he cultivates it, the fuqaha differ as to its ruling. Ash-Shafi'i is of the opinion that there is no 'ushr (tenth) nor kharaj to pay. Abu Hanifah, however, submits it to the kharaj and considers that this is not annulled even after the person becomes Muslim. Abu Yusuf says that twice the amount of tax payable by a Muslim is exacted from him, and then the extra amount is annulled if he becomes Muslim. Muhammad ibn al-Hasan and Sufyan ath-Thawri say that the tax payable by a Muslim is taken, and it is not doubled up.

If a Muslim cultivates some kharaj land, a tenth of the crops together with the kharaj tax of the land is taken, according to ash-Shafi'i; Abu Hanifah prohibits this combination of the two.

Payment is restricted to the kharaj tax alone for the person renting out the kharaj land, and to a tenth for the cultivator. Abu Hanifah, however, says that the tenth part is payable by the person renting out, as well as by the cultivator.

These three types of goods are all those classified as manifest.

4. As for the fourth kind of wealth, silver and gold, they are counted among the hidden goods. Two and a half per cent is payable, since the Prophet, may the peace and blessings of Allah be upon him, said: "On silver, a quarter of a tenth." The nisab of silver is two hundred dirhams, using Islamic weighting, that is six *daniq* to a dirham, ten dirhams weighing seven *mithqal*. On two hundred dirhams, five dirhams are payable, that is a quarter of a tenth; there is nothing to pay on less than two hundred, but anything over this sum is calculated according to the additional amount. Abu Hanifah, however, says there is no zakah payable until this addition to two hundred amounts to forty dirhams, in which case, a sixth dirham is due. Minted silver and ingot silver are both treated in the same manner.

As for gold, its nisab is twenty *mithqals*, according to Islamic weighting, and two and a half per cent is payable, that is half a *mithqal*, and then proportionally for any amount over this; both ingot-gold and minted gold are treated alike.

Silver is not included with gold, and the nisab of each is considered individually, although Malik and Abu Hanifah add the smaller quantity of one together with the larger quantity of the other, and calculate the former in relation to the latter.

When trade is undertaken by means of dirhams and dinars, zakah is payable on them both, and any profit made on these monies is added to them when one year has passed, as the zakah of silver and gold becomes obligatory after a year has passed on them. Dawud exempts zakah on the monies used in trade, and thus represents an isolated opinion in opposition to the general consensus.

If silver and gold are transformed into jewellery whose use is permitted, no zakah is payable, according to the better of the two opinions from ash-Shafi'i, and this is also the opinion of Malik; according, however, to the weaker of the two, it is obligatory, and this is also the opinion of Abu Hanifah. When, however, they are used for jewellery which is not permitted, or for vases, then zakah is obligatory, according to all jurists.

※

※　※

As for mines, they belong to the class of manifest goods. The fuqaha differ as to what materials zakah must be paid on. Abu Hanifah considers it is obligatory on all materials which are minted, namely, silver, gold, copper and brass, and he exempts those which cannot be minted, like liquids and stone; Abu Yusuf considers payment obligatory on those materials from which jewellery is made, such as precious stones; according to the madhhab of ash-Shafi'i, it is obligatory on the produce of silver and gold mines only, when the quantity extracted attains the nisab, after smelting and refining.

As for the amount of tax which is levied on these materials, there are three opinions: the first that it is two and a half per cent, like gold and silver that has been acquired; the second, that it is a fifth, like buried treasure; the third, that the circumstances should be taken into account: if the cost (of extraction) is great, then two and a half per cent, and if insignificant, then a fifth. The passing of a year is not taken into consideration as it is treated as a gain whose zakah is taken immediately.

As for treasure, that is any wealth from the pre-Islamic age found buried in disused ground or a public pathway, it belongs to the person who finds it, and he must pay a fifth, the proceeds of which are utilised like that of zakah, based on the saying of the Prophet, may the peace and blessings of Allah be upon him: "There is a fifth to pay on buried treasure." According to Abu Hanifah, the finder has the option of either making it known or hiding it, and the Imam has the choice, if it is made known to him, of either taking a fifth or renouncing it.

Whatever is found in land which is owned, it obviously belongs to the owner of the land, and the finder has no claim over it; he cannot claim anything off the owner except the zakah if he has already paid it on behalf of the owner.

As for treasure, be it buried or otherwise, of an Islamic minting, it is treated as objects found which must be made public for a year: either the owner appears, or the finder may take possession of it, but remains liable for replacing its value to the owner should he appear.

✳
✳ ✳

The tax collector should make a supplication for those paying the zakah in order to encourage them to do it promptly, to distinguish them from the dhimmis who pay the jizyah poll-tax, and because of the words of Allah: **"Take from their wealth a sadaqah, that it might cleanse and purify them thereby, and pray for them; surely your prayer will be a tranquillity for them"** (Qur'an 9: 104). **"Cleanse and purify them thereby,"** means cleanse them of their wrong actions and purify their actions; **"pray for them,"** may either mean "seek forgiveness for them," and this is the opinion of Ibn 'Abbas, may Allah be pleased with him, or "make supplication for them," and this is the opinion of the majority; **"surely your prayer will be a tranquillity for them,"** has four interpretations: **i.** as a means of bringing them closer (to Allah), and this is the opinion of Ibn 'Abbas, may Allah be pleased with him; **ii.** as a mercy for them, according to Talhah; **iii.** in order to establish them firmly, according to Ibn Qutaybah; and **iv.** to give assurance to them. This is recommended of the collector if he is not asked; as for his obligation to do it if asked, then it is recommended according to some, and an obligation according to others.

If a man coneeals the zakah payable on his wealth from the collector and hides it from the collector, who is a just (collector), then the latter should seize it if he is able and investigate the reason for its concealment: if he did it in order to take responsibility for its payment himself, then he imposes no discretionary punishment; if its concealment was in order to defraud and deny a right of Allah over it, then he should impose a discretionary punishment, although he does not inflict any additional penalty. According to Malik, however, he should take a half of his wealth, in accordance with the saying of the Prophet, may the peace and blessings of Allah be upon him: "Whoever tries to defraud regarding the tax, then I shall take it, together with half of his wealth, this being one of the decrees of Allah, but the family of Muhammad has no portion in it." His saying, may the peace and blessings of Allah be upon him, "There is no claim to someone's wealth other than the zakah," allows the former hadith to be interpreted as a reproach and a threat, rather than an obligation just as his saying, "The person who kills his slave, then we will kill him," since the murderer is not killed for the murder of his slave.

If the collector acts unfairly in collectiing the zakah, but is just in its distribution, then it is permitted to conceal it from him, but it is also acceptable to hand it over to him. If he is fair in its collection, but unjust in its distribution, then it must be hidden from him and it is not permitted to hand it over to him, as those subject to the zakah are not thereby relieved of Allah's right on their wealth, whether the zakah is handed over willingly or under coercion, and they must pay it themselves to those belonging to the various categories entitled to it. Malik says, however, that it is accepted of them, and they do not have to pay it a second time.

If the tax-collector, be he a delegatory or ann executory agent, affirms that he has collected the zakah from those liable to it, then his word is accepted as long as he is in authority; if, however, he is no longer in office, there are two opinions as to whether his word is accepted, based on the two opinions concerning the payment of the zakah on apparent wealth – that is, those who say that it is recommended, and those that it is obligatory: if it is recommended, then his word is accepted after he is no longer in office; if it is obligatory, his word is not accepted except with proof; it is also not sufficient that he bear witness to having collected it, even if he is a just person.

If the owner of the wealth claims to have paid it, then if this happens when the agent has been delayed in coming to him, and after a period in which he would have been able to pay it, then his word is accepted, but the agent may ask him to take an oath if he suspects him of lying. There are two opinions as to the legal consequences of this oath: the first, is that it is legally binding, and that if he refuses to swear an oath, the zakah is taken from him; and the other, is that it merely has an affirmative status, in which case it is not taken from him if he refuses to make the oath. When the person makes this claim in the presence of the collector, his word – as to having made the payment – is not acepted in the case of those who say that this payment is obligatory, although it is accepted in the case of those who say that it is merely recommended.

＊

＊　＊

As for the division of the zakah among those who are entitled to it, it is distributed amongst those mentioned by Allah, may He be exalted, in His noble Book: **"Surely the sadaqah is for the poor, and the indigent, and those who collect it, and those whose hearts may be brought closer thereby, and for the setting free of slaves, and for (the relief of) debtors, and those fighting in the way of Allah, and those travelling – an obligation from Allah, and Allah is the Knowing, the Wise"** (Qur'an 9: 60). The Messenger of Allah, may the peace and blessings of Allah be upon him, used to divide between them in accordance with his judgement and ijtihad until one of the munafiqun approached him saying: "Be fair, O Messenger of Allah!" to which he replied: "May your mother overburden you – if I am not just, then who is?" Then the above-mentioned ayah was revealed to him, and the Prophet, may the peace and blessings of Allah, said: "Surely Allah, may He be exalted, is not contented that the division of the wealth be done by one of the close-standing angels or a prophet who has been sent – so He has taken charge of its division Himself!" Thus it is obligatory that the division of the tax on animals, and the 'ushr ('tenth' which becomes a twentieth if irrigation is used) of crops and fruit, the zakah of wealth and mines, and the fifth on treasure, be made into eight parts, and paid to the eight various categories if they exist, as these taxes are all included in zakah, and it is not permitted to omit any one of them. Abu Hanifah, however, says that it is permitted to pay it to just one of the eight categories, even though the others exist, and it is not obligatory to pay it to all of them. But the equal treatment accorded them all by Allah in the ayah referring to the tax prevents one from restricting it to one of them; thus the collector must, after having gathered together the complete amount, and when all eight categories exist, divide it into eight portions equally:

180

First, he gives a portion to the poor (*faqir*), the poor being those who possess nothing;

Second, then he pays the second portion to the indigent (*miskin*): the indigent are those who do not possess enough wealth to make do – so the faqir is in a worse state than him. Abu Hanifah, however, says that the miskin is in a worse state than the faqir, arguing that it refers to those who have been immobilised by their lack of everything. Thus it is paid to each of these categories, if there is sufficient zakah, such that they are brought out of their state of poverty or indigence to the lowest state of wealth – and this is relative to their situation: for some, a dinar will be enough to make them (relatively) rich, if he is a person of the markets and he is able to make a profit enough to suffice him, in which case it is not permitted to give him any more than this; for others, a hundred dinars would hardly be enough, in which case it is permitted to give him more than this; there is also the man of vigour who earns enough to make his living by manufacturing, in which case it is not permitted for him to be given any of this tax, even if he does not possess so much as a dirham. Abu Hanifah, may Allah be content with him, estimates the maximum that may be given the faqir or the miskin to be a sum less than two hundred dirhams of silver, or less than twenty dinars of gold, so that he himself does not become liable for the zakah because of the amount he has taken in zakah.

Third, this is the portion for the agents, of whom there are two kinds: those who demand and collect, and those who divide and distribute – including treasurers, collectors, those in charge and those who obey orders. Allah has ordered that their remuneration be from the zakah monies, so that no other tax besides the zakah be taken from the owners of the wealth. An amount is paid to them from their portion which is equal to the wages of other officials like them; if their portion amounts to more than their wages, then this surplus is returned to the other portions; if it is less, then their wages are made up from the zakah wealth, according to one method, or from the part used for the public good, according to another;

Fourth, this portion is for those whose hearts may be induced to come closer by giving to them, and they are of four kinds: **i.** those who are brought closer so that they may help the Muslims; or **ii.** those whom one brings closer so that they may desist from harming the Muslims; **iii.** those brought closer because of their desire for Islam; **iv.** those brought closer in order to stimulate the desire in their people and family for Islam. If those among these four types are Muslims, it is permitted to give them from the portion of the zakah allotted to **"those whose hearts may be brought closer"**; those among them who are mushrikun (idol worshippers) are given from the portion allotted to the public interest from the *fay* booty and booty itself (*ghaneemah*) rather than from the zakah wealth;

Fifth, according to ash-Shafi'i and Abu Hanifah, the portion allotted for slaves is used so that makatib slaves may complete their instalment payments towards buying their own freedom, while Malik says it is used to buy slaves in order to set them free;

Sixth, this portion is for debtors and they are of two types: **i.** those who have incurred debts for their own personal benefit in which case, if they are poor, enough is given to pay their debts, but not if they are wealthy; **ii.** those who have incurred debts for the benefit of the Muslims as a whole, in which case an amount is given them which covers their debts and no more, irrespective of whether they are poor or wealthy;

Seventh, this portion is for those fighting in the way of Allah, namely the members of the raiding parties; an amount from their portion is paid which is enough to cover their needs for conducting their jihad ; if they go to a ribat on the frontier, the cost of travel there is given them, and if possible an amount for the expenses which will be incurred during their stay; if they return after having completed the jihad, they are given for the expenses incurred in their travel there and their return;

Eighth, this portion is for travellers who do not find the means to travel: it is given to them from their portion as long as their journey does not involve any act of disobedience – that is, an amount which suffices them, irrespective of whether they are setting out or in the middle of their journey, although Abu Hanifah says that it is only given to those who are in the middle of their journey, and not to those who are setting out.

When the zakah has been apportioned to the eight categories, then they will necessarily be in one of five situations:

First, the payment made suffices them, there being no lack or surplus involved, in which case they cease to be entitled to the tax, and it is forbidden for them to make any further claim to it;

Second, the payment made is less than their need, and so they still have a claim to it, and the part owing to them is made up from another zakah-portion;

Third, it is enough for some but not for others, in which case the former cease to be entitled to it, while the rest remain entitled;

Fourth, it provides more than enough to meet the needs of all of them, in which case entitlement ceases for all, and the surplus from their portions is given to others who are entitled to it, living in the regions nearest to them;

Fifth, it provides more than enough for some of them, while not enough for others, in which case the surplus from the former is given to the rest until both groups have enough.

If one of the eight categories is lacking, the zakah is divided amongst those which exist, even if it is only one category. The portion of someone who is absent is not given to his like in the same category, except the portion allotted to those in the way of Allah: the whole is given to them, as they reside on the frontiers for the most part.

The zakah of each region is distributed amongst those of that same region, and it is not permitted to transfer the zakah of one region to another, unless no categories entitled to it exist in it; if it is transferred and such categories exist, it cannot be accepted (from those who contribute), according to one of two opinions, while it can, according to another, and this is the madhhab of Abu Hanifah.

It is not permitted to give zakah to a nonbeliever, although Abu Hanifah permits the fitr-zakah paid at the end of Ramadan in particular to be paid to a dhimmi, but not a mu'aahid kafir (one permitted by special contract to reside amongst Muslims). It is not permitted to be paid to the family of the Prophet amongst the Bani Hashim, nor the Bani 'Abd al-Muttalib, in order to avoid their being tainted with the stain of wrong-actions (the zakah is paid as a purification from wrong actions), although Abu Hanifah permits payment being made to them. It is also not permitted to pay it to a slave, or a mudabbar slave freed on the death of his owner, or an umm walad slave who gives birth to the son of her owner, or to a partially owned slave. Moreover, a man may not give it to his wife, but she may give it to her husband, although Abu Hanifah forbids this. It is also not permitted for someone to pay his zakah to someone for whose upkeep he is responsible, be it a father or son, as they have no need of it in these circumstances – except from the portion of the debtors, if these latter figure amongst them; he is, however, permitted to give it to relations other than these, and it is preferable to give it to them rather than strangers, just as it is better to give it to neighbours rather than people who are distant. When someone subject to zakah brings his relations to the official in order to have his zakah paid to them, it is given specifically to them if his zakah has not been mixed with others' zakah; if it has been mixed up, his relations are treated in the same way as others; the collector must not, however, exclude them from it, as they have a greater and more particular right to it.

If the owner of wealth has doubts as to the official's use of his zakah and asks to oversee its distribution, he does not have to accept this request, as the owner has been freed of all further connection with it by his handing it over to him. Likewise, if the official asks the owner of the wealth to be present at its distribution, he does not have to be present, as he is freed of all connection to it by his handing it over. If the zakah perishes in the hands of the official before its distribution, the contribution of the owner of the wealth is acceptable (in the eyes of Allah), and the official is not liable, except in cases of fraud. If the zakah perishes in the hands of the owner of the wealth before it reaches the official, his zakah is not acceptable and he must give it again; if his wealth perishes before the zakah has been paid on it, then he is exempt from payment as long as it perished before there was any possibility of payment, but he is not exempted if it perishes after payment was possible. If the owner of the wealth claims that his goods have been destroyed before he has to submit it to zakah, his word is accepted, although if the official has any suspicions, he should make him swear an oath by way of confirmation.

The official may not take any bribes from the owners of wealth, nor receive any gifts from them. The Prophet, may the peace and blessings of Allah be upon him, said: "Making gifts to officials is fraud." The difference between bribes and gifts is that the former is what is taken after a request, while the latter is given voluntarily.

If any duplicitous behaviour on the part of the official manifests, it is up to the Imam, and not the owners of the property, to investigate him. Moreover, it is not up to those persons entitled to the zakah to engage in litigation against him, rather they should take their grievance to the Imam and make a complaint, in the same way as for any other abuse. Their testimony against the official is also not accepted, because of the suspicion that they have an interest in the matter. Testimony on behalf of the owners of the property against him is not entertained if it concerns the zakah taken from them, but it is if it is a matter of the official's misuse of it.

When the owners of property claim to have paid the zakah to the official, and the latter denies this, the former are made to swear an oath on their claim, in which case they are freed of all further liability; the official is also made to swear an oath on his denial, and is also exonerated. When some of the owners of the property bear witness in favour of one another, for example, that one of them has paid the zakah to the official, their testimony is not accepted if it is made after the parties involved have already made contradictory declarations and begun the dispute, although it is accepted if it happens before this, in which case the official is pronounced liable.

If, after the testimonies, he claims to have distributed the zakah amongst the various categories, his word is not accepted, as his previous denial (of having received the zakah) contradicts this affirmation; if the categories entitled to it bear witness that they have received their due from him, their word is not accepted, as it contradicts his denying having received it.

When the official affirms that he has received and distributed the zakah to those entitled to it, but the latter reject this, then his claim that he has distributed it is accepted, as he has been entrusted with it – although their denial of this is accepted if their state of poverty and need has remained unchanged.

The word of someone who claims poverty – and is thus entitled to the zakah – is accepted, while the word of someone who claims to be in debt is not accepted unless accompanied by proof.

If the owner of property states how much zakah he has to pay, but does not inform the collector of the amount of property he has, he may take this zakah from him on the basis of his affirmation, but must not compel him to bring the property before him.

If the official makes a mistake in his division of the zakah and gives it to someone who is not entitled to it, he does not become liable when the persons in question are wealthy, but their situation was not known. As for his liability when the situation of the persons in question is known, such as their being from among the family of the Prophet, or their being nonbelievers or slaves, then there are two opinions. If it is the owner of the goods who has made a mistake in the division, then he does become liable when it concerns the family of the Prophet, or slaves, whose situation is known; as for his liability concerning the wealthy, whose condition is not known, there are two views. There is more latitude given in any judgement regarding the exemption of the official from liability, as his participation in this affair is greater (than others), and his excuse for any mistake is all the more readily accepted.

Chapter 12

The Division of the Fay and the Ghaneemah

The wealth of fay and ghaneemah booty is that which comes directly or indirectly from the mushrikun. These two types of wealth are governed by different rulings and they differ from zakah-wealth in four ways: **i.** zakah is taken from the Muslims as a purification for them, while the fay and ghaneemah are taken from the nonbelievers as a way of exacting revenge; **ii.** the use made of zakah is prescribed in the (Qur'anic) text, and the Imams do not have to make ijtihad concerning it, while the use made of the wealth of fay and ghaneemah is dependent upon the ijtihad of the Imams; **iii.** those who pay the zakah may distribute it themselves to those entitled to it, whereas those from whom the fay and ghaneemah are exacted may not give it themselves to those entitled to it, until such time as the people of ijtihad take responsibility for it; **iv.** the use made of each kind is different, as we shall explain.

As for the fay and the ghaneemah booty, they are the same in two respects, and different in two respects. The first way in which they are identical is that each of the two kinds of wealth have their origin in the nonbelievers; and the second way is that the use of the khums (fifth) tax thereof is the same. The first way in which they differ is that the fay is taken without force, while the ghaneemah is taken by force; and the second, the use of four-fifths of the fay is different from the four-fifths of the booty, as we shall explain below.

We shall begin with the fay: all wealth which derives from the mushrikun, and is freely given without battle, and which has not resulted from the use of galloping horses and camel mounts (of war) – that is wealth resulting from a treaty, the jizyah tax, the 'ushr tax on their trade, or from something connected to them, like the wealth of the kharaj tax – then on all these a fifth is taken for those entitled to it, which is then also divided into fifths. Although Abu Hanifah says that "there is no fifth on the fay," the Qur'anic text prohibits any other interpretation: Allah ta'ala says: **"Whatever Allah has given in**

fay to His Messenger from the wealth of the people of the towns, then it belongs to Allah, to the Messenger, his family, the orphans, the indigent and travellers" (Qur'an 59: 7).

The fay is thus divided in five equal parts:

First, this portion was for the Messenger of Allah, may the peace and blessings of Allah be upon him, during his lifetime, and he spent of it to feed himself and his wives, and for his needs and those of the Muslims. People have differed concerning it after his death: those who consider that Prophets may bequeath inheritance say that it is used by his descendants; Abu Thawr says that it is wealth for use by the Imam after him, so that, in place of the Prophet, he may see to the affairs of the Muslims; Abu Hanifah says that it is annulled by the death of the Prophet; ash-Shafi'i, may Allah have mercy on him, considers that it should be used in the interests of the Muslims, such as provisioning the army, equipping horses, arming soldiers, constructing forts and bridges, providing wages for qadis and imams, and any other matters of public interest;

Second, this portion is for the close relations of the Prophet. Abu Hanifah claims that their claim to it no longer stands today, while for ash-Shafi'i it still does. The close relations refer to the Banu Hashim and the Banu Muttalib, the (descendants of the) two sons of 'Abd Manaf especially – and no others from the Quraysh have any other claim. Ash-Shafi'i treats the young and the old, the rich and the poor in equal manner, but he allows more to men than to women, that is, the male gets twice the portion of the female, basing his judgement on the fact that they are granted it because they are related (as in the laws of inheritance). Their freed client slaves and the offspring of their slave-girls have no right to it, but if someone dies after his right has been established, but before its distribution has been made, then his portion goes to his inheritors;

Third, this portion goes to needy orphans. The orphan refers to the person whose father dies when he is young, and this applies both to boys and girls; when they reach puberty this description no longer applies to them – as the Prophet said, may the peace and blessings of Allah be upon him: "The state of being an orphan ceases at puberty;"

Fourth, this portion is for the *miskin* (the indigent). This refers to those who do not find enough to live on, from amongst those entitled to the fay – these miskin being different from those of the zakah, because of the different uses to which the two kinds of wealth are put;

Fifth, this portion is for travellers, referring to those entitled to the fay, who travel and do not have enough to keep them going, irrespective of whether they are setting out, or are in the middle of their journey.

This is how the fifth from the fay is divided. As for the other four-fifths, there are two opinions: the first, that it is for the army only, and no others share in it, and it is used for their provisioning; the second, that it is used for the public interest, which would include the provisioning of the army, and other concerns which the Muslims cannot be without.

The fay tax is not to be used for the people entitled to the zakah, nor *vice-versa*: each tax is given to its particular people. The zakah is for those who have not emigrated, who are not combatants defending the Muslims, and who are not among those defending the cities. The people of fay are those who emigrate, who are defending the cities, those protecting what is sacred to them, and those making jihad against the enemy. The word "emigrate" only refers to those who left their homes to go to Madinah in search of Islam: all tribes which accepted Islam and made hijrah with all their members were called the "righteous" (*al-bararah*), and those tribes of whom only a part had emigrated were called the "good" (*al-khirah*), and so the Muhajirun were righteous and good; then the definition of hijrah was dropped after the conquest of Makkah, and the Muslims were known only as Muhajirun, or as "Arab" bedouins; the people entitled to the zakah in the time of the Prophet, may the peace and blessing of Allah be upon him, were called Arab bedouins, and the people entitled to fay were called Muhajirun, as is manifest in their poems; thus one of them said:

> *The night has enveloped her with a strong and intelligent man, able to escape from sickness, a muhajir and not an Arab bedouin.*

The difference between the two groups arises from the difference between the rulings governing the two types of wealth, although Abu Hanifah treats them the same, and permits each type of wealth to be used for either of the two groups.

If the Imam wants to make a gift to someone, in the interests of the Muslims – to ambassadors, for example, or to people he wishes to conciliate – he may do it from the fay wealth. The Prophet, may the peace and blessings of Allah be upon him, gave gifts to those whose hearts he wished to draw closer, on the Day of Hunayn: a hundred camels to 'Ubaidah ibn Hisn al-Fuzari, the same to Al-Aqra' ibn Habis at-Tamimi, and fifty to al-'Abbas ibn Mirdas as-Sulami, who, annoyed at the amount, reproached the Messenger, may the peace and blessings of Allah be upon him, saying:

I underwent a terrible test on returning to the battle on my horse in the plain and on waking up the troops from their inertia; although they rested I was not resting: so my booty and that of 'Ubaid is going to 'Uyaynah and al-Aqra'. I was full of power in the battle and yet I have not been given anything but – and this I could not very well be refused – as many young camels as the four legs of my camel. Neither Hisn nor Habis (their fathers) were superior to my father Mirdas. I am no less of a man than these two. The one whom you bring low today will not be able to rise up again.

The Messenger, may the peace and blessings of Allah be upon him, then spoke to 'Ali ibn Abi Talib, saying: "Go and cut his tongue away from me!" When he brought him Mirdas the latter said: "Do you want to cut off my tongue?" He replied: "No, but rather to give you, such that you will be content," and he gave to him, with the result that he cut off his tongue (from further speech).

If the gift made by the Imam will not result in general benefit to the Muslims, and its aim is only to benefit the donor, then it should be made from his own wealth. It is narrated that a Bedouin Arab came to 'Umar ibn al-Khattab, may Allah be pleased with him, saying:

O 'Umar the Good, may your reward be the Garden! Clothe my girls and their mother, and be a shield for us against these times. I swear by Allah that you will certainly do this!

'Umar then replied, may Allah be pleased with him, "If I do not then what?" and the other replied, "Then, O Abu Hafs, I shall certainly depart." 'Umar then said: "And after you have departed, then what?" The man replied:

You will certainly be asked about my circumstances on the Day when divine recompenses will be allotted, and the one who is asked will find himself either with those of the Fire or with those of the Garden.

Then 'Umar began to weep so much that his beard became wet, and he said: "Boy, give him this khamis (long shirt) of mine for that Day, but not for his verses. By Allah, I do not possess anything else." Thus the gift he made was from his own wealth, and not that of the Muslims, as his gift would not be of benefit to other than him, and was not therefore to be counted of public interest. A man like this Bedouin would be among those entitled to zakah, although 'Umar, may Allah have mercy on him, did not in fact give him any of it – either because his verses caused him not to consider him for this za-kah, or because the zakah had already been used for the neighbours of his area, and he was not among them. One of the reasons for the people's resent-ment of 'Uthman, may Allah be pleased with him, was that he used to make gifts from the fay wealth, without distinguishing between (personal or public benefit).

The Imam may give of the fay wealth to his male sons as they are entitled to it: if they are underage, they are included among those children of distin-guished and prominent persons; when they are adult, they are given from the portion reserved for combatants like them. Ibn Ishaq narrates that when 'Abd-allah ibn 'Umar, may Allah be pleased with them both, reached puberty, he went to his father 'Umar ibn al-Khattab, may Allah be pleased with him, and asked him to allot him his portion; so he allotted him two thousand coins; then a young man from the Ansar, who had attained puberty, also came to ask him for his portion, and 'Umar gave him three thousand coins. 'Abdallah then said to his father, "O Commander of the Believers, you gave me two thousand and to him, three thousand, and the father of this man has not been a witness to what you have been a witness." 'Umar assented to this but added: "But I have seen the father of your mother fight the Prophet, may the peace and blessings of Allah be upon him, and I have seen the father of the mother of this man fight with the Prophet, may the peace and blessings of Allah be upon him, and this difference in mothers is worth more than a thousand!"

The Imam may not give some of the fay to his daughters, as they are counted amongst those who are included in his share. As for his slaves, or those belonging to others, then if they are not among the combatants, their sustenance comes from his wealth or that of their masters; if they are com-batants, then Abu Bakr, may Allah be pleased with him, used to include them in the apportioning, although 'Umar, may Allah be pleased with him, did not; ash-Shafi'i, basing his judgement on that of 'Umar's, may Allah be pleased with him, does not apportion them anything, although he increases the por-tion given to their masters on their behalf, as any increase of the portion is based on the number of dependants. If they have been freed, then it is permit-ted to apportion them a part.

It is permitted to apportion some to the naqeeb-judges from among those entitled to the fay from the fay, although it is not permitted to apportion anything to their collectors, as the naqeeb-judges are chosen from amongst the people entitled to fay, while the collectors take a salary for their work.

The fay collectors may be chosen from the near-relations of the Prophet, from among the Banu Hashim and the Banu Muttalib, but not from the zakah collectors who want their part of this tax, unless one does it voluntarily (for free): this is because the Banu Hashim and the Banu Muttalib are forbidden to receive zakah, but not the fay.

The fay-collector may not distribute what he has collected without permission, while the zakah-collector may, as long as he has not been denied this capacity. We have already mentioned that the use to which the fay is put is decided upon by the Imam's ijtihad, while the use of the zakah is stipulated by Qur'anic text.

The qualities required of the fay-collector, assuming that he is trustworthy and astute, vary according to the different kinds of authority involved:

First, he is responsible for the assessment of the fay-wealth, and the assessment of its distribution amongst those entitled to it is like that of the kharaj and the jizyah. Among the conditions of this kind of authority is that the collector be free, a Muslim, capable of ijtihad concerning the rulings of the shari'ah, and knowledgeable of accounting and measuring.

Second, he has a general authority to collect all the tax from the fay wealth which has been clearly fixed and decided upon; for his authority to be valid, he must be Muslim, free, and knowledgeable of accounting and measuring, although he does not have to be a faqih capable of ijtihad, as he is responsible for collecting what has already been determined by others;

Third, he has a particular authority extending to one kind of fay wealth in particular, in which case this authority is examined: if he is not prevented from appointing another to take his place, he must be Muslim, free, and knowledgeable of the accounting and measurements necessary for his responsibilities; he may not be a dhimmi or a slave, as the task carries responsibility. If he is restricted from appointing another in his place, he may be a slave, as he is like a messenger carrying out an order. As to whether he may be a dhimmi, one has to examine the nature of the fay handed over to him: if his transactions involve other dhimmis, as in the collection of the jizyah, or the exacting of the 'ushr (tenth taken the goods of dhimmis when they come into Muslim lands to trade from other lands) from their goods, then he may be a dhimmi; if his transactions involve the Muslims, as in the collection of the kharaj-tax imposed on the kharaj-land which has fallen into the hands of the Muslims, then there are two aspects regarding the permissibility of his being a dhimmi.

If the authority of the tax-official ends, and he has taken some fay without valid authority, then the one who has given the fay is freed of all further obligation, as long as he did not prevent him from taking it – since the collector has permission to do this, despite his authority being invalid, and he assumes the role of a messenger in the collection of it. The difference between the validity of his authority and its invalidity is that in the former he is empowered to compel the person to pay, while in the latter he does not: thus if he refuses to allow its collection while the collector's authority is invalid, then the latter must not undertake collection and there is no compulsion. The person who does hand it over to the collector, knowing that he can refuse, is not freed of further obligation. There are two ways of looking at the question as to whether he is freed of further obligation, if he does not know of this possibility of refusal, as in the case of person with the power of agency (a *wakeel*).

As for the ghaneemah booty, it has more divisions and rulings, since it is the root of the matter, the fay being merely one of its branches, and thus the meaning of ghaneemah is more general. It comprises the four categories of prisoners of war, women and children captured in war, lands and goods.

1. Prisoners of war refers to the fighting men from amongst the unbelievers taken alive by the Muslims. The fuqaha differ as to the ruling concerning them. According to ash-Shafi'i, may Allah have mercy on him, the Imam, or his representative for the purposes of jihad, may choose the most expedient solution from amongst four possibilities – if they remain unbelievers: either to put them to death, or to enslave them, or to exchange them for a ransom or for other captives, or to spare them without ransom. If they surrender, they cannot be put to death, and he can only choose between one of the other three alternatives. Malik, however, says that he only has a choice between three options: putting them to death, enslaving them, or exchanging them for other male-prisoners but not for money, and he does not therefore have the option of setting them free. Abu Hanifah says that he has the choice of two things, putting them to death or enslaving them, and he does not have the option of sparing them or exchanging them for money – although the Qur'an mentions letting them go and ransoming them: Allah, may He be exalted, says: **"After that either spare them or ransom them, until the war has laid down its burdens"** (Qur'an 47: 5).

The Prophet, may the peace and blessings of Allah be upon him, set Abu 'Uzza Jumahi free after the battle of Badr, although he stipulated that he should not return to fight him; he returned, however, to fight him at the battle of Uhud and was taken prisoner, whereupon the Prophet, may the peace and blessings of Allah be upon him, ordered him to be killed. The latter then asked to be spared, and the Prophet replied: "The believer does not let himself be stung from the same hole twice."

After he had an-Nadr ibn al-Harith killed at as-Safraa, as he was leaving Badr, his daughter Qutaylah then asked the Prophet on the day of the conquest of Makkah to stop and listen to the following:

O Horseman, al-Uthayl is at a distance of five dawns travel away: if you arrive safely, give my greetings to the dead man, for mounted horsemen will not cease from sending him my greetings, together with a profusion of tears for him who is their cause, and other tears which are suffocating me. O Muhammad, the best of a noble progeny amongst his people, a hero amongst high born heroes, an-Nadr was the most deserving and the most entitled to be set free if any were to be set free; it would not have done you any harm to have set him free – many a time a valorous man has granted freedom when he himself is full of anger and rage.

Then the Prophet, may the peace and blessings of Allah be upon him, said: "If I had heard her verses before, I would not have killed him." This shows that if sparing someone were forbidden, he would not have said this – and his very words have the force of legal rulings.

As for ransoming, the Messenger of Allah, may the peace and blessings of Allah be upon him, accepted the ransoming of prisoners taken at Badr, and thereafter exchanged prisoners at a ratio of one for two (of his).

If he delays his decision regarding those of the prisoners who do not surrender in one of the four (above mentioned) ways, the Imam examines the state they are in, and makes his judgement concerning them based on his own ijtihad: those he recognises have a strength and capacity for harm, and for whom he entertains no hope of their becoming Muslims, and those whose death will inflict loss on their people – these he has bound and killed, but without chastising them; those whom he recognises as possessing vigour and strength for work, and from whom he fears no treachery or ill-behaviour, he enslaves, so that they may help the cause of the Muslims; those whom he hopes will become Muslims, or who are obeyed by their people – and who, it is hoped, by his sparing them, will either become Muslims or bring their people closer – then they are spared and set free; those who are found to have wealth and fortune – and there is some lack or need amongst the Muslims – are ransomed off, and the money used to help fortify Islam and the strength of the Muslims; if amongst the tribe of the prisoner, there is a captive man or woman from amongst the Muslims, he is ransomed off in return for setting the other free. Thus his choice of one of the four options is made on the basis of what is most prudent and most advantageous.

Any money taken in exchange for ransomed persons is treated as booty and added to the other objects of booty, but it is not handed over to those who actually took the prisoners. The Prophet, may the peace and blessings of Allah be upon him, did hand over the ransom to those who had taken the prisoners at Badr, but this was before the revelation of how booty is to be apportioned amongst those who acquire it.

If the Imam has sanctioned the killing of some of the mushrikun, because of the severity of their misdeeds or the great harm they have done, and then they are made prisoner, he may still spare and pardon them. In the year of the Conquest (of Makkah), the Prophet, may the peace and blessings of Allah be upon him, ordered six persons to be put to death, even if they were to cling to the coverings of the Ka'bah: they were 'Abdallah ibn Sa'd ibn Abi Sarh, who had written down the revelations of the Prophet, may the peace and blessings of Allah be upon him, but who, when the latter said: "Write: **'The Forgiving, the Merciful,'** wrote instead, 'The Knowing, the Wise,' and then reneged on his Islam and joined the Quraysh, saying, "I change (the words of) Muhammad as I wish." Then His words, may He be exalted, were revealed: **"And he who says, 'I will reveal the like of what Allah has revealed'"** (Qur'an 6: 93). There was also 'Abdallah ibn Khatal, who had two musicians who used to sing songs insulting the Messenger, may the peace and blessings of Allah be upon him. There was al-Huwayrith ibn Nuqayth, who caused harm to the Messenger, may the peace and blessings of Allah be upon him; then Miqyas ibn Hubabah, whose brother had been killed accidentally by one of the Ansar, and who had received the blood-price for him, but had still treacherously killed his brother's killer; he had then returned to Makkah reneging on his Islam and composed the following:

My soul is healed now that he is lying the night on the ground, the blood from his veins staining his clothes; before killing him my soul's troubles were paining me and were stopping me from resting in my bed; I have taken my revenge by force and transferred his blood-money to the Bani Najjar, the masters of Fari'; now that I have found vengeance, I can rest on my pillow, and I am the first to renounce my Islam.

There was also Sarah, the freed slave of one of the Banu 'Abd al- Muttalib, who used to insult and harm the Prophet; and 'Ikrimah ibn Abi Jahl who used to repeatedly provoke the Prophet, may the peace and blessings of Allah be upon him, seeking thereby revenge for the killing of his father.

As for 'Abdallah ibn Sa'd ibn Abi Sarh, when 'Uthman sought his pardon from the Messenger of Allah, may the peace and blessings of Allah be upon him, the latter turned away from him, and then he sought his pardon again (and obtained it). After he had left, the Prophet said: "Was there no one among you to kill him when I turned away from him?" "Why then," they replied, "did you not indicate this with your eye?" He then said: "It is not for a Prophet to indicate an act of treachery with his eyes." As for 'Abdallah ibn Khatal, he was killed by Sa'd ibn Hurayth Makhzumi and Abu Birza al-Aslami. As for Miqyas ibn Hubabah, he was killed by Numaylah ibn 'Abdallah, a man from his tribe. As for Huwayrith ibn Nuqaydh, he was killed in cold blood by 'Ali ibn Abi Talib, on the orders of the Messenger of Allah, may Allah bless him and grant him peace. The latter then said: "Hereafter no one from the Quraysh will be killed in cold blood, except when exacting the blood-price." As for the two singers of Ibn Khatal, one of them was killed, while the other escaped; pardon was later sought on her behalf from the Prophet of Allah, may Allah bless him and grant him peace, and he granted this. As for Sarah, she hid until someone sought her pardon from the Prophet, may Allah bless him and grant him peace, which he granted her; after this she concealed herself once more, until a man from among the Muslims made his horse trample her at al-Abtah, and so killed her – and this occurred at the time of 'Umar ibn al-Khattab. As for 'Ikrimah ibn Abi Jahl, he made towards the sea, saying, "I will not live with a man who has killed Abu'l-Hakam," that is, referring to his father. When he had boarded the boat, the captain of the boat said to him, "Be sincere (towards Allah)," to which he replied, "And why should I?" The captain then said, "Sincerity is all that is acceptable at sea!" "By Allah!" 'Ikrimah said, "If sincerity is the only thing acceptable at sea, then nothing else should be acceptable on land!" He then returned, and his wife, Umm Hakeem bint al-Harith, who had accepted Islam, succeeded in having him spared by the Messenger of Allah, may the peace and

195

blessings of Allah be upon him. According to others, however, she went out to meet him at sea with the promise of pardon, and when the Prophet later saw him he said, "Welcome to the sailor of emigration," and he became a Muslim, to which the Prophet, may Allah bless him and grant him peace, said, "There is nothing you would ask me for today but that I would give it to you." He then replied, "I ask that you ask Allah to forgive everything I have spent putting obstacles in the path of Allah, and all the measures I have taken to put obstacles in the way of Allah," to which the Messenger, may Allah bless him and grant him peace said, "O Allah forgive him what he has asked." He then said, "By Allah, O Messenger of Allah, for every dirham I have spent in the state of shirk, I will spend two in its place in Islam, and for every stand I have taken in shirk, I will take two stands in Islam." He was later killed at the battle of al-Yarmuk, may Allah be pleased with him.

We have described these incidents from the life of the Prophet, may the peace and blessings of Allah be upon him, because various rulings are dependent upon them.

As for the killing of those who are weakened by old-age, or affected by chronic paralysis, or those amongst the monks and inhabitants of cloisters retired from the world, they may be put to death on capturing them, if they had helped the combatants, by giving advice, or they had instigated them to battle: thus they are treated in the same way as combatants after being made captive. If, however, they were not involved in giving advice, there are two opinions as to whether they may be killed or not.

2. As for the *sabi*, the captive women and children, it is not permitted to kill them if they are of the People of the Book, because of the prohibition of the Messenger, may Allah bless him and grant him peace, of killing them; they are enslaved and distributed as part of the booty. If the women are from a people without a Book, like the Dahriyyah or the idol-worshippers, and they refuse to accept Islam, then they are killed, according to ash-Shafi'i, while according to Abu Hanifah, they are enslaved. If enslaved, then the mothers are not separated from their children, as the Prophet, may the peace and blessings of Allah be upon him, said: "Do not cause grief by separating the mother from her child." If, however, a ransom is given for prisoners, then this separation is permitted, as this ransom is treated as a sale.

The money paid in ransom is treated as booty, in place of the persons and it is not necessary to obtain the agreement of those who took the captives. If the Imam wishes to use them in exchange for Muslims held captive by relatives of the former, he awards those who took them captive an equivalent amount from the portion reserved for the public interest; if he wishes to spare them, then it is not permitted, unless those who captured them are in agreement, either by their renouncing their claim over them, or by his compensating them accordingly; if their pardon is in the public interest, it is permitted for them to be compensated from the portion reserved for the public interest; if, however, he wishes to do so for personal reasons, then he should compensate them out of his own wealth. Whoever among the booty-takers refuses to renounce his right over them, then he is not to be forced in the matter: this is different from the ruling concerning men who are captured – the consent of the booty-takers is not needed to spare them, as putting the men to death is permitted, while putting the women and children to death is forbidden: thus these women and children are treated as part of the wealth of the booty, and they cannot be made to renounce their claim to it, unless it is of their own free will.

The Hawazin sought the goodwill of the Prophet, may Allah bless him and grant him peace, after he had made some of them captive at the battle of Hunayn; deputations came to him. The booty and the women and children had already been distributed, so they reminded him of the honour to be accorded to the Prophet's wet-nurse who had suckled him, namely Halimah, who was from the Hawazin. Ibn Ishaq narrates that the Hawazin, when their women and children and their wealth had been captured at Hunayn, came to the Prophet, may Allah bless him and grant him peace, claiming to be Muslims, while he was at Ji'ranah, saying: "O Messenger of Allah, we have a common origin and tribe, and we have been afflicted by a disaster which is not hidden from you. Treat us as well as Allah has treated you." Then from among them Abu Surd Zuhayr ibn Surd got up saying, "O Messenger of Allah, surely amongst those you hold captive are your own paternal and maternal aunts, and wet-nurses who used to care for you. If we had suckled (the famous) al-Harith ibn Abi Shimr or (the prince) an-Nu'man ibn al-Mundhir, and then we had found ourselves in the situation in which we now find ourselves, we would hope for their forbearance and pity: you, however, are the best of guardians," and then he recited the following:

Be generous and gracious with us, O Messenger of Allah, for surely you are the man in whom we have hope, and for whom we wait; act well towards a country afflicted by fate, whose unity has been shattered, visited by a calamity of time; be gracious with the women by whom you have been suckled and who filled your mouth with the purest milk in the time of your childhood while they nursed you and brought you up as you walked to and fro. Do not split us up, and spare those among us who are a distinct group; even though you may not shower blessings on us, you will act with forbearance towards us, O you who are the best of men when put to the test; surely we will be grateful for such blessings, however, great they are, and we shall guard them in our memory after this day.

The Messenger, may the peace and blessings of Allah be upon him, then said, "Are your sons and your women dearer to you than your wealth?" to which they replied, "You would have us choose between our wealth and our honour! Give us back our sons and our women, for they are more dear to us." Then the Messenger said: "As for what is with me and the Bani 'Abd al-Muttalib, it is yours." Then the Quraysh added, "Whatever is ours, it belongs to the Messenger of Allah, may the peace and blessings of Allah be upon him," and the Ansar also said, "Whatever is ours, it belongs to the Messenger of Allah." Then al-Aqra' ibn Habis said, "As for myself and the Banu Tamim, we refuse"; then 'Utaybah ibn Hisn also said, "As for myself and the Banu Fizara, we refuse"; and then al-'Abbas ibn Mirdas as-Sulami said, "As for myself and the Banu Saleem, we refuse"; but then they themselves said, "Whatever is ours, it belongs to the Messenger of Allah, may the peace and blessing of Allah be upon him," and then al-'Abbas responded by saying to the Banu Saleem, "You have belittled me." Then the Messenger, may the peace and blessings of Allah be upon him, said: "Those among you who would hold to their claim over these captive women and children, they will have six young camels for each head – so give back to the people their children and their women." They were then given back. 'Uyaynah had taken an old woman from the Banu Hawazin, saying that he supposed she had relations in the tribe, and expecting that her ransom would be higher; he refused to give her back for six young camels. Then Abu Surd said: "Let her go! by Allah, she has neither a moist mouth, nor a full breast, nor a child-bearing womb, nor a husband who would miss her, nor abundant milk," – then he gave her back for six camels. Later, 'Uyaynah met al-Aqra' and complained to him; the latter then replied, "You certainly did not take her fresh and inexperienced, nor middle-aged and full of flesh."

Among the prisoners, there was ash-Shaymah, the daughter of al-Harith ibn 'Abd al-'Uzza, a sister by suckling of the Messenger, may the peace and blessings of Allah be upon him; she was treated harshly for saying, "I am the sister by suckling of the Messenger of Allah, may the peace and blessings of Allah be upon him;" when she was finally brought to him, she said, "I am your sister," to which the Messenger replied, "What mark is there of this?" She said, "A bite which you gave me while you were riding on my back"; he then recognised the mark and, spreading out his cloak for her, he bade her sit down, and gave her the choice of either staying, honoured, with him, or of returning to her people at her ease; she chose that he release her to return at ease, and this he did. All this happened before the delegation came, and before he returned their captives to them. He also gave her back a young servant of hers, called Mikhul, and a young servant girl, and she married them off to each other, and to this day there are still descendants of this couple amongst the Hawazin.

These incidents, together with the rules which may be deduced from them, form a code of behaviour which those in authority must follow – and it is for this reason that we have described them in full.

If among the captives, there are married women, their marriage is annulled by their captivity, irrespective of whether their husbands have been made prisoner with them or not. Abu Hanifah, however, says that if they are made prisoner along with their husbands, then they are still married. If a married woman becomes Muslim before being made captive, she is still a free women, but her marriage is annulled as soon as the 'iddah waiting period comes to an end. When the captive women have been distributed amongst the booty-takers, it is forbidden to have intercourse with them until they have completed the *istibra* waiting period, lasting for one of their periods – if they still have periods – or by giving birth, if they are pregnant. It is narrated that the Messenger passed by a captive woman of the Hawazin and said: "Do not have intercourse with a pregnant woman, until she has given birth, nor any other woman who is not pregnant, until she has had her period."

Any goods belonging to the Muslims which have been taken by the mushrikun, and which have been deposited somewhere for safekeeping, do not become their property, and they remain the property of their Muslim owners; if the Muslims take them in booty, they are returned to their owners without demand for compensation. Abu Hanifah, however, says that the mushrikun do become the owners of them, if they have seized them: thus in the case of a slave-girl, for example, if her Muslim master crosses over into enemy territory (Dar al-Harb), it is forbidden for him to have intercourse with her; if it is a land conquered by a mushrik who then becomes Muslim in order to keep her, then he is more entitled to her; if these goods are seized as booty by the Muslims, they are more entitled to them than their owners. Malik says that if the owner of these goods comes across his goods before the sharing out, then he is more entitled to them; if he finds them afterwards, then the owner is more entitled to their value, and the booty-taker is more entitled to the things themselves.

One may buy children of people residing in enemy territory, just as one may make them captive, but one may not buy children of dhimmi peoples or take them captive.

Whatever is taken by one or two persons is subject to the same ruling as booty, namely regarding the taking of a fifth. Abu Hanifah and his followers, however, say that a fifth is not taken unless the booty-takers constitute a *sariyyah* (raiding party); there is a difference of opinion as to this sariyyah: Abu Hanifah and Muhammad say that it is a group capable of mounting resistance; for Abu Yusuf, it is nine men or more, since the sariyyah (raiding party) of 'Abdallah ibn Jahsh consisted of nine persons. Most of the fuqaha do not take this opinion into consideration, however, as the Messenger of Allah, may the peace and blessings of Allah be upon him, sent 'Abdallah ibn Unays alone as a sariyyah against Khalid ibn Sufyan Hudhali, and he killed him; he also sent 'Amr ibn Umayyah Damri with another person as a sariyyah.

If one of the two parents become Muslim, then the male and female children all become Muslim too, although not those who have reached puberty, unless they are insane. Malik, however, says that if the father becomes a Muslim, it results in them becoming Muslims, but not if the mother becomes a Muslim. The children's acceptance of Islam does not in itself constitute their being Muslims, nor does their claim to deny Islam constitute that they are in fact renegades, although Abu Hanifah says that a child's Islam is accepted as such, just as his denial is accepted as such, if he has an intellect and is capable of discrimination; he may not, however, be put to death until he reaches puberty. Abu Yusuf says that a child's Islam is accepted of him, whereas his claim of denial is not. Malik narrates from Ma'an that a child's Islam is valid as long as he has knowledge of himself, while it is not if he does not.

3. As for land seized by the Muslims, it is of three types:

First, that seized by force and violence, when its inhabitants abandon it by their own deaths, or they are taken captive, or they emigrate. The fuqaha differ as to its judgement after the Muslims have seized it. Ash-Shafi'i, may Allah be pleased with him, is of the opinion that it is treated as booty, like any other goods, and is divided amongst the booty-takers, unless they renounce any claim over it, of their own free will, in which case it is made into waqf-property for the benefit of the Muslims. Malik, however, considers that it becomes waqf as soon as it is seized, and that it may not be divided between the booty-takers. Abu Hanifah says that the Imam has the choice of either dividing it between the booty-takers, in which case the 'ushr tax is payable on it; or of returning it to the hands of the mushrikun, and imposing the kharaj tax on them, in which case it is considered as kharaj land, and the mushrikun are treated as the people of dhimmah regarding this land; or it is made into waqf property for the Muslims as a whole, and this land is treated as Dar al-Islam, irrespective of whether Muslims inhabit it, or the mushrikun return to it, because the land still actually belongs to the Muslims; the Muslims, if they are the inhabitants, may not be compelled to cede it to the mushrikun, so that it becomes Dar al-Harb territory.

Second, land which is acquired from them (its inhabitants) without violence, because they have abandoned it out of fear: it becomes part of the waqf by virtue of seizing possession of it, although some say that it does not become part of the waqf until the Imam declares it as such; the kharaj tax is exacted on it, as a hire-charge on those dependant on it, be they Muslims or nonbelievers who work it. The kharaj-tax and the 'ushr on its crops and its fruits are taken together – except for the fruit of the date-palms, as the palms together with the fruit are treated as waqf, and an 'ushr is not obligatory on the fruit. The Imam has the option of either imposing the kharaj on them or granting a *masaqah*-sharecropping arrangement (renting out the palms in return) for some of the dates. Any palms which are later planted are subject to the 'ushr, and the land thereof to the kharaj. Abu Hanifah, however, says that the 'ushr and the kharaj are not combined, the 'ushr being annulled by kharaj, and this land becomes part of Dar al-Islam. It is not permitted to sell it, or put it up for pledge, although it is permitted to sell any date-palms or other trees which have been freshly planted;

Third, land which is taken through treaty, but which remains in their (its inhabitants) hands, on the understanding they pay the kharaj on it, is of two kinds: **i.** the treaty is made on the understanding that the land is ours, and that it becomes waqf within Dar al-Islam by way of the treaty: it is not permitted to sell it, or pledge it, and the kharaj is a rental charge which is not annulled by their becoming Muslims: thus its kharaj is also taken, if it is transferred to others who are Muslims. Such persons become people of treaty by this agreement, and, if they pay the jizyah, they may stay there indefinitely. If they refuse to pay the jizyah, they are not compelled to pay it, but they may only stay for the same length of time that the "people of treaty" may stay, that is four months, but (certainly) no longer than a year. There are two points of view as to whether they may stay for a period between four months and a year; **ii.** A treaty is made such that the lands remain theirs and the kharaj tax is imposed on them, and this has the same force of law as the jizyah, so that if they become Muslims, it is cancelled; their land does not become part of Dar al-Islam, but remains Dar al-'Ahd (treaty territory) such that they may sell it and pledge it, and if it is transferred to a Muslim, the kharaj is not taken; they may remain there as long as they respect the treaty, and the jizyah is not taken from them because they are outside Dar al-Islam – although Abu Hanifah says that their territory does become Dar al-Islam by the treaty, that they themselves become dhimmis, and that the jizyah is taken from them.

If they violate the treaty after it has been concluded with them, there is a difference of opinion: ash-Shafi'i, may Allah have mercy on him, considers that if their lands have been seized from them, then the ruling concerning them remains as it was; if they have not been seized, then they become Dar al-Harb. Abu Hanifah says that if there is a Muslim in their territory, or there is a territory of Muslims between them and the Dar al-Harb, then it is treated as Dar al-Islam, and those who have broken the treaty are treated as rebels. If there is no Muslim and no territory of Muslims between them and the Dar al-Harb, it is treated as Dar al-Harb. Abu Yusuf and Muhammad say that this territory is treated as Dar al-Harb in both cases.

4. Movable goods constitute the normal form of booty. The Messenger, may the peace and blessings of Allah be upon him, would divide them according to his judgement; when, on the day of Badr, the Muhajirun and the Ansar disputed over them, Allah, may He be glorified, made them the property of the Messenger of Allah – for him to distribute as he wished. Abu Umamah al-Bahili narrated that: "I asked 'Ubadah ibn as-Samit about the booty, that is about Allah's words, **'They ask you about the booty: say, "The booty belongs to Allah and his Messenger, so have taqwa of Allah and come to an agreement between yourselves"'** (Qur'an 8: 1), and 'Ubadah replied, 'This ayah was revealed about the participants of Badr at a moment when we were disputing about the booty and the dispute was becoming ugly, and then Allah, glory be to Him, took it from our hands and made it over to His Messenger, who then distributed it equally amongst the Muslims.'"

He himself chose his sword Dhu'l-Fiqar, which had belonged to Munabbih ibn al-Hajjaj, from the booty of Badr, and he took his full part, but did not pay the khums-fifth until Allah revealed the following after Badr: **"Know that whatever you take in booty then there is a fifth for Allah and the Messenger and for the close relations, for the orphans, and for the travellers"** (Qur'an 8: 42). Thus it was Allah Who was responsible for the division of the booty, just as He was responsible for the division of the zakah; the first booty from which the Messenger paid the khums, may Allah bless him and grant him peace, after the battle of Badr, was the booty taken from the Bani Qaynuqa'.

After the booty has been gathered together, it is not divided until the fighting has come to an end, so that it may be certain that victory is assured and the property is secure, and so the combatants do not get diverted by it and end up being defeated; when the fighting finishes, its distribution should be carried out immediately, in the actual Dar al-Harb, although it is permitted to delay it until the return to Dar al-Islam, that is, in accordance with whatever the army commander considers to be expedient. Abu Hanifah, however, says that it may not be divided in Dar al-Harb, but rather on return to Dar al-Islam.

If the Imam wishes to make the division, he should begin with the personal effects of those killed: they are given to the same combatants who killed them, irrespective of whether the Imam has stipulated this or not. Abu Hanifah and Malik say that if he stipulates these effects for them, they are entitled to them, otherwise they are treated as ghaneemah booty in which they all share. After the booty had been seized, the herald of the Messenger would call out: "Whoever has killed someone, then to him belong his effects." The stipulation of the Imam precedes the seizing of the booty, and does not come after it. Abu Qatadah was given the effects of those he had killed, amounting to twenty persons. As for these personal effects (*salb*), they refer to the combatants' defensive and offensive arms, and the horse he is fighting on but whatever is still in camp is not treated as his salb-property. As for whether what is around his middle (on a belt) or in a saddle bag counts as salb, there are two opinions. There is no khums on the personal effects, although according to Malik it is taken for those who are entitled to it.

There is a difference of opinion regarding what the Imam should do after he has finished this distribution of personal effects. Of the two opinions, that which is correct is that he should exact the khums from the whole of the booty, and then distribute it to those entitled to it, according to the five portions stipulated by Allah: **"Know that whatever you take in booty, then a fifth is for Allah and His Messenger ..."** (Qur'an 8: 42).

Abu Hanifah, Abu Yusuf, Muhammad and Malik say that the khums is divided into three parts, that is for the orphans, the indigent and the travellers, although Ibn 'Abbas says that it is divided into six parts, one of which is for Allah, may He be exalted, which is used to benefit the Ka'bah.

Those entitled to the khums of the booty are the same as those entitled to the khums of the fay: thus the portion of the khums for the Messenger of Allah, may the peace and blessings of Allah be upon him, is used, after his death, for the public interest; the second portion is for his close relations from amongst the Banu Hashim and the Banu Muttalib; the third is for orphans; the fourth is for the indigent; the fifth is for travellers.

Once the khums has been taken, a small gift is given to those known as "those of the small portion" (*ahl ar-radkh*) – who, according to a second opinion however, are given it before the khums is taken. The ahl ar-radkh are those among the slaves, women, children, the sick and the dhimmis who were present at the battle but are not entitled to a portion: they are given a small amount from the booty in recognition of the trouble they took (in assisting the combatants), but not so much as to equal the portion given to a mounted horseman or foot-soldier. If, after being present at the battle, the imperfection attributed to their status disappears, such that the slave is freed, or the child attains puberty, or the nonbeliever becomes a Muslim, then if this occurs before the end of the fighting, they are awarded a portion of the khums and are not treated as ahl ar-radkh; if, however, it occurs after the end of the fighting, a small gift is made to them, but they are not awarded a full portion.

After the khums and radkh portion have been taken, the ghaneemah booty is divided between those who took part in the battle, that is, free, Muslim men of good health, both those who fought and those who did not, since the latter are an aid to the combatants and a help to them in time of need. There is a difference of opinion about the words of Allah: **"It was said to them: 'Come and fight in the way of Allah or repulse'"** (Qur'an 3: 160); some interpret it as referring to an increase in the number of troops, and this is the view of as-Suddi and Ibn Jurayh, while others, to those ready on their mounts, and this is the view of Ibn 'Awn.

The booty is divided between them, that is to those entitled by right, and the matter does not depend on the choice of the person making the division, or the commander of the jihad. Malik says, however, that the booty is dependant upon the judgement of the Imam: if he wishes, he divides it between the booty-takers equally or in unequal parts, and if he wishes, he may have others who have not participated in the battle share with them. The saying of the Prophet, however, may the peace and blessings of Allah be upon him, "The booty is for those who participated in the battle," negates this view. Thus, having awarded it solely to those who have participated, he must give preference to the mounted horseman over the foot-soldier, because of the greater trouble the former must take in battle, although there is a difference of opinion as to how much preference must be given: Abu Hanifah says that the horseman is given twice as much as the foot-soldier, while ash-Shafi'i, that he is given three times as much. The portion awarded the mounted combatant is only given to the horse cavalry: those mounted on mules and asses, camels and elephants are given the portion of a foot-soldier, and no distinction is made between racing horses or normal horses – although Sulayman ibn Rabi'ah says that this portion is only given to thoroughbred racing horses.

Those who are present at the battle on a horse, but who do not actually fight mounted, receive the portion of a horseman, but those who leave their horse behind in the camp do not receive this; those who come to battle with several horses only receive the portion of one rider, according to the view of Abu Hanifah and Muhammad. Abu Yusuf says that they are awarded the portion of two horsemen, and this is also the view of al-Awza'i; Ibn 'Uyaynah says that they are awarded a portion for any horse they have had need of, but not if they have had no need. Anyone whose horse dies after being present is awarded a portion, while if it dies beforehand, then he is not – and likewise if he himself dies. Abu Hanifah says that if he or his horse dies after entering the battle zone, he is awarded the portion. Those who arrive to assist the combatants before the end of the fighting participate with them in the booty, but if they arrive after the end of the battle, they do not – although Abu Hanifah says that if they have entered the Dar al-Harb before the fighting has ended, they do take a share with them. The booty is divided equally between the regulars and volunteers amongst the army, as long as they all took part in the battle. If a party take part in a ghazwah without the permission of the Imam, then whatever booty they seize is subjected to the khums; Abu Hanifah, however, says that they do not pay khums, and al-Hasan that they cannot keep what they have taken in booty.

If a Muslim enters Dar al-Harb with a guarantee of safe-conduct, or is taken captive but then freed with a safe-conduct, he may not attack the enemy – neither their persons nor their goods, and he must guarantee them safe-passage. Dawud, however, says that it is permitted to attack them – both their persons and their property – unless they have sought safe-passage from him and he has obtained it from them: in which case he must spare them and not attack them.

If amongst the combatants there is someone who has clearly taken great trouble and pains by his courage and audacity, he takes his portion from the booty like the others and is also given a portion from the public interest share, in proportion to the trouble he has taken: in effect, those of particular pre-eminence and bravery have a right which must not be ignored.

The Messenger, may the peace and blessings of Allah be upon him, handed over the standard for the first time in Islam – that is, after giving it to his uncle Hamzah ibn 'Abd al-Muttalib – to 'Ubaidah ibn al-Harith in the month of Rabi' al-Awwal in the second year of the Hijrah; with him, Sa'd ibn Abi Waqqas made his way towards the nearest water to the Hijaz. 'Ikrimah ibn Abu Jahl was the amir of the mushrikun. Sa'd shot arrows and wounded the enemy, he being the first to do so in the way of Allah, and he recited:

Has it not reached the ear of the Messenger of Allah that I have protected my companions by the points of my arrow; with them I am able to repulse the most advanced of them, be the terrain difficult or easy; no one has shot arrows into the enemy before me, O Messenger of Allah, and that is because your deen which you have brought is the deen of sincerity, truth and justice.

When he returned, the Messenger of Allah, may the peace and blessings of Allah be upon him, took account of his pre-eminence and bravery.

Chapter 13
The Imposition of the Jizyah and the Kharaj

The jizyah and the kharaj are two rights which Allah, may He be exalted, has accorded the Muslims, and which are to be exacted from the mushrikun: they have three aspects in common, and three in which they differ, and the rulings thereof vary accordingly. The three points which they share in common consist of: **i.** both taxes are taken from the mushrikun as a mark of their subjugation and humiliation; **ii.** they are both treated as fay and are distributed to those entitled to the fay; **iii.** they are both payable after the passing of a year and they may not be exacted before this time. The three aspects in which they differ consist of: **i.** the jizyah is prescribed by a text, and the kharaj is based on ijtihad; **ii.** the minimum amount of the jizyah is laid down by the shari'ah, and the maximum amount is prescribed by ijtihad, whereas the minimum and maximum for the kharaj is determined by ijtihad; **iii.** the jizyah is taken as long as a person remains a kafir, and it is annulled when he becomes Muslim, whereas the kharaj is taken irrespective of a person's disbelief in or acceptance of Islam.

The jizyah is imposed as a poll-tax – and the word is derived from *jazaa* (he penalised, compensated) – either as a penalty for their disbelief, in which case it is exacted to humiliate them, or as compensation paid in return for their being guaranteed safe-passage, in which case it is taken with gentleness from them.

The basis of these interpretations is the saying of Allah: **"Fight those amongst the people of the Book who do not believe in Allah and the last Day, who do not prohibit what Allah and His Messenger have prohibited, and who do not adopt the deen of truth, until they pay the jizyah from their own hand in a state of humiliation"** (Qur'an 9: 29). As for Allah's words, **"those who do not believe in Allah"**, then given that the people of the Book acknowledge that Allah, glorious is He, is One, this denial may be interpreted in two ways: either they do not believe in the Book of Allah, namely the

Qur'an, or they do not believe in His Messenger, Muhammad, may the peace and blessings of Allah be upon him, as acknowledgment of the Messengers is a belief in the One who sent them. His words, **"and not in the Last Day"**, may be interpreted in two ways: either that they do not fear the threat of the Last Day, even though they acknowledge the Reward and Punishment, or they do not acknowledge the exactness of Allah's description regarding the different kinds of punishment. His words, **"and who do not prohibit what Allah and His Messenger have prohibited"**, may also be interpreted in two ways: either they refer to those of their laws Allah has commanded be abrogated, or to whatever Allah has made permissible for them or prohibited them. His words, **"and who do not adopt the deen of truth"**, may have two interpretations: either that it refers to those parts of the Tawrah and the Injeel which talk of following the Messenger – and this is the opinion of al-Kalbi – or to their entry into Islam, and this is the opinion of the majority. His saying, **"from amongst those who have been given the Book"**, has two interpretations: either it refers to the children of those who have been given the Book, or to those amongst whom there is a Book – as being its followers they are also like its sons. His words, **"until they give the jizyah in a state of humiliation"**, also has two interpretations: either until they give the jizyah, or until they undertake to give it – as this undertaking entails that they will be left alone. There are two interpretations of the word jizyah: either that it is among the words of more than one meaning whose precise import is only made clear in context, or that it is a word of general meaning whose general import must be understood, unless there is an indication that a particular meaning is implied. Allah's words, **"from their own hand"**, may either imply that they have independence and strength, or that they believe that we have the power and strength to exact it of them. His words, **"in a state of humiliation"**, refers either to the fact that they are mean and low, or that the laws of Islam apply to them.

The amir in authority must impose the jizyah on all those who come under dhimmi protection from amongst the people of the Book, so that they be established thereby as residents in Dar al-Islam. Their payment of this tax assures them two rights: that they be left in peace and they be protected; their domestic security is assured by the former, and their defence from outside attack is guaranteed by the latter. Nafi' has narrated from 'Umar that the last words spoken by the Prophet, may the peace and blessings be upon him, were: "Guarantee dhimmi contracts for me."

Arabs, like any other peoples, are subject to the jizyah, although Abu Hanifah says: "I will not take it from the Arabs, lest they be humiliated." It is not taken from a renegade, nor a dahri (materialist), or an idol worshipper, although Abu Hanifah considers that it is taken from the latter, as they are non-Arabs, while it is not taken if they are Arabs.

The People of the Book are the Jews and the Christians, and their books are the Tawrah and the Injeel; the Majus (Magians) are treated the same as jizyah peoples, even though it is forbidden to eat their meat or to marry their women.

It is taken from the Sabians and the Samaritans, when their beliefs concord basically with those of the Jews and the Christians, even though they may differ as to the details.

Whoever became a Jew or a Christian before these two religions were corrupted may be left in his belief, although not if he becomes one afterwards.

As for those whose situation is unknown, the jizyah is taken from them but their meat is not eaten. Those who convert from the Jewish to the Christian faith are not allowed to do so according to the most correct of two opinions, and they must accept Islam. There are two opinions as to whether or not the person who returns to the deen he has left stays in it or not. The Jews of Khaybar and any others are treated in the same way regarding the jizyah, according to the consensus of the fuqaha.

The jizyah is only obligatory on free men of sane mind and it is not an obligation on women, children, mad persons or slaves, as they are dependants and protected persons within a household. If a woman amongst them lives in isolation (and would seem subject to this tax), given the fact she is (no longer) dependent on her husband or family relations, the jizyah is nevertheless not taken from her as she is (considered) a dependent of the men of her people even if they are not related to her; if a woman living alone in Dar al-Harb pays the jizyah in order to reside in Dar al-Islam she is not bound to pay it and this payment is treated as a kind of gift which may not be exacted from her if she refuses to pay it; she must, however, be protected even if she is not dependent on her people.

The jizyah is not taken from a hermaphrodite of dubious status; if this doubt disappears and it becomes clear that the person is a man then it is taken from him from then on but what he missed in the past is not.

The fuqaha differ as to the amount of the jizyah. Abu Hanifah considers that those subject to this tax are of three kinds: the rich from whom forty-eight dirhams are taken; those of average means from whom twenty-four are taken, and the poor from whom twelve dirhams are taken: he thus stipulates the minimum and maximum amounts and prohibits any further judgement on behalf of those responsible for its collection. Malik, however, does not fix its minimum and maximum amount and considers that those responsible should make their own judgement as to the minimum and maximum. Ash-Shafi'i considers that the minimum is a dinar, and that it is not permitted to go below this while he does not stipulate the maximum, the latter being dependent upon the ijtihad of those responsible: the Imam, however, should try to harmonise between the different amounts, or to exact an amount in accordance with people's means. If he has used his judgement to conclude the contract of jizyah to the satisfaction of the leaders of the people to be taxed, then it becomes binding on all of them and their descendants, generation after generation, and a leader may not afterwards change this amount, be it to decrease or increase it.

If a peace agreement is made in return for their paying double the tax, this is executed: 'Umar ibn al-Khattab, may Allah be pleased with him, did this with the Tanukh, the Bihra and the Bani Taghlib in Syria. This double tax is not taken from women and children as it is a kind of jizyah for the benefit of those entitled to the fay and differs from the zakah which is taken from women and children. If this tax is combined with the jizyah, they are collected together; if there is only one of them, then it is treated as the jizyah as long as it does not amount to less than a dinar for a year.

If a peace agreement is made in return for providing hospitality for any Muslims who travel amongst them, then they are liable to do so for three days, but no longer: 'Umar came to an agreement with the Christians of Syria in return for their providing hospitality for three days to any Muslims who travelled amongst them – that is, to feed them (in the customary manner) without obliging them to slaughter a sheep or chicken, and to give shelter during the night to their animals without being liable to feed them barley; moreover this was the responsibility of the country-people but not the townsfolk. If the Imam does not stipulate their obligation to provide hospitality or pay double the tax, they do not have to pay any tax on crops or fruit and do not have to provide hospitality for any who ask or travellers.

The contract of the jizyah contains two kinds of conditions: obligatory and recommended. The first comprises six conditions: **i.** they may not denigrate or misquote the Book of Allah; **ii.** they may not accuse the Messenger, may the peace and blessings of Allah be upon him, of lying, or speak of him disparagingly; **iii.** nor mention the deen of Islam with slander or calumny; **iv.** nor approach a Muslim woman to commit fornication or with a view to marriage; **v.** nor try to undermine a Muslim's faith in his deen or to cause harm to his wealth or deen; **vi.** nor help the enemy or any of their spies. These six count as obligatory duties and must be adhered to without condition: they are only stipulated as a way of averting such situations and of emphasising the severity of the contract binding them, and that if they fail in fulfilling them it will result in the breaking of the contract.

The recommended conditions are six in number: **i.** the changing of their outward form by imposing the wearing of distinctive clothes and a special zunnar belt; **ii.** they are not to erect any buildings higher than those of the Muslims and must either be of equal or lesser height; **iii.** they must not allow the sound of their bells, the reciting of their books or their talk of 'Uzayr or Jesus to reach the ears of the Muslims; **iv.** they must not drink their wine in front of the Muslims, display their crosses or allow their pigs to be seen openly; **v.** they must conceal the burial of their dead and not lament or wail openly for them; **vi.** they are prevented from riding horses, be they thoroughbred or of mixed race, but not from riding mules or asses. These six are recommended but are not a binding part of the dhimmi contract unless they are stipulated, in which case they become obligatory; if they are not fulfilled, however, it does not entail the breaking of the contract – although they are held to it by force and are chastised accordingly. They are not, however, reprimanded if this has not been made a condition for them.

The terms which are fixed regarding the contractually binding peace-agreement with them are recorded by the Imam in the diwan offices of the large towns so that reference may be made to them if the subject peoples do not fulfil these terms; each people's peace-agreement may differ from that concluded with others.

The jizyah only becomes an obligation after the passing of a lunar year, and then only once therein. Anyone who dies during this year, then this tax is exacted from whatever he leaves behind in proportion to the time which has elapsed. Whoever becomes a Muslim, then his jizyah is treated as a debt which he must be made to pay, although Abu Hanifah considers that it is annulled when he becomes Muslim or dies. Anyone who reaches puberty or recovers after a period of insanity is allowed to wait until the following full year before payment is taken. It is exacted from a poor person as long as this is easy for him while his case is examined if it is difficult for him; neither the old nor the chronically sick are exempted from it, although according to some, both they and the poor are exempt.

If the subject people dispute amongst themselves concerning their deen and differ concerning their beliefs, no attempt is made to interfere or resolve their differences; if they argue about a right and have recourse to their judge they are not stopped from doing this; if they have recourse to our judge, he should pass judgement between them in accordance with the criteria of the deen of Islam and the hadd-punishments are imposed on them if they merit them. Anyone who breaks his contract may be allowed to leave for a place of safety but he is treated as an enemy.

A people with whom there is a peace-treaty are guaranteed safety for themselves and their property if they enter Dar al-Islam, and they may reside for four months without payment of the jizyah; they may not, however, stay a year without paying the jizyah. There is a difference of opinion regarding a period between these two times. They must be left in peace, like dhimmi peoples, but it is not obligatory to defend them like dhimmi peoples.

If a Muslim of sane mind who has reached puberty gives a guarantee of safety to an enemy, then all the other Muslims are obliged to guarantee his safety; a woman may give this guarantee just like a man and a slave may give it just like a free person. Abu Hanifah, however, considers that the guarantee of a slave is not valid unless he has been given permission to fight. The guarantee accorded by a child or a mad person is not valid; anyone who is given a guarantee from either them is still treated as an enemy unless he is ignorant of its invalidity, in which case he is treated as an enemy only when he has gone to his place of safety.

If the peoples of an agreement and the dhimmis openly manifest hostility towards the Muslims, they are immediately treated as enemies and their combatants are killed; the rest are treated in accordance with the support or condemnation they showed towards the hostilities. If the dhimmis refuse to pay the jizyah, they break their contract, although Abu Hanifah only considers it a violation if they reach Dar al-Harb. It is taken from them by force like any other debt. It is not permitted to build a new synagogue or church in Dar al-Islam; if they do, it is destroyed; it is, however, permitted to rebuild an old synagogue or church if they fall into ruin.

If the dhimmis violate their agreement, it is not then permitted to put them to death or to take their property as booty or their women and children as captives as long as they do not fight: they must be expelled from the Muslim territories with a guarantee of safe passage until they reach a place of safety in the nearest adjoining region inhabited by the people of shirk; if they do not leave willingly they must be forced to do so.

The kharaj is a tax imposed on land, the obligation of which must be fulfilled. The Qur'anic text regarding it is manifestly different from the text about the jizyah, and for this reason its implementation is dependent upon the ijtihad of the Imam. Allah says: **"Would you demand a tribute (*kharj*) of them when the sustenance (*kharaj*) of your Lord is better?"** (Qur'an 23: 74). There are two aspects concerning His words, **"Would you demand a tribute (*kharj*)"**, the first that it refers to a wage, the second, to a benefit; the word **"*kharaj*"** has two meanings: either that provision from your Lord in this world is better, and this is the opinion of al-Kalbi or the wage of your Lord in the next world is better than it, and this is al-Hasan's opinion. Abu 'Amr ibn al-'Ala says that the difference between the kharj and the kharaj is that the former is a tax incumbent on the neck of a person while the latter is a tax on the land. The kharaj refers also, in the language of the Arabs to the hiring out of land or the harvest and it is in this latter sense that the saying of the Prophet, may Allah bless him and grant him peace, may be understood: "Revenue taken is based on responsibility."

Kharaj land differs from 'ushr land regarding the property rights and rulings governing them. All lands may be classified in four ways:

First, those lands which the Muslims have revived are 'ushr lands and it is not permitted to impose the kharaj tax on them. Mention will be made later of these lands which are revived;

Second, lands whose owners have become Muslims, in which case they are more entitled to them. According to ash-Shafi'i, may Allah have mercy on him, these are 'ushr lands and it is not permitted to impose the kharaj on them. Abu Hanifah, however, says that the Imam has the option of either treating them as kharaj or 'ushr lands; if he treats them as kharaj lands then he is not allowed to change them into 'ushr lands although if he treats them into 'ushr lands it is permitted to change them into kharaj land;

Third, lands which have been seized from the mushrikun by force and violence; according to ash-Shafi'i's teaching, may Allah have mercy on him, they are treated as booty and divided amongst the booty-takers: it is treated as 'ushr land and it is not permitted to impose the kharaj on it. Malik considers that it is a waqf for the Muslims based on the kharaj imposed upon it. Abu Hanifah says that the Imam may choose either option;

Fourth, land upon which an agreement has been concluded with the mushrikun and which is characterised by the imposition of the kharaj; it is of two types:

A. Those lands abandoned by their people and which the Muslims have acquired without fighting, in which case they become waqf for the benefit of the Muslims and the kharaj is imposed on them; this kharaj becomes a revenue in perpetuity – not for a restricted period – because of the general interest attached to it. Its status does not change if the inhabitant is a Muslim or a dhimmi; one may not sell such land or the liabilities thereof – given that it is governed by a waqf ruling;

B. Those lands on which the former owners still remain: an agreement is made for them to stay on their lands in return for the imposition of the kharaj on them: this is of two kinds: **i.** those who renounce all claims, in our favour, to possession of such lands when they make the peace treaty with us, in which case these lands become waqf for the Muslims, as in the case of lands abandoned by their inhabitants; the kharaj is imposed on them as a retribution and they are not exempted if they become Muslim; they are not permitted to sell the liability thereof although they are more entitled to occupy these lands as long as they honour the peace-agreement; these lands may not be taken from them irrespective of whether they remain in shirk or become Muslims, just as rented lands may not be taken from the one who rents them. Their payment of the kharaj does not, however, exempt them from the jizyah if they become dhimmis and take up residence; if they do not become dhimmis but still honour the terms of the agreement, they are not permitted to stay there for a year, although their residence is permitted for a shorter period, without having to pay the jizyah; **ii.** those who remain property-holders and who do not renounce their responsibility for these lands and who come to an agreement in return for a kharaj payment imposed on them: in this case, the kharaj is in fact the jizyah which is taken from them as long as they remain in the state of shirk and from which they are exempted when they become Muslims. It is thus permitted not to exact the actual jizyah poll-tax. They may sell this land to whomever they wish among themselves, or to Muslims, or to dhimmis. If they sell it among themselves, it retains the same status regarding the kharaj; if it is sold to a Muslim, he is exempt from paying the kharaj on it; if it is sold to a dhimmi, it may well be that he is not exempted from the kharaj because he remains in a state of disbelief; it may also be that he is exempted because he is outside the contract made with those of the peace-agreement, by his being a dhimmi.

The kharaj exacted on these lands must be examined as to whether it is imposed according to surface area such that an amount of silver is exacted on each measure of area. If a certain area becomes exempt because the inhabitants become Muslims, the remaining areas continue to pay as before without, however, having to pay the kharaj which would have been due on the exempted lands. If the kharaj is imposed by way of a peace-agreement and is for a fixed sum, then the amount cannot be decreased in proportion to the areas which cease to be subject to this tax. Ash-Shafi'i says that the sum fixed in return for the agreement is decreased accordingly if the inhabitants become Muslim; Abu Hanifah, however, says that the sum fixed by the agreement remains in full and the person who becomes a Muslim is not exempt but must pay his part.

The amount of kharaj imposed is in accordance with what the land can bear. When 'Umar, may Allah be pleased with him, imposed the kharaj on the Sawad of Iraq he stipulated that a *qafeez* and a dirham be paid for each acre in certain districts, following the example, which he made his own, of the Khusroes ibn Qubadh. This latter was the first to assess as-Sawad, to impose the kharaj, to establish the boundaries and the diwan offices; he took account of the capacity of the land (for tax) without prejudice to the owner's interest or that of the farmers, and he took a qafeez and a dirham for every *jareeb* (a measure of arable land) – a qafeez weighing eight pounds and having a value of three dirhams of the mithqal weight; this was so well known that it appears amongst the Jahiliyyah Arabs for as Zuhayr ibn Abi Silma has declaimed:

And the war will bring you what the inhabitants of the towns in Iraq do not bring you, namely qafeez and dirhams.

In other parts of Iraq, 'Umar, may Allah be pleased with him, imposed another amount employing 'Uthman ibn Hunayf for the task of measuring and imposing what the land was capable of supporting in tax. He thus made the measurements and imposed the following amounts for each *jareeb*: vines and trees in rows, ten dirhams; date-palms, eight dirhams; sugar cane, six dirhams; fodder crops, five dirhams; wheat, four dirhams; barley, two dirhams. He wrote to 'Umar ibn al-Khattab, may Allah be pleased with him, and the latter let him do this.

'Umar, however, operated another tariff in some parts of Syria but it is known that he always took account of the capacity of the land to bear tax: thus it is incumbent upon the person imposing the kharaj thereafter to take this into account: this varies in three ways and each results in an increase or decrease in the kharaj: the first, concerns the goodness of the earth and the corresponding effect it has on the crops, or the badness of the earth which slows down their growth; the second, concerns the different kinds of produce, that is the grains and fruits some of which are of more value than others, and the kharaj is imposed accordingly; the third, concerns irrigation and watering because the costs involved in irrigation machinery and water wheels mean that the kharaj exacted is not the same as may be exacted on land watered naturally by streams and rains.

The irrigation of crops and trees may be classified in four ways

First, that undertaken by man without the use of equipment – like allowing the flow of water from springs and streams when needed and stopping it when there is no need; this is the most profitable kind of watering and the one involving the least expense;

Second, that undertaken by man using equipment like irrigation machinery and water-wheels; this is the most costly and difficult form of irrigation;

Third, land which the sky waters in the form of rain, snow or dew – the latter known as *al-idhy* land;

Fourth, land which is watered by the natural humidity of the earth or by naturally trapped water from which the crops drink and which is absorbed by the trees through their roots – this type of land is called *al-baal.*

Ghayl refers to water absorbed into the earth by means of a canal; if the water therein is flowing, then it is classified in the first category; if not, then in the second. *Kidhaa'im* refers to water which is absorbed from wells; if it is drawn by buckets, it belongs to the second category, and if it is brought by canal, it is called ghayl and belongs to the first.

It is essential that the person responsible for imposing the kharaj should take these three aspects into account, namely the type of land, of the crops, and of the irrigation in order to ascertain the amount of tax the land can sustain: he should aim to act fairly, taking into consideration the people of the land and those entitled to the fay without imposing any excess which would harm those paying kharaj, or tolerating any shortfall which would be to the detriment of the people entitled to the fay, that is he should examine the interests of both parties.

Some take a fourth element into consideration, that is the proximity or distance of towns and markets and the corresponding effect on the value of the land: this is taken into consideration when the kharaj is taken in silver but not if it is in grains – whereas the previous three elements are considered irrespective of whether payment is made in silver or grains. As the kharaj is subject to what we have described above, its amount varies accordingly: thus the kharaj of one district may be different from that of another district.

One should not attempt to exact the maximum amount of kharaj that the land will sustain lest there is not enough left over to compensate those responsible for the land in times of calamity and drought.

It is related that al-Hajjaj wrote to 'Abd al-Malik ibn Marwan to seek permission to take the excess wealth of the Sawad (held in reserve), but he prohibited him from doing so and wrote: "Do not be more zealous with the dirham already collected than with the dirham you have left with them: leave them some meat for them to cook with their fat."

The kharaj having been fixed according to the capacity of the land and with regard to the elements mentioned above, the Imam should take care to choose the most expedient method of assessment from among three: either according to the surface area of the land; or to the size of the harvest; or by making it payable in kind based on a proportion of the produce (*muqasamah*). If assessed on the surface area, the lunar year is used; if on the size of the harvest, the solar year; if by muqasamah then it is done on completion of the harvest, and after the threshing or separation, and cleaning of the fruit.

If one of these methods is adopted and assessed according to the necessary conditions, it is fixed for ever and it is not permitted to increase it or decrease it as long as the land remains in the same state with respect to its irrigation and yield. If a change occurs in the irrigation or yield, be it an increase or decrease, then it is of two kinds: first, the cause of this increase or decrease is man-made, like the increase resulting from altering the course of a river or raising its water-level, or a decrease brought about by neglecting the cultivation or not fulfilling its requirements, in which case the kharaj stays as it was: it is not increased because of increased cultivation or decreased because of neglect – rather cultivation must be continued lest this abandonment results in its reverting to wilderness; second, it is not man-made – rather the decrease is caused by a fissure opening up in the water-course or a stream drying up: if it is possible to block it up and do work on it, it is incumbent on the Imam to have it done from the treasury – from the portion allotted to the public interest – and the kharaj is annulled as long as work is being carried out; if work is not possible on it, the kharaj is annulled for the people of the land, if no more benefit may be had from it; if benefit may be had from it other than from cultivation, as a hunting reserve or as pasture, kharaj may be exacted again at a rate sustainable by the hunting or pasture. Thus this land is not like that of mawat ("dead" or undeveloped) lands on which it is not permitted to exact kharaj for hunting or pasturing on it as the former is owned land and the mawat lands are open to all. As for any increase brought about by Allah, like a stream formed by a flood such that the earth is watered by running water whereas before it was irrigated by equipment, then if it is an occasional event which does not look like lasting, the kharaj may be increased; if it does look like lasting, the Imam should take into account the interests of the farmers and those entitled to the fay and should act with fairness when deciding between the two parties as to whether to increase the kharaj or leave it as it was.

Kharaj is exacted on a land where agriculture is possible, even if it is not being cultivated. Malik, however, says that there is no kharaj on it irrespective of whether it was deliberately abandoned or for some valid reason. Abu Hanifah says it is taken if abandoned deliberately and is exempt if there is some valid reason.

If an area, subject to various kinds of kharaj because it has various kinds of crops, stops producing some of its crops, then the lightest of the various rates is taken on this area as the cultivator is at liberty to cultivate only the crop subject to the lightest tax and could not be opposed in this.

If a kharaj land cannot be cultivated each year but rather must lie fallow one year and be planted the next, then one should take account of its condition at the outset of the imposition of the kharaj, and then the most practical method from among three methods is adopted, taking into account the interests of the cultivators and the people entitled to the fay: **i.** the kharaj is exacted at half the rate of what would normally be exacted in a year, and thus it is taken on what is cultivated and what is fallow; **ii.** one out of every two jareebs only is measured such that one is for what is cultivated and one for what is fallow; **iii.** the tax is imposed on the land-surface as a whole both cultivated and fallow but (the kharaj) is exacted from only a half of the cultivators' harvest of the land.

If the kharaj varies according to the different kinds of crops and fruits and the cultivator plants something of which no mention has been made, then the kharaj is based on a plant which has been mentioned specifically and which most resembles the unknown one in form and use. If the kharaj land is cultivated such that it is subject to the 'ushr, this 'ushr is not annulled by payment of the kharaj and these two obligations are combined according to ash-Shafi'i's teaching, may Allah have mercy on him. Abu Hanifah, however, says that they are not added to each other and only the kharaj is taken and the 'ushr is annulled. Kharaj land cannot be changed into 'ushr land nor *vice versa* although Abu Hanifah permits this.

If 'ushr land is irrigated by kharaj water (from streams and irrigation canals) the 'ushr is taken, and if kharaj land is irrigated with 'ushr water (i.e. rain, springs, lakes), the kharaj is taken, taking account of the type of land rather than the type of water. Abu Hanifah, however, says that the water must be taken into account such that the kharaj is taken on 'ushr land watered by kharaj water and the 'ushr when kharaj land is watered by 'ushr water, that is he takes account of the water and not the land. It is preferable to take the land rather than the water into account, however, as the kharaj is taken on the land and the 'ushr is taken on the crops and there is no kharaj or 'ushr on the water itself and so it is not taken into account in either case. This difference of opinion causes Abu Hanifah to prohibit the person responsible for kharaj land from irrigating with 'ushr water and the person responsible for 'ushr land from irrigating with kharaj water; ash-Shafi'i, however, may Allah have mercy on him, does not prevent either of them from irrigating with any water he wishes.

If buildings are erected on kharaj land, that is houses or shops, the kharaj is still due as it is up to the owner of the land to derive benefit from it as he wishes; Abu Hanifah, however, annuls it unless the land is planted. My view is that if the building is needed for the cultivator of the kharaj land to reside in – in order to carry out the cultivation, then the kharaj is not payable on this portion as the cultivator can only reside by building a place in which to live; the kharaj, however, is exacted if this exceeds a basic need. If kharaj land is rented out or lent, the kharaj is payable by the owner but not by the person renting or borrowing, although Abu Hanifah says the opposite.

If the tax collector and the owner of the land dispute as to the status of the land and the collector claims that it is kharaj land while the owner that it is 'ushr land and both their claims are possible, then the word of the owner is accepted, not that of the collector – although if he is suspected in any way then he should take an oath by way of confirmation. It is permitted, in such disputes, to have recourse to the records of the Sultan's diwan-offices if their accuracy is known and the scribes are trustworthy; such disputes are rare, except about the boundaries between different types of land.

If the owner of the land claims to have paid the kharaj, his word is not accepted – although if he claims to have paid the 'ushr, it is. It is permitted to check on payment of the kharaj in the records of the Sultan's diwan offices if they are known to be correct – as long as customary practice in the matter is considered. If a person has difficulties in paying the kharaj, he is accorded a delay until he is able to do so. According to Abu Hanifah, it is obligatory only on someone who is able to pay, and anyone who is not is exempt. Anyone who delays payment when able to pay is locked up, unless goods of his are found which are then sold for him to pay his kharaj, as in the case of debts. If nothing other than the kharaj land of his is found, then a portion of it is sold on his behalf for an amount equalling the kharaj, if the Sultan considers this sale permissible; if he does not, then it is rented out for him and the kharaj is taken from the proceeds of the person renting it; if the rent amounts to more than the amount, the excess is for the owner, if it is less, then he owes the shortfall.

If the person in charge of the land is incapable of cultivating it, he is asked either to rent it out or to renounce it in favour of someone who can; it is not left and abandoned, even if the kharaj is paid, lest it become a wilderness and a dead land.

The validity of the kharaj-agent's authority is established by his being a free, trustworthy and capable person; his capacities may vary, however, in accordance with the differing nature of his authority: if he is responsible for exacting the kharaj, then he should be a faqih and a man of ijtihad; if he is only responsible for its collection, his authority is valid even if he is not a faqih or a mujtahid. The wages of the kharaj agent are taken from the kharaj revenue just as the zakah agent is paid from the zakah revenue, from the portion reserved for the agents – as are the wages of those responsible for making assessments. As for those who distribute (*qassaam*), the fuqaha differ about them: ash-Shafi'i, may Allah have mercy on him, says that the wages of the distributors for both the 'ushr and the kharaj are taken from the revenue received from both of them by the Sultan. Abu Hanifah says that both their wages are taken from the total of the measured quantity received, while Sufyan ath-Thawri says that the wages for the kharaj are paid by the Sultan while the wages of the 'ushr are paid by the people of the land. Malik, however, says that the 'ushr wages are paid by those of the land and the kharaj wages taken from the total revenue collected.

$$*$$
$$*\quad *$$

The kharaj is a tax whose amount is quantifiable and based on measurements which are known by means of three elements: namely the measurement – based on the cubit – used to determine the area, the value of the dirham used in payment, and the type of measure used to assess the produce.

As for the *jareeb* (surface area) it amounts to ten *qasabah* (fathoms) squared; the *qafeez* is ten qasabah by one qasabah; the *'asheer* is one qasabah by one qasabah and a *qasabah* is six cubits; so the jareeb is three thousand and six hundred square cubits; and the qafeez is three hundred and sixty cubits that is a tenth of a jareeb; and the 'asheer is thirty six square cubits, that is a tenth of a qafeez.

As for the cubit, there are seven kinds: **1.** the shortest being the *qadiyyah*; **2.** then the *yusufiyyah*; **3.** then the *sawda*; **4.** then the lesser *hashimiyyah*, that is the *bilaliyyah*; **5.** then the greater *hashimiyyah*, that is the *ziyadiyyah;* **6.** then the *'umariyyah;* **7.** then the *mizaniyyah.*

As for the qadiyyah it is also called the house cubit and it is less than the sawda cubit by a finger and two thirds; the first to establish it was Ibn Abi Layla the Qadi and this is the one used by the people of Kilwadha.

As for the yusufiyyah it is the one used by the qadis of Madinat as-Salaam (Baghdad) to measure the houses and it is less than the sawda by two thirds of a finger; and the first to establish its use was Abu Yusuf the Qadi.

As for the sawda, it is longer than the house cubit by a finger and two thirds, and the first to establish its use was ar-Rashid, may Allah have mercy on him, who took its measure from the cubit of a black servant guarding him; and this is used to measure material, trade goods and buildings and for measuring the height of the Nile.

As for the smaller hashimiyyah, that is the bilaliyyah, it is longer than the sawda by two fingers and two thirds; it was instigated by Bilal ibn Abi Burda and it is said that it is the cubit of his grandfather Abu Musa al-Ash'ari, may Allah have mercy on him, and it is less than the ziyadiyyah by three quarters of a tenth; it is used by the people of Basra and Kufa.

As for the greater hashimiyyah, that is the king's cubit, the first to call it a hashimiyyah was al-Mansur, may Allah have mercy on him: it is longer than the sawda by five fingers and two thirds of a finger, that is, it represents a sawda plus a tenth and an eighth and the lesser hashimiyyah has three quarters of a tenth less than the greater. It is also called a ziyadiyyah because it was used by Ziyad as a measure for the land of Sawad and it is the one used by the people of Ahwaz.

The 'umariyyah is based on that of 'Umar ibn al-Khattab, may Allah be pleased with him with which he measured the land of Sawad. Musa ibn Talhah said: "I saw the cubit of 'Umar Ibn al-Khattab, may Allah have mercy on him, with which he measured the land of the Sawad and it was the length of the forearm and a palm and the outstretched thumb." Al-Hakam ibn 'Uyaynah said that 'Umar, may Allah be pleased with him, added up the longest, the shortest and the average cubits, then divided them by three, and added a palm-length and an outstretched thumb; then he sealed each end of the measure with lead and sent it to Hudhayfah and 'Uthman ibn Hunayf who used it to measure the Sawad; the first person to use it after this was 'Umar ibn Hubayrah.

The mizaniyyah is equal to two sawdas plus two-thirds and two-thirds of a finger: the first to establish it was al-Ma'mun, may Allah be pleased with him, and it is used to measure the miles between post-stages, houses, markets and the lengths of rivers and wells.

✻

✻ ✻

As for the dirham, its weight and quality of metal must be known: as for its weight, it was established that under Islam it was six daniqs and that ten dirhams weighed seven mithqals. There is a difference of opinion as to how this weight was established. Some explain it by saying that at the time of the Persians three types of dirham were minted: one weighing a mithqal of twenty *qiraat*, the second of twelve qiraat and the third of ten qiraat. When Islam required a measure for the zakah, the average was taken of the three weights, (forty-two in total) thus making fourteen qiraat, on average, to a mithqal. When the Islamic dirhams were minted based on the average weight of the three weights, it was said that ten dirhams equalled seven mithqal, which in fact was so. Others said that the reason was that when 'Umar ibn al-Khattab, may Allah have mercy on him, saw the different dirhams – amongst them the *baghli* of eight daniq, the *tabari* of four, the *maghribi* of three, the *yemeni* of one daniq – then he said: "Find out which is used most amongst the people, both the strongest and the weakest among them;" as it was found to be the baghli and the tabari, he added both together amounting to twelve daniqs and divided it in half, that is six daniqs and so made the Islamic dirham of six daniqs. When three sevenths are added to the latter a mithqal is obtained and when there are three tenths below a mithqal it is a dirham, and ten dirhams is equal to seven mithqals and ten mithqals is fourteen dirhams and two sevenths.

As for the quality of the metal it must be pure silver; any of alloy are not legal currency. As the empire of the Persians became corrupted so did their currency but when Islam came, Persian coins of impure gold and silver still continued as currency as if they were real pure ones. Their impurity was tolerated as it was of no significance to them until the Islamic dirhams were minted and the impure became clearly distinguishable from the pure.

There is a difference of opinion as to who made the first minting in Islam. Sa'id ibn al-Musayyab said that the first person to mint engraved dirhams was 'Abd al-Malik ibn Marwan and that up until then the dirhams had been the *rumiyyah*, the *khusriyyah* and, in small quantities, the *himriyyah*. Abu'z-Zinad related that 'Abd al-Malik ibn Marwan then ordered al-Hajjaj to mint dirhams in Iraq and he did so in 74 AH. Al-Mada'ini says, however, that al-Hajjaj had them minted at the end of 75 AH and then 'Abd al- Malik ordered them to be minted in the surrounding regions in 76 AH.

It was said that al-Hajjaj did not use metal of an absolute purity and had **"Allah is One, Allah is Eternal"** written on them. They were called *makruh* (disliked) and there is a difference of opinion as to why they were designated thus: some say that the fuqaha disliked them because of the Qur'an on them – lest people in a state of ritual impurity carried them. Others say that the non-Arabs disliked their lack of purity and designated them accordingly. After al-Hajjaj, it was 'Umar ibn Hubayrah who became governor (of Iraq) during the reign of Yazid ibn 'Abd al-Malik and he had coins of a better quality minted; he was succeeded by Khalid ibn 'Abdallah al-Qasri who took great pains to ensure their quality; after him, Yusuf ibn 'Umar had others minted and was extremely meticulous in ensuring their good quality: thus the *hubayriyyah*, the *khalidiyyah* and the *yusufiyyah* were the best coins from the Umayyads and al-Mansur, may Allah be pleased with him, did not accept any other for payment of the kharaj.

Yahya ibn an-Nu'man al-Ghifari narrates from his father that Mus'ab ibn az-Zubayr was the first, on the order of 'Abdallah ibn az-Zubayr, to have dirhams minted in 70 AH, in the manner of Khusroes; on one side was "blessing" (barakah) and on the other "Allah". Then a year later, al-Hajjaj altered it and had "In the name of Allah" written on one side and "al-Hajjaj" on the other. Pure gold and silver coins free from adulteration were what were accepted as legal currency. Those minted with the mark of the Sultan, whose purity could be relied on, for the absence of any counterfeited or substituted material was guaranteed, were accepted as authentic – but not silver pieces or gold ingots as the latter cannot be relied on unless melted down, refined, and minted in an acceptable form; it is for this reason that this coinage has been established as the currency for repayment of any debt regarding the prices of things sold and the value of baled goods.

If there are minted coins of varying value – although accepted by all as good – and if the kharaj official demands the ones with the highest value, then they should be examined: if they are minted by the reigning Sultan, one is obliged to accept his demand as any refusal would represent a lack of obedience towards the Sultan; if they are of another mint, then they must be further examined: if they are the same coins as were accepted by the previous official, one should respond to his demand, following the preceding instance as an example; if they were not taken by the previous official, the present demand for them is fraudulent and unjust.

There is no obligation to accept broken dirhams and dinars as there is the possibility of mistaking their identity or their being adulterated: for this reason their value is less than whole, minted coins. The fuqaha differ as to why they are disliked (makruh) when broken. Malik and most of the Madinan fuqaha consider they are disliked as they constitute one of the elements contributing to **"corruption on earth"** and that those responsible are to be blamed. It is narrated that the Prophet, may the peace and blessing of Allah be upon him, forbad the breaking of coins (sikkah) of the Muslims which were currency.

The word "sikkah" refers to the die of iron with which the dirham is minted and so minted dirhams are called sikkah.

The Umayyad rulers disliked this practice of breaking coins to such an excessive degree that it is narrated that Marwan ibn al-Hakam had a man's hand cut off after he had cut up a Persian dirham; this, however, is a quite vindictive act and there is no justification for it in the interpretation of the law. Waqidi narrates that when Abban ibn 'Uthman was in charge of Madinah he inflicted thirty strokes on those guilty of cutting up dirhams and had them paraded around the town; he also said: "This is what we do to those who cut them up, who recast them or who add some base metal to them." If the situation was as Waqidi describes, then what Abban ibn 'Uthman did was not a vindictive act as he did not exceed the bounds of a discretionary punishment thereby; he was entitled to inflict a discretionary punishment on someone acting in a fraudulent manner. As for what Marwan did, it was an unjust and vindictive act.

Abu Hanifah and the fuqaha of Iraq consider that it is not makruh to cut them. Salih ibn Ja'far relates from Ubayy ibn Ka'b that Allah's words, **"Or that we should cease dealing with our property as we wish"** (Qur'an 11: 89), refer to the cutting of dirhams. Ash-Shafi'i, may Allah have mercy on him, says that it is not makruh if it is done out of need, but it is when there is no need, as anything which causes damage to property is a waste. Ahmad ibn Hanbal says that if the name of Allah is on it, it is makruh to cut it while if it is not it then is not. As for the hadith narrating the prohibition of cutting sikkah, Muhammad ibn 'Abdallah al-Ansari, the Qadi of Basra interprets it as a prohibition against cutting them up to reduce them to ingot-form: some people do not want to leave coins in their original form – as currency – as they would be susceptible to being used up for (day to day) expenses. Others consider that the prohibition refers to their being broken down to be used for making containers and ornaments, while still others, that it refers to a prohibition from cutting off the edges of the coins with scissors: such coins were used in transactions at the outset of Islam with their edges cut off but any payment made using them was in fact at a discount, not the full price.

As for the measure (scoop), then if the kharaj is of a muqasamah type (paid, proportionally, in kind) then any qafeez scoop which amounts to the payment required may be used; if, however, the kharaj is a specific amount, then it has been narrated that the qafeez imposed by 'Uthman ibn Hunayf on the territory of Sawad and approved of by 'Umar, may Allah be pleased with him, was a measure used by them known as *shaborqan*. Yahya ibn Adam says that it is also known as al-makhtum al-Hajjaji and it is said that it weighed thirty ritl (pounds).

If the imposition of the kharaj as a specific measure is initiated in a particular country, one should take care to use the measure most commonly in use amongst the people of that country.

Chapter 14
The Different Statuses of the Regions

The territory of Islam may be divided into three types: the Haram, the Hijaz and all other territories.

As for the Haram, it comprises Makkah and the surrounding areas which are recognised as inviolate. Allah, may He be exalted, mentions it by two names in His Book: Makkah and Bakkah, mentioning the first in His words: **"He it is who has restrained their hands from reaching you and your hands from reaching them, in the valley of Makkah after he had given you victory over them"** (Qur'an 48: 24). The word "Makkah" is derived from a word meaning "to suck the marrow from the bone, to extract it" as it sucks out the corrupt from itself, according to what al-Asma'i has narrated, who cites the following poem written as a kind of homage (*talbiyah*):

O Makkah, the sucker of the corrupt, suck – but not those who reside nor those who are strong.

Bakkah is mentioned in His words: **"Surely the first House established for mankind was the one in Bakkah as a blessing"** (Qur'an 3: 90). Al-Asma'i says that it was called Bakkah as the people there jostle each other, that is, push each other and he cites the following:

When a bad humour seizes the person who drinks with you then leave him until he is jostled.

There is a difference of opinion regarding these two names: some say that they are two names for the same thing as the Arabs substitute for the "mim" a "baa," pronouncing *lazim* as *lazib*, because the two sounds are closely situated (in the mouth), and this is the opinion of Mujahid; others, however, say that they are two names for two different things as a difference in names necessarily indicates a difference in what is named. Those who are of this opinion, however, differ as to what they refer to: either that Makkah refers to the name of the whole area and that Bakkah is only the House, and this is the

227

opinion of Ibrahim an-Nakha'i and Yahya ibn Abi Ayyub, or that Makkah refers to the whole of the Haram and Bakkah to the Mosque, and this is the opinion of az-Zuhri and Zayd ibn Aslam.

Mus'ab ibn 'Abdallah az-Zubayri relates that Makkah, during the time of the Jahiliyyah, was called Salah (peace) because of the security it enjoyed, and he cites the following lines from Abu Sufyan ibn Harb ibn Umayyah addressed to ibn al-Hadrami:

> *O Abu Matar come to Salah, and table-companions from the Quraysh will suffice you; you will be a guest in a town whose honour dates from an age past and you will rest assured that no army chief will visit you.*

Mujahid narrates that among the other names of Makkah is Umm Zahm and al-Baassah: the former refers to the fact that the people are crowded there and jostle each other; the latter refers to the crushing of those who leave the straight path there and that they are broken and destroyed, the word being the same as in Allah's words, **"and the mountains are crushed to powder"** (Qur'an 56: 5). The word an-Naassah has also been reported, its meaning referring to the fact that it repulses those who leave the straight path, that is, it drives them out and forces them into exile.

The origin of Makkah's inviolability lies in the importance that Allah, subhanahu, has attached to the inviolability of its House, his establishing it as the Mother of cities and His establishing it expressly for this House, the foundations of which He commanded to be set up and which He has made a Qiblah for His slaves – as He himself has said: **"So that you might warn the Mother of Cities and those around it"** (Qur'an 6: 92). Ja'far ibn Muhammad narrates from his father, Muhammad ibn 'Ali, may Allah have mercy on them, that the reason for the establishment of the House and its circumambulation was that Allah said to the angels: **"'Surely I am establishing a Khalifah on earth;' they said, 'Are You establishing therein someone who will work corruption in it and will shed blood while we glorify You with praise and we honour Your sanctity?' He replied, 'Surely I know what you do not know'"** (Qur'an 2: 28). Allah thus became angry with them; they sought refuge in the Throne and they went round it seven times so that their Lord might be content with them again; He was content with them and He said to them, "Build a house for Me on earth in which those among the sons of Adam with whom I am angry may find refuge and around which they may make tawaf just as you did around the Throne so that I may be satisfied with those that do it." And so they built this House for Him and it was the first

House which was established for the people as Allah says: **"Surely the first House to be established for the people was that of Bakkah, as a blessing and a guidance for all the worlds"** (Qur'an 3: 96).

The people of knowledge do not differ as to its being the first House established for the people for the purpose of worship although they do differ as to whether it was the first to be built for another purpose. Al-Hasan and a group of others say that there were many other houses before this one, while Mujahid and Qatadah say that there were no others before it. As for His words, **"as a blessing"**, there are two interpretations: the first, that its blessing derives from the reward contained in making it one's goal; and the second, that it refers to the security enjoyed by those entering it, for even wild animals such that the gazelle and the wolf live side by side in it. The words, **"as a guidance for all the worlds"**, also have two interpretations: the first, a guidance for them towards His tawhid (an understanding of His oneness); and the second, towards His worship on the Hajj and in the prayer. **"In it there are clear signs like that of the Station of Ibrahim; those who enter it are safe"** (Qur'an 3: 91). The sign relating to the Station of Ibrahim refers to the imprint of his feet on the hard rock, and the sign referring to other than this refers to the security from fear and the awe inspired in those who see it, the fact that the birds avoid flying over it and the swift punishment of those who behave insolently there, like the Companions of the Elephant in the pre-Islamic era; there is the fact, too, that it held such a high place in the hearts of the Arabs of that era and anyone entering it – who was not of the People of the Book and who did not follow any law-abiding religion – was granted safety: indeed a man from among them caught sight of the killer of his brother and father there but did not demand requital – so all these are signs from Allah ta'ala, which He has placed in the hearts of His slaves.

As for the security which it provided at the time of Islam this is referred to in His words, **"and whoever enters it is in safety"**; this has two interpretations: the first, that he is safe from the Fire, and this is the opinion of Yahya ibn Ja'dah; the second, that he is safe from being killed – as Allah has obliged all those entering it to be in a state of ihram and has prohibited them from being in a state of ihlal (that is, man's normal situation). The Messenger, may the peace and blessings of Allah be upon him, said on entering it the year of its conquest in an ihlal state: "It has been permitted for me (in this state) for an hour of a day but not for anyone else before me, and it will not be permitted for anyone else after me." Then Allah says: **"The people have an obligation to Allah to make a Hajj to the House, those that are able to find a**

way there" (Qur'an 3: 91). Thus He made the Hajj for Him an obligation after it had become a qiblah (direction) of the prayer – as praying towards the Ka'bah was made an obligation in 2 AH and the Hajj was made an obligation in 6 AH.

As there are two fundamental acts of worship connected to the Ka'bah at Makkah and as its inviolability makes it different from all other cities, we must describe it in detail and then mention the ruling concerning its inviolability. As for its construction, the person responsible for building it after the Flood was Ibrahim, on whom be peace, as Allah says of him: **"And when Ibrahim set up the foundations of the House, together with Isma'il, saying, 'O our Lord, accept our supplication, for surely You are the Hearer, the Knower'"** (Qur'an 2: 121). The fact that they both made this request to Him for acceptance is proof that they had been commanded to erect the building. It is called the Ka'bah because of its height, derived from the saying, "The woman *ka'abat*" meaning her breasts were prominent, and also the word *ka'b*, denoting the ankle bone, because of its prominence. After Ibrahim, may Allah bless him and grant him peace, the Ka'bah was with the tribes of Jurhum and the 'Amaliqah and stayed with them until their disappearance. 'Amir ibn al-Harith said of them:

> *It is as if there never was an intimate friend or people talking in the night at Makkah from the time of the al-Hajun to that of as-Safa, although we were there, but the alternating nights and the changing times have brought us far from it.*

These were followed by the Quraysh who seized the Haram when they became numerous after having been few and when they became powerful after having been insignificant – and thus paved the way for Allah's subsequent manifesting of prophethood amongst them. The first to renew the construction of the Ka'bah from amongst the Quraysh after Ibrahim, on whom be peace, was Qusayy ibn Kilab who covered it with a roof of *doum* wood and palm branches. Al-A'sha said:

> *I swear by the two robes of the monk of Syria and by the (Ka'bah) built by Qusayy, his forefather (Ibrahim) and ibn Jurhum: if the fires of enmity break out between us, he will leave me on the back of Shayham.*

Thereafter the Quraysh reconstructed it, at a time when the Messenger was twenty-five years old. The latter witnessed its construction and when its door was being established on the ground, Abu Hudhayfah ibn Mughirah said: "O people, raise the door of the Ka'bah so that entry can only be made by ladder; then only those persons you want to enter will enter, for if anyone comes you dislike, then you can throw things at him and he will fall and that will be an example to those who see it." The Quraysh did as he said. The reason for their rebuilding it was that it had fallen into ruin – although it was still above a man's height; they wanted to make it higher: the sea had thrown up a boat of a Roman trader at Jiddah and so they recovered its wood; there was also a snake in the Ka'bah feared by people and it came out on the wall of the Ka'bah; then a bird descended and snatched it up. The Quraysh said: "We hope that Allah will be pleased with what we want." They thus destroyed it and rebuilt it from the ship's wood.

It stayed like this until the day when Ibn az-Zubayr was besieged in the mosque by al-Husayn ibn Numayr and the army of Syria: they fought Ibn az-Zubayr in 64 AH during the time of Yazid ibn Mu'awiyyah; one of his men had attached a flaming torch to the top of his lance: a violent wind caused a spark to fly off which landed on the covering of the Ka'bah and it caught fire; the fire spread up the walls, blackened them and stones fell off. When Yazid died and Husayn ibn Numayr withdrew, 'Abdallah ibn az-Zubayr consulted his companions as to whether it should be demolished and then reconstructed; Jabir ibn 'Abdallah and 'Ubaid ibn 'Umayr supported the idea while 'Abdallah ibn 'Abbas was against it, saying: "Do not destroy the House of Allah;" then Ibn az-Zubayr said: "Can you not see the pigeons are alighting on the walls of the House and the stones are falling down: would you repair your own house but not the House of Allah? Surely I shall demolish it tomorrow. I have heard that the Messenger of Allah said, 'If I had the means I would reconstruct it on the foundations of Ibrahim and I would put two doors in it, one to the east and one to the west.'" He then asked Aswad whether he had heard anything about this from A'ishah, may Allah be pleased with her, and he replied: "Yes, she informed me that the Prophet, may the peace and blessings of Allah be upon him, had told her, 'The means at the disposal of your people have diminished so restrict your expenditure; if their time of disbelief were not so recent I would have demolished it and would have restored what they had abandoned.'" Ibn az-Zubayr's opinion that it should be demolished thus prevailed, and the next morning he sent someone to 'Ubaid ibn Umayr but it was said that he was sleeping; he then sent someone again and he woke him up saying: "Have you not heard that the Messenger of Allah, may the peace and blessings of Allah be upon him, said, 'The earth cries out to Allah when the people of knowledge sleep during the early morning'?" He then set about demolishing it and Ibn 'Abbas sent someone to him to say: "If you are demolishing it then do not leave the people without a qiblah." When it had been demolished, the people said: "How should we pray without the qiblah?" Jabir and Zayd said: "Pray towards the site itself for that is the actual qiblah." Ibn az-Zubayr then ordered the site to be covered and placed the Black Stone in a chest wrapped in a piece of silk. 'Ikrimah said: "I saw it: it was a cubit or more and the inside was white like silver." The ornaments of the Ka'bah were placed in a store of the Ka'bah and guarded. When he wanted to begin reconstruction, he had the al-Hateem side dug out until the foundations of Ibrahim, on whom be peace, were exposed; he gathered the people around saying: "Do you realise that these are the foundations of Ibrahim?" They replied: "Yes," and he had the building constructed on these foundations and he included six cubits of the Hijr in one part and left four cubits of it out in another, although according to some he included six but left out three. He placed two doors in it at floor level, one to the east and the other to the west such that one entered through one and left through the other, and they were both ornamented with gold strips and the keys were also made of gold.

Among the Qurayshi men who participated in the construction was Abu'l-Jahm ibn Hudhayfah al-'Adawi who said: "I have twice worked on the construction of the Ka'bah, once during the Jahiliyyah with the strength and usefulness of a young man and again in Islam with the strength of an old, failing man."

Az-Zubayr ibn Bakkar narrates that 'Abdallah ibn az-Zubayr found some green stone slabs which had lain over a tomb and that 'Abdallah ibn Safwan had said that it was the tomb of the Prophet Ismail and that he avoided moving those stones. Then, during the rule of Ibn az-Zubayr, it stayed in this state until the day when al-Hajjaj came to fight, laid siege to him in the mosque and had ballistas set up against him until he seized it; as the stones from the ballista had split the building of the Ka'bah, al-Hajjaj, on the orders of 'Abd al-Malik ibn Marwan, demolished it and had it rebuilt: in doing so he recovered the stones from it and reconstructed it as it had been built by the Quraysh. 'Abd al-Malik ibn Marwan said: "I would have preferred to have entrusted Ibn az-Zubayr with the business of the reconstruction of the Ka'bah as he had done it before."

As for the covering of the Ka'bah, it is narrated that Abu Hurairah, may Allah be pleased with him, related from the Prophet, may Allah bless him and grant him peace, that he said: "The first person to cover the House was

Sa'd al-Yamani." After this the Messenger of Allah, may the peace and blessing of Allah be upon him, covered it with Yemeni cloth; then 'Umar ibn al-Khattab and 'Uthman, may Allah be pleased with them, covered it with Coptic cloth; then Yazid ibn Mu'awiyyah covered it with Persian brocade. Muharib ibn Dithar, however, relates that the first to cover the Ka'bah with brocade was Khalid ibn Ja'far ibn Kilab who had seized a caravan during the Jahiliyyah in which there was some brocade and this he hung on the Ka'bah; then Ibn az-Zubayr and al-Hajjaj covered it with brocade; then the Umayyads covered it for a certain period with robes from the people of Najran – given as a tribute following the war against them – and put some brocade on top of it; al-Mutawakkil renewed the marble of the Ka'bah, surrounded it with silver, covered all the walls and the roof with gold and then clothed the columns in brocade; the brocade has continued to be used as a covering during the whole of the Abbasid dynasty.

As for the Masjid al-Haram, it was originally the space surrounding the Ka'bah used by those doing the tawaf and it was not encompassed by a wall at the time of the Messenger, may the peace and blessings of Allah be upon him, nor that of Abu Bakr, may Allah be pleased with him. When 'Umar became the Khalifah, may Allah be pleased with him, and the number of people multiplied, he extended the Mosque by buying houses which he then had demolished and increased the space thereby; he even demolished the houses of some people adjacent to the mosque who had refused to sell: he had set aside a price for these houses which they later accepted. A low wall, less than a man's height was built around the mosque, and torches were placed on it. 'Umar, may Allah be pleased with him, was the first to put a wall around the mosque; when 'Uthman became Khalifah, may Allah be pleased with him, he purchased more houses and enlarged the mosque thereby. When he wanted to take the people's houses (who were unwilling to sell), he too put aside the price of their houses but they came and clamoured for him at the House. He then said: "Your audacity is the result of my forbearance towards you. 'Umar did this to you, may Allah be pleased with him, and you affirmed and accepted it." He then ordered them to be put in prison until 'Abdallah ibn Khalid ibn Asad spoke on their behalf and he released them. 'Uthman had galleries constructed in the mosque when he enlarged it. Then al-Waleed ibn 'Abd al-Malik enlarged the mosque and had stone and marble columns brought in; then al-Mansur, may Allah have mercy on him increased it further with more construction and then al-Mahdi did the same after him and it has stayed in this state until today.

As for Makkah, it was not a significant place of habitation and after the Jurhum and the 'Amaliqah, the Quraysh pastured their flocks in the mountains and valleys but did not go outside its inviolable area (*haram*), attaching themselves to the Ka'bah so as to remain in control of it: they particularly held to the Haram by virtue of their long residence in it and considered that it would be of importance for them in the future. When their numbers grew and their leadership was established, their aspirations became stronger and they became aware that they would be eminent among the Arabs. Those of excellence, judgement and experience among them foresaw that it would be for taking leadership in the deen and the establishment of future prophethood – as their attachment to the Ka'bah was particularly apparent in matters of the deen.

The first person to sense this and to receive inspiration in the matter was Ka'b ibn Lu'ayy ibn Ghalib. The Qurayshis would gather with him every Friday, the day known as 'Arubah during the Jahiliyyah, and the day which Ka'b called Jumu'ah – and according to az-Zubayr ibn Bakkar, he would address the Quraysh saying: "So listen and realise and understand: know that the night passes on and the day declaims; the earth is a cradle and the mountains are pegs, the sky is an edifice and the stars are banners; the first are as the last; the male and female are a couple until the day when all will shake; so maintain close ties with your family, guard your relations and make your wealth bear fruit; have you ever seen someone who has perished return, or a dead person rise up? The (true) abode is ahead of you and whatever one may think it is not what you say. Decorate your Haram, treat it with awe and hold firmly to it for a great news will come to it and a noble prophet will emerge from it;" then he recited:

Day and night bring new events every moment; day and night have become one for us; they bring events upon us and also blessings which cover us with their abundance; vicissitudes and news in which those involved are overwhelmed, they contain knots which cannot be undone; suddenly the Prophet, Muhammad, will appear, who will give news of which he will be the authentic source.

Then he said: "By Allah, if I had hearing and sight, hands and feet, I would move with the speed of a camel and the strutting of a stallion," and he declaimed the following:

If only I could witness his call being plainly made at a time when my tribe will be seeking humbly for the truth.

This came from an understanding whose origin derives from inspiration – when the intellects imagine something which then becomes true, when the spirit conjures up an image which then comes into being.

Then the leadership after him passed to Qusayy ibn Kilab who built the assembly house to pass judgements between the Quraysh; thereafter it became a place for their consultations and where the banners were knotted whenever they waged war. Al-Kalbi said that it was the first building to be erected in Makkah, but thereafter the people built other houses to live in; the nearer the time of Islam approached, the stronger they became and the greater their numbers: so much so that the Bedouin Arabs inclined to them. Thus the first presentiment that they would take over the leadership of the Arabs came true. Then Allah, subhanahu, raised his Prophet as a Messenger and the second presentiment, concerning the arrival of a Prophet amongst them, came true. Those amongst them who accepted the guidance believed in him and those who refuted it denied him. When the harassment of him increased, he made Hijrah, may the peace and blessings of Allah be upon him – until the day that he returned victorious eight years after this Hijrah.

There is a difference of opinion as to whether he entered Makkah, the year of the Conquest, by force or peacefully, although they are agreed that he did not take any of their wealth and did not take any captives. Abu Hanifah and Malik consider that he did enter by force and that he renounced the booty and set the captives free: thus when an Imam conquers a town by force, he may renounce the booty and set the captives free. Ash-Shafi'i considers that he entered peacefully, having made a treaty with Abu Sufyan which stipulated that, "those who closed their doors would be safe and those who clung to the covering of the Ka'bah would be safe and those entering the house of Abu Sufyan would be safe," – all that is, except for six persons who would be put to death even if they did cling to the covering of the Ka'bah, and they have been mentioned above. It was because of this peace treaty that no booty and no captives were taken. The Imam may not, if he has conquered a town by force, renounce the booty or free the captives – because of Allah's claim in the matter and that of the booty-takers. Thus Makkah and the Haram, as they were not taken as booty, are treated as 'ushr lands, if they are cultivated; it is not permitted for the kharaj to be imposed on them.

The fuqaha differ as to the sale and renting of the houses of Makkah; Abu Hanifah prohibits their sale while he permits them to be rented outside the time of Hajj; he prohibits both during the time of the Hajj because of the narration of al-A'mash, from Mujahid that the Prophet, may the peace and blessings of Allah be upon him, said: "Makkah is an inviolate area (*haram*): it is not permitted to sell its large buildings nor to rent its houses." Ash-Shafi'i, may Allah have mercy on him, considers that it is permitted to sell and rent them, as the Messenger of Allah, peace and blessings of Allah be upon him, let the status of their ownership after the advent of Islam be the same as that before Islam and he did not take their property as booty: he thus did not oppose their rights therein and they would buy and sell to each other before Islam just as they did afterwards. The assembly-house, the first house to be built in Makkah came into the hands of 'Abd ad-Dar ibn Qusayy, after Qusayy himself and Mu'awiyyah purchased it at the time of Islam from 'Ikrimah ibn Amir ibn Hashim ibn 'Abd ad-Dar ibn Qusayy and made it the House of Amirate: the purchase of this house was exceedingly famous, the one about which the people spoke the most, and none of the Companions rejected the sale. 'Umar and 'Uthman, may Allah be pleased with them, also bought houses in Makkah which enabled them to enlarge the mosque, the owners receiving a price for them: if the transaction had not been permitted they would not have spent the money belonging to the Muslims. This work (on the mosque) continued in this manner until today and all are in agreement that such precedents may be followed.

As for the narration of Mujahid, despite the omission of the name of the companion in its chain of narration, it is understood thereby that it is not permitted to sell the large buildings of Makkah to the detriment of their owners as they were not taken as booty and the right of property was not taken from those dwelling therein – and it is for this reason that they are not sold, and the rule is the same for renting.

As for the Haram, it refers to the area surrounding Makkah in all different directions: when coming from Madinah, beyond at-Tan'im by the houses of the Bani Nifar, at three miles distance; coming from Iraq, at the Munqati' pass at seven miles; coming from al-Ji'ranah at the mountain paths of the people of 'Abdallah ibn Khalid, at nine miles; coming from Ta'if, at a high point in the valley of Namirah, at seven miles; coming from Jiddah, at Munqati' al-'Asha'ir, at ten miles.

These are the boundaries which Allah has defined as Haram (inviolate) because of its inviolate character and because it is governed by a ruling which is different from other towns. Allah, ta'ala, says, **"And when Ibrahim said: 'O Lord, make this a place of security'"** (Qur'an 2: 120), referring to Makkah and its Haram, **"and provide its people with fruits"**, being a valley without cultivation, he was asking Allah ta'ala, that He grant safety and fertility for its inhabitants so that they might enjoy ease in their life by means of these two things. Allah responded to what he had asked and made it a Haram of, **"safety while those surrounding it were being held up and robbed"** (Qur'an 29: 67), and He brought fruits from all countries and gathered them together there.

There is a difference of opinion as to whether Makkah and its surroundings became an inviolate place of safety by virtue of Ibrahim's request, peace be upon him, or whether it was such before this. According to some, it had always been an inviolate place of safety, even before Ibrahim's request, on whom be peace, that is safe from tyrants, (unjust) rulers, eclipses and earthquakes; Ibrahim, peace be upon him, requested his Lord to make it inviolate and safe from drought and dearth and that He provide its inhabitants with various fruits; this is based on the narration of Sa'id ibn Abi Sa'id who said: "I heard Abu Shurayh al-Khuza'i say that when the Messenger of Allah conquered Makkah he got up and addressed the people, saying: 'O people, surely Allah has made Makkah a Haram the day He created the heavens and the earth and it will be an inviolate place until the Day of Raising Up. It is not permitted for anyone who believes in Allah and the Final Day to shed blood or to cut a tree therein; it will not become "a permitted place" (for fighting) for anyone after me and it will not be permitted, even for me, except at this moment, out of anger at its inhabitants. So it has returned to the state it had yesterday; may the person hearing this inform those who are absent: anyone who says that the Messenger of Allah has killed someone therein then say to them that Allah, ta'ala, permitted this for His Messenger but He has not permitted it for you.'"

Others say that Makkah was a "permitted place" before the supplication of Ibrahim, on whom be peace, just like any other city, and that it became a Haram because of his supplication and became a place of safety when he made it inviolate – just as Madinah became a Haram, after it had been "a permitted place", when the Messenger made it such. This we know from the tradition of al-Ashhab from Nafi' from Abu Hurairah who said that the Messenger of Allah, may the peace and blessings of Allah be upon him, said:

"Ibrahim, on whom be peace and blessings, was the slave of Allah and His Friend and I am the slave of Allah and His Messenger: surely Ibrahim made Makkah a Haram and surely I have made Madinah a Haram between its two *laaba* (boundary marks) for its acacias and for its game; no one will carry weapons for fighting in it and no one will cut any plants except as fodder for camels."

The Haram (of Makkah) is characterised by seven aspects which distinguish it from other cities: first, no one enters the Haram, approaching in the state of ihlal, unless he first takes on the state of ihram, be it for the Hajj or for the 'Umrah, after which he may revert back to the state of ihlal. Abu Hanifah, however, says that someone who does not want to make the Hajj or the 'Umrah may enter in the state of ihlal. But the Prophet's words, on whom be blessings and peace, as he entered Makkah in the year of the Conquest in a state of ihlal – "An hour of the day has been made halal for me while it will not be made halal for anyone after me" – prove that ihram is obligatory when entering it, except for those who enter repeatedly as a service to its people, like those bringing wood or water who leave in the morning and return in the evening; such people may enter it in the state of ihlal because it would be difficult for them to be in ihram every time they entered; the 'ulama of Makkah confirm that they can enter in ihlal and oppose those who would give a different ruling arguing that those who arrive in ihlal would be committing a wrong action for which there is no way to make amends (either by doing it again or compensating for it with a sacrifice); since repeating it would be impossible, for if a person left to do it again, the ihram which he renewed would be specific to his second entry and renewing his action for his first entry would be invalid; thus any attempt to make it up by doing it again is impossible and without effect; as for the sacrifice, this is not incumbent on him as the sacrifice is only obligatory to compensate for an incomplete rite and is not obligatory as a substitute for the rite itself.

Second, its inhabitants may not be attacked as the Messenger of Allah, may the peace and blessings of Allah be upon him, prohibited this. If they act outrageously towards honourable people, then some of the fuqaha go so far as to prohibit their being attacked, despite their outrageous acts – rather they should be constrained until they renounce their outrageous behaviour and return within the bounds of the people of justice. Most of the fuqaha, however, consider that they should be fought because of their rebellious acts if this will deter them from rebellion: fighting the rebellious is one of the demands of Allah ta'ala, which may not be ignored; moreover this should be upheld all the more rigorously in the Haram of Allah rather than showing laxness.

As for imposing the hadd-punishments in the Haram, ash-Shafi'i may Allah have mercy on him, considers that they should be imposed on those who merit them arguing that the fact that it is a Haram does not prevent this, irrespective of whether they incurred the hadd-punishment within Haram territory, or in territory outside it and then took refuge in the Haram. Abu Hanifah says that if they committed the wrong in the Haram then the hadd is imposed therein but if they were outside in the state of ihlal and then seek refuge in the Haram, it is not imposed on him while he remains in it; rather he is compelled to leave and then it is imposed on him;

Third, hunting is forbidden in it both to those in ihram and in ihlal state. Anyone who crosses into it and catches his prey therein must let it go again and if it perishes in his hands then he is liable for its compensation-price, just like someone who is in ihram. Likewise, if he throws from within the Haram and strikes his prey in the area outside it, he is liable for compensation as he killed it while in the Haram; if he throws from the area outside the Haram and strikes his prey in the Haram he is liable as the animal is killed in the Haram. If he hunts in the area outside the Haram, but then brings the game into the Haram, it is permitted for him, according to ash-Shafi'i, may Allah have mercy on him, although, according to Abu Hanifah, it is forbidden him. It is not prohibited to kill harmful creatures, be they wild animals or insects.

Fourth, it is forbidden to cut down any tree which Allah has caused to grow but it is not forbidden to cut those planted by man; nor is it forbidden to sacrifice domesticated animals or to let them feed on pasture. Compensatory payment must be paid for those trees which one is prohibited from cutting: a cow for a large tree, a sheep for a small one; a branch from either of them must be compensated for proportionally and planting a replacement for a cut tree does not exempt the person responsible from paying compensation;

Fifth, no person from amongst those who oppose Islam, be they dhimmis or protected by treaty, may enter the Haram – irrespective of whether they wish to be resident or are passing by – and this is the teaching of ash-Shafi'i, may Allah have mercy on him, and most of the fuqaha. Abu Hanifah, however, permits their entry as long as they do not take up residence although the words of Allah, ta'ala: **"The mushrikun are filthy and they are not to come close to the Haram mosque, after this year"** (Qur'an 9: 28) prohibit this. If a mushrik does enter, then he is given a discretionary punishment, if he did it without permission although it is not permitted to have him killed; if he has entered with permission, then the discretionary punishment is not inflicted on him, and the person who gave the permission is blamed and he is given a discretionary punishment if his rank demands it, and the mushrik is expelled and guaranteed safe passage. If the mushrik wants to enter the Haram to become a Muslim there, he is prevented from this until he has become a Muslim before entering; if a mushrik dies in the Haram, it is forbidden to bury him therein and he is buried in the territory outside it; if he has been buried in the Haram, he is transferred to the territory outside it unless the body has decomposed, in which case he is left there, as were the dead of the Jahiliyyah time.

It is permitted to allow them to enter other mosques as long as they do not wish to waste this opportunity by eating or sleeping there, in which case they are refused permission. Malik, however, says that they are not permitted to enter under any circumstances.

✳

✳ ✳

As for the Hijaz, al-Asma'i has said that this name (meaning barrier) refers to its acting as a barrier between Najd and Tihamah, while Ibn Kalbi says that it is called so because of the mountains that enclose it. Apart from the Haram within it, it is different from the other territories in four ways:

First, the mushrikun may not reside in it, be they dhimmis or people of treaty. Abu Hanifah, however, permits it - although 'Ubaidullah ibn 'Abdallah ibn 'Utbah ibn Mas'ud has narrated that A'ishah, may Allah be pleased with her, said that the last thing to be confirmed by the Messenger, may the peace and blessings of Allah be upon him, was that: "Two deens will not exist together in the Arab peninsula." 'Umar ibn al-Khattab, may Allah be pleased with him, expelled the dhimmis from the Hijaz, but accorded traders and artisans three days, after which they were expelled. This practice became current and established itself as law; the dhimmis were prevented from taking up residence in the Hijaz, but they could enter it as long as they did not stay in any place for more than three days; at the end of this term, they were sent to another place, where they could stay for another three days, but if they stayed for more than this, then they were given a discretionary punishment, unless they had a valid excuse;

Second, their corpses may not be buried there, and they are transferred elsewhere if this happens – as their burial would imply their continued presence and that they had become residents – unless the distance involved is too great and they would decompose, in which case it is permitted to leave them buried in cases of necessity;

Third, the Madinah of the Messenger in the Hijaz, may the peace and blessings of Allah be upon him, also has a Haram which is inviolate territory within special boundary marks: it is forbidden to hunt in it or to cut down its trees, just as in the Haram of Makkah. Abu Hanifah, however, permits all this and treats it as a town like any other - although in the above-mentioned hadith of Abu Hurairah, there is proof that the Haram of Madinah is inviolate. If someone kills its game or cuts down one of its trees, it is said by some that he must be stripped of his clothes in compensation, and by others, that he be given a discretionary punishment;

Fourth, the land of the Hijaz may be divided in two ways by virtue of the special fact that the Messenger of Allah himself, may the peace and blessings of Allah be upon him, conquered it:

A. This part refers to the Prophet's Sadaqat-wealth, may the peace and blessings of Allah be upon him, which he was entitled to take in two ways: the first, a fifth of the khums derived from the fay and the booty; and the second, four fifths of the fay accorded by Allah to His Messenger from what had been acquired by the Muslims while not mounted on horses or camels (i.e. without fight). Thus from what came to him from these to entitlements, he gave a small portion to some of his Companions, and retained the rest for his own expenses, and for the needs of the Muslims. When he died, however, may Allah bless him and grant him peace, the people differed as to the ruling in this matter: some considered that it was inherited from him, and that as such should be divided amongst the inheritors, just like any other property; others, however, considered that it should be made over to the Imam, who in effect had taken over responsibility from him for the defence of the territories of Islam and the jihad against the enemy; the majority of the fuqaha, however, say that this kind of wealth has an inviolate character, and that it is to be put to special use, that is, spent on various public needs;

B. Besides his Sadaqat-wealth there is the 'ushr-land which is not subject to the kharaj as it is either property taken as booty, or left to the original owners in return for their becoming Muslim – and in both cases, it is the 'ushr and not the kharaj which is exacted.

As for the sadaqat-wealth of the Prophet, on whom be blessings and peace, it is of a specific nature, being what he left after his death and as such well-known. It is of eight kinds:

First, the land which was the first to be acquired by the Messenger, may the peace and blessings of Allah be upon him, and which was assigned to him by the Jew Mukhayriq from the wealth of the Banu Nadir. Al-Waqidi narrates that he was a rabbi from among the learned men of the Banu Nadir who believed in the Messenger, may the peace and blessings of Allah be upon him, on the day of Uhud; he owned seven gardens, namely al-Manbat, as-Safiyah, ad-Dilal, al-Husna, Barqah, al-A'raaf and al-Masrabah, and he left them to the Messenger, may the peace and blessings of Allah be upon him, after making over the zakah-tax on them to him; he also fought with the Prophet at Uhud and died there, may Allah have mercy on him;

Second, this sadaqat comprises land from the Banu an-Nadir in Madinah; it was the first land which Allah accorded the Messenger, may the peace and blessings of Allah be upon him, as fay; he expelled them, but was lenient towards them and allowed them to carry as much as their camels could bear, as well as their arms; so they left with what their camels were carrying, to Khaybar and Syria, and abandoned all their land to the Messenger, may the peace and blessings of Allah be upon him, except what belonged to Yameen ibn 'Umayr and Abu Sa'd ibn Wahb, as they had both become Muslims before the victory and their Islam allowed them to keep all their wealth. The Messenger, may the peace and blessings of Allah be upon him, divided the rest of the property, besides the land, between the first of the Muhajirun, but not the Ansar – apart from Sahl ibn Hunayf and Abu Dujanah Simak Kharashah, because they drew attention to their poverty, and so he gave to them; as for the land, he reserved it for himself, and it became part of his Sadaqat-wealth which he disposed of as he wished, spending on his wives therefrom. Later 'Umar gave them to al-'Abbas and 'Ali, may Allah be pleased with them both, for them to dispose of;

Third, Fourth, and **Fifth,** are three of the eight forts of Khaybar: Na'im, al-Qamus, Shiqq, an-Natat, al-Kutaybah, al-Wateeh, as-Sulaalim, and the fort of as-Sa'b ibn Mu'adh. The first to be conquered by the Messenger of Allah was that of Na'im, where Mahmud ibn Maslamah, the brother of Muhammad ibn Maslamah, was killed; the second was al-Qamus, the fort of Ibn Abi al-Huqayq: among the captives taken was Safiyyah bint Huyay ibn Akhtab, whom the Messenger, may the peace and blessings of Allah be upon, chose to marry for himself - and she had been the wife of Kinanah ibn ar-Rabi' ibn Abu'l-Huqayq; he set her free and gave her this freedom as a dowry; the third was the fort of as-Sa'b ibn Mu'adh, the largest of the forts at Khaybar and the one containing the most wealth, food and animals; then Shiqq, an-Natat, and al-Kutaybah - these six being taken by force; then al-Wateeh and as-Sulaalim which were the last to be conquered and which were taken when terms were agreed after a siege lasting some ten days, during which the inhabitants requested to leave and be spared and this was accepted. The Prophet acquired three of these eight forts, those of al-Kutaybah, al-Wateeh and as-Sulaalim. The first he acquired as the khums (fifth) of the booty, but al-Wateeh and as-Sulaalim he was given by Allah as fay, since they were conquered by a peace-agreement: all three, both as khums and fay, became the absolute property of the Messenger, may the peace and blessings of Allah be upon him, and so he was entitled to give them away, as they formed part of his Sadaqat-wealth.

As for the five remaining forts, he divided them between the booty-takers and they included the two Khaybar valleys of as-Sareer and Hadir, which together represented eighteen portions. Those who shared in it numbered one thousand four hundred, that is, those who had taken part in al-Hudaybiy-yah, irrespective of whether they had been at Khaybar or not; no one had in fact been absent, except for Jabir ibn 'Abdallah, and he was given a portion like those who had participated. Amongst them were two hundred horsemen - and they were given six hundred parts, while one thousand two hundred portions were given to one thousand two hundred infantry: to each group of a hundred he gave a portion (of a hundred parts), so that Khaybar consisted of eighteen portions;

Sixth, this consists of a half of Fadak: when the Prophet, may the peace and blessings of Allah be upon him, conquered Khaybar, the people of Fadak approached him through the embassy of Muhayyisah ibn Mas'ud, in order to make a peace-agreement with him, in return for his having a half of their land and their date-palms – which they would work for him – and they would keep the other half. This half became part of his Sadaqat-wealth which was worked by them in return for half of its produce; the other half remained theirs until 'Umar ibn al-Khattab, may Allah be pleased with him, expelled them, along with the other dhimmis whom he expelled from the Hijaz – after having assessed the value of Fadak, and after giving them half of this, that is, sixty thousand dirhams; those who assessed it were Malik ibn at-Tayyihan, Sahl ibn Abi Haythamah and Zayd ibn Thabit; thus half of it remained part of

243

the Sadaqat-wealth of the Messenger, may the peace and blessings of Allah be upon him, and the other half was for the rest of the Muslims, although the use to which both halves are put now is the same;

Seventh, this consists of a third of the land of Wadi al-Qura as a third had belonged to the Banu 'Udhrah and two thirds to the Jews; then the Messenger of Allah, may the peace and blessings of Allah be upon him, made a peace agreement with them in return for a half, such that it was divided into thirds, one third for the Messenger of Allah, may the peace and blessings of Allah be upon him, which was part of his Sadaqat-wealth, a third for the Jews, and a third for the Bani 'Udhrah - until the time when 'Umar, may Allah be pleased with him, expelled the Jews and assessed what compensation they were due: this amounted to ninety thousand dinars which he gave to them; he said to the Banu 'Udhrah that if they wished, they could pay a half of what he had given and that he would give them a half of the land: they thus gave him forty-five thousand dinars, and so half of the Wadi became the property of the Banu 'Udhrah, and the other half was divided such that a third of it belonged to the Sadaqat-wealth of the Messenger, may the peace and blessings of Allah be upon him, and a sixth for the Muslims as a whole - although the use to which the whole of this half is now put is the same;

Eighth, this consists of the site of the market in Madinah known as Mahrudh. Marwan demanded it as a fief from 'Uthman, may Allah be pleased with him, and the people reproached him for it. It is possible that the fief was merely farmed out (to him), and not taken as a property which might have been a reason for his being allowed to do this.

These then are the eight types of Sadaqat-wealth reported by the biographers of the Prophet; the various aspects of this wealth have also been narrated by the authors of the accounts of the raiding parties; but Allah has more knowledge of the correctness of what we have mentioned.

As for his other properties besides these eight kinds of Sadaqat-wealth, al-Waqidi narrates that the Messenger of Allah, may the peace and blessings of Allah be upon him, inherited Umm Ayman the Abyssinian, whose name was Barakah, five camels and a flock of sheep and goats from his father, 'Abdallah: some say also his freed-slave, Shuqran and his son Salih, who were both at Badr. From his mother, Aminah bint Wahb az-Zuhriyyah, he inherited her house in which he was born, in the valley of the Banu 'Ali. From his wife Khadijah bint Khuwaylid, may Allah be pleased with her, he inherited her house in Makkah, between Safa and Marwa behind the perfume sellers, together with other properties. Hakeem ibn Hizam had bought Zayd ibn Harithah for Khadijah for four hundred dirhams from the 'Ukadh market; the Prophet asked her for him as a gift, and then set him free and married him off to Umm Ayman, who gave birth to 'Usamah after the beginning of prophethood. As for the two houses, 'Aqil ibn Abi Talib sold them after the Hijrah of the Messenger of Allah, may the peace and blessings of Allah be upon him; when he returned to Makkah for the final Hajj he was asked: "Which house will you stay in?" He said: "Has 'Aqil left us any property?" but he did not try to recover what 'Aqil had sold, as he had become his conqueror, and Makkah had been enemy territory at that time; thus he applied the ruling making him responsible for this loss, and so these two houses were excluded from his Sadaqat-wealth. As for the houses of his wives, he gave away to each the house they lived in and bequeathed it to them; if this gift was one of property, it is excluded from his Sadaqat-wealth, but if it was merely a gift of the right to residence, then it was still included in his Sadaqat-wealth. Today they constitute part of the mosque and I do not think that any part of them is outside it.

As for the movable effects of the Messenger of Allah, may the peace and blessings of Allah be upon him and his family, Hisham al-Kalbi narrates from 'Awanah ibn al-Hakam that Abu Bakr as-Siddiq gave away the armour, the riding beast and the sandals of the Messenger, may the peace and blessings of Allah be upon him, and said that the rest was given in sadaqah. Al-Aswadi reports that A'ishah, may Allah be pleased with her, said: "When the Messenger of Allah died, his breastplate was in pledge to a Jew for thirty saa' of wheat." If this was the breastplate known as al-Batra then it is reported that it was worn by al-Hussein ibn 'Ali, may Allah be pleased with both of them on, the day that he was killed, and that 'Ubaidullah ibn Ziyad took it; when al-Mukhtar killed 'Ubaidullah ibn Ziyad, the breastplate passed to 'Abbad ibn al-Husayn Handhali; then Khalid ibn 'Abdallah ibn Khalid ibn Usayd, the amir of Basra, requested it from 'Abbad, but the latter refused to give it to him, and so he then had him whipped a hundred times. Then 'Abd al-Malik ibn Marwan wrote to him saying: "The like of 'Abbad should not be whipped - rather he should have either been killed or pardoned." Thereafter the whereabouts of the breastplate were not known.

As for his cloak, the people differ about it. Abban ibn Tha'lab narrates that the Messenger of Allah, may the peace and blessings of Allah be upon him, had given it to Ka'b ibn Zuhayr and that Mu'awiyyah, may Allah be pleased with him, then bought it from him, and that this was the cloak worn by the Khulafa. Damra ibn Rabi'ah narrates that the Messenger of Allah, may the peace and blessings of Allah be upon him, gave this cloak to the people of Ayla in trust; then Sa'id ibn Khalid ibn Abi Awfa, who was the tax official among them on behalf of Marwan ibn Muhammad, took it from them and sent it to this Khalifah, and it remained among his treasures until it was taken from him after his death; it is said that Abu'l-Abbas as-Saffah bought it for three hundred dinars.

As for his staff, it was part of what was left by him which was treated as sadaqah; together with the cloak, it became one of the marks of Khilafah.

As for his signet ring it was worn after the Messenger of Allah by Abu Bakr, then by 'Umar, then by 'Uthman, may Allah be pleased with them, until the latter dropped it in a well and could not find it.

This then is a description of what was received from the Messenger of Allah as Sadaqat or inherited wealth.

✳

✳ ✳

As for all other land outside the Haram and the Hijaz, we have already said that it may be classified in four ways: first, that whose inhabitants have become Muslim and which is treated as 'ushr land; second, that which has been revived by the Muslims and as such becomes 'ushr land; third, that taken by force by the booty-takers and which is subject to the 'ushr; fourth, that whose inhabitants have entered into a treaty and it is considered that fay and the kharaj are imposed: this in turn may be divided into two parts: **A.** those with whom a treaty has been made in return for their renouncing their right to its ownership, in which case such land may not be sold and the is kharaj imposed in the form of a hire-charge, from which the inhabitants are not exempted if they become Muslim – as it is taken both from the Muslim and the dhimmi; **B.** those with whom a treaty is contracted on the understanding that they remain entitled to the property, in which case the kharaj is treated as jizyah from which they are exempt if they become Muslims, as it is only taken from dhimmis, but not from Muslims.

Having explained that such land is classified in this way, we shall explain the ruling applied to the Sawad territory, since it serves as a legal precedent for the fuqaha in other analogous situations.

The Sawad refers to the Sawad of Khusroes (a generic term for the Persian Emperor) which was conquered by the Muslims in the time of 'Umar ibn al-Khattab, may Allah be pleased with him, and which was part of Iraq. It was called Sawad (Arabic: black) because of the intensity of cultivation and trees there: when the Arabs left the peninsula, which contained no cultivation or trees, the greenness of its cultivation and trees was what manifested (itself most strongly to them) and for them the colour green and black were synonymous – as al-Fadl ibn 'Abbas ibn 'Utbah ibn Abi Lahab, who was black makes clear in the following:

> *I am the Green - who then will know me, of the green skin, as being of the Arabs.*

Thus they called the green of Iraq, Sawad (black) and it was called Iraq because of the level nature of the land where no mountains rise up and no valleys descend, the word in Arabic meaning level. As a poet has said:

> *You have striven to accord justice to them ,while they are striving like those who have no equitable measure, that is, no level measure (*iraq*).*

The Sawad extends lengthways from Hadithah al-Mawsil to Abadan and in breadth from Uthayb al-Qadisiyyah to Hulwan, that is, it is one hundred and sixty parasangs long by eighty wide. As for the term Iraq, it traditionally encompasses the land of the Sawad in its breadth but is shorter in length, as it begins in the east at al-Ilth on the Tigris, and to the west at Harbi, and then extends to the last provinces of Basra in the peninsula of Abadan: its length is one hundred and twenty five parasangs, thus being shorter than the Sawad by thirty five parasangs; its breadth, including what is traditionally dependant upon it, is eighty parasangs, like the Sawad. Qudamah ibn Ja'far says that this comes to a surface area of ten thousand parasangs.

A parasang has a length of twelve thousand cubits - that is, the mursal cubit - making nine thousand hashimiyyah cubits. When squared, a parasang equals twenty-two thousand five hundred jareebs, and if this is multiplied by the number of parasangs it amounts to 225 million jareebs. From this figure must be estimated a deduction of a third for the area occupied by towns, hills, marshes, brush-land, pathways, roads, riverbeds, suburbs of towns and villages, mills, mail-stages, bridges, reservoirs, ports, sugar cane depots, brick works and other places, which represent 75 million jareebs; as for the rest, that is 150 million jareebs, half is left fallow and the other half is cultivated, besides what exists in the whole area of date-palms, vines and other trees. If one adds the extra part included in the Sawad as mentioned by Qudamah, that is thirty-five parasangs, to the area of Iraq, then this is the equivalent of a quarter of the former and gives us the total area which may be cultivated and planted in the Sawad; but it is difficult for the whole area to be suitable for cultivation and for various reasons which may arise, an indeterminate portion of this area cannot be used.

It is said that during the reign of the Khusroes Qubadh, the area of the Sawad amounted to 150 million jareebs, yielding a profit of 277 (or 287) million dirhams of the seven weight, because for every jareeb a dirham and a qafeez was taken, a qafeez being worth three dirhams with the weight of a mithqal. The area cultivated at the time of 'Umar, may Allah be pleased with him, varied between 32 and 36 million jareebs.

The above mentioned boundaries of the Sawad and its cultivated area have remained constant. The fuqaha differ regarding its conquest and its status. The people of Iraq consider that it was conquered by force, although 'Umar, may Allah be pleased with him, did not divide it among the booty-takers: rather he let it remain in the hands of its inhabitants and imposed the kharaj on the land. The clear teaching of ash-Shafi'i, may Allah have mercy on him, regarding the Sawad, is that it was conquered by force: the booty-takers divided it among themselves as property, but then 'Umar asked them to renounce it - which they did, except a group whose willing acceptance was only forthcoming when they were given money in compensation for what they were entitled to; when, however, it became clearly under the control of the Muslims, 'Umar imposed the kharaj.

The followers of ash-Shafi'i, however, differ as to its status. Abu Sa'id al-Astakhri, among many others, is of the opinion that 'Umar, may Allah be pleased with him, made it a waqf for all the Muslims and left it in the hands of its (previous) owners in return for the kharaj, imposed as a mark of their (temporary) purchase and paid as a kind of rent every year, although the period was not stipulated on account of the general interest involved. His making it a waqf gave it the same status as what Allah gave in fay to his Messenger at Khaybar, al-'Awaali and the property of the Bani an-Nadir- and so what is taken in its kharaj is used for the public interest: it is not a fay from which a fifth is taken, because the khums (fifth) has already been taken; moreover, it is not restricted to the use of the army, as it is a waqf for the Muslims as a whole and it is thus used in their general interest: part of this interest is provisioning the army, fortifying outposts, building Jumah-mosques and bridges, dredging canals, and paying salaries of public servants, such as judges, witnesses, fuqaha, reciters of the Qur'an, imams and muadhdhins. This therefore prohibits the sale of property-rights and any transaction involving a transfer of title from one person's hands to another; any right of disposal thereof only concerns the rights to its profits, and not the creation of any (new) property rights, other than over what has been planted or constructed after the conquest.

It is said that 'Umar, may Allah be pleased with him, made the Sawad a waqf on the advice of 'Ali ibn Abi Talib and Mu'adh ibn Jabal, may Allah be pleased with them both.

Abu'l-'Abbas ibn Surayj among the followers of ash-Shafi'i said that 'Umar, may Allah be pleased with him, after requesting the booty-takers to renounce the Sawad, sold it to the farmers and the land-holders for money to be paid as an annual kharaj. Thus the kharaj was a kind of purchase price: this is permitted concerning matters of public interest just as it is said that the like is permitted in cases of renting; thus (its is argued) the sale of the Sawad land was permitted, and this sale resulted in the acquisition of property rights.

As for the amount of kharaj imposed on it, 'Amr ibn Maymun narrates that 'Umar, may Allah be pleased with him, after securing the Sawad, appointed Hudhayfah to govern the region beyond the Tigris, and 'Uthman ibn Hunayf to govern the region below it. Ash-Sha'bi said that the latter measured the Sawad, and found it to be 36 million jareebs, and imposed a dirham and a qafeez on each jareeb. Al-Qasim said: "I have heard that the qafeez is a measure of theirs called shaburqan", and Yahya ibn Adam said that it was the same as (described by) al-Makhtum al-Hajjaji. Qatadah narrates that Abu Makhlad said that 'Uthman ibn Hunayf imposed a tax of ten dirhams for every jareeb of vines, eight dirhams for a jareeb of dates, six for a jareeb of sugar cane, five dirhams for every jareeb of fodder crop, four for a jareeb of wheat, and two for a jareeb of barley. Thus the kharaj of wheat and barley are different in this narration to that of the other narration, and this is because of the difference in the regions, and the different yields which they can sustain.

The cubit of Hudhayfah and 'Uthman ibn Hunayf is the length of a forearm plus a palm and an outstretched thumb.

At the beginning of the Persian era, the Sawad was subject to the muqasamah payment in kind until Qubadh ibn Fayruz had it measured and imposed the kharaj: thereafter it yielded 150 million dirhams of a mithqal weight. The reason why he imposed the kharaj on this designated area, after it used to be imposed as a muqasamah, has been recorded in the following way: he went out one day to hunt, and came to an area overgrown with trees, into which the game disappeared; he then mounted a hill so as to see whereabouts in the wood the game was, when he caught sight of a woman who was digging in an orchard of date-palms and pomegranates full of fruit; with her was a child who tried to take one of the pomegranates, but whom she prevented from doing so; he was surprised at her action and so he sent someone to ask her why she had prevented her child from taking the pomegranate. She replied that the King was entitled to a share, and the official in charge had not yet come to take it, and she was afraid to take anything before he had taken his due. The King felt pity at her words and was filled with sympathy for his subject; he therefore charged his ministers with measuring the land so that roughly the same tax as had been taken in kind could now be collected based on measurement, so that anyone could dispose of his own property whenever the need arose. This continued until the end of the reign of the Persians.

'Umar ibn al-Khattab continued to base the tax on the surface area and to impose the kharaj, which amounted to 120 million during his time. 'Ubaidullah ibn Ziyad collected 135 million in tax on account of his incorrect and unjust methods; al-Hajjaj collected 118 million, likewise on account of his incorrect and wasteful methods; 'Umar ibn 'Abd al-'Aziz collected 120 million on account of his just methods and his revitalisation of agriculture; Ibn Hubayrah collected 100 million, besides food for the army and provisioning the combatants; Yusuf ibn 'Umar took 60 to 70 million annually, having already accounted for 16 million spent on the people of Syria, 4 million on postal expenses, 1 million on roads, and 10 million on various kinds of hostels for young and the sick. 'Abd ar-Rahman ibn Ja'far ibn Sulayman said that the total amount produced by this region was a thousand million for the two entitled parties: anything lacking from the portion for the subjects was supplemented from the Sultan's wealth, and whatever was lacking in the Sultan's wealth was made good from the people's wealth.

The Sawad continued to be subject to the kharaj based on surface area until al-Mansur, may Allah have mercy on him, during the Abbasid era, changed the system from the kharaj back to the muqasamah, because the sale-price of the produce did not cover the amount of the kharaj and the Sawad was failing. Abu 'Ubaidullah advised al-Mahdi to change the kharaj land into muqasamah land, based on half the rate for land watered naturally, a third for that irrigated using machinery, and a quarter when irrigated by hydraulic wheels - and they had no other tax to pay; he also advised that the surface area of plantations of date-palms, vines and fruit-trees be taken as a basis for the kharaj, and that it be estimated according to its proximity to the markets and seaports, and that the same distinction be established as for the muqasamah - that is, that if the produce amounts to twice the kharaj tax, then the kharaj is taken in its entirety, but not if it does not amount to this.

This is what was done with the Sawad land: thus it was subject to the kharaj in the first instance, but was then changed to muqasamah, because of new circumstances which gave rise to the need for ijtihad by the imams: thus this new situation remains as long as the original reason for the change remains – otherwise one reverts to the original situation when the reason no longer exists, for the Imam should not annul the ijtihad of his predecessors.

It is invalid to make the tax-officials liable for the wealth derived from the 'ushr and the kharaj, and there is no law in the shari'ah that says this: this is because the official is trusted to collect what is due, and to distribute what he collects, and he is like the wakeel (agent in a commercial venture) who, if he hands over what he has been entrusted with, is not liable for any shortfall and cannot keep any excess: if he were liable for goods of a specific value, this would mean that he was the sole owner of whatever excess existed, and that he would be the person responsible for any - deficit and this contradicts the nature of the official who enjoys a position of trust, and it is therefore invalid.

It is reported that when a man came to Ibn 'Abbas, may Allah be pleased with him, to take possession of Ubullah for 100,000 dirhams, the latter had him whipped a hundred times and crucified alive as a discretionary punishment and as a lesson.

'Umar ibn al-Khattab, may Allah be pleased with him, addressed the people thus, speaking both of their status as subjects and of his authority over them, and of the management, in a correct and legitimate manner, of the wealth for which he was responsible: "O people, read the Qur'an and you will learn from it, act in accordance with what is in it and you will be amongst its people. No one will ever fulfil its claim if it means disobedience to Allah; surely no man can lose provision or come closer to his death merely by declaring the truth; surely I have only discovered what is good in that which Allah has given me authority over by means of three things: fulfilling a trust, taking by means of force, and ruling by what Allah has revealed; surely I have only found the good in this wealth by means of three things: that it is taken justly, that it is distributed justly, and that it is prevented from being spent on unjustifiable things; surely I am like the guardian of an orphan regarding your wealth: if I am able to do without, I abstain from using it, and if I am in need, then I use it in a reasonable way, just as the animals of the Bedouin feed."

Chapter 15
Reviving Dead Lands and Drawing Water

Whoever revives a dead land becomes its owner with or without the permission of the Imam, although Abu Hanifah says that it is not permitted to revive it without the permission of the Imam, based on the saying of the Prophet, may the peace and blessings of Allah be upon him, "No one may have anything unless his Imam is happy about it," - but in another of his sayings, "Whoever revives a dead land, then it is his," there is a proof that ownership of dead lands is validated by means of its revival without the permission of the Imam.

Dead land (*mawat*), according to ash-Shafi'i is any land which is not cultivated nor constitutes a hareem reserve of cultivated land- even if it is adjacent to a cultivated land. Abu Hanifah says that mawat land is that which, is distant from cultivated land and which water does not reach. Abu Yusuf says it may be defined as that land which, when someone stands on its point which is nearest to a cultivated land and cries out at the top of his voice, he cannot be heard by anyone standing at the nearest point in the cultivated land. These two opinions, however, depart from what is traditionally accepted regarding the connection between cultivated lands.

Those living near the dead land and those living at a distance both enjoy the same rights concerning the reviving of land, although Malik says that those living on neighbouring land are more entitled to revive it than those living far away.

The nature of the revival is determined by custom, with regard to the purpose of the revival, as the Messenger of Allah, may the peace and blessings of Allah be upon him, referred to it in terms of usual customary practice in the matter: thus if someone wishes to revive a dead land by way of residence, then revival is obtained by constructing and roofing a building on it, as this represents the minimum necessary for residence. If someone wants to revive it for cultivation or planting trees, three conditions must be observed: first, the earth at the edges of the area should be heaped up to form a barrier between it and other areas; second, it should be irrigated with water if it is dry, or water should be stopped from reaching it if it is marshy – because reviving dry land consists in irrigating it, and reviving marshy land is by stopping water from reaching it - so as to make cultivation and planting possible in both cases; third, tilling the earth should be by ploughing up flat ground, flattening out any mounds, and filling in any holes. If these three conditions are fulfilled, the revival is complete and ownership is transferred to the person who revives it. One of the followers of ash-Shafi'i is mistaken when he says that ownership is not established until the person cultivates or plants trees; this is incorrect, as both of these actions correspond to taking up residence in a residential property but not to the acquisition of a place of residence (prior to taking up residence).

The cultivator of a land which has been revived is the one who works and cultivates it: the person responsible for reviving it remains the owner, and the cultivator is the owner of what is produced. If the owner of the land wishes to sell it, he may do so, but there is a difference of opinion as to whether the owner of the cultivation may sell his right. Abu Hanifah says that he may sell it if he has worked the land, but not if he has not worked it. Malik says that the sale of the right of cultivation is permitted whatever the circumstances, and the cultivator is treated as a partner in ownership by virtue of his work. Ash-Shafi'i says that it is not permitted for him to sell the right to cultivation under any circumstances, except if he owns specific things there, like trees or crops, in which case it is permitted for him to sell these specific objects, but not the right to cultivation.

If someone has marked out a defining boundary around the dead land, he has more right to its revive it than any other; if, however, he is superseded by someone else who revives it, then the latter is more entitled to it than the one who defined it. If the person who encloses it wishes to sell it before having revived it, this is not permitted, according to the clear meaning of ash-Shafi'i's teaching, although many of his followers have permitted it, arguing that as the person who encloses it is the most entitled to it, he may sell it, as with any other property. If, in this instance, he sells it, and the person who has actually revived it takes it over after it has passed into the hands of the buyer, then Ibn Abi Hurairah, from among the followers of ash-Shafi'i, claims that the buyer is still liable to pay for it since the article has, as it were, been lost while in his hands after his having taken possession of it. Others of his followers who permit its sale are of the opinion that he is exempted from making payment, as possession has not really been established.

If someone has enclosed and irrigated some land but has not worked it, then he becomes the owner of the water and of the dead-land, and of any adjoining hareem land over which it has flowed, but he does not own anything more than this; he may sell land over which water has flowed; as to the permissibility of selling any other portion of the enclosed area, it is subject to the two aspects discussed above.

If a dead land which is subject to the 'ushr is revived, it is not permitted to impose the kharaj on it, irrespective of whether it has been irrigated with 'ushr water or with kharaj water. Abu Hanifah and Abu Yusuf say that if what has been revived has been irrigated with 'ushr water, then it is 'ushr land; if irrigated with kharaj water, then it is kharaj land. Muhammad ibn al-Hasan says that if the land is revived by canals which have been excavated by non-Arabs, then it is kharaj land, and if it is by rivers created by Allah, ta'ala, like the Tigris or the Euphrates, then it is 'ushr land. The Iraqis and others are unanimous that the dead-lands of Basra and its salt-marshes are 'ushr lands. As for the opinion of Muhammad ibn al-Hasan, it is based on the fact that the Tigris of Basra is a river, whose flow has been brought about by Allah; any dependent canals are treated as revived areas which have been excavated by the Muslims in dead-lands. As for the saying of Abu Hanifah, his followers differ in their explanation of this: some say that the kharaj water flows down into the Tigris at Basra at the time of its ebbing and that the land of Basra absorbs it at the time of the flow – but this flow comes from the sea and not from the Tigris or the Euphrates. This reasoning is incorrect, since this flow prevents the sweet water from flowing into the sea and does not mix with it, and the earth does not absorb it; it is not the flow water which waters it, but rather that of the Tigris and the Euphrates. His followers, among them Talhah ibn Adam, say that the reason is that water of the Tigris and the Euphrates gathers in the marshes, but that it can no longer be absorbed and so its benefit has ceased; it then flows towards the Tigris of Basra, and so it is not kharaj water, because the marshes are not part of the kharaj canals. This reasoning is also false, as the marshes of Iraq were formed before Islam - so the ruling governing the land changes: it became dead land and the status of the water is not taken into account. The true reason is that related by the authors of the histories, namely that the water of the Tigris itself flowed into that part of the Tigris known as al-Ghawr, which joins the Tigris at Basra: it came from al-Mada'in, passing through straight openings and well-protected banks, and the present site of the marshes was taken up by cultivated lands and villages and houses; then, during the reign of Qubadh ibn Fayruz, a large fissure appeared in the river bank in the lower reaches of Kaskar; no one was aware of this until the water flooded over and submerged the cultivated land upstream. When his son Anushirvan succeeded him, he ordered the water to be pushed back with the aid of dykes, with the result that some of the land was returned to cultivation.

The situation remained like this until 6 AH, when the Messenger of Allah, may the peace and blessings of Allah be upon him, sent 'Abdallah ibn Hudhafah as-Sahmi to Khusroes, that is Khusroes Parviz. At that time the height of the Tigris and the Euphrates increased to levels never before seen and resulted in huge fissures appearing in the banks; Parviz went to great efforts to shore up the banks and even once closed up seventy gaps in one day. He had money spread out on mats (to remind the workers of the reward they could expect), but no amount of innovative methods allowed them to get the better of the water. Then the Muslims entered Iraq, and the Persians became occupied with waging war on them, and so the bursting of the dykes continued unabated; they were unable to concern themselves with them, and the local leaders were unable to contain them. As a result, the marshes grew and became deeper.

When Mu'awiyyah, may Allah be pleased with him, entrusted his freed slave 'Abdallah ibn Darraaj with the responsibility for the kharaj of Iraq and the area of the marshes, he collected a sum of 5 million dirhams. After him, Hassan Nabati (cultivated and) collected a large amount from these marsh lands for al-Waleed ibn 'Abd al-Malik and then for Hisham, who succeeded al-Waleed. People have continued this work (of reclamation) up until today, with the result that the area of drained cultivatable land now amounts to the same area as that of the marsh lands or even greater.

The reasons given by the followers of Abu Hanifah are excusable, given the above mentioned explanation of the changing states of the marsh land: they saw too that the Companions were agreed that the dead lands of Basra were revived and became 'ushr lands, and that the reason for their becoming subject to the 'ushr lands was their revivification.

As for the hareem lands adjacent to the revived lands which have been reserved for habitation or cultivation, then according to ash-Shafi'i their status derives from the fact that the revived land is dependent on them for (access via) a road or pathway, or that it forms open (living) space, or that it contains streams or canals necessary for irrigation. Abu Hanifah says that the hareem extends as far as the point where the water of the cultivated land does not reach; Abu Yusuf says that its extent reaches as far as the voice of someone standing at the edge of the cultivated land. If, however, either of these two views applied, then no two cultivated areas would touch, nor any two houses lie adjacent to each other.

When the Companions, may Allah be pleased with them, established Basra at the time of 'Umar, may Allah be pleased with him, and they divided it into sections for the various tribes of their people, they made the width of its widest street – and it also served as a camel stable – sixty cubits, and they made the width of the rest of the streets twenty cubits, and the width of the alleyways seven cubits. In the middle of every district they established a wide space to stable their horses and to serve as the burial-grounds of their dead, and all these lay adjacent to houses: this they would not have done unless there had been recourse to a judgement agreed upon by the fuqaha, or to some text of an irrefutable nature. Bashir ibn Ka'b narrates from Abu Hurairah that the Messenger of Allah, may the peace and blessings of Allah be upon him, said: "If people are in disagreement concerning a road, then make it with a width of seven cubits."

✻
✻ ✻

As for water which is taken or drawn out, it may be classified in three ways: that of rivers, of wells, and of springs:

1. Rivers may be divided into three kinds:

First, those large rivers whose flow has been created by Allah and which have not been excavated by man, like the Tigris and the Euphrates, which are called the Two Tributary Rivers (*raafidaan*); the water from these two rivers is enough for both agriculture and for drinking and is so abundant that any insufficiency or any situation giving rise to dispute and haggling is unimaginable; people may use it for watering and irrigation as they wish, and no one can be prevented from using it for watering or from creating irrigation canals.

Second, small rivers created by Allah and these are of two types:

A. That whose depth is such that even without a dam, it is sufficient for all the adjacent inhabitants: there is no deficiency - anyone with land among them may take water for irrigation when he needs it, and no one should stop another from doing so; if some people wish to channel a small canal off from it and direct it to another non-adjacent area, or connect it to an empty irrigation canal, then one should examine whether this would harm the people adjacent to the rivers: if it would not harm them, they are not stopped from doing this;

B. A river in which there is little water and which is not deep enough for irrigation unless it is dammed up: so those further up the river should be the first to dam it up and irrigate their land; when their irrigation is complete, then it is the turn of those below them, and so on, until those at the end of the river are the last to dam it up. 'Ubadah ibn as-Samit narrates that the Prophet, may the peace and blessings of Allah be upon him, decided that the irrigation of date-palms from flowing water should be taken from upstream before downstream and then the remaining water should be allowed to flow downstream, until each (area of) land had been (successively) watered.

As for the amount of water which may be retained for each area, Muhammad ibn Ishaq has narrated from Abu Malik ibn Tha'labah, from his father, that the Messenger of Allah, may the peace and blessings of Allah be upon him, decided that the water in the Wadi Mahzur could be dammed up to ankle-height after which it should be allowed to flow on to the next area. Malik says that he took the same decision regarding the flowing water of Bat'han, namely up to the ankles. This decision is not to be applied in a general manner at all times and in all places, as he gave this measure in accordance with the need, and this need varies in five ways: **i.** because of the different kinds of land, some requiring a little water and some a lot; **ii.** because of the difference of the agriculture: crops require one amount of irrigation while trees require another; **iii.** the difference between summer and winter, each having its own required amount; **iv.** the varying amount required before sowing and after it; **v.** the differing flow of water, sometimes uninterrupted and sometimes interrupted: in the latter case, only as much is taken as can be stored, while in the former, it is taken whenever it is needed. Given differences of this nature, it cannot always be measured to the same degree decided upon by the Messenger of Allah, may the peace and blessings of Allah be upon him, but rather depends on custom and local need.

If a man irrigates his land or causes water to flow (in a canal), and this water flows onto and floods his neighbours' land, he is not liable as he is making legitimate use of it on his property; if however, there are fish in the water then the second person is more entitled to catch them than the first, as he is the owner of the land (beneath the water);

Third, this consists of canals excavated by people for the (benefit of the) land which they have revived: such canals are owned in partnership, like alleyways between two houses, neither of the two owners having a sole right to it. If such a canal is at Basra, and the flow-waters enter it, then it may be used by all the inhabitants, and no dispute between them is acceptable because of the abundance of the water; they have no need to dam it, as its level at flow-time is high enough for all lands, and this water then recedes after irrigation with the flow. If the land is not in Basra, and there is no ebb or flow, then the canal is owned by those of the land owners who have excavated it, and no others have the right to draw from it or divert water from it; none of its people may set up a bridge or walkway over it, nor raise the water to drive a mill, unless all the others agree, because they are all partners: it is forbidden to set up something individually – as in a cul-de-sac, where no-one can open up a door to it, or set up a protruding wing or an archway, unless all agree.

The water of such canals is used for irrigation in one of three ways:

A. the participants use it in turn, either on a daily basis if there are few of them, or on an hourly basis if they are numerous. If there is disagreement, then lots are drawn to see who will be the first and then who will follow, and then each must keep to his turn and no one else shares it with him: once established, this order is retained;

B. the opening of the canal is divided by a wooden barrier which extends from one bank to the other: channels are dug from it, corresponding in size to how much water the various participants are entitled to - five or ten for example, each taking his turn to draw off water to his land;

C. each digs a channel to his land whose irrigating-capacity they have mutually agreed upon, or which corresponds to the surface area of their property: in this way they draw off the amount of water to which they are entitled, and all the participants have an equal share; no one may increase his amount, and no one can restrict another's amount; now may anyone set his irrigation-channel downstream after having established it upstream – just as no one in a cul-de-sac may change the position of his (shared) door from up the alley to further down it; nor may he place it upstream after having it downstream, even though it is permitted for a door to be placed further up (a cul-de-sac), as this represents a restriction of his right - since in the case of resetting the channel upstream, this represents an increase in his right.

As for the hareem of this type of canal when it has been excavated in a dead land, then according to ash-Shafi'i, it is as dictated by custom in similar circumstances; this same ruling applies to qanaat canals, as they are nothing other than covered canals. Abu Hanifah, however, says that the hareem of a canal extends as far as the muddy land resulting from it (on either side); Abu Yousuf says that the hareem of a qanaat is the actual area of the canal as long as it does not come to the surface and contains the water (underground) – and this opinion has an aspect which is helpful.

✳
✳   ✳

2. As for wells, the person responsible for digging them will be in one of three situations:

A. He has dug it for the use of those using a particular road, in which case its water is common property and the person who dug it is like any other 'Uthman, radiy'Allahu 'anhu, made the Rumah well a waqf-property and would draw water from it with his bucket along with other people. The water is shared by all when there is enough to water animals and to irrigate crops, but if there is less water, then watering the animals has priority over irrigating the crops, and people and animals share it together; if, however, there is not enough for the latter two, then people have priority over the animals;

B. People have dug it for their own use, like the nomads who find pasture land and dig a well in it to have water for their own use and for their animals: they are more entitled to it, as long as they stay there to pasture, but they must give any excess water to those who wish to drink, but to no others. If they leave, the well becomes open to use for those passing by: thus from a particular use in the beginning it reverts to public use at the end. If they return to it after having left it, they are on a par with others, and those who arrive first have priority.

C. A person digs it for himself and as his own property. However until he actually reaches water, his right of property is not established: his right to it is established when he is able to draw water from it, as only then is it considered a complete revival of the land – unless it needs to be bricked up, in which case the completion of this work signals that the revival is complete, and that the right of ownership to this well and the adjacent hareem areas is established.

The fuqaha differ as to the extent of this hareem. Ash-Shafi'i is of the opinion, may Allah have mercy on him, that it depends on custom and tradition concerning other similar wells. Abu Hanifah says that for a well where an animal is used to draw the water, it is fifty cubits, while Abu Yusuf says that it is sixty cubits - unless the length of the well-rope is longer than this, in which case it extends as long as its length; he also says that for a well around which camels gather, it is forty cubits. These measurements may only be soundly established on the basis of a text: if there is a text, then it should be followed, and opinion is defective. As for the measurement based on the length of the rope, it is valid to consider this as it forms part of common usage and as such is worthy of consideration.

If the property right to a well and its hareem area is established for someone, then this person is more entitled to its water. The followers of ash-Shafi'i differ as to whether he acquires the property right to it before having drawn water from it and taken complete possession: some of them consider that it becomes his property before he takes complete possession of it – just as the person acquiring a mine acquires the property right to it before extracting from it; thus he may sell it before having drawn from it; whoever draws from it without the owner's permission therefore may be held liable for the return of the water he has used. Others, however, say that he does not own it until he has taken full possession of it, as the site is potentially open to all: he may stop others from using it by drawing from it but if someone does succeed in drawing from it (before him), then he has no claim over him.

If the property rights of the person (who has dug it) are established for him alone and he is entitled to the water, then he may water his animals and his crops, his date-palms and his fruit-trees; if there is no excess after he has used what he needs, he does not have to give any of it away, unless someone is in extreme need. Al-Hasan, may Allah have mercy on him, narrates that a man came to some people with water and requested them to give him a drink; they did not, with the result that he died - and 'Umar made them liable for payment of the blood-money. If, after having taken enough for themselves there remains an excess, he must give it to those who wish to water their animals, but not for their agriculture or fruit-trees, according to the teaching of ash-Shafi'i, although Abu 'Ubaidah ibn Jarthunah says that he does not have to give away the excess, neither for animals nor agriculture. Others say that he must give the excess to animals but not for agriculture. Ash-Shafi'i's teaching that there is an obligation to give it to animals but not for agriculture, is the shari'ah-ruling. Abu'z-Zinad narrates from al-A'raj, from Abu

Hurairah, that the Messenger of Allah, may the peace and blessings of Allah be upon him, said: "As for whoever stops excess water from being used to increase pasture land, Allah will cut him off from the overflow of His mercy on the Day of Rising."

The giving of this excess is dependent on four conditions: first, that the water is still lying in the well: if it has been drawn then it does not have to be given away; second, that the pasture land must be adjacent: if it does not lie near the pasture, he does not have to give it away; third, that the animals cannot find any other water; if they can find some which is available to all, he does not have to give it away, and the animals should go to this water which is open to all; if there is another well, but it is owned privately, then both owners of the wells must provide their excess water for those who come to them: if there is sufficient water for the animals from the excess of one of the wells, then the obligation of the other is annulled; fourth, that the animals which come to drink must not cause any damage to his crops or animals, and if this happens, then they should be prevented from watering these but their keepers may draw the excess water for them. If these four conditions are fulfilled then he must give the excess water, and it is forbidden for him to take payment for it; if, however, any of the conditions are lacking then he may take payment as long as he sells it by the measure or by weight, but not if he sells it en bloc, or according to the quantity needed by the animals or the crops.

If someone digs a well or becomes the owner of it and its hareem, and then another digs a second well at the edge of his hareem, and the water of the first flows into and collects in the second, then his right to it is established and he is not to be prevented from using this second well; the same is true if the second digs deeper in order to find cleaner water and this changes the water in the first. Malik says, however, that if it does flow to the second, or if there is a change in the first as a result, then the owner of the second is prevented from doing it, and his well is filled in.

3. Springs may be divided into three categories:

First, those which Allah has caused to flow and which have not been the work of man: their status is the same as those rivers which Allah has caused to flow; anyone who revives a land by means of its water, then he may take sufficient for his needs. If there is cause for dispute because of the small quantity of water, then the dead-lands for which it is used should be considered: those who were the first to revive a land should take what they need to irrigate their land, and then (it is the turn of) the others after them; if there is a lack of water for some, then this lack must be borne by the last persons; if there are several persons who all contributed equally to the revival, and not one of them has precedence over another, then they divide it between them or take it in turns;

Second, those created by man – such a spring belongs to the person who activated it, together with its hareem, which is determined, according to the madhhab of ash-Shafi'i, by custom and comparison with other similar sites, and whose size is determined by how much is needed. Abu Hanifah says that the hareem of a spring is five hundred cubits, and that the person who has activated the spring may draw off water to wherever he wishes, and that the place wherein the water flows is his property and his hareem;

Third, those which a man activates in his property: he is the most entitled to its water for the irrigation of his land; if it is enough for his needs, then no one is entitled to it other than someone in extreme need of a drink; if there is an excess after seeing to his needs, and he wishes to revive a dead land with this excess, then he is more entitled to do this; if he does not require it to revive a dead land, he is obliged to give it away to those with animals, but not for watering crops, as in the case of excess well-water; if he seeks compensation for this from cultivators, this is permitted, but not if he asks it of live-stock-holders.

The person who digs a well in the countryside and establishes ownership of it, or the person who activates a spring, may sell either of them and cannot be prohibited from taking payment for it. However, Sa'id ibn al-Musayyab and Ibn Abi Dhi'b say they may not sell or take payment for them. 'Umar ibn 'Abd al-'Aziz and Abu'z-Zinad say that it may be sold if it is sought after, but not merely because he is leaving – in which case those living closest to the owner are more entitled to it without payment; if the person who has left returns, he is more entitled to the property.

Chapter 16
Reserves (*hima*) and Common Lands

Dead-land which has been made into a reserve (*hima*) is that which cannot be revived or converted into private property, so that it may remain available for all, for the purpose of a pasture for   animals. The Messenger of Allah, may the peace and blessings of Allah be upon him, created a reserve in Madinah: he went up the hill of al-Baqi' – or an-Naqi', according to Abu 'Ubaid – and said, "This is my reserve," and he indicated al-Qaa' with his hand, one mile by six in extent, which he made a reserve for the horses of the Muslims amongst the Ansar and Muhajirun.

As for the reserves created by the imams after him, if they established all the dead-land as a reserve or the greater part of it, then it is not permitted; likewise it is not permitted if they reserved a small part just for particular persons, or the rich. If, however, a reserve has been made for all the Muslims, or for the poor or indigent, then there are two opinions in the matter: the first, that this is not permitted, and that reserves may only be created by the Messenger, may the peace and blessings of Allah be upon him; this is based on the narration of As-Sa'b ibn Juthamah, that the Messenger, on creating the reserve of al-Baqi', said, "There are no reserves except for Allah and his Messenger;" the second, that the reserves made by the imams after him are permitted, just as he was permitted to do, as he made them for the benefit of the Muslims and not for himself: thus the same principle applies to those who stand in for him when it is in the public interest. Abu Bakr, may Allah be content with him, created a reserve at ar-Rabadhah for the people entitled to a share of the zakah-tax, and he put his freed slave Abu Salamah in charge of it; 'Umar, may Allah be pleased with him, made a reserve of as-Sarif, just as Abu Bakr had done with ar-Rabadhah, and put his freed slave Hunayy in charge, saying, "Behave kindly towards people, and shield yourself from the supplication of the oppressed person, for surely the prayer of the oppressed is answered, and allow entry to the master of a few camels or few sheep; but beware of the flocks of

'Uthman ibn 'Affan and 'Abd ar-Rahman ibn 'Awf, for if their animals perish, they can always have recourse to their date-palms and crops; if the owner of a few camels or sheep comes to me with his children, saying, 'O Amir of the Believers!' should I abandon them? As for me, know that the pasture land is worth less to me than the dinar and the dirham. By the One in Whose hand is my self, if it were not for the wealth that I have been made responsible for in the way of Allah, I would not make an inch of this land into a reserve."

As for the saying of the Messenger, may the peace and blessings of Allah be upon him, "There are no reserves but for Allah and His Messenger," it means that there should be no reserve made but for the same purpose as those made by Allah and His Messenger, for the poor and the indigent, and for the benefit of all the Muslims - and not in the way that they were made in the Jahiliyyah, for the particular use of a powerful person, reserved for himself. Kulayb ibn Wa'il, for example, brought a dog to a high point in a certain area and then made him bark, declaring that he had created a reserve for as far as his barking could be heard in all directions, and that the people could share any land beyond this. This was the cause of his being killed, and al-'Abbas ibn al-Mardas recited the following about it:

It is thus that Kulayb seized – unjustly by his position of power until he fell and was killed by it – the land of the Wa'il, when he had the dog bark and prevented his brothers from living there.

If a land acquires the status of a reserve, because its dead lands remain available to all and are prevented from becoming private property after their being revived, then it should be examined: if it is open equally to all, be they rich or poor, Muslim or dhimmi, for the pasture of their horses and animals; if it has been reserved for the Muslims in particular, both rich and poor among them may use it, while the dhimmis are excluded; if it has been reserved for the poor and the indigent, then the rich are excluded as well as the dhimmis; it is not permitted to reserve it especially for the rich to the exclusion of the poor, nor for the dhimmis to the exclusion of the Muslims; if it is reserved for the animals taken in payment of the zakah, or for the horses of those in jihad, then no other animals may share in it.

Once established as a particular or general reserve, then it should remain as such; if a place has been reserved for a particular use, and then it is extended for the general use of all, it is permitted for all to share in it, as those who had a particular use for it before, suffer no harm. If a place reserved for general use does not suffice for all the people, it is not permitted for the rich among them to use it just for themselves; there are two opinions as to the permissibility of allowing the poor among them to have exclusive use of it.

If the status of a reserve is established for a certain area, and then someone comes and revives it and violates its status, then its character as a reserve should be considered:

A. If it is among those reserves created by the Messenger of Allah, may the peace and blessings of Allah be upon him, then its status as a reserve is upheld, and its revival is annulled, and the person responsible is rejected and reprimanded – especially if the reason for its original by being made a reserve still exists – for it is not permitted to contravene a decision of the Messenger of Allah, may the peace and blessings of Allah be upon him, either by violating or by annulling it.

B. If it is one of the reserves established by the imams after him, then there are two opinions concerning its revival: the first, is that it may not remain as such, and its status as a reserve is reconfirmed, just as in the case of the reserves created by the Messenger of Allah, may the peace and blessings of Allah be upon him, because its status has been created with proper authority; the second, is that it is confirmed as a revived land, and that this status is more secure than that of a reserve, since the Messenger, may the peace and blessings of Allah be upon him, made it clear that: "Whoever revives a dead land, then it belongs to him."

No person in authority may take payment from the owners of animals for (allowing them to) pasture in dead-lands or reserves, based on the saying of the Messenger of Allah, may the peace and blessings of Allah be upon him, "The Muslims have a share in three things: water, fire and pasture."

As for public or common land (*arfaq*), it refers to those areas given to people for their use, namely the areas surrounding markets, the open spaces on either side of the streets, the hareem of the towns, and the stopping places of travellers. These may be classified in three ways: the first, applies in particular to the countryside and deserts; the second, to open spaces adjacent to properties; the third, to the streets and roads:

First, this category applies both to the countryside and to deserts, as well as to the stopping places of travellers and watering places. These are of two types:

i. those used by caravans and places of rest for travellers. The Sultan has no say in these, because of their distance from him, and their being indispensable for the caravans, except for his particular responsibility of removing any difficulties from the path, maintaining water supplies, and allowing people to stop over in these places. The person who arrives first at a stopping place is more entitled to stop there than someone who arrives later, until the latter leaves, since the Messenger said, may the peace and blessings of Allah be upon him: "Mina is a stopping place for camels for the first to arrive." If several parties arrive at the same time and dispute the site, then the matter should be appraised fairly, so that their dispute comes to an end. Likewise in the case of nomads who occupy an area, seeking pasture to feed their animals, and moving from place to place - they are treated the same as the caravans, that is, they must not be impeded in their movement and search for pasture;

ii. this type concerns people who intend to stay on a (piece of) land and take up residence. The Sultan examines their stay there and makes the most expedient decision: if this would cause harm to the caravans, they are prevented from stopping or are prohibited from doing so (if they are already there); if there would be no harm to the caravans, then he should consider the most practical solution, namely whether to allow or prevent them from stopping there, or to have others come to live there, as 'Umar did when he established the cities of Basra and Kufa, transferring to each of them those whom he judged would be of benefit, and preventing travellers from gathering there who might cause trouble and bloodshed; the Sultan acts likewise in according fief-rights over dead-lands, as he sees fit; if he does not give them permission until after they have stopped, then he should not prevent them from staying there, just as he is not to prohibit them if they revive a dead-land without his permission; rather he arranges their affair in a manner which he judges to be of benefit for them, but prohibits them from proceeding to add any more thereafter without first obtaining his permission.

Kathir ibn 'Abdallah narrated from his father, from his grandfather, saying: "We were with 'Umar ibn al-Khattab on his 'Umrah-visit to Makkah in the year 17 AH, and the people responsible for the watering places along the way spoke to him concerning their intention to build houses between Makkah and

Madinah where none had been before: he gave them permission to do this, and stipulated that travellers were more entitled to the water and the shade;"

Second, this is specific to the open spaces surrounding houses and properties; if, however, this causes harm to their owners, those taking advantage of this (the general public) should be prevented from using them, unless they give permission that this harm may continue, and then their stay becomes possible. If no harm is being done to them, then there are two opinions as to their being able to make free use of these places without permission: the first, is that they may make free use of them even without the permission of their owners, because a hareem area should be made available if its people are to have access to whatever is theirs – the latter being on a par with everyone else (once access has been gained); the second, is that general use may not be made of the owners' hareem unless they grant permission, as their property, is dependent on the space and they are more entitled to dispose of it, and have a particular right to it.

As for the hareems of the Friday mosques and the other mosques, if their general use causes harm to the people of the mosques and Friday mosques, then they (the general public) are prohibited from using them and the Sultan may not give permission for them to use them, as those praying are more entitled to dispose of it; if no harm is caused to them, then they are given permission to make free use of the hareems. As to whether consideration should be given to permission from the Sultan, there are two opinions, as in the case of the hareems of properties;

Third, this concerns in particular the open spaces of the streets and the roads, and open access to these is dependent upon the authority of the Sultan; there are two aspects regarding the ruling regarding this authority: the first, is that it is restricted to stopping any transgression, preventing people from causing any harm, and making peace between disputing parties; he may not, however, make someone who is sitting to stand up, or put someone who is at the back in front, as those who are the first to come are more entitled to their place than those who arrive after them; the second, is that his authority is on a par with that of the mujtahid: in seating anybody, or preventing entry to others, or placing some in front, he may act whenever he judges it to be expedient – just as the mujtahid acts with the wealth of the bait al-mal, and in his granting fief rights to dead land; he may not, however, give more entitlement to the one who goes in front; he is not to take payment, according to two views, for the seating. When he leaves people to come to an agreement amongst themselves, then the person who arrives before another is more entitled to the place; when he leaves, then he and any others who arrive the following morning are on an equal footing, and the first to arrive has priority, although Malik says that if one of them is known to occupy a certain place, and this becomes well-known, then he is the most entitled to it as such – and no further discussion or dispute is entertained. This should be considered a valid judgement, even if there is an element of general benefit involved: in effect this means that the status (governing the place) is changed from being one of general access to that of (limited) ownership.

*

* *

As for the 'ulama and the fuqaha who sit in the Friday mosques and other mosques to teach and give fatwas, it is up to each to restrict himself from undertaking something which he is not qualified to do, lest he lead astray those who seek guidance and cause those who seek the right path to stumble – for the (following) hadith has been transmitted: "The most forward of you in giving fatwa will also be the most forward in bearing the torment of Jahannam." The Sultan has authority over them, and he must decide whether they should be affirmed in their position, or rejected.

If a qualified person wants to establish himself in a mosque in order to teach or give fatwas, and if it is a local mosque whose imams are not under the supervision of the Sultan, then he is not obliged to seek the permission of the Sultan – just as the person seeking to establish himself as its Imam does not have to seek permission for this; if, however, it is one of the Friday mosques, or one of the greater mosques where the imams are appointed by the Sultan, then the custom and practice of the region should be taken into account regarding the teaching of such persons: **i.** if it is up to the Sultan to appoint such persons, then they should not take up such positions without his permission, just as those intending to become imams should not take up the post without his permission, lest they infringe his authority; **ii.** if the Sultan has no established authority in such cases, it is not necessary for them to seek his permission, and such mosques are treated as any other.

If someone becomes known for having a particular place in a Friday mosque or any other mosque, then Malik considers that he is more entitled to it than anyone else; the majority of the fuqaha, however, consider that this is only a beneficial practice sanctioned by custom, and that it does not have any legal status; when, however, such a person relinquishes his place, he no longer has any right to it, and the first person to take it is the most entitled to it, for Allah ta'ala has said: **"alike, those who are present there or those who are away,"** (Qur'an 22: 25).

Those who try and make a way through the circles of the fuqaha or the reciters in the Friday mosques and other mosques are to be prevented from doing so, out of respect for the inviolate nature of such circles: it has been narrated of the Prophet, may the peace and blessings of Allah be upon him, that he said: "There are no reserved places except in three instances: the space around a well, the corral of a horse, and the circles of people." The space around a well is the area reserved for those using the well; the corral is the area in which a horse may move around, that is to the extent of his lead-rein if he is tethered, and the circles of people are their gatherings for consultation and conversation.

If those following different madhhabs dispute concerning matters in which ijtihad is permissible, no attempt should be made to prevent them lest this leads to enmity and so discussion ceases. If a dispute arises in which ijtihad is not permitted, then this should be prevented and forbidden; if someone insists on this, and appears to be leading astray those whom he is addressing, then the Sultan must stop the manifestation of this innovation by using the constraints of authority, and by making plain the corruption of his argument by means of legal proofs – most certainly, since for every innovation there are people who listen, and for everyone who leads astray there are those that follow. Those who act correctly in the outward, but who conceal something else in their inward, are left alone - but those who make a show of knowledge when they have none, are exposed: in effect, the one who calls to good action without actually practising himself does good, while the one who calls to a knowledge which he does not have, leads others astray.

Chapter 17
Grants and Concessions

Grants accorded by the Sultan are restricted to those which he is permitted to make, and the administration of which is dependent upon his orders; this does not extend to property which has a specific owner or a particular claimant. Grants may be of two kinds: that which concedes the right of ownership and that which concedes the right to produce:

1. As for that which gives the right of ownership, such grant-land may either be dead-land, cultivated land, or mines:

First, dead-land is of two types:

A. that which has always been dead for as long as anyone can remember such that no cultivation exists, and no property rights have been established. Such land may be conceded in a grant by the Sultan to anyone who wishes to revive it or cultivate it; according to the madhhab of Abu Hanifah, this grant-concession is also a condition for the permissibility of reviving it as he forbids the revival of a dead-land without the permission of the Imam. According to the madhhab of ash-Shafi'i, a grant-concession gives him more right to revive it than any one else, even though it is not a condition for its permissibility, since it is permitted to revive a dead-land without the permission of the Imam. Thus according to both of these madhhabs, the person to whom the grant has been conceded has more right to the land than anyone else. The Messenger of Allah, may the peace and blessings of Allah be upon him, conceded to az-Zubayr ibn al-'Awwam a grant-right whose extent was to be determined by the gallop of his horse in the dead-lands of an-Naqi': after doing this, he threw his whip ahead, hoping to extend it further and the Messenger of Allah, may the peace and blessings of Allah be upon him, said: "Give it to him, right up to where his whip reached;"

B. This applies to dead-land which was once cultivated, but which has since become dead and unused, and it is of two kinds:

i. Those lands belonging to the Jahiliyyah, like the land of 'Ad and Thamud: these are treated as dead lands which have never been cultivated, and they may be conceded in grant. The Messenger of Allah, may the peace and blessing of Allah be upon him, said, "The 'Adi land belongs to Allah and His Messenger, then it belongs to you from me," that is, the Land of 'Ad;

ii. That, dating from the Islamic era, which became the property of Muslims and then was neglected, and became dead-land and unused. The fuqaha differ in three ways as to its legal status if it is revived: first, ash-Shafi'i is of the opinion that it does not become someone's property by being revived, irrespective of whether the (previous) owners are known or not; second, Malik says that it does become someone's property through being revived, irrespective of whether the owners are known or not; third, Abu Hanifah, may Allah have mercy on him, says that if the owners are known, property rights are not gained through reviving it, and if they are not, then revival confers the right of ownership - even though it is not permitted, according to his teaching, to gain possession of anything other than by grant or concession. If the previous owners are known, the Sultan may not concede it as grant land, and they are more entitled to sell it and revive it; if they are not known, it may be granted as grant land - and its being grant land is a precondition of the permissibility of reviving it.

If a dead-land is given as a grant in the manner which we have described above, ownership is not established for the person designated by the Imam – who nevertheless becomes the most entitled to it by virtue of this grant – until the revival has taken place: if he begins its revival, it is only by the completion thereof that he gains full possession; if he ceases to revive it, he is still the most entitled to it, even though he has not gained full possession. Then the reason for his ceasing are examined: if he has a valid and justifiable excuse, he is not disturbed and is allowed to retain it until the disappearance of the excuse; if, however, he has no excuse, then Abu Hanifah says that he is not taken to task concerning it until three years have elapsed; if he revives it within this period, all well and good - but if not, then the grant concession is annulled, as 'Umar, may Allah be pleased with him, set the term of the concession at three years.

Ash-Shafi'i does not consider that this term is binding, but argues rather that one should take account of the person's ability to revive the land; if the term does come to an end, one says to him: "Either you must revive it and then it will remain in your hands, or you must leave it to return to its former state which it had before it was granted in concession." As for the term set by 'Umar, it was applied to a particular situation and may have been for a special reason or because of the benefit he saw in it.

If someone takes over a dead-land granted in concession to another and revives it, then the 'ulama differ as to the ruling thereon in three ways. According to the madhhab of ash-Shafi'i, the person who revives it is more entitled to it than the one granted the concession. Abu Hanifah says that if he revives it before the three years is up, then it is the property of the grant-holder - but that if he revives it after this, then it is the property of the one who revives it. Malik says that if the person who revives it is aware of the grant-right, then the property belongs to the grant-holder, and if he is not, then the grant-holder has the option of either taking possession of it and compensating the person who has revived it with the cost of its cultivation, or of leaving it to the one who has revived it and seeking to recover from his its value as dead land before it was revived.

Second, Cultivated land is of two kinds:

A. That whose owner is known: in this case the Sultan has no authority over it, except regarding any claim on it from the bait al-mal - that is, if it is situated in Dar al-Islam, irrespective of whether it belongs to a Muslim or to a dhimmi; if it is in Dar al-Harb, the possession of which cannot be firmly established by the Muslims, and the Imam wants to concede it as a grant so that the grant-holder may then acquire possession of it – when it is conquered – this is permitted. Thus Tamim ad-Dari asked the Messenger of Allah, may the peace and blessings of Allah be upon him, to give him the grant-right over some springs in a region of his in Syria – that is before it had been conquered – and he did this. Abu Talib al-Khushani also asked him for a land which was in the hands of the people of Rum and this amazed the Prophet who said: "Did you hear what he said?" Then he replied: "By the One Who has sent you with the Truth, He will conquer it for you." So he wrote it down in writing for him.

Likewise it is permitted for the Imam to accept the request of someone who seeks something still belonging to its owner in Dar al-Harb, or some prisoners, or women and children not yet captured, so that he will be more entitled to them when the land is conquered: such a gift is valid even if the (precise nature of the) thing is unknown because it is connected with questions of a general nature. Ash-Sha'bi narrates that Huraym ibn Aws ibn Harithah at-Ta'i said to the Prophet, may the peace and blessings of Allah be upon him: "If Allah conquers al-Hira for you, then give me the daughter of Nufaylah." When, later, Khalid ibn al-Walid wanted to make a peace treaty with the people of al-Hira, Huraym told him: "The Messenger of Allah, may the peace and blessings of Allah be upon him, gave bint Nufaylah to me, so do not make her part of the peace terms." Bashir ibn Sa'd and Muhammad ibn Maslamah testified for him, and so Khalid excluded her from the peace terms and handed her over to Huraym; she was then bought from him for a thousand dirhams – for she was now an old woman and had changed since the time he first knew of her. Someone said to him, "Woe on you: you have sold her off cheaply - her people would have paid double what you were asking," to which he replied, "I did not think there was a number greater than a thousand."

Thus, given that there are such grant-concessions and property rights secured through such means, examination should be made of the nature of the conquest: if it is by means of a peace-agreement, the land conceded in a grant should be set on one side and is excluded from the terms of the agreement by virtue of the prior grant-concession; if the conquest was achieved by force, then those who had asked for a grant-concession or property rights are more entitled to whatever was requested than the booty-takers. As for the latter, one should investigate whether they were aware of the grant-concession or gift of ownership before the conquest: if they were, then they may not seek compensation for what has been requested as a grant or granted; if they were not aware until the moment of the conquest, the Imam has to compensate them to their satisfaction, either for this – just as they should be compensated to their satisfaction for anything else deducted from the booty. Abu Hanifah, however, says that they do not have to be compensated to their satisfaction, either for this or for any other thing which he deems should be deducted from the booty.

B. This applies to cultivated land whose owners are not clearly known or whose property rights have not been defined. They are of three types:

i. land which has been chosen by the Imam for the bait al-mal at the time of conquest of various regions, either by reason of the khums which is taken in order to fulfil the rights of those entitled to it, or what has been taken in order to satisfy the booty-takers. 'Umar ibn al-Khattab, may Allah be pleased with him, set aside the Sawad land belonging to the Khusroes and his family, or belonging to those who had fled or perished; the revenue there from amounted to 9 million dirhams which he spent in the general interests of the Muslims, and he did not give anything in grant. Later, 'Uthman, may Allah be pleased with him, gave these lands as grants, because he judged that as grants, their revenue would be greater than if they were left fallow - but he stipulated to those to whom he granted a concession that the fay tax would be exacted from them. Thus this was a kind of hire-grant and not a property grant. The revenue was abundant: it was said that it amounted to 50 million dirhams, from which he used to make gifts and grants. The khulafa after him transmitted this revenue (from one to the next) as they succeeded each other; in 82 AH, known as "the Year of the Skulls," at the time of the discord caused by Ibn al-Ash'ath, the diwan records were burnt, and each group seized what lay around it.

The Sultan may not give a grant-right of ownership to this type of cultivated land: his setting it aside for the bait al-mal means that it is for the Muslims as a whole, and its status is that of a waqf-property in perpetuity. The revenue there from is used to make grants, and it is up to the Sultan to choose, after examination, what is of most benefit: he may either keep the revenue for the bait al-mal as 'Umar did, may Allah be pleased with him, or grant it to those who have the capacity to work at cultivating this land, in return for payment of the kharaj, the amount of which is assessed in accordance with the revenue, just as 'Uthman did, may Allah be pleased with him. Thus the kharaj is a hire-payment which is used for various matters of general need, unless it is taken as a khums - in which case it is spent on those entitled to the khums.

The kharaj payment may be paid in kind (*muqasamah*), at a rate of half of the fruit in the case of date-palms - since the Messenger of Allah, may the peace and blessings of Allah be upon him, granted the people of Khaybar use of their land in return for a half of the produce of their date-palms. As for whether this is permitted in the case of crops, this depends on the varying opinions of the fuqaha regarding payment in kind: those who accept muqasamah, permit the kharaj to be paid in this way; those who do not, do not permit the kharaj payment to be made in this way, although some say that it is permitted, as it involves a matter of general interest for which the rules are wider than for specific contracts. The 'ushr is imposed on crops, but not on fruit, as the crops are the property of those who sowed them, and the fruit is the property of the Muslims as a whole and is spent in their general interest.

ii. this type of cultivated land is that which is subject to the kharaj - in which case it is not allowed to be granted as a property-grant, as it is of two kinds: the first, is that whose status is a waqf, and its kharaj is a kind of hire-charge; property rights over waqf property cannot be acquired, neither by way of grant-concessions, sale or gift; the second, is that whose status is that of a property, and so its kharaj is a jizyah; whatever is owned - and whose owners are clearly known - may not be granted as a property-grant. As for granting the kharaj of this land, we shall discuss this later, in the section on granting revenue;

iii. this comprises property whose owners have died, and there is no claim to it by any inheritor or other tribe member: such property is transferred to the bait al-mal, and is inherited by all the Muslims and spent in their general interests. Abu Hanifah, however, says that the inheritance of someone who has no inheritors is spent on the poor as a kind of sadaqah from the dead person. According to ash-Shafi'i, it is to be used for more general purposes of a general benefit – since what was once private property has now become public property, after having been transferred to the bait al-mal.

The followers of ash-Shafi'i differ concerning the status of property which is transferred to the bait al-mal - as to whether it becomes waqf-property by the mere fact of transference: according to some, it does become waqf, as it is to be spent in a general way - in which case it is not permitted to sell it or grant it in grant; according to others, it does not become waqf-property, unless the Imam makes it a waqf - in which case he may sell it instead, if he thinks that the sale would be of more benefit to the bait al-mal: the sum raised is spent in the public interest, and on those in need amongst those entitled to the fay or those entitled to the zakah. As for giving it as a grant, according to this second opinion, there are some who say that it is permitted, arguing that as it may be sold and as he may use the sum raised for those whom he considers to be in need, or those who might benefit by it, then he may also give it as a grant: thus the property rights may be bestowed in the same way as the sale-price may be bestowed. There are others, however, who say that it may not be granted as a grant, but that it may be sold – because something is paid in return for the sale, whereas the grant is a gift; as for the sale-price, if it is paid in cash then it is subject, if it is a question of gifts, to a rule other than that of buildings, even though the difference is slight.

The above discussion covers the nature of a grant of the right of ownership.

2. As for the granting of (produce or) revenue, this may be of two kinds: the 'ushr or the kharaj:

First, as for the 'ushr, any type of grant is not permitted, because it is a zakah for a specific category of persons whose claim to it is established at the time it is allotted to them; it may be that they are not entitled at the moment that they make the claim, as it may only be handed over when certain conditions are fulfilled, and these may not be satisfied. If the claim is valid and the person receiving the 'ushr has a right to it at the time of transfer, then this transfer from the person paying it to the person entitled to it is valid: it may be handed over to the person, although the latter has no claim to it – merely as something owed to him – until he takes possession of it: zakah is only owned when possession has been taken. If someone is refused the 'ushr, he has no basis for argument and the official in charge of the 'ushr has more right to make a claim.

Second, as for the kharaj, the rulings governing its being granted vary according to the status of the grantee:

A. If the person is among those entitled to zakah, then he is not entitled to be granted some of the kharaj revenue, because the kharaj is fay and those entitled to zakah are not entitled to it – just as those entitled to fay are not entitled to zakah. Abu Hanifah, however, permits it - just as he allows the fay revenue to be spent on those entitled to zakah;

B. Amongst those who undertake works of public interest are those who have no fixed salary: it is not correct under any circumstances to make any grant to them, although it is permitted to give them something from the kharaj-revenue – because it is an extra benefit for those entitled to fay and not an obligatory right. Anything given to them is considered as being from the portion of what is given for works of public interest; if any of the kharaj is given to them it is treated as a payment to cover reasonable costs which are to be repaid, and not as a grant; moreover, its permissibility is dependent upon two conditions: the first, that it is for a specific amount and for a legitimate reason; the second, that the kharaj revenue involved has fallen due and may be exacted, so that a legitimate claim may be made on it, and a payment for what is owed completed. These two conditions necessarily exclude it from being a grant.

C. Those entitled to the fay and recorded in the diwan register are army personnel: they have more claim than others to grants, as they receive specific salaries accorded them by virtue of their right and as compensation for their devoting themselves to defending territory and protecting women and children.

If they claim to be among those entitled to a grant, then the kharaj revenue is examined: it is of two types, that originating from jizyah, and that from the revenue of rent:

A. The jizyah is not instituted in perpetuity, but is only exacted as long as a person remains an unbeliever, and is annulled as soon as a person accepts Islam. Thus it is not permitted to make a concession from it for more than a year, as it cannot be assured after this: thus if the concession is made after the year has elapsed, and the time for exacting the Jizyah has arrived, then it is valid; if the concession is made before payment (of the Jizyah) is due at the end of the year, then there are two aspects to its permissibility: it is permitted if it is said that payment is dependent upon the Jizyah payment falling due, but it is not if it is said that payment will be obligatory when the Jizyah falls due.

B. If it involves kharaj which is paid as a rent, then it is in perpetuity, and so it is valid to grant it for several years; it is not necessary to restrict it for a single year, as opposed to the Jizyah, which is not established in perpetuity. This being so, then the grant will necessarily be one of three kinds:

1. The grant is made for a specific number of years, say ten for example: this will be valid on fulfilment of two conditions: **i.** that the amount of the salary is known to the person making the concession: if not, then it is not valid; **ii.** that the amount of the kharaj is known to the person receiving the concession and the person making it: if it is not known by either or both of them, then it is not valid.

This being so, the kharaj will necessarily be of one of two types, either muqaasama, paid in kind, or paid according to the measure. If paid in kind, then those fuqaha who permit payment in kind for the kharaj consider that it involves a specific amount and that therefore concessions may consequently be made; those who prohibit payment made in kind consider that it is an unknown amount, and that as such it is not permitted to make a concession of it. If it is paid according to the measure, then it is of two types: the first, is that which does not vary according to the varying yield of the crops - in which case the amount is known, and so it is valid to give it as a concession; the second, is that which does vary according to the yield of the crops - in which case the salary of the grantee must be investigated: if it is equal to the highest amount of the two types of kharaj then it is valid to give it as a concession, as the person receiving it will accept a lesser amount if it occurs; if the salary is equal to the lowest amount of the two types of kharaj, then it is not valid to give it as a concession, as there might turn out to be more than this, and he would not have a right to it.

Having established the validity of the concession (in the first example) one must take account of the circumstances of the grantee during the period of the concession: he will necessarily be one of three types:

i. he remains in a good state of health until the end of the concession, in which case he is entitled to it until the end of the term;

ii. he dies before the end of the term, in which case the concession is annulled for the rest of the period and it reverts back to the bait al-mal; if he has children, they share in the funds reserved for children and not in the salaries for the army: what they are given is an extra amount from the fay in order to sustain them - and not a concession;

iii. he falls chronically ill, such that he no longer enjoys good health for the rest of his life, in which case there are two opinions as to whether his concession is still valid after the onset of his illness: the first, that it remains valid until the end of the term; and the second, that his salary is annulled at the onset of the chronic illness.

These then are the rulings regarding the first kind, that is a concession made for a fixed period.

2. This refers to the person who seeks a concession for the duration of his life, and then for his descendants and inheritors after his death: this concession is invalid, as it would go beyond the jurisdiction of the bait al-mal and become a kind of inherited property; whatever he did take as a concession (in these circumstances) would be taken with permission, but by virtue of a corrupt contract: thus those who gave the kharaj would be released from their responsibility. (In these circumstances) the amount is deducted from his salary as a whole, and if he has received more than his due, he must repay it and if less, then he should claim the missing amount. The Sultan then makes the invalidity of the concession known, so that the person is prevented from taking it, and the people of kharaj from giving it; if, however, they do pay it after its invalidity has been publicised, then they are not released from their liability;

3. This applies to someone who seeks a concession for the duration of his life. There are two opinions on this matter: the first, is that it is valid if it is stated (at the outset) that the onset of a chronic disease will not result in the annulment of his salary; the second, that it is invalid if it is said that the onset of a chronic disease will necessarily result in the annulment of his salary. If it is valid, and the Sultan wants to take it back from the grantee, then it is permitted after the year in question, and his salary reverts back to the diwan in charge of funds. As for the year in question, if his salary falls due before the kharaj falls due, then it is not taken back from him, as he still has a claim over the kharaj; if, however, the kharaj falls due before his salary falls due, then it is permitted to withdraw it and set it aside as payment of a debt falling due in the future; it is not, however, obligatory.

As for payment of non-army personnel, if they are granted concessions from the kharaj revenue, then it will be one of three kinds:

First, those granted payment for some work which is not of a permanent nature, like works of public benefit or the collection of the kharaj - such salaries are invalid, and whatever they receive of it from the kharaj revenue is treated as an extra payment made from the fay for a particular reason and given after their claim has been made, at the time that the kharaj falls due;

Second, those who receive payment for work of a permanent nature, in which case this payment is like a wage; such persons are those who do works of public good which are valid when undertaken voluntarily; if they receive a salary for it, like the job of the mu'adhdhin, or the Imam, then giving them something from the kharaj as a salary is not a concession, but a lump sum paid from the fay for a particular reason and treated as a debt which must be paid.

Third, those who receive payment for work of a permanent nature, in which case it is like a salary; this applies to persons whose jurisdiction is only valid when they are given authority and appointed to the post, like qadis, judges and diwan scribes: it is permitted to make a concession for them to be paid from the kharaj for one single year; permission to grant this for more than one year has two aspects: the first where it is permitted, as in the case of the army; the second; where it is not – in the case where they may be dismissed or replaced.

3. As for granting concessions from mines, that is, those areas in which Allah has deposited the precious materials of the earth, they consist of two types: open and concealed.

The open are those where the precious deposits are on the surface, like mines of antimony, salt, tar and naptha; these are treated in the same category as water which may not be given as a concession: everyone has an equal right to them, and anyone who comes to them may take from them. Thabit ibn Sa'id narrates from his father, from his grandfather, that al-Abyad ibn Hammal sought a concession for the salt of Ma'arab from the Messenger of Allah, may the peace and blessings of Allah be upon him, and he granted it to him. Then al-Aqra' ibn Habis at-Tamimi said: "O Messenger of Allah, in the Jahiliyyah era, I came to this salt deposit and there was no other in the region; whoever comes to it may take from it, and it is like *'idd*-water in a land which keeps renewing itself." He then asked al-Abyad to renounce this concession for the salt. He replied: "I renounce it to you, but on condition that you consider it a sadaqah from me." Then the Prophet, on whom be peace and blessings, said: "It is a sadaqah from you, and it is like water which does not dry up and anyone who comes to it may take it." Abu 'Ubaid said: "Water which is called *'idd*-water is that which is renewed from springs or wells," while another has said that it is (a large expanse of water) which has been collected.

If, however, open mines such as these are given in a concession, there is no legal ruling and the grantee and any others are on an equal footing: all those who come to such areas may participate equally in them; if the grantee tries to prevent them from having access to them, then he is committing a wrong action, although he is still the owner of what he has taken, and is only in the wrong in preventing access. He should be stopped from preventing access and from working the mine continuously, so that his "concession" is not established as valid, and so that he does not become treated as the owner.

As for concealed mines, these mean those whose precious materials are hidden and may only be reached by working them, like mines for gold, silver, copper or iron: these and the like are known as concealed mines, irrespective of whether the material extracted needs to be smelted and refined or not.

There are two opinions as to the permissibility of granting them as concessions: the first, is that like open mines, it is not permitted, and that everyone has an equal right to them; the second, is that this is permitted, since Kathir ibn 'Abdallah ibn 'Amr ibn 'Awf al-Muzani narrated from his father, from his grandfather, that the Messenger of Allah, may the peace and blessings of Allah be upon him, granted a concession to Bilal ibn al-Harith of the Qabiliyyah mines, including both the Jalsi and the Ghawri areas, and also the area of al-Quds which was good for agriculture - but in granting him this concession, he did not infringe on the rights of any other Muslim. There are two interpretations of the Jalsi and the Ghawri: one, that they refer to the high part and the low part of the area, and this is what 'Abdallah ibn Wahb says; and the second, that Jalsi means the region of Najd, and Ghawri, the region of Tihamah, and this is what Abu 'Ubaidah says. This is affirmed by ash-Shimakh in the following:

> *She passed by the water of al-'Udhayb and her eye was like an empty socket (full) of pebbles – her Najd (Jalsi) had become Tihamah (Ghawri).*

If one follows this point of view then the grantee is more entitled to it, and may prevent others from gaining access to it.

As for the status of this concession, there are two opinions: the first, that it also grants the right of ownership, so that the grantee becomes the owner of the actual mine just in the same way as he would for any other property of his which he is working; when he ceases, he may sell it during his lifetime, and it is transferred to his inheritors after his death; the second, is that it is a concession only granting the use thereof, and that he does not own the actual mine, but only owns the right to use it as long as he works it: no one may dispute his right to it as long as he is working it; if he abandons it, then the right to this concession is annulled, and it reverts to open access to all.

If someone revives a dead land – whether by means of a concession or not – and an open or concealed mine is uncovered in the course of this revival, then the one responsible becomes its owner in perpetuity, just as he would become the owner of a spring which he activates, or a well which he digs.

Chapter 18
The Diwan and the Rulings Governing It

The diwan is set up to maintain the rights of the authorities under the Sultan regarding (public) works, finance and those employed in these authorities.

There are two interpretations of the name diwan: the first, is that one day Khusroes caught sight of the scribes of his diwan settling the accounts among themselves and he said, "diwaneh", meaning "mad persons", and thus this name came to be attached to this place; then the "eh" was omitted through continual use and it became abbreviated to diwan; the second, is that "diwan" is the Persian for "demons", and the scribes were so called because of their cunningness in affairs, and their capacity to make something public or keep it secret and to place together things which are different or separate – and so the place where they worked came to have the same name as themselves, namely, diwan.

The first person to set up a diwan in the Islamic era was 'Umar ibn al-Khattab, may Allah be pleased with him. There is a difference of opinion as to why he set it up. Some say that the reason for it was that Abu Hurairah came to him with wealth from Bahrain and 'Umar asked him what he had come with. When he replied, "500,000 dirhams" 'Umar thought the amount was rather large and said: "Do you realise what you are saying?" He replied: "Yes, five times a hundred thousand." 'Umar then said, "Is that good?" to which the other replied, "I do not know." Then 'Umar mounted the mimbar and after praising and extolling Allah, ta'ala, he said: "O people, a great amount of wealth has come to us and we shall either weigh it or count it, as you wish." Then a man stood up and approached him saying: "O Amir of the Believers, I have seen the non-Arabs set up diwans for themselves, so set one up for us." Others say that the reason was that 'Umar was sending off a party amongst whom was Hurmuzan, who said to him: "You have given expenses to this party: if one of the men stays behind and remains at home, how then will your companion (in charge) know this? So set up a diwan for them!" 'Umar then asked him about this and he explained what it was.

'Abid ibn Yahya narrates from al-Harith ibn Nufail that 'Umar, may Allah be pleased with him, sought advice of the Muslims regarding the setting up of the diwan and 'Ali ibn Abi Talib, may Allah be pleased with him, replied: "Distribute the wealth that you accumulate each year, and do not keep any back." 'Uthman ibn 'Affan, may Allah be pleased with him, said: "I consider that there is enough wealth for everyone, but I fear that the matter will get out of hand if we do not take account of who has received something and who has not." Al-Waleed ibn Hisham said: "I was in Syria and I saw their rulers set up diwans and armies, so set up diwans and set up armies." 'Umar accepted this and called for 'Aqeel ibn Abi Talib, Makhramah ibn Nawfil and Jubayr ibn Mut'im, who were amongst the young men of the Quraysh, saying: "Write down the people according to their ranks." They thus started with the Banu Hashim, followed by Abu Bakr and his people, then 'Umar and his people, and then wrote down the tribes and their differences in rank, and then they handed it over to 'Umar. When he saw it, he said: "No, I did not want it to be like this: begin with the nearest of the family of the Messenger of Allah, may the peace and blessings of Allah be upon him, and then the nearest after them, so that you put 'Umar where Allah has put him." Al-'Abbas, may Allah be content with him, thanked him for this, and he said: "Your bond is a tie of kinship."

Zayd ibn Aslam narrates from his father that the Banu 'Adi came to 'Umar, saying: "You are the Khalifah of the Messenger of Allah and the Khalifah of Abu Bakr, and Abu Bakr is the Khalifah of the Messenger of Allah – why do you not place yourself where Allah, may He be praised, has placed you, and where those who wrote the lists placed you?" He replied: "Excellent! O Banu 'Adi, do you want to eat off my back and that I grant you my good actions? No! However, until your turn comes and you are included in the register – meaning even if you are registered the last of those listed – I have two companions with me on the journey, and if they were to follow them on the journey, they would do the same for me. By Allah, any excellence of this world which has come to us, any reward that we might hope for with Allah ta'ala for our work, is but by Muhammad, may the peace and blessings of Allah be upon him, for he is all our honour, and his people are the most noble of the Arabs, and then those nearest in lineage after him in their turn; by Allah, if the non-Arabs come with actions and we come with none, they would have greater priority with Muhammad, may the peace and blessings of Allah be upon him, than us on the Day of Raising Up: those who are lacking in action will not be speeded along by virtue of their genealogy."

'Amir narrates that when 'Umar wanted to set down the register, may Allah be pleased with him, he said: "With whom should I begin?" 'Abd ar-Rahman said that he should begin with himself. 'Umar replied: "You remind me of the time when I was with the Messenger, may the peace and blessings of Allah be upon him, and he began with the Banu Hashim and the Banu 'Abd al-Muttalib." Thus 'Umar began with them, and then followed them with the various tribes of the Quraysh, clan by clan, until he had included all of the Quraysh, and then he went on to the Ansar. 'Umar said: "Begin with the family of Sa'd ibn Mu'adh from the Aws, and then with those closest to him." Az-Zuhri narrates from Sa'id ibn al-Musayyab that this took place in Muharram, 10 AH.

When the list of people had been drawn up in the diwan registers according to the proximity of their relationship to the Messenger of Allah, may the peace and blessings of Allah be upon him, he granted proportionally more to those who had entered earliest into Islam, and in accordance with their proximity in lineage to the Messenger of Allah, may the peace and blessings of Allah be upon him. Abu Bakr, may Allah be pleased with him, had considered that they should all be treated equally, and that those who had entered Islam before others should not be given proportionally more; likewise 'Ali, may Allah be pleased with him, did the same in his khilafah, and this was adopted by ash-Shafi'i and Malik. 'Umar, may Allah be pleased with him, considered that preference be given to those who had entered Islam first, and this was likewise the view of 'Uthman, may Allah be pleased with him. This view was adopted by Abu Hanifah and the fuqaha of Iraq. 'Umar had discussed the matter with Abu Bakr, when the latter had treated people equally, saying: "Would you treat as the same those who participated in the two hijrahs and prayed to the two qiblahs and those who became Muslim in the Year of the Conquest under the threat of the sword?" Abu Bakr then replied: "Surely they acted for Allah, and their reward will be from Allah, and this world is only a means of reaching (the next) for the rider." 'Umar: "I will not treat those who fought against the Messenger of Allah like those who fought with him."

Thus when he set up the diwan, he gave correspondingly more to those who had preceded others in Islam: he granted 5,000 dirhams annually to each person who had been at Badr from amongst the first of the Muhajirun; among them were 'Ali ibn Abi Talib, 'Uthman ibn 'Affan, Talhah ibn 'Ubaidullah, az-Zubayr ibn al-'Awwam and 'Abd ar-Rahman ibn 'Awf, may Allah be pleased with them. He also awarded 5,000 to himself together with the others, and included al-'Abbas ibn 'Abd al-Muttalib and al-Hasan and al-

Hussein, may Allah be pleased with them, by virtue of their rank in the eyes of the Messenger of Allah, may the peace and blessings of Allah be upon him. It is also said, however, that he gave preference to al-'Abbas, granting him 7,000 dirhams. To all those at Badr from amongst the Ansar he granted 4,000 dirhams, and he did not prefer anyone over the people of Badr except the wives of the Messenger of Allah, may the peace and blessings of Allah be upon him, each of whom he gave 10,000, except for A'ishah, to whom he gave 12,000; he also included Juwayriyyah bint al-Harith and Safiyyah bint Huyayy amongst them. According to others, he gave each 6,000. To those who had made the Hijrah before the Conquest, he gave 3,000, and to those who had become Muslims after the Conquest, he gave 2,000; the young men whose fathers were either from amongst those who made the Hijrah or from amongst the Ansar were treated as those who had become Muslim after the Conquest. 'Umar ibn Abi Salamah al-Makhzumi was given 4,000 dirhams , because his mother Umm Salamah was a wife of the Prophet, may Allah grant him peace and blessings. Muhammad ibn 'Abdallah ibn Jahsh then said: "Why do you prefer 'Umar (ibn Abi Salamah) to us, when our fathers made the Hijrah and were at Badr?" 'Umar then replied: "I have given preference to him because of his rank in the eyes of the Messenger of Allah, may the peace and blessings of Allah be upon him. Anyone who can demand to be pleased because he has a mother like Umm Salamah, then I will please him." He granted 4,000 dirhams to 'Usamah ibn Zayd, and then 'Abdallah ibn 'Umar, said, "You give me 3,000, and 4,000 to 'Usamah, and I have been present at times when he has not!" - "I gave him more," said 'Umar, "because he was more beloved to the Messenger of Allah than you were, and his father was more beloved to the Messenger of Allah than your father." Then, to the others, he granted in proportion to their rank, to their recitation of the Qur'an, and to their jihad. To the people of Yemen, the Qays in Syria, and Iraq, he granted to each man an amount varying between two thousand, a thousand, five hundred and three hundred - and he did not go below this amount, saying: "If there was more money, I would give 4,000 to each man - 1,000 for his horse, 1,000 for his arms, 1,000 for his travel expenses and 1,000 to leave with his people."

He gave 100 dirhams to newborn babies, and 200 if they were older, and increased this if they had reached puberty. He had not granted anything for a child until he had been weaned – until the night he heard a mother discouraging her child from breast feeding; the child was crying, and he asked her about it, to which she replied: "Umar does not grant anything to a child until he has been weaned: I am discouraging him from breast-feeding, so that he will be granted his share." Then he said: "O woe to 'Umar - how many mistakes he makes without knowing it." Then he gave orders to his herald to announce: "Do not hurry to wean your children. We will grant a portion to every child in Islam." Then he wrote to the people of al-'Awali, to whom he gave subsistence, and ordered that they be given a measure (jareeb) of wheat which he had milled, and made into bread, and then steeped in soup; then he called thirty persons and fed them their morning meal from it until they were satisfied. He did the same for the evening meal, and said: "Two jareebs is thus enough for each man every month." So he stipulated for each man or woman or slave-girl two jareebs every month; such was the custom, that if a man wanted to make a supplication against another, he would say to him: "May Allah cut off your two jareebs from you."

The diwan was set up in accordance with the call to the Arabs (made by the Prophet) and the order was in accordance with their genealogy; preference, regarding the amount, was given in proportion to the precedence of a person's entry into Islam, and to his good works in the deen; when the first to become Muslims were no longer alive, preferential amounts were accorded in proportion to their bravery and the trials undergone in their jihad.

This is the ruling regarding the diwan of the army at the outset, based on how soon people became Muslim and on their being categorised according to (their service to) the shari'ah.

As for the diwan responsible for settling payments and collecting monies, it continued in this way, after the arrival of Islam in Syria and Iraq, as it had done before. The diwan of Syria used the language of Rum, as it had been among the territories of Rum, and that of Iraq used the Persian language, as it had belonged to those of Persia; this situation continued during the reign of 'Abd al-Malik ibn Marwan until the diwan of Syria began to use Arabic in 81 AH. The reason for this change, according to al-Mada'ini, was that one of the scribes of Rum in his diwan needed some water for his inkwell, and so he urinated in it instead of using water. 'Abd al-Malik reprimanded him for this and ordered Sulayman ibn Sa'd to translate the diwan (records) into Arabic; the latter then asked if he could be placed in charge of the kharaj of Jordan for a year – which the Khalifah granted – and it amounted to 180,000 dinars. The year was not out, before he had completed the diwan records and translated them into Arabic. He came with these records to 'Abd al-Malik ibn Marwan, and the latter called his scribe Sarjun and showed them to him: they troubled him, and he went out aggrieved; he was met by a group of the scribes of Rum and he told them: "Look for a means of living other than this trade, for Allah has cut this off from you."

As for the Persian diwan in Iraq, the reason for its records being translated into Arabic was that al-Hajjaj's scribe was called Zadan Farrukh, and there was along with him Salih ibn 'Abd ar-Rahman, who wrote under his supervision in Arabic and in Persian, and whom Zadan Farrukh attached to al-Hajjaj, for he was important in his view. Salih said to Zadan Farrukh: "Al-Hajjaj has brought me close to him, and I have no guarantee that he will not show more favour to me than to you." He then replied: "Do not think that, for he has more need of me than of you, because he has no one who can do his accounts for him other than me." Then Salih said: "By Allah, if I wished, I could translate the accounts into Arabic", to which the other replied: "Then translate a page or a line of them, so that I may see." And this he did. Then later Zadan Farrukh was killed at the time of 'Abd ar-Rahman ibn al-Ash'ath, and al-Hajjaj replaced him with Salih. He then mentioned to him what had occurred between him and Zadan Farrukh, and al-Hajjaj commanded him to translate the records into Arabic; this he accepted, and he completed it in the time accorded to him. When Mardanshah ibn Zadan Farrukh realised this, he offered 100,000 dirhams to Salih for him to feign incapacity for the task. This, however, he did not do and so he said to him: "May Allah cut you off from all your earthly connections just as you have cut the connection with Persian." 'Abd al-Hameed ibn Yahya, Marwan's scribe, then said: "How great is Salih, what a vast gift he has bestowed on the scribes."

The diwan of the Sultan may be divided into four divisions: the first, is specific to the army, the assignment of its posts and its expenditure; the second, to the various provinces and their taxes and claims; the third, to the provinces with respect to their officials, that is, their appointment and their dismissal; the fourth, to the bait al-mal, that is, its income and expenditure. These four divisions are governed by the relevant laws of the shari'ah, although the details relative to each individual diwan-department are often better known by its scribes.

1. This division is specific to the assignment of posts and the expenditure of the army. Their assignment to the diwan-records is dependent upon three conditions: that is, the description (of their rank) by which they may be entered into the diwan, the reason for their entitlement to a particular rank, and the criteria by means of which their salaries may be assessed.

As for the conditions by a virtue of which they may be recorded in the diwan, five characteristics must be taken into account:

First, puberty, since those under age are treated as children and dependants: they are thus not permitted to be recorded in the diwan of the army, although they are covered by the grants accorded to children;

Second, being free, since any person who is owned is dependent upon his master, and is included with the grant to the latter. Abu Hanifah, however, does not consider it a condition that he be a freeman, and permits the slave to be recorded in the register of combatants, and to receive his own grant: this was the opinion of Abu Bakr, but he was opposed in this by 'Umar, who considered that a person should be free in order to receive a salary, and this view is adopted by ash-Shafi'i;

Third, Islam, since he will find himself in a position of having to defend the nation by virtue of his beliefs, and he will be trusted regarding his sincerity and his efforts; if a dhimmi is recorded amongst them, this is not permitted, and anyone who reneges on his Islam is struck off;

Fourth, free of any sickness which would preclude him from fighting: thus he may not be chronically sick, or blind, or missing a limb - but he may be deaf and dumb; as for the lame person, he may be registered as a rider but not as a foot-soldier;

Fifth, prowess in war and knowledge of fighting: those whose ability to go forward is weak, and who have little knowledge of fighting, may not be registered, since they would be attempting what they are incapable of doing.

If these five qualities are fulfilled in someone, then his being registered in the diwan of the army is dependent upon his demand it and then its being accepted; the one making the request must be free of other work, in which case the person in charge should accept his request if there is a need for him.

If the person in question is well-known and important, it is not good to describe or qualify his name when registering him; if, however, he is among the ordinary, a description of his qualities should be made, mentioning his age, his size, his colour, his facial characteristics and any distinguishing marks, so that those bearing the same name may not be confused; at the time of being given his salary, he is called in the presence of the chief officer or lieutenant, so that they may be witnesses of his having received it.

As for the order in which they are registered in the diwan, this may be either in a general or in a particular order. As for the general, this applies to the order of tribes and races, so that each tribe is distinguished from the other and each race from that which is different to it. Those among whom differences may exist are not put together, and those between whom harmony reigns are not separated, with the result that when the diwan calls people up, there is an established order based on lineage, and any possibility of dispute or contention is avoided.

This being so, the people will necessarily be either Arabs or non-Arabs. If they are Arabs, then they are both united and distinguished by their lineage, and their tribes are arranged in order, depending on their proximity to the Messenger of Allah, may the peace and blessings of Allah be upon him, just as was done by 'Umar, may Allah be pleased with him, when he first registered them. One begins the order with the origin of the lineage, and then with its branches. The Arabs are descended from either 'Adnan or Qahtan, and the 'Adnan precedes the Qahtan because prophethood appeared among them; the 'Adnan are descended either from Rabi'ah or Mudar, and the latter precede the former because prophethood appeared amongst them; the Mudar consist of both the Quraysh and the non-Quraysh, and the former take precedence, as prophethood manifested amongst them; the Quraysh comprise the Banu Hashim and those who are not Banu Hashim, and the former take precedence likewise, and they constitute the pivotal point of the ordering, others following them according to their proximity of lineage, until all of the Quraysh are listed; likewise, by proximity of lineage, until all of the Mudar are listed, and then likewise for those of the 'Adnan.

The genealogy of the Arabs is composed of six ranks, the different levels being known as *sha'b, qabeelah, 'imarah, batn, fakhidh* and *faseelah.*

The sha'b ('a people' lit. 'branch') is the most distant lineage, like the 'Adnan and the Qahtan and it is called thus because in Arabic it refers to that from which the tribes branch out; the qabeelah ('tribe') refers to the genealogical divisions of the sha'b, such as the Rabi'ah and the Mudar; it is thus described because the word qabeelah in Arabic refers to how the different tribes face each other (genealogically); the 'imarah ('house' lit. 'building' or 'structure') refers to the divisions resulting from the qabeelah, such as the Quraysh and the Kinanah; the batn refers to the genealogical divisions of the 'imarah, such as the Banu 'Abd al-Manaf and the Banu Makhzum; the fakhidh refers to the divisions resulting from the batn, such as the Banu Hashim and the Banu Umayyah, and finally, the faseelah refers to the divisions of the fakhidh, such as the Banu Abu Talib and the Banu 'Abbas. Thus the fakhidh encompasses the faseelahs, the batn encompasses the fakhidhs, the 'imarah encompasses the batns, the qabeelah encompasses the 'imarahs and the sha'b encompasses the qabeelahs. As the generations become more and more distant from each other, the qabeelahs become sha'bs and the 'imarahs become qabeelahs.

Even though the non-Arabs are not encompassed by a genealogy, they are affiliated by two elements, namely by race and by country. Those who are distinguished by race, such as the Turks and the Indians, are themselves subdivided into other races; those who are distinguished by country, such as those of Daylam and Jabal, are also subdivided into regions. Thus having distinguished them by race or by country, they are entered in the diwan in order of those who first became Muslims; and if they have not become Muslims, then according to the degree of the blood-relationship with their leader; and if they are alike in this degree, then according to when they gave their allegiance to him.

With regards to the particular order, this refers to the individuals who are listed according to when they became Muslims; if they became Muslims at the same time, then they are listed according to (their excellence in) the deen; and if they are alike in this, then according to their age; and if they are alike in age, then according to their degree of courage; and if they are alike in this, then the leader has the option of either listing them on the basis of lots, or according to his opinion and judgement.

*

*   *

As for the amount of the salary, it should be enough so that the person does not need to seek elsewhere for anything, lest his defence of the territory be interrupted. Three elements are taken into account regarding this sufficiency: **i.** the number of dependants he has, that is women, children and slaves; **ii.** the number of horses and mounts he keeps at the ready; **iii.** the relative cost of the place he is in. An amount sufficient to cover his expenses and clothing is assessed for the whole year, and this is reckoned with his salary; his situation is then examined each year, and if his outgoings have increased, it is raised, and if they have decreased, it is lowered.

The fuqaha differ as to whether it is permitted to increase his salary after he has been given an assessment for an amount sufficient for his provision. Ash-Shafi'i prohibits any increase above what is sufficient, even if there are ample funds, as the wealth of the bait al-mal may only be spent on necessary claims; Abu Hanifah, however, permits an increase over what suffices if there are ample funds.

Payment of the salary is on a specific date, and army personnel may attend when their claim becomes due. This date is determined by the time when the bait al-mal has received all that is due: if what is due is paid at one time of the year, then the salaries are paid at the beginning of each year; if what is due is paid twice a year, the salaries are paid twice a year; if paid every month, the salaries are paid at the beginning of each month, so that the monies are paid to them after they have been received. Thus they are not prevented from receiving them if they are there, but also they may not demand them if what is due has not yet been collected.

If there is a delay in payment to those with a claim, and it exists in the bait al-mal, then they may demand it just like any claim for a debt. If the bait al-mal has been emptied because of some event, and this has caused the annulment of his claim or caused a delay to it, then his provision is treated as a debt against the bait al-mal, but he cannot demand it from the person in power, just as the creditor cannot demand repayment from someone without the means to pay.

If the person in authority wants to disband part of the army because of some reason which makes it necessary, or for some valid excuse, then this is permitted; if there is no reason, then this is not permitted, as the soldiers constitute the army of the Muslims, responsible for defending the Muslims.

If someone from the army wishes to withdraw his name from the diwan register, this is permitted as long as he is not needed, but it is not permitted if he is needed, unless he has an excuse.

If an army is sent into combat and they refuse to fight when their numbers are equal to those whom they are fighting, then their salaries are annulled; if they are fewer in number, they are not annulled.

If someone's mount perishes in the fighting, he is compensated for it, but if it does not, he is not; if someone uses up his arms in the fighting, he is compensated for them, as long as provision has not been made for them in the assessment of his salary, in which case no compensation is made. Someone who is sent out on a journey receives the expenses of that journey, as long as this has not already been assessed in his salary, in which case he does not. If someone dies or is killed, then what is due to him as his salary is inherited from him in accordance with the proportions fixed by Allah, ta'ala: it is treated as a debt which is owed to his inheritors from the bait al-mal.

The fuqaha differ as to whether the expenses necessary for the upkeep of his children should continue to be paid from his salary: some say that the diwan of the army is no longer liable for their expenses, since the person entitled to the salary no longer exists: rather, these expenses are met by the revenue from the 'ushr and the zakah; according to others, the expenses for his children continue to be drawn from his salary, in order to encourage him to stand his ground in battle and to stimulate him into attacking (when he is still alive).

They also differ as to whether his salary is annulled if he becomes chronically sick: according to some it is annulled, as it otherwise is paid in return for work which is not being done; according to a second opinion, payment is continued – to encourage recruitment by stimulating those who seek provision thereby.

2. This section is concerned with the taxes and claims of the various provinces and is comprised of six parts:

First, this concerns defining the province by those features which distinguish it from others, and then dividing it into various districts which may be governed by different rules; thus each region is defined by a border which separates it from others, and each region is divided into different districts, if the rulings thereof differ from each other. If the rulings of the estates within each district differ, then these are divided in the same manner as the district is divided; if they do not, then division is restricted to districts;

Second, reference is made as to whether the region was conquered by force or by treaty; reference is also made as to what has been established regarding the rulings governing its land, namely, whether it is 'ushr or kharaj, and whether the rulings governing its districts are different or the same, there being necessarily one of three possible situations: either the whole land is 'ushr-land, or it is all kharaj land, or it is a mixture of the two:

i. if it is all 'ushr land, it is not measure to establish its surface area as the 'ushr is based on the harvest and not on area: whenever sowing takes place, the 'ushr-diwan is informed and so no kharaj is imposed on this land; the names of the farmers must be mentioned when the diwan is informed, as the 'ushr is an obligation on them, not on those who actually own the land; if the date of sowing and the names of the farmers are given, then mention is also made of the measure (of the harvest) and the manner of its irrigation - whether it is natural or artificial - as the ruling (regarding the amount of 'ushr) differs accordingly;

ii. if the whole land is kharaj, the surface area must be measured as the kharaj is based on the surface area. If the kharaj is paid as a kind of rent, then it is not necessary to name those working the land, as it does not make any difference if they are Muslims or not; if it is given as a jizyah, then the names of the farmers must be given and also whether they are Muslims or not, as the ruling varies depending on the difference (in religions) of its people;

iii. if some of the land is subject to the 'ushr and some to the kharaj, then whatever is 'ushr-land is registered in the 'ushr-diwan, and whatever is kharaj in the kharaj diwan because they are each governed by a different ruling and each is treated according to its own particular ruling;

Third, this concerns the rulings governing the kharaj of each province and what has been established concerning their surface areas, namely whether it is paid in kind from the crops, or as a specific sum: if paid in kind, then when the measurements of the surface areas are given to the kharaj-diwan, mention is also made of the proportion which is paid in kind - whether a quarter, a third or a half - and the sizes of the measures used are also reported to the diwan, so that the correct amount in kind may be taken. If the kharaj is paid in silver coins, then it is necessarily either a fixed amount, independent of the diversity of the crops, or a variable amount dependent on the diversity of the crops. If the amount is fixed, despite the diversity of crops, then the surface areas are ascertained from the kharaj-diwan, in order to establish the amount of the kharaj, and only the amount collected is made over to the diwan; if the kharaj varies according to the diversity of the crops, then the surface areas must be ascertained from the diwan, and the various kinds of crops must be reported, so that the kharaj paid from each area is in accordance with the amounts connected with each crop.

Fourth, reference is made as to all the dhimmis in each region, and the amount which has been established as payable by the contract of jizyah; if the amount varies according to whether the persons have difficulty or not in paying, then they are named, along with their numbers, in the diwan, so that their relative financial ease or difficulty may be examined. If it does not vary according to their financial circumstances, then it is permitted to restrict oneself to recording their numbers. Account must be taken each year of those who have reached the age of puberty, of those who have died – so that their names may be removed– and of those who have become Muslims, so that the total amount due for their jizyah may be established;

Fifth, if the province comprises a mining area, then reference is made of the different kinds of mines and the number of each kind, so that the amount due from each may be gathered: this does not depend on the surface area or on an evaluation, because of the changing circumstances; rather, it depends on what is extracted from them, that is, what they produce.

It is not necessary, regarding the status of mines, to describe in the diwan how they were conquered or whether they exist in 'ushr land or kharaj land as the diwan is only concerned with collecting a tax based on the output of the mine - which it does not depend on how it was conquered, or on what type of land it is: rather, any differences are to do with the rights of those working it, and how much may be taken. We have already discussed the differences amongst the fuqaha as to what tax is imposed on which minerals or metals and how much is to be taken. If there is no precedent concerning a particular material, then the person in authority at the time should make ijtihad in order to arrive at a judgement as to whether the material is taxable and the amount to be taken: people should act in accordance with this judgement in both cases, if he is someone capable of ijtihad; if, however, there exists a precedent from one of the imams or governors, concerning which materials must be subject to the tax and the amount taken, then this ruling remains valid with regard to the materials in question, but not with regard to the amount to be paid on them - because the ruling governing the material was made regarding existing mines, but that governing the amount, was made on materials not yet mined;

Sixth, if the region is at the frontier, adjacent to Dar al-Harb, and their goods are allowed to come into the territory of Islam in return for a tenth, as agreed by treaty with them, then this is recorded in the diwan as well as the amount to be taken from them, be it a tenth, a fifth, or more or less, and if it depends on the kind of baggage and goods, then these differences are also recorded. The diwan is set up, in effect, to collect the taxes of the region, and to exact a levy on the goods passing through it in proportion to their volume.

As for exacting a tenth on goods being transported within Dar al-Islam, from region to region, this is forbidden; it is neither permitted by the shari'ah nor allowed by ijtihad; it is neither a just policy nor an equitable decision, and it rarely exists – other than in those countries where it is tolerated (but is nevertheless unjust). Moreover, it is narrated of the Prophet, may the peace and blessings of Allah be upon him that: "The worst of people are those who collect the 'ushr and taxes."

If governors change the legal status of regions and the amount of taxes imposed, then what they have done must be examined: if this has been justified by ijtihad for some necessary matter which has arisen, and is not prohibited by the shari'ah, then an increase or decrease may be warranted, in which case this second amount of tax is exacted and not the first. If information concerning the practice of tax collection is required from the diwan, it is permitted to restrict this information to this second amount, and to omit the first, although as a precaution, it is better to supply information concerning both amounts, as the reason for the new amount may disappear, and then the first amount may have to be re-imposed.

If what is collected by the governors in accordance with to the modified amount is not permitted by the shari'ah, and has no justification according to ijtihad, then the tax should be re-imposed according to the old amount, and the first amount is annulled, irrespective of whether it represents an increase or a decrease, as any increase would be an injustice to those subject to the tax, and any decrease would be an injustice to the claim to it exercised by the bait al-mal. When the diwan is asked to supply information about fiscal practice, the scribe responsible should give the two amounts if the governor does not know what previous practice was; if, however, he is aware of previous practice then it is not necessary to inform him of the first amount as he already has knowledge of it, and so it is permitted for the scribe to restrict information to the second amount, mentioning simply that it represents a new amount.

∗

∗ ∗

3. This section is concerned particularly with the appointment and dismissal of finance officials and comprises six parts:

First, this concerns those who may appoint such officials, namely those empowered to issue orders and to exercise authority: thus all those who exercise authority in a matter have the right to issue orders, and it is valid that they appoint those responsible for carrying out these orders. Such a person will be one of three kinds: either the Sultan, who has authority over all matters, or the delegatory minister, or the governor, who has a general authority over a province or large town, for example, and who may appoint others for particular functions. As for the wazir of delegation, it is not correct for him to appoint an official until he has investigated the matter and has been ordered to do so;

Second, this concerns those who may validly be appointed as officials, that is, those who satisfy the necessary requirements of the post, and who are trustworthy; if they are officials of delegation, in whom the capacity to make judgements of ijtihad are required, then one ensures that they are freemen and Muslims; if they are merely executory officials, and have no need to make ijtihad, then it is not necessary that they be freemen or Muslims;

Third, here reference is made as to the task for which he is appointed, and this is dependent upon three conditions: **i.** defining the region, so that it is clearly distinguishable from others; **ii.** the nature of the work with which he is to be entrusted, be it zakah-, kharaj- or 'ushr-collection; **iii.** a detailed knowledge of the taxes and the claims thereon, so that he will not be ignorant of any matter. If these three conditions are fulfilled and are known both to the person appointing and the person appointed, then the appointment is valid and may be carried out.

Fourth, this concerns the duration of the person's authority, and it is of three kinds:

A. This kind is restricted to a particular period of months or years, such that it is permitted for the person to operate during it, and prohibited after this period has elapsed. The person responsible for his appointment is not, however, bound by this stipulated time and he may dismiss and replace him if he sees fit. As for whether this period is binding on the official, this depends on the circumstances: if his office has the nature of a salaried post, then he must continue his work until the end of the period, as he has in effect simply been hired for this task, and so the official is compelled, if necessary, to work until the end of the term. The difference between the two – between, that is, the freedom of choice exercised by the person in authority, and the binding nature for the post of the appointed person – lies in the fact that the first is charged with contracts of a general nature: he is responsible for seeing that the task is completed and must therefore choose the person best able to fill the post; the second is concerned with contracts of a particular nature, and his contract is undertaken for himself personally, and so it becomes binding upon him. If, however, it does not represent a salaried position, then the person appointed is not bound to stay for the whole period, and he may leave the task if he wishes, after having informed the person who appointed him of his intention to leave, so that the post is not left vacant;

B. In this case, the period is determined by the task. The person in charge says, for example, "I have appointed you over the kharaj for such and such a region for this year", or, "I have appointed you over the zakah for such and such a country for this year", – and so the period of his authority lasts until the completion of his task, and on completion, his appointment ends; however, as we have discussed above, he may be dismissed by the person in charge; as for his leaving of his own accord, this is dependent on the validity or otherwise of this act depending on the nature of his appointment;

C. In this case, the appointment is of an absolute nature, and the period and task are not defined: thus the person in charge may say, "I have appointed you over the kharaj of Kufa or the 'ushr of Basra, or the tax-collection of Baghdad." This appointment is valid, even if the period involved is not known, since the purpose is to grant permission for the exercise of authority, and not to compel someone into a binding contract, as in the case of salaried positions. Thus if the appointment is valid, and the authority is permitted, then it must necessarily be either of a lasting nature or interrupted:

i. if it is of a lasting nature, such as authority over tax collection, the judiciary, or the claims and rights concerning mines, then it is valid for him to operate year after year, as long as he is not dismissed;

ii. if it is interrupted, it is of two kinds: either that in which he does not undertake to return to the task every year, such as the person in charge of dividing the booty - in which case his responsibility ceases after he has completed the task, and he may not undertake the division of any other booty; the second kind is that in which he returns to the task every year, like in the case of the kharaj, such that if he collects it one year he returns for the next: the fuqaha differ as to whether this absolute appointment is restricted to his involvement for a year, or whether it is carried over to each following year for as long as he is not dismissed: according to some, he is restricted to operating for the year in question, and when he has collected the kharaj or the 'ushr, his authority ceases thereafter and he may not operate the following year, unless his appointment is renewed – this opinion is restrictive in nature, but it safeguards the certainty of its legal effect; according to others, however, he may continue every year thereafter as long as he is not dismissed – and this is based on customary practice;

Fifth, This concerns the amount paid to the official and is necessarily one of three kinds: it is a fixed amount, or an indeterminate amount, or neither of the two:

A. If fixed, then he is entitled to the amount as soon as he has completed his task; if he falls short in its completion, then this shortfall should be examined: if it is because he has abandoned some part of the task, then he is not entitled to payment for it; if, although he has completed the task, it is because of some fraudulent practice, then he is paid in full, but returns whatever he has acquired fraudulently. If he has collected a surplus, then this surplus must be examined: if it has come from a source beyond the jurisdiction of his task, his authority over it is annulled and is not executed; if it has come from a source within his jurisdiction, then it will necessarily have been taken either for a just reason, or for an unjust one; if he has taken it justly, then he has done so at his own expense and is not entitled to an excess wage; if he has done so unjustly, then he must return the extra to the person unjustly treated: this is treated as a wrong action committed by the official, and he is punished accordingly;

B. If the amount of his salary is not fixed, then he is entitled to an amount corresponding to his task. If the salary for the task is assessed by the diwan, and a number of others work in the same manner, then what they are paid should be treated as a reasonable rate; if there is only one other person working in the same manner, then this is not treated as a suitable salary-level;

C. If there is no indication that it is for a determinate or an indeterminate amount, then there is a difference of opinion amongst the fuqaha, namely ash-Shafi'i and his followers, as to his entitlement to a rate which is equitable in relation to his work: **i.** ash-Shafi'i says that he is not entitled to a salary for his work and that he is undertaking it voluntarily – until he requests a fixed amount, or otherwise, so that his work does not remain without remuneration; **ii.** al-Muzani says that he should have a salary which corresponds to his work, even if it has not been fixed, because he is carrying out a task with the permission (of the authorities); **iii.** Abu'l-'Abbas ibn Surayj says that if he is known to usually take a salary for his work, then he should have a corresponding remuneration, but if not, then he does not receive one; **iv.** Abu Ishaq al-Marwazi, from amongst the followers of ash-Shafi'i, says that if he has been asked or ordered to do the work at the outset then he should have a fitting remuneration; but if he requested it at the outset, and was then given permission to do it, then he does not receive a salary.

If his work comprises the collection (of taxes in the form) of money then his salary is taken from it, but if not, then it is taken from that portion of the bait al-mal which is reserved for the public interest;

Sixth, this concerns the validity of the appointment. If it is made orally by the person in charge, then the appointment is valid, just as any other contract would be valid; if it issues from a signed letter from the person in charge of making the appointment, and is not oral, it is also valid, since appointments contracted by the Sultan may be made in this way if the circumstances demand it – even though this is not the case with contracts of a private nature – as this is sanctioned by custom and usage. This is the case if the appointment is restricted, and does not extend to anyone standing in for him; it is not valid if the appointment is general and extends to other persons.

Thus if the relevant conditions are fulfilled, and the appointment is valid, and if the post has been empty before him, and the person appointed holds it alone, then he is entitled to his salary from the moment he takes up the appointment; if, however, the post is occupied before his appointment, then the matter should be examined: if the work is such that it is not correct for it to be shared, then the appointment of the second brings about the dismissal of the first; if it may be shared, then account should be taken of customary practice: if it is not customary for it to be shared, then it results in the dismissal of the first; if custom does sanction it, then the appointment of the second does not result in the dismissal of the first, and they both do the work and are responsible together.

If an inspector is appointed, then it is the official who actually carries out the work and the inspector who sees that it is completed properly, so that no excess is demanded or any shortfall accepted, and so that officials do not carry out their work unsupervised. The ruling governing inspectors differs to that governing the director of posts in three ways:

i. an official may not undertake work independently of the inspector, while he may work independently of the director of posts;

ii. the inspector may prevent the official from doing something wrong, while the director of posts may not do so;

iii. the inspector does not have to draw attention to every right or wrong action of the official if he comes to know of it, while the director of posts must do so, because a complaint made by the inspector is a demand for judicial intervention, while that of the director of posts is merely passing on information. The difference between passing on information and making a complaint which requires advice from the judiciary is twofold: the first is that passing on information relates to both invalid and valid actions, whereas a request for advice is made only in the case of invalid action - but not in the case of valid action; the second, is that passing on information includes both those acts renounced by the official and those which he has not renounced, while a complaint which requires judicial advice relates only to those acts which he has not renounced - and not to those which he no longer exercises.

If the official denies whatever it is that the inspector has alerted the authorities to, or the information given by the director of posts, then the word of neither party is accepted until it is supported by proof; if both the information of the direction and the complaint of the inspector concur, then their word is accepted against him – as they are both witnesses – if they are both trustworthy.

If it is demanded of the official that he submit his accounts, then he must submit them with regard to kharaj-transactions, but he does not have to submit them for 'ushr-transactions, because the kharaj revenue comes to the bait al-mal, and that of the 'ushr to the people entitled to the zakah. According to the madhhab of Abu Hanifah, both accounts must be submitted, as both revenues are treated in common, according to him.

If the official responsible for the 'ushr claims to have spent the revenue on those who are entitled to it, his word is accepted - but if the official in charge of the kharaj, claims to have spent it on those entitled to it, his word is not accepted unless it is verified or evidence is provided.

If the official wants to appoint someone in his place to do his work, then this may take two forms: the first, is that he puts someone in his place to work independently of him, in which case this is not permitted, as he is, in effect, replacing himself with another: he may not replace himself with another person, even if he is entitled to resign; the second, is that he wishes to appoint someone as an assistant, in which case one must take account of the circumstances in which the appointment is made: these may be of three kinds:

i. that he has permission to appoint another, in which case he may appoint another, but only as his representative, so that the other is dismissed if he himself is dismissed – if he has not been named when permission was given. If the person acting as his representative has been named, then the fuqaha differ as to whether he is also to be dismissed if the official is dismissed: according to some he is, and to others, he is not;

ii. that he is prohibited from having a representative, in which case it is not permitted for him to appoint another, and he alone must complete the task if he is able; if he is not, then his appointment becomes invalid; if he continues to work despite the invalidity of his appointment, then that part of his work which is concerned with granting permission to people to carry out something or to prohibit them from doing something, is valid - but not that part concerned with authorising or dissolving a contract;

iii. that this appointment is of general nature and does not grant permission or forbid, in which case the kind of work he does must be considered: if he can do it alone, he may not appoint a representative to do it; if he is unable, he may appoint someone to undertake that which he is incapable of doing: he may not have a representative do what he himself is able to do.

4. This department deals with the income and expenditure of the bait al-mal, that is with all the wealth to which the Muslims are entitled, but which is not owned by a specific person: thus if such wealth is collected, then by the act of collection it is added to the resources of the bait al-mal, irrespective of whether it has actually gone into the coffers or not – since the term "bait al-mal" refers to a financial sphere and not to a particular place. The bait al-mal becomes liable for the expenses of any activity of public utility which must be paid for from the bait al-mal; if anything is paid out, then this expense is added to the expenditure of the bait al-mal, irrespective of whether it is actually paid out from the coffers themselves or not – because anything which is handed over to the officials of the Muslims or which leaves their hands is treated as income or expenditure of the bait al-mal.

The wealth to which the Muslims are entitled is of three kinds: fay, ghaneemah and zakah:

A. As for the fay, it is the responsibility of the bait al-mal as its use depends upon the judgement of the Imam and his ijtihad;

B. As for the ghaneemah, it is not the responsibility of the bait al-mal as it goes to the booty-takers who are identified by their presence at the battle - and the judgement of the Imam cannot alter the way in which it is divided, nor can his ijtihad prevent them from being given it: thus it is not the responsibility of the bait al-mal;

As for the fifth part which is deducted from the fay, it is divided three ways: one portion becomes part of the bait al-mal and this is the portion of the Prophet, may the peace and blessings of Allah be upon him, and it is spent in the public interest – as its use is determined by the judgement and ijtihad of the Imam; another portion does not become part of the bait al-mal and this is the portion of the close relations of the Prophet – as this group is entitled to it and the owners are identifiable: this portion does not form part of the bait al-mal as it is not subject to the judgement and ijtihad of the Imam; the third portion is that which is kept within the bait al-mal for the purpose allocated to it, namely for the orphans, the destitute and travellers - who are given of this wealth if they are to be found, and which is kept in trust for them if not;

C. As for the zakah, it is of two kinds: that of hidden wealth which does not become part of the bait al-mal, as those who are liable may distribute this zakah directly to those entitled to it; the second is that of manifest wealth, like the tax on crops, fruits and animals. According to Abu Hanifah, this forms part of the bait al-mal, as it may be used according to the judgement and ijtihad of the Imam, who does not treat it as wealth to which the various categories are entitled; according to the madhhab of ash-Shafi'i, it does not form part of the bait al-mal, as those to whom it is given are identifiable and it is not permitted to use it for other than its original purpose. He has two opinions, however, regarding whether or not the bait al-mal keeps it when those entitled to it are not to be found; according to his first opinion, the bait al-mal keeps custody of it if they cannot be found, until such time as they are found – as he considered that this wealth should be handed over to the Imam; however, later, he was of the opinion that it was not to be kept in the bait al-mal to be used when claimed, as he no longer considered that it had to be handed over to the Imam, even though this was permissible: thus its custody in the bait al-mal was not necessary, although permitted.

That which may be claimed from the bait al-mal is of two kinds:

First, that which is kept in the bait al-mal and which may be claimed when the person in question is available: as long, that is, as the wealth still exists it may be claimed by the person entitled to it, but if not, then no claim may be made;

Second, that to which the bait al-mal is entitled, and this is of two kinds: **i.** that which is used to be paid as a compensation - like military salaries, and the price of horses and arms - in which case entitlement to it is not dependent on its existence in the coffers, but rather it is a binding liability whether it exists or not; if it does exist, then payment is made immediately, as with any debt which may be paid without difficulty by the debtor; if it does not exist, it becomes an obligation which is delayed, just as in the case of a debt which can only be paid with difficulty; **ii.** that which is used for the public interest and amenities, rather than compensation; such money must exist: if it is present in the bait al-mal, it must be paid out and the obligation on the rest of the Muslims is annulled; if it is not, then there is no longer any obligation on the bait al-mal; if, however, this would cause extensive harm, then it becomes a communal obligation on all the Muslims, such that someone must take responsibility for it, as in the case of the communal obligation of the jihad; if the harm would not be serious, such as in the case of the bad state of repair of a road which can be circumvented by taking a longer route, or where a water source ceases but another is available, then – just as the obligation on the bait al-mal is annulled when the funds are not available – this obligation is also lifted from the Muslims as a whole, by virtue of the existence of alternatives.

If two claims are made on the bait al-mal which can hardly meet both, but which is able to meet the claim of one of them, then it should nevertheless meet the claim of both, by becoming indebted itself; if it cannot meet the claim of either, then the person in charge may, if he fears that harm will be done, charge the bait al-mal with any debts incurred, as long as it is not for any non-essential expenses; it is then up to his successor to repay the debt once there is enough in the bait al-mal.

If the funds available in the bait al-mal exceed expenditure, then the fu-qaha differ as to this surplus: Abu Hanifah considers that it should be stored in the bait al-mal for such contingencies as might befall the Muslims; ash-Shafi'i, however, considers that this wealth should be used for those projects which are of general benefit to the Muslims and should not be stored – as any contingencies which may occur will be their responsibility.

These, then, are the four divisions upon which the foundations of the diwan are built.

*

* *

As for the secretary of the Diwan, that is, the person in charge, the validity of his authority is dependent upon two conditions, that he be just, and that he be capable of the task: he should be just, because he is entrusted with responsibility for the bait al-mal and for the populace which requires the qualities of justice and trustworthiness; as for his capability, this is necessary, because he is actively working and must be able to work independently, just as any official who works with others.

If his appointment is valid, then he is charged with six things: upholding the laws, the collection of what is due, the verification of any documents which are submitted, the accounts of officials, the investigation of circumstances, and the examination of injustices:

First, upholding the laws, so that the taxes are just, neither so excessive, that they are a burden on the subjects, nor so insufficient, that this infringes upon the right of the bait al-mal. If these laws are first established during the life of the secretary, because a country has been newly conquered, or a dead territory has been revived, then they are recorded in the regional diwan and in that of the bait al-mal, together with the tax-ruling governing that territory; if already-established laws exist, then he should have recourse to them as long as they have been made by trusted scribes, whose handwriting can be recognised, and provided that he receives them from trusted persons amongst them, accompanied by their seals. Documents in writing which fulfil these conditions are acceptable and may be acted upon – both regarding the diwan tax-assessments and the rights and claims concerning the Sultan – and even though this is not the case regarding the laws in court and giving testimony: this is based on customary practice – in the same manner as the muhaddith may narrate something as if he has heard it, when he finds it in writing, as long as it is to be trusted. According to Abu Hanifah, however, the secretary of the diwan may not base any practice on a written document alone, unless he has heard it from the official himself and learns it from him by heart – just as he could narrate a hadith according to the same practice current in matters of giving judicial judgements and bearing testimony, although this presents difficulties and is hardly plausible. The difference between the two is that the judicial process and bearing testimony are rights of a special kind: many people come into contact with them, and many invoke them, so that memorising them by heart is not difficult; for this reason, it is not permitted to rely solely on written documents; the laws of the diwan, however, count as rights of a general character with which few people come into contact, despite their number and widespread nature: it is thus difficult to remember them by heart, and so for this reason it is permitted to rely on written documents alone just as in the narration of hadith;

Second, the collection of taxes is of two kinds: collection by those officials on whom collecting is an obligation and collection by those governors who happen to receive it from them.

i. As for what is collected from the former, it is processed in accordance with the testimonies of those who collected it; as regards the practice in the case of documents written by officials to confirm receipts, the custom amongst the diwan scribes is that if the handwriting is known, then it is proof of receipt, irrespective of whether or not the official confirms that it is his writing – that is, as long as it may be compared to any other piece of writing known to be his. The fuqaha, however, consider that if he does not acknowledge it as his and if he denies it, then the (import of the) document is not binding on him, and is not a proof of receipt; moreover, it is not permitted to compare it with another example of his writing, so as to make it binding on him and to compel him to recognise it, but rather this comparison is made in order to put pressure on him, so that he confirms it of his own accord. If he confirms the writing but denies receipt, then according to the literal meaning of ash-Shafi'i is teaching on the matter, it is a proof of payment, as regards the rights and claims of the Sultan, only for the collectors, and a proof against the officials of receipt – and this is based on customary practice; the clear meaning of Abu Hanifah's madhhab is that it is not a proof either against them or in favour of the collectors until there is confirmation, given orally, just as in the case of debts between individuals. What we have already mentioned above is sufficient to describe this difference.

ii. As for the receipt of monies collected by officials, if they are to be paid into the bait al-mal, the person in charge does not have to make out a signed order, and the acknowledgement of the treasurer of the bait al-mal of its receipt is proof of the official's paying it in. As for a written document without his acknowledgement, this is like the written documents of the officials concerned expressly with collection as we have described above, namely, that it is treated as proof, according to the clear meaning of ash-Shafi'i's teaching, while it is not, according to that of Abu Hanifah's. If, however, it is a question of outgoing money and not income, then the officials cannot proceed with this without the signed order of the person in charge; this signed order, therefore, if it is known to be authentic, would amount to satisfactory evidence allowing payment to be made. As for proof of payment, this may be of two kinds: either it depends on the acknowledgement of the beneficiary of the signed order that he has received the payment in question - since the signed order is proof that the payment is to be made to him, but not that the beneficiary has received it; or else one presumes that the official is in debt to the bait al-mal, and if the beneficiary of the signed order denies its receipt, then a claim is made against the official and judgement is given against him, if proof is forthcoming; if it is not, then the beneficiary of the signed order is made to testify on oath, and then the official is judged to be in the wrong. This latter practice is particularly customary in the diwan, while the former resembles more precise legal practice.

If the secretary of the diwan is suspicious of the signed order, he does not hold the official to account in either of the two ways, until he has shown it to the person who signed it; if the latter recognises it, then the matter is in order, and the official is checked in the above mentioned manner. If, however, he denies it, the official is not held accountable, and he investigates how it has been spent: if it has been given to someone who still exists, then the official recovers it from him; and if it is not possible to recover it, then the official is asked to have the person who signed it swear an oath with respect to his denial. If it is not known if the amount has been validly spent, the signatory may not make the official swear an oath, neither according to the practice in the Sultan's sphere of authority, nor according to judicial practice. If it is known that the amount has been validly spent, then according to the practice of the Sultan, it is prohibited from making the person who signed the order swear an oath, although according to judicial ruling this is acceptable.

Third, documents to be registered and verified are of three kinds: those relating to surveys and surveying operations, those relating to collection and payments taken in trust, and those concerned with costs and expenses: **A.** If the original registrations relating to survey measurements are held in the diwan, then any copy submitted is valid if it corresponds to this original and if so, then it is thus registered; if the original is not in the diwan, then the document is registered in accordance with the person submitting them; **B.** collections and payments taken in trust are registered solely on the basis of the word of the person submitting the documents, as his avowal renders himself liable and is not to his benefit; **C.** if the documents relating to costs and expenses submitted by a person represent a claim which is to his benefit, then this claim is only accepted if clear proofs are provided: if proof comes in the form of signed orders from persons in authority, they are required to be shown, and the ruling with regard to them is the same as that discussed above concerning rulings governing signed orders;

Fourth, as for the accounts of the officials, their status varies according to the various ways in which they were appointed, and this we have discussed above: kharaj officials must submit accounts, and the diwan secretary has to check that what they submit is correct; if they are 'ushr officials, they do not have to do this, according to ash-Shafi'i's madhhab, nor does the diwan secretary have to call them to account, as, according to him, the 'ushr is a sadaqah, the use of which does not depend on the ijtihad of the governors: it is acceptable if those who benefit use it by themselves. According to Abu Hanifah, however, they must submit accounts and the diwan secretary has to verify them, as the use to which the kharaj and the 'ushr are put is common to both, according to him.

If an official whose accounts must be checked is investigated, then one must examine the matter: if there is no disparity between the official and the secretary of the diwan, then the latter is believed regarding the rest of the accounts; if the person in authority is suspicious, however, then he demands that he produce proof and testimony: if he no longer has any doubts, there is no need for the oath to be sworn but if doubts persist and the person in authority wants him to swear an oath, then he has the official but not the diwan secretary swear – as any claim is against the former and not the latter.

If they differ concerning the accounts, and if it concerns income, then the word of the official is accepted, as he is denying it; if it concerns an expense, the word of the secretary is accepted, as he is denying it. If their difference concerns a measurement which can be recalculated, then the corrected calculation is utilised.

Fifth, this concerns a description of circumstances, that is, a demand made to the secretary of the diwan to declare which rulings and claims have been established: it is treated as a testimony and is subject to two conditions: **i.** he should only render account for amounts which he knows to be correct just as he would only bear testimony for what he knows and has verified; **ii.** he should not take the initiative in this, (but should wait) until he is requested, just as he would not bear witness until his testimony was sought. The person who demands a clarification of circumstances is someone whose signed orders are carried out, just as the person before whom a testimony is made is someone whose decisions are executed. If an account of the state of affairs is made, the signatory of the order to render this account is held to it and must keep to it - just as the judge must execute the order in accordance with the testimonies made before him. If the person who has demanded the statement of affairs still entertains doubts, then he may ask the secretary where he obtained such information, and he may ask him for proofs from the diwan that testify to this state of affairs - even though a judge may not ask a witness the reason for his testimony. If these proofs are forthcoming, and he is satisfied as to their validity, then the doubt is removed; if however, the director does not furnish proofs and states that he has described the situation from memory, by virtue of his knowledge of what happened previously, then his word is in doubt and the person who demanded an account of the situation has the choice of either accepting it of him or not – although he may not demand that he swear on oath;

Sixth, the investigation of injustices varies in accordance with the different kinds of injustice. The claim of injustice will necessarily be either from the taxpayer or from an official. If a taxpayer claims that an official has dealt unjustly with him, then the secretary of the diwan is the judge between them, and he may investigate the injustice and put an end to any harm being done, irrespective of whether he has been given express authority to conduct this investigation or not – because he is charged with the preservation of the laws and with seeing that rights are fulfilled: thus by the contract conferring his authority on him, he becomes empowered to investigate injustices. If, however, he is prohibited from this, then he should leave it alone and is restricted regarding the full authority of the post. If it is the official who is making the complaint, because he has been cheated in the accounts or been deceived in a transaction, then it is the secretary of the diwan who becomes the defendant, and it is the person in authority who must investigate.

Chapter 19
Rulings Governing Criminal Actions

Criminal actions refer to those prohibited by the shari'ah which Allah punishes with a hadd or discretionary punishment; in the case of mere suspicion of such an act, immunity is required by the dictates of the deen; when the occurrence of a criminal act has been properly established, then the full consequences, necessitated by rulings of the shari'ah ensue.

When there is suspicion, but before the act has been firmly established, then one must take account of the person who is investigating: if it is a judge, before whom a person has been brought accused of stealing or fornication, then this accusation is of no effect for him: he may not imprison him, be it to investigate, or to await his being proved innocent, and he may not proceed after compelling him to confess. Any claim against him is only entertained, in the case of theft, if it issues from a litigant entitled to the thing stolen, and one must take into account what issues from an avowal of the accusation or its denial. If he has been accused of fornication, the claim against him is not heard until he (the person making the accusation) has named the woman with whom he has fornicated, and has described what he did with her, as fornication carries the hadd-punishment: if he confesses, then he is given the hadd-punishment in accordance with his confession; if he denies it, and there are witnesses, then these are given a hearing; if there are no witnesses, then he is made to swear an oath – for the sake of man's rights but not for the sake of Allah's rights – if the litigant demands this.

If the investigator before whom the accused person is brought is an amir or his deputy and assistant, he has access to means of investigation and examination which are not available to the qadis and judges. There are nine points of difference between the two:

First, it is not permitted for the amir to hear about the crime of the accused from the assistants of the amirate without checking the claim and without considering their statements regarding the circumstances of the accused: that is, whether he is of suspicious character, or whether he is known to have committed similar deeds. If he is innocent of similar acts, then the accusation against him carries less weight, and he is released as soon as possible and is not subjected to any rough treatment; if they affirm that he has committed similar crimes and they identify him with the like, then the accusation is strengthened, and an investigation is instigated in the manner we shall describe below. Qadis may not act in this way;

Second, the amir must take account of the circumstances of the case and the character of the accused – both of which are important as regards the strength or weakness of the case. Thus if the accusation is of fornication and the accused is susceptible to women, full of jest and charm, then the accusation is strengthened, and if the opposite of these is true, then it is weakened. If the accusation is regarding theft, and the accused is a scoundrel, or there are signs of blows on his body, or he was found with a sharp instrument at the time, then the accusation is strengthened; if, however, the opposite is true, then it is weakened. Qadis may not proceed in this manner either;

Third, the amir may imprison the accused for the purposes of an investigation and enquiry. There is a difference of opinion as to how long he may be imprisoned. Abu 'Abdallah az-Zubayri, from amongst the followers of ash-Shafi'i, says that his confinement for an enquiry or investigation should be for one month and no longer, while others say that it is not for a specific time, but rather depends on the judgement of the Imam and his ijtihad – and this is a more likely approach. Qadis, however, may not imprison anyone, except for a specific legal cause;

Fourth, if the grounds for the accusation are sufficiently strong, the amir may have the accused beaten as a discretionary measure, not as a hadd-punishment, in order to compel him to be truthful regarding his situation and the crime of which he has been accused ; if he confesses during the beating, then account must be taken of the reason for the beating: if he has been beaten to compel him to confess, this confession has no legal status; if, however, it was to extract the truth about his situation, and he confesses during the beating, then the beating is stopped and he is asked to confess again; if he confesses, then he is judged according to this second confession, and not the first; if he restricts himself to the first confession, and a second is not asked of him, then he is not put under any more pressure, because one proceeds according to the first confession – although we dislike this.

Fifth, the amir may keep someone in prison until he dies if he repeatedly commits crimes, if he is not deterred by the application of the hadd-punishments, and if the people are being harmed by his crimes – that is, after he has arranged for his sustenance and clothing to be paid for by the bait al-mal; this he may do in order to remove this harm from the people, although qadis do not have this power;

Sixth, the amir may compel the accused to swear on oath, in order to clarify his situation, and to exert pressure on him during the course of the investigation of his affair, be he accused of infringing one of Allah's rights, or one of man's rights; he does not, however, make him swear upon his own divorce, or on the setting free of a slave, or on the giving away of property in sadaqah – as might be the case when swearing, in the Name of Allah, an oath of allegiance to the Sultan Qadis may not compel anyone to make an oath which has a specific legal consequence, and may not go so far as to make someone swear upon their divorce or freeing a slave;

Seventh, the amir can compel criminals to make tawbah, and may make threats so that they turn in tawbah of their own accord; he may not, however, go so far as to threaten them with death in a matter which does not carry the death sentence, as this threat is made to intimidate and, as such, is not considered a lie but rather a part of discretionary and correctional measures. He may not carry out his death-threat and have him killed for a matter which does not carry the death-sentence;

Eighth, the amir may hear the testimonies of people of other religions, if they are numerous, whereas the Qadi may not;

Ninth, it is up to the amir to investigate incidents of assault, even if there is no fine or hadd-punishment prescribed. If none of them has any marks on him, he should hear the one who made the charge first; if one of them does have marks on him, some of the jurists consider that he should hear this person first, and not consider the person who was the first to lay the charge; most of the fuqaha, however, consider that he should hear the one who first made the charge. The one who began the attack is the most to blame, and is the one who suffers the more severe discretionary punishment. It is permitted to impose a different punishment on each, for two reasons: the first, because of the difference between their crimes and the degree of outrage; and the second, because of the difference of respect and self-esteem between the two of them: thus if he considers there is a benefit in making public and proclaiming the crimes of some low and mean persons, then he may do this.

These, then, are the differences between the ways amirs and qadis may deal with the investigation of crimes, before, that is, it is established that any hadd-punishment (is necessitated): these differences arise because of the amir's concern with administration, and the qadi's concern with the laws.

*

* *

If it is established that a crime has been committed, then amirs and qadis are alike in their execution of the hadd-punishments. Establishing that a crime has been committed is done in two ways, either by a confession or by proof and each is governed by a specific ruling, which will be discussed in the appropriate place.

The hadd-punishments are restraints imposed by Allah ta'ala, to prevent people committing what He has forbidden, or from abandoning what He has commanded them to do: this is because of what is contained in man's nature, which allows him to be dominated by pleasurable desires, and to forget the Next World for the sake of immediate gratification; thus Allah ta'ala has imposed these restraints to protect the ignorant from the torment, punishment and shame attached to such crimes, so that he is prevented from engaging in what He has forbidden, and so that what He has ordered is obeyed: from this ensues a benefit of the greatest significance which ensures that each carries out his responsibilities in the most complete manner. Allah ta'ala has said, **"I have not sent you but as a mercy to all the worlds"** (Qur'an 21: 107), that is, in order to save them from ignorance, and to guide them away from error, and to prevent them from acts of disobedience, and to urge them to obedience.

This being so, then these restraints are of two kinds: the hadd and the discretionary punishments. The hadd-punishments are also of two kinds: those regarding the rights of Allah, and those regarding the rights of man. As for the former they are also of two kinds: the first, those punishments resulting from abandoning obligations; and the second, those resulting from committing something which is forbidden.

1. As for those resulting from abandoning obligations, these are:

i. not performing the obligatory prayer until after its time, in which case the person in question is asked why he has not done it: if he replies that he had forgotten to do it, then he is ordered to make it up at the very moment that he has been reminded, and that he should not wait until the corresponding time (the next day). The Messenger of Allah, may the peace and blessings of Allah be upon him, said: "Whoever sleeps through the prayer, or forgets it, then he should pray it as soon as he remembers it, and then this counts as its (true) time, and there is nothing else to be made up apart from this." If the person has not done it because of illness then he should pray it as he is able, sitting or reclining: Allah ta'ala says: **"Allah only burdens someone according to his capacity"** (Qur'an 2: 286). If the person abandons it, claiming that it is not an obligation, then he is a nonbeliever, and the same ruling as that governing the renegade applies – that is, he is killed for his denial, unless he turns for forgiveness. If he has not done it because he claims it is too difficult to do, but while acknowledging its obligation, then the fuqaha differ as to the ruling: Abu Hanifah considers that he should be beaten at the time of every prayer, but that he is not killed; Ahmad ibn Hanbal and a group of his later followers say that he becomes a kafir by his abandoning it, and is killed for this denial; ash-Shafi'i considers that he does not become a kafir by not doing it, that he is not killed as a hadd-punishment and that he is not considered a heretic; he is not put to death until he has been asked to turn in tawbah: if he does turn in tawbah and does it then he is left alone, but while ordering him to do it; if he says, "I will do it in my house," then he is trusted in his promise, and he is not compelled to do it in front of people. If he refuses to make tawbah, and does not accept to do the prayer, then he is killed for abandoning it – immediately, according to some, after three days, according to others. He is killed in cold blood by the sword, although Abu'l-Abbas ibn Surayj says that he is beaten with a wooden stick until he dies – since the irrevocability of the sword is avoided by this method, and thus more time is allowed in which the person may make tawbah.

The followers of ash-Shafi'i differ as to the obligation to kill him if he refuses to make up the prayers he has missed: some consider that he should be killed for missing them as for any of the other prayers at their time while others that he should not as the prayers missed still remain his responsibility.

Prayers are said over him after he has been put to death and he is buried in the Muslim cemetery as he is still counted as a Muslim and his wealth still belongs to those who inherit from him.

ii. As for the person who does not fast, he is not put to death according to the consensus of the fuqaha, but rather he is prevented from eating or drinking during the period of the fast in the month of Ramadan, and he is given a discretionary punishment to teach him a lesson; if he accepts the (necessity to) fast, he is left alone and is entrusted to do it; if he is then seen eating, he is given a discretionary punishment, but he is not killed;

iii. As for the person who does not pay the zakah, he is not put to death, but rather some of his wealth is taken by force; he is given a discretionary punishment if he keeps it hidden without a reason; if it is difficult to collect because he prevents this, he is attacked for it, even if getting it from him leads to his death, just as Abu Bakr as-Siddiq fought those who refused the zakah;

iv. As for the Hajj, it is an obligation, according to ash-Shafi'i, at any time a person is able, right up to his death: it is thus not conceivable, according to his madhhab, that someone can delay it beyond its time; according to Abu Hanifah, however, it is to be performed as soon as possible, and so it is conceivable, according to his madhhab, that someone might delay it beyond its stipulated time, but he is not put to death for it, and he is not given a discretionary punishment, as his doing it after the time is counted as performing it properly – and not just as making up something missed.

If someone dies before carrying it out, then someone should do the Hajj for him using money from his capital.

As for someone who refuses to fulfil one of the claims of man (as opposed to a claim of Allah), such as a debt or something else, then it is exacted from him by force if the person is able to pay; he is imprisoned if it is difficult unless he has no means, in which case one waits for his financial state to become easier.

These then are the rulings concerning those who abandon what is obligatory.

2. As for someone who commits something which is forbidden this is one of two kinds: the first concerns the rights of Allah, and they are four in number: the hadd for fornication, the hadd for drinking wine, the hadd for theft and the hadd for brigandage; the second involves the rights of man, and they are two in number: the hadd-punishment for false accusation of fornication, and the blood-money necessary for harm caused to someone. We shall describe each separately.

❋

❋ ❋

A. The hadd-punishment for fornication. This refers to the act in which the head of the penis of the sane adult penetrates one of the two orifices, at the front or the back, of a person with whom he has no protecting tie, and without valid reason; Abu Hanifah considers that it refers only to the front orifice and not the back. The hadd-punishment for the male and female fornicator is the same; each will either be a virgin, or a muhsan-married person:

The virgin is the person who has not had intercourse with a spouse in marriage. The hadd-punishment, if he is a free person, is a hundred strokes applied all over his body – other than his face and those parts which would result in death – such that each member receives its due, and this is done with a whip which is not so new as to kill him, nor so worn as to cause no pain; the fuqaha differ as to whether he should be banished as well as being whipped; Abu Hanifah forbids this, confining it to a whipping; Malik says that a man is exiled, but not a woman; ash-Shafi'i says that she must be banished for a year from her land, that is, at least to a distance of a day's and night's travel away, basing his judgement on the saying of the Prophet, may the peace and blessings of Allah be upon him, "Take this from me – Allah has made a way for them: a virgin with a virgin, a hundred strokes and banishment for a year, a married person with a married person, a hundred strokes and stoning." The hadd of whipping and banishment is the same for the kafir as for the Muslim according to ash-Shafi'i.

As for the slave and those considered still to be slaves amongst the mudabbar slaves (who are to be freed after their master's death), the mukatab slaves (who are buying their freedom), and the umm walad (who have given birth to children of their masters), then the hadd for them is fifty lashes for fornication – that is, a half of the hadd for a free person, because of their lower status, i.e. of servitude. There is a difference of opinion as to whether slaves should be banished: some say that they are not, because of the harm it would cause their masters, and this is the opinion of Malik, while others say that they are banished for a year, like free persons, and this is the opinion of Dawud; the literal teaching of ash-Shafi'i is that he is banished for half a year, just as the lashes are half in number.

The muhsan is the man who has had intercourse with his wife in a valid marriage: his hadd is stoning with stones, or something similar, until death, and it is not necessary to protect the parts of the body likely to cause this fatality – unlike in the case of lashes – as the purpose of this stoning is death. Lashes are not given as well as the stoning, although Dawud says that a hundred lashes are given and then the stoning. But the lashes have been abrogated in the case of the muhsan: The Prophet, may the peace and blessings of Allah be upon him, had Ma'iz stoned but did not have him lashed. Being a muhsan is not conditional upon being a Muslim: thus both the kafir and the Muslim are stoned, although Abu Hanifah says that the situation is such that if a kafir commits fornication, he is whipped but not stoned, and that the Prophet, may the peace and blessings of Allah be upon him, had two Jews whipped for fornication. And only the muhsan is stoned. The state of being free is a precondition of being a muhsan: thus if the slave fornicates, he is not stoned, and if he has a wife, then he still receives fifty lashes, although Dawud says that he is stoned, like the free person. As for sodomites and those fornicating with animals, then the virgin is whipped and the muhsan is stoned, although it is also said that both are to be put to death. Abu Hanifah says that there is no hadd applicable to them – although the Prophet, may the peace and blessings of Allah be upon him, said: "Kill the animal and the person who has fornicated with it."

If a virgin male fornicates with a muhsan female, or a muhsan male with a virgin female, then the virgin is whipped and the muhsan is stoned; if they repeat fornication after the hadd-punishment, then the hadd is imposed again. If someone has fornicated several times before the hadd is imposed, then only one hadd-punishment is imposed for all of them.

Fornication is established in one of two ways: either by confession or by proof: **i.** as for confession, if the person is adult and of sane mind, and confesses once of his own accord, then the hadd is imposed – although Abu Hanifah says that he is not punished until he has confessed four times; if the hadd-punishment becomes obligatory by his confession, and then he withdraws it before the whipping, the hadd is annulled – although Abu Hanifah says that the hadd is not annulled by his withdrawing it; **ii.** as for proof, this is that four just men bear witness to his having committed fornication, there being no women amongst them, and they declare that they saw his penis entering the vagina, just as the bodkin enters the eye-black bottle; if they have not seen this according to this description, then it is not treated as a testimony; if they do bear testimony in this manner, be it at the same time as each other or separately, then their testimony is accepted. Abu Hanifah and Malik, however, both say that: "I do not accept it if it is made separately, and then I treat them as slanderers." If they bear witness to fornication after a year or more, their testimony is heard – although Abu Hanifah says: "I do not listen to it after a year, and then I treat them as slanderers." If there are less than four witnesses, then they are treated as slanderers, according to one opinion, and are given the hadd-punishment, although according to a second, they are not. If people have witnessed his confession to fornication, then it is permissible to accept only two witnesses according to one of two opinions,, although according to another, it is not permitted to accept less than four.

If a person's fornication has been proved, then a hole is dug so that when he is put in, it comes up half way and prevents him from escaping; if he does escape, he is pursued and stoned until he dies; if he is stoned on his own confession, a hole is not dug for him and if he then escapes, he is not pursued.

The Imam or the governor who has made the decision to stone the person is permitted to attend the stoning; they may also not attend; Abu Hanifah, however, says that it is not permitted to stone someone unless the person who pronounced the sentence of stoning attends. The Prophet, may the peace and blessings of Allah be upon him, said: "O Unays, bring the woman to me tomorrow morning, and if she confesses, then stone her." It is permitted for the witnesses not to attend the stoning, although Abu Hanifah says that they must attend, and that they must be the first to start the stoning. The pregnant person is not given the hadd-punishment until after she has given birth, and then only after there is someone to suckle her child.

If the accused offers a reasonable excuse for the fornication, such as that it was a legally imperfect marriage, or that he had mistakenly thought her to be his own wife, or that he was unaware that fornication was forbidden as he had only recently entered Islam, then he is spared the hadd. The Prophet, may the peace and blessings of Allah be upon him, said: "Spare the imposition of the hadd-punishments if there are likely excuses." Abu Hanifah says that if he mistakenly took the other woman for his wife, this is not a likely excuse, and the person responsible is given the hadd. If he marries someone of his close family, with whom marriage is forbidden, and has intercourse with her, then the hadd is also applied, because this type of marriage – given that it has been forbidden expressly in a (Qur'anic) text – does not represent an excuse sufficient to ward off the hadd; Abu Hanifah does, however, consider that it is sufficient excuse, and that the hadd-punishment is not to be applied. If the fornicator turns in tawbah after he has been apprehended, the hadd is not annulled, whereas if he turns in tawbah before he is apprehended, the hadd is annulled according to the clearest of two opinions: Allah ta'ala says: **"So surely your Lord is Merciful and Forgiving towards those who**

do evil whilst ignorant and then turn in tawbah after that and then perform good actions" (Qur'an 16: 119). There are two interpretations of "**whilst
ignorant**", the first, that they were ignorant of the evil, and the second, that
they were overwhelmed by lust, although aware that it was evil, and this is
the more obvious of the two interpretations: since anyone who is unaware
that it is evil has not committed a crime.

It is not permitted for anyone to mediate in order to have the hadd annulled for a fornicator or any other – just as it is not permitted for the person
for whom mediation is made to intercede on his own behalf: Allah ta'ala
says: "**Whoever intercedes with a good intercession, then he will have a
portion of it, and whoever intercedes with an evil intercession, then he
will have the equivalent of it**" (Qur'an 4: 85). There are three interpretations of "**good**" and "**evil**": the first, is to ask for good for the person for
whom one is interceding , or to ask for evil for him, and this is the opinion of
al-Hasan and al-Mujahid; the second, is that the "**good**" is a prayer for the
men and women believers, and the "**evil**" is a supplication against them; the
third, and this is likely, is that the "**good**" is to deliver them from injustice,
and the "**evil**" is to exempt them from the law. As for "**equivalent**", there are
two interpretations: the first, is that it will be equivalent to the crime, according to al-Hasan; and the second, is that it will be a portion (of the evil) and
this is the opinion of as-Suddi.

*

* *

B. Concerning cutting off the hand for theft: if an adult, sane person
steals an article of property kept in a safe place, whose value is of a specific
minimum amount, and there is no doubt concerning this article or concerning the place of safekeeping, then his right hand is cut off at the wrist; if he
steals again after having had his hand cut off, be it the same article from its
place of safekeeping, or another article, then his left foot is amputated at the
ankle; if he steals again, then according to Abu Hanifah, there is no further
amputation, while according to ash-Shafi'i, the left hand is cut off, and if he
commits it a fourth time, then the right foot; if he steals a fifth time, he is
given a discretionary punishment, but is not put to death. If he steals several
times before any amputation, then this entails only one amputation.

The fuqaha differ as to the minimum value of the article stolen which would lead to amputation of the hand: ash-Shafi'i is of the opinion that its value should amount to at least a quarter of a dinar of the good type mostly in circulation; Abu Hanifah says that the amount is ten dirhams or a dinar and no amputation is made if it is less than this; Ibrahim an-Nakha'i sets the amount at forty dirhams or four dinars, while Ibn Abi Layla sets it at five dirhams, and Malik at three dirhams; Dawud, however, says that amputation ensues, be the amount large or small.

The fuqaha differ as to the kind of property which, if stolen, results in amputation: ash-Shafi'i considers that amputation ensues regarding any property which it is forbidden to steal; Abu Hanifah says that there is no amputation if the thing in question is essentially common to all, like game, wood, and grass; according to ash-Shafi'i, however, there is amputation when these things have become the property of someone; Abu Hanifah says that there is no amputation with respect to fresh food, while according to ash-Shafi'i there is; Abu Hanifah says that there is no amputation when someone steals a copy of the Qur'an, while for ash-Shafi'i there is; Abu Hanifah says that there is no amputation for someone who steals the candles from a mosque, or the covering of the Ka'bah, while for ash-Shafi'i there is; if a slave who is underage and who has not attained to full intellect, or a non-Arab who does not understand, is stolen, then amputation ensues, but for Abu Hanifah it does not; if a young child is stolen, there is no amputation, but for Malik there is.

There is a difference among the fuqaha regarding what constitutes safekeeping. Dawud is at odds with the rest in that he does not take the place of safekeeping into account, and says that amputation ensues irrespective of whether the object was in a place of safekeeping or not; the majority, however, do consider that amputation can only ensue if the thing was in a safe place, and that there is no amputation if it was not in such a place: it has been narrated of the Prophet, may the peace and blessings of Allah be upon him, that he said: "There is no amputation for taking horses unless they were safe in their corrals." Likewise, there is no amputation if someone borrows something and then denies having borrowed it; Ahmad ibn Hanbal, however, says that amputation ensues.

Those who stipulate this condition of safekeeping differ as to its nature: Abu Hanifah considers that safekeeping is the same for all objects, and treats the safekeeping of minor objects in the same way as major ones; for ash-Shafi'i, however, it varies in accordance with the various kinds of property and the customary practice regarding them: he thus deems the place of safe-keeping of little significance with regard to things of little value, like wood and kindling, but he is strict with regard to things of great value, like gold and silver: thus he does not consider the place of safekeeping for kindling to be on a par with that of gold and silver – so he would amputate the hand of someone stealing wood from such a place, but not if someone stole gold and silver from the same place. Someone who violates graves and steals the shrouds of the dead suffers amputation, as graves are customarily a place of safekeeping for these things, although not for other property; Abu Hanifah says that someone who violates graves does not suffer amputation, as nothing is kept in them other than these shrouds. If a man secures his baggage on a moving animal in the customary manner, and then someone steals something from it whose value amounts to at least a quarter of a dinar, then his hand is amputated, because he has stolen from a place of safekeeping; if however, he steals both the animal and what is on it, then he does not suffer amputation, as he has stolen both the place of safekeeping and that which is being kept safe. If a person steals a beaker made of silver or gold, he suffers amputation – even though use of such a container is forbidden – as this article belongs to someone; this is irrespective of whether there is foodstuff in it or not, although Abu Hanifah says that if there is food or drink or water in the stolen container, then he does not suffer amputation; if however, he empties it of the food or drink and then steals it, his hand is amputated.

If two persons participate in violating a place of safekeeping, but just one of them takes some article of property, then only the one who took the thing suffers amputation, and not the other who participated in the violation of the place of safekeeping; if two persons act together, and one of them breaks into a place of safekeeping but does not take anything, and the other person does, but has not broken into the place, then neither of them suffers amputation; it is concerning circumstances such as these that ash-Shafi'i said: "The clever thief does not suffer amputation."

If someone enters a place of safekeeping and destroys the property, he is held liable but does not suffer amputation. If a thief suffers amputation and the article in question still exists, then it is returned to its owner; if the thief then returns after having had his hand amputated and steals it again after it has been put in a place of safekeeping, he suffers further amputation – although Abu Hanifah says that there is no further amputation for a theft of the same thing twice.

If the thief destroys what he has stolen, then suffers amputation, he is held liable for it; Abu Hanifah says that if he suffers amputation, then he does not have to pay back its value, and that if he does pay, then he does not suffer amputation. Even if the thing stolen is (subsequently) given to him, he still suffers amputation – although Abu Hanifah says that he does not.

If the owner of the property pardons the thief, the amputation is not annulled: when Safwan ibn Umayyah pardoned the person who had stolen his cloak ,the Messenger of Allah said, may the peace and blessings of Allah be upon him, "Allah would not pardon me if I were to pardon," and he ordered his hand to be amputated. It is narrated that Mu'awiyyah had thieves brought to him and he had their hands amputated one by one, until only one of them was left, and as he was about to suffer amputation, he said:

My right hand, O Amir of the Believers, I seek refuge for it by your pardon from this punishment which will cut if off; my hand will be Beauty itself if its covering is whole, so do not bring imperfection to this Beauty and so deform it: there would be no good left in this world, and it would be ugly if the right hand was parted from the left.

Then Mu'awiyyah said: "What should I do with you, seeing as I have cut off the hands of your companions?" Then the mother of the thief said: "Make what you are doing (by pardoning my son) just one of the wrong actions for which you will turn to Allah in tawbah"; so he let him go, this being the first time that the hadd-punishment had been abandoned in Islam.

Men, women, the free and slaves, Muslims and non-Muslims are all subject to amputation, but not children or anyone who steals when he has lost his senses; nor is the slave who steals from his master subject to amputation nor a father who steals from the property of his son, although Dawud says that both suffer amputation.

C. Concerning the hadd for drinking wine: any kind of wine or nabidh (date wine), be it a small or a large amount, which causes intoxication, is prohibited, and the person who drinks them is given the hadd-punishment, irrespective of whether he becomes drunk or not, although Abu Hanifah says that the hadd is imposed on anyone who drinks wine even if he does not get drunk, but not on someone who drinks nabidh unless he gets intoxicated from it.

The hadd is that the person is beaten forty times with the hand and the ends of cloth, and he is severely rebuked with words of reprimand, as this has been narrated in a hadith; it has also been said that he is whipped with the lash, as with the other hadd-punishments. It is permitted to go beyond forty, up to as many as eighty, if the person does not learn his lesson: 'Umar, may Allah be pleased with him, used to give the hadd of forty to someone who had drunk wine until he saw how people were beginning to drink in larger numbers, and so he consulted the Companions about it, saying: "I see how more and more people are taking to drinking wine – what is your opinion?" 'Ali then replied, may Allah ennoble his face: "I think that you should give them a hadd-punishment of eighty lashes, for if someone drinks wine he becomes drunk, and if he becomes drunk, he talks irrationally, and if he talks irrationally, he slanders – so give him the hadd-punishment of eighty for slander." 'Umar for the rest of his life, and the imams who followed him, imposed this number. 'Ali later said: "I have not reproached myself for imposing the hadd-punishment on anyone who has died as a result – except the wine-drinker, for we have set the punishment after the Messenger of Allah, may the peace and blessings of Allah be upon him: thus if the wine-drinker is given the hadd of forty and he dies as a result, then his blood has been shed with impunity, but if he is given the hadd of eighty and he dies, then there is liability for him." There are two opinions as to what this liability amounts to: the first, is that the full blood-money is to be paid as the text referring to the hadd-punishment has been exceeded; the second, is that half is to be paid, as a half of the hadd-punishment is contained in the text, and the other half has been added.

There is no hadd against anyone who is forced to drink wine, or who drinks it unaware that it is forbidden; if someone drinks it to quench his thirst, he suffers the hadd, as wine will not quench thirst; if he drinks it for some illness, he does not suffer the hadd, as sometimes he may be cured by it; if a person believes that nabidh is permitted and drinks it, he is given the hadd although he is still treated as a just person. The intoxicated person is not given the hadd until he confesses to having drunk intoxicating wine, or two witnesses testify that he drank it of his own free will, knowing that it was intoxicating. Abu 'Abdallah az-Zubayri says that he is given the hadd for being intoxicated – but this is a mistake, as he might have been forced to drink something intoxicating.

The ruling governing an intoxicated person who is convicted of acts of disobedience while drunk is the same as that governing a sober person; however, he is excluded from responsibility for an act of disobedience if he was forced to drink wine, or if he drank it unaware that it was intoxicating – like someone who temporarily loses his senses.

There is a difference of opinion as to the definition of intoxication: Abu Hanifah considers that it refers to a person who no longer has his intellect, such that he cannot distinguish between the earth and the sky, and he cannot tell the difference between his slave-girl and his wife; ash-Shafi'i defines it as that which causes a person to talk disjointedly and unintelligibly, to move without co-ordination and to sway while walking – thus if his speech is affected both if he understands and communicates, and in the way his movement is affected in the way he walks and stands then he may be described as being intoxicated, and the worse his state is, the worse his degree of intoxication.

D. Concerning the hadd for slander, and mutual cursing: the hadd for slander alleging fornication is eighty lashes, there being a specific text supporting this; there is a consensus about it, such that this number is not to be decreased or increased; it is one of the rights of man, and is applied in response to a demand, and is annulled if the person is pardoned. If five conditions are fulfilled regarding the person accused of fornication, and three regarding the accuser, then the imposition of the hadd becomes obligatory: thus the accused must be adult, of sane mind, Muslim, a free person and of moral character; if he is below age, or mad, or a slave, or a non-Muslim or someone whose moral character has been tainted by a previous hadd-conviction, then no hadd is imposed on the accuser, although he is given a discretionary punishment because of the harm he has caused and the looseness of his tongue. As for the accuser, he must be of age, of sane mind and free; if he is under age, or mad, then the hadd is not imposed and he is not given a discretionary punishment; if he is a slave, he is given the hadd-punishment of forty, half of that for a free man, because he is enslaved; the non-Muslim is given the hadd like the Muslim, and a woman is given the hadd like a man. The accuser's legal status is thus impaired and his testimony is not accepted thereafter; if he turns in tawbah, then his status is no longer impaired and his testimony is accepted, both before the imposition of the hadd and after it – although Abu Hanifah says that his testimony is accepted if he makes tawbah before the hadd, but not *vice versa*.

The person who falsely accuses someone of sodomy, or of fornication with animals, is punished in the same manner as the one who accuses another of fornication; there is no hadd for someone who accuses another of kufr or stealing, but he is given a discretionary punishment because of the harm done. False accusation of fornication occurs when there is a clear statement to that effect such as someone saying, "O fornicator," or, "You have committed fornication," or, "I say you commit fornication;"; if, however, he only says, "O dissolute one," or, "O corrupt one," or, "O Luti, (i.e. describing him with an adjective derived from the name of the Prophet Lut, peace be upon him, as he was the Prophet first to be confronted with sodomites)," then this is metaphorical by its ambiguity, and the hadd is not obligatory unless he meant to slander; if the person says, "O whore," then this is metaphorical according to some of the followers of ash-Shafi'i because of its ambiguity, while for others it is a clear statement, because of the saying of the Prophet, may the peace and blessings of Allah be upon him: "The child is attributed to the bed (where it was conceived), and the stoning is for the whore." Malik, may Allah have mercy on him, considers that an allusion is to be treated as a clear statement with regard to the obligation of the hadd. An allusion may be made in a state of anger or dispute when the person says, "*I* have not committed fornication," thereby implying that, "*You* have committed fornication;" according to ash-Shafi'i and Abu Hanifah, may Allah have mercy on them, there is no hadd for allusion unless he confesses that he meant to slander thereby; if he says, "O son of fornicators," this is treated as slander of his parents, not of him, and he is given the hadd on their behalf if they demand it, or if one of them demands it – unless they are dead, in which case the hadd may be demanded by their inheritors, although Abu Hanifah says that it is not transferred to the inheritors; if the slandered person wants to come to be paid compensation for dropping the hadd of the slanderer, this is not permitted; if a man slanders his father, he is given the hadd, but if he slanders his son, he is not; if the slanderer has not yet received the hadd-punishment, and the slandered person then commits fornication, the hadd-punishment for his previous false accusation is not annulled; Abu Hanifah, however, says that it is annulled; if a man slanders his wife with fornication, he is given the hadd-punishment, unless he pronounces the mutual curse (*li'an*). The li'an is that he says in the Friday Mosque on the mimbar, or next to it, in the presence of the governor and at least four witnesses: "I bear witness by Allah that I am among the truthful when I accuse this, my wife, of fornication with such and such a person, and that this child is by fornication and not from me," – these last words if he wishes to deny that the child is his – and the former he repeats four times; the fifth time he says, "May Allah's curse be on me if I am among the liars when I accuse her of fornication with such and such a person (that is if he mentions the name of the person who fornicated with her) and that this child is from fornication and not from me." So if he says this, he has completed the li'an-cursing and the hadd for slander is not applicable to him, and the hadd for fornication must be imposed on his wife, unless she makes a counter-curse saying: "I bear witness by Allah that this husband of mine is one of the liars by accusing me of fornication with such and such a person, and that this child is from him and not from fornication," and she repeats this four times and on the fifth occasion, "and may the anger of Allah be on me if this my husband is of the truthful in accusing me of fornication with such and such;" if she completes this, the hadd is not applicable to her, and the child is banished from the husband, and there is a separation between them, and the woman becomes prohibited to her husband forever. The fuqaha differ as to the way the separation is effected: ash-Shafi'i considers that this separation occurs by the li'an of the husband alone, while Malik says that it occurs by their both declaring the li'an; Abu Hanifah says that the mutual li'an does not bring about separation until they are separated by the governor.

If a woman slanders her husband, she suffers the hadd and she does not make the declaration of li'an. If the husband retracts his statement after making the li'an, the child is recognised as his, and he is given the hadd-punishment for slander; his wife is no longer permitted for him according to ash-Shafi'i, while Abu Hanifah says that she is.

E. Concerning the retaliation and blood money for bodily harm: there are three kinds of bodily harm, intentional, accidental and an intentional bodily harm which resembles the accidental.

As for the purely intentional, it is when a person intends to kill someone with a sharp instrument, such as an iron blade or anything which could cut into flesh like a blade, or something that would usually kill by its weight like a stone or wood, in which case this is treated as intentional killing and the hadd is obligatory. Abu Hanifah says that injury caused with intent which obligates the retaliation is that in which the killing is done with a sharp instrument of iron or anything else which penetrates the flesh, but that a killing or pain caused by something heavy made of stone or wood is not treated as intentional and does not obligate retaliation. The ruling regarding the intentional act, according to ash-Shafi'i, is that the person who represents the person killed is free to exact either retaliation or the blood money, as long as there exists equality of status between the killer and killed. Abu Hanifah says that the person who represents the victim is only entitled to retaliation, but not to the blood money, unless the killer agrees.

The wali – the person who represents the victim – is the person who inherits his or her property, be they male or female, either by the normal right of inheritance, or by tribal link; Malik, however, says that this right applies only to males who inherit, but not females. There is no right of retaliation unless they all are in accord to exact it; if one of them accords a pardon, then the right of retaliation is annulled, and the diyah blood-money becomes due; Malik, however, says that it is not annulled. If there is a person who is underage, or a mad person, then the right to retaliation is not solely exercised by the adult of sane mind.

Equality of status between the killer and the killed, according to ash-Shafi'i, is that the former should not be superior to the latter by his being free and a Muslim: if he is superior to him by one of these qualities, for example, if a free person kills a slave, or a Muslim a non-Muslim, then there is no retaliation – although Abu Hanifah says that this equality of status is not taken into account, and that a free person may be put to death for a slave, or a Muslim for a non-Muslim, just as a slave is put to death for a free person, and a kafir for a Muslim. However, as people take care not to do this, or refuse even to do it, those who are of this opinion do not put it into practice. It is narrated that a Muslim who had killed a non-Muslim was referred to the Qadi Abu Yusuf, who pronounced the right of retaliation against him, and then a man came to him with a note which he threw to him on which was written:

> *O killer of a Muslim for a kafir, you have done wrong, for the just person is not the same as the unjust person. O whoever is among the 'ulama and poets of Baghdad and its surroundings, remind yourselves of the return to your Lord, and lament for your deen, and be patient, for the reward is with the patient; Abu Yusuf has committed a wrong regarding the deen by killing a believer for a kafir.*

Abu Yusuf then went to ar-Rashid, and told him what had happened, and read out the note. Ar-Rashid replied: "Deal discreetly with the affair, so as to avoid any discord;" then Abu Yusuf left and demanded of those who had the right of retaliation evidence of the liability which had been duly established; they did not provide it, and so he annulled the right of retaliation. Recourse to such action is permitted if there is benefit to be seen in it.

A slave is killed for killing a slave, even if the value of the killer is greater than that of the killed, although Abu Hanifah says that there is no retaliation against the killer if he is worth more than the value of the person killed. If there is a difference of religions amongst the non-Muslims involved, the right of retaliation is still established amongst them: a man may be entitled to the right of retaliation for a woman, and a woman for a man, an adult person for a person who is underage, and a person of sane mind for a mad person; there is no right of retaliation, however, against a child or a mad person, nor against a father who kills his son, but there is against the son who kills his father, or against a brother who kills his brother.

As for a purely accidental killing, where someone causes the death of another without intention, there is no right of retaliation against the killer – such as when a man throws something down (from on high) and kills someone, or when someone digs a well and someone falls in it, or if he starts the construction of an overhang and this falls on someone, or if he mounts an animal which bolts and tramples someone, or if he lays down a stone over which someone trips – if this or anything like it causes someone's death, purely accidentally, then the blood-money but not retaliation is required.

This blood money is owed by the clan of the killer, and it is not a fine on his own wealth, and it is to be paid within three years of the killing of the person, although Abu Hanifah says that it is from the time the judge pronounces the blood-money; this clan comprises his tribe – other than his father or sons – such that neither the father nor any other ascendant is liable for it, nor any sons and their descendants – although Abu Hanifah and Malik include the fathers and the sons in the clan. The killer is not liable for paying this blood-money along with the clan, although Abu Hanifah and Malik consider that the killer is treated as one of the clan. For the person of ample means, he should pay half a dinar each year, or its value in camels; for the person of average means, a quarter of a dinar, or its value in camels; the poor do not have to pay anything of it; whoever acquires ample means after being poor must contribute, and whoever becomes poverty-stricken after enjoying ample means does not have to contribute.

The blood money for a free Muslim, if assessed in gold, is a thousand dinars of the most common gold coins of good quality; if assessed in silver, then it is twelve thousand dirhams; Abu Hanifah says it is a thousand dirhams; if it is in camels, then a hundred camels divided into fifths – that is, twenty two-year olds, twenty female three-year olds, twenty male three-year olds, twenty four-year olds and twenty five-year olds. The blood money is based on payment in camels, and any other form of payment is by way of substitution. The blood money for a woman is half that of a man, both regarding her life and her limbs. There is a difference of opinion concerning the blood money for a Jew and a Christian. Abu Hanifah considers that it is the same as that of a Muslim; Malik says that it is half the blood money of Muslim, and according to ash-Shafi'i, a third. As for aMajusi (Zoroastrian), it is three tenths, that is, eight hundred dirhams; as for a slave, it is equivalent to his value, whatever it is, even if it is many times more than that of a free man, according to ash-Shafi'i; Abu Hanifah, however, said: "I do not consider that it attains the value of the blood money of a free person, even if it amounts to more than this, but rather I would reduce it by ten dirhams."

As for a killing which resembles the accidental, this refers to an act done intentionally but not with the aim of killing, as, for example, when a man hits another with a piece of wood of throws a stone at him, from which he might escape death or perish, but it does cause his death, or when a teacher hits a pupil in the customary manner, or the Sultan inflicts a discretionary punishment on a man for a crime, and they perish – then there is no right of retaliation, but rather an extra payment of blood money is due from the clan, that is, an increase of a third in gold or silver; or in the case of camels, they are paid in thirds, that is, a third of four-year olds, a third of five year olds and a third pregnant with young. It is reported of the Prophet, may the peace and blessings of Allah be upon him, that he said: "The clan does not have to contribute for a slave, nor for an intentional murder, nor as terms of an agreement, nor for a confession." The diyah (blood money) for a purely accidental killing in the Haram sanctuary, and in the sacred months of Muharram, Rajab, Dhu'l-Qa'dah and Dhu'l-Hijjah, and for a related person, is of the increased amount. The diyah for killing with intent, when there is a pardon instead of retaliation, is also of the increased amount and may be taken immediately from the wealth of the murderer.

If a group of persons took part in the killing of someone, then the right of retaliation is against all of them, but they only have to pay one diyah, even if there are many of them; the person who represents the person killed may pardon whom he wishes of them and may have the rest killed; if he pardons all of them, only one diyah is to be paid, and its payment exonerates all of them; if one of them was the person who actually did the killing, another wounded the victim, and another only inflicted some (minor) injury, then the right to take life in retaliation is only against the person who killed, while those who wounded or injured are subject to the ruling governing injury and not the taking of a life. If one person kills a group of persons, he is put to death for killing the first, and the diyah for the rest is to be paid from his wealth – although Abu Hanifah says that his being put to death is for all of them, and no diyah is to be paid. If he kills them all at the same time, then lots are drawn between them, and the right of retaliation is for the person who draws the lot, unless the persons who represent the killed persons agree amongst themselves to give the right of retaliation to one of them, in which case, the diyah is to be paid for each of the others from the wealth of the killer.

If a person in authority orders a man to kill someone, then the right of retaliation is against the person who gave the order and the person who carried it out; if the person giving the order is not a superior (officer) obeyed by subordinates, then the right of retaliation is against the person who carries out the order, and not the one who gave it; if a person is forced to kill, the right of retaliation must be against the person who forced him; there are two opinions as to whether it must also be against the person who was forced.

As for the right of retaliation for a part of the body which has been severed from the joint, an arm may be taken for an arm, a leg for a leg, a finger for a finger, the end of a finger for the end of a finger, a tooth for a similar tooth, but not a right for a left, nor an upper for a lower, and not a molar for another kind, nor a full tooth for a milk tooth, nor a healthy hand for a paralysed one, and not a tongue of someone who can speak for a tongue of a dumb person; however, the hand of someone who can write or make things may be taken in retaliation for the hand of someone who cannot write or make things; an eye is taken for an eye, be it a healthy eye, or one with a squint, or one that is night blind, although not for an unseeing fixed eyeball – or for a withered hand – unless it is like for like; the nose that can smell may be taken for one that cannot, and the ear that can hear for one that cannot, although Malik does not allow the right of retaliation for the latter. The retaliation takes place between Arabs and non-Arabs, and between nobles and those of lower status.

If the right of retaliation is renounced in favour of the diyah for these parts of the body, then the full diyah is payable for both hands, and half the amount for one; for every finger a tenth of the diyah is payable, that is ten camels; for each of the lower fingers, three camels and a third, except for the end of the thumb for which five camels is due; the two feet are the same amount as the two hands, except that for each toe five camels are due; for both eyes the full diyah, and for one eye, a half, no extra being paid for the eye of a one-eyed person – although Malik, may Allah have mercy on him, considers that the full diyah must be paid in this case; for the four eyelids the full diyah, and for each a quarter; for the nose the full diyah; for both ears the full diyah, and for each a half; for the tongue the full diyah; for both lips a quarter; for each tooth, five camels, irrespective of whether they are molars, or incisors or wisdom teeth; for the loss of hearing the full diyah, and if both ears have been cut off and also loss of hearing, then two diyahs, just as when the nose has been cut off and there is loss of smell, two diyahs are due; for loss of speech a diyah, and if the tongue has been cut off and there is loss of speech, then still only one diyah; for the loss of intellect, one diyah; for the loss of the penis, a diyah, irrespective of whether he is a eunuch, or the person is impotent, or anything else – although Abu Hanifah says that for the eunuch and the impotent, there must be a judicial ruling; for both testicles the diyah, and for one, a half; for the loss of a woman's breasts her full diyah, and for one a half; for a man's breast a judicial ruling is made, although some have said that the full diyah is to be paid.

As for head wounds: if the skin has been broken there is no right of retaliation or diyah to be paid, but rather a ruling is made; if blood is drawn, there is a ruling; if the blood comes out like tears after the skin has been cut, there is a ruling; if the flesh has been cut, a ruling is made; if the flesh is penetrated, a ruling is made; if after the skin is completely cut, only a thin covering over the skull remains, a ruling is made. These rulings are increased in severity according to the degree of the head-wound. Thereafter, there is the wound known as the *mudihah* where the skin, the flesh and the covering membrane have been pierced and the skull has been exposed, in which case, retaliation is due; if a pardon is granted five camels are due; if the flesh is exposed and the skull has been splintered in the wound known as the *hashimah*, ten camels are due; there is no retaliation for this latter (wound), but for the mudihah there is; when the hashimah is particularly severe, an extra five are paid, although Malik says that it is subject to a judicial ruling; as for the wound known as the *munaqqalah* ,where the skull is showing, has been fractured and is dislocated, so that it must be put back in place, fifteen camels are due; if retaliation of the mudihah is sought, ten camels are given for the hashimah and munaqqalah wounds; the *ma'munah*, also known as the *damighah*, refers to a wound which penetrates to the core of the skull, and a third of the diyah is due.

As for wounds to other parts of the body, the diyah is not payable except if the stomach is pierced, in which case a third of the diyah is due; there is no right of retaliation for a body wound, except if the bone is exposed, in which case, it is subject to a judicial ruling. If various limbs have been severed and have formed scars, then the diyahs are due for each, even if it amounts to many more times the amount of the diyah for loss of life; if the person dies of these wounds before scars have formed, then the diyah for loss of life is due and the various diyahs for the (missing) limbs are not payable; if death follows the formation of scar tissue on some of the wounds, a full diyah is payable for what has not healed, together with the diyah for each of the limbs; if healing takes place in the case of a tongue which cannot produce speech, or a paralysed hand, or a useless finger, or an eye still in place but not functioning, then a judicial ruling is necessary. This ruling consists in the judge assessing the victim as if he were a slave without any wound; he then assesses the difference in value after the wounds, this difference in value being the amount of the diyah – and it is this amount which is in the judicial ruling.

If a woman's stomach is hit, resulting in a still birth, and if it would have been a free person, payment of a slave or a slave-girl must be made by the clan; if it would have itself been a slave, then a tenth of the value of its mother is payable, irrespective of whether it is male or female; if it gave out a cry at the time of birth, a full diyah is payable, and then a distinction is made between a male and a female. Whoever kills someone and must pay the diyah is also obliged to pay a kaffarah-expiation, irrespective of whether it was intentional or accidental; Abu Hanifah makes it an obligation in the case of accidental death, but not for one with intent. This kaffarah consists of freeing a believing slave who is free from any defect which would be detrimental to his capacity to work; if this is not possible, he must fast for two consecutive months, and if he is incapable of this, then he must feed sixty destitute persons, according to one of two opinions; according to another, then he is no longer liable.

If a people claims from another people that there has been a killing and this claim is vigorous, that is, they want to convince others of the truth of their claim, then such a claim is accepted, and they are made to swear to it on oath fifty times, and then the judge grants them the right to the diyah, but not to retaliation; if the litigants refuse to make the oath, or part of it, then the accused must swear and is thus acquitted.

If there is to be retaliation for someone's murder, or for the loss of a limb, the person entitled to it cannot exact it on his own initiative, but only with the permission of the Sultan; in the case of the loss of a limb, the Sultan cannot authorise a retaliation unless he has failed to find someone else to do it; the fee for this is born by the person being punished, and not the person exacting it although – Abu Hanifah says that it is the other way round. If the retribution is to take the murderer's life, the Sultan may allow the person who represents the victim to exact vengeance himself if he is of strong character; otherwise the Sultan has it done for him by someone who is surer in his use of the sword.

If the person entitled to retaliate for a murder or the loss of a limb carries out the retaliation on his own initiative, without, however, going beyond the limits, then the Sultan imposes a discretionary punishment on him for having infringed the Sultan's own prerogative; however, he is not liable for any further penalty, as he only inflicted what he had a right to inflict.

✻

✻   ✻

F. Concerning discretionary punishments: these are imposed for wrong actions, but are not defined as hadd-punishments by the law. These vary according to different circumstances and the situation of the person who imposes them. In one respect, they do resemble the hadd-punishments, in that they are a reprimand which seeks to reform the behaviour of the person in question, and to deter others; they vary in accordance with the different kinds of crime. They differ from the hadd-punishments in three ways:

First, the correction inflicted on respectable persons of the noble class is lighter than that inflicted on the meaner and lower classes based on the saying of the Prophet, may the peace and blessings of Allah be upon him: "Pardon the faults of those who command respect." Thus people are treated according to their station, even though they are treated equally with respect to the hadd-punishments: thus the discretionary punishment inflicted on a prominent person might consist in merely turning away from him, and for a less significant person, in speaking roughly to him, and for another, in reproaching him in humiliating terms, while not, however, slandering or insulting him; for persons of a lower class, it consists in imprisonment for a length of time corresponding to their wrongdoing, so that for some it is a day, and for others, a longer indeterminate period. Abu 'Abdallah az-Zubayri, one of the followers of ash-Shafi'i, fixes the maximum for detention at a month in order to clarify and investigate the affair, and at six months as a means of correction and setting aright. For others, it consists in banishment if their crimes have involved others and caused them harm. There is a difference of opinion as to the maximum term of banishment; the clear meaning of ash-Shafi'i's madhhab is that it should be less than a year, even by one day, so that it is not as long as that inflicted as a punishment for fornication; the clear ruling in the madhhab of Malik is that it is permitted to impose more than a year depending on the reasons for the punishment. For others beatings are inflicted in accordance with the nature of the crime, and the degree or quality of the persons in question. There is a difference of opinion as to the maximum amount of beating that may be inflicted; the clear teaching of ash-Shafi'i is that for the free person, it should not exceed thirty-nine lashes, so as to be below the minimum number for the hadd of drinking wine: thus for the free person it should not be as much as forty, and for the slave, not as much as twenty; Abu Hanifah says that the maximum inflicted is thirty-nine for a free person and a slave alike, while Abu Yusuf says that it is seventy-five, and Malik, that there is no upper limit and it may be more than that of the hadd-punishments. Abu 'Abdallah az-Zubayri says that the discretionary punishment for any wrong action is deduced from the hadd-punishment associated with it, and that the maximum is seventy-five, that is, five less than the hadd for slander; if the discretionary punishment is for a crime associated with fornication, then account is taken of the circumstances: if the two are surprised before he has penetrated her vagina, they are both given the maximum discretionary punishment, that is seventy-five lashes; if they are found beneath a sheet, with nothing between them, embracing each other but not committing fornication, then they are given sixty lashes; if they are found thus but not embracing, then forty; if they are found together in a house both clothed, then thirty; if found in the road and they are speaking with each other, then twenty; if discovered making signs to each other but without speaking, then ten; and if he is discovered following her but nothing else is seen, then a few light strokes.

The same is true for the discretionary punishment for theft when no amputation is necessary: if someone steals something whose value is the value for which a limb is amputated, but which was not in a place of safekeeping, then the maximum number is given, that is, seventy-five lashes; if the person has stolen less than the legal minimum from a place of safekeeping, he is given sixty; if less than the legal minimum from other than a place of safe-keeping, then fifty; if he had started to gather up property from a place of safekeeping, but then returned it before taking it away, then forty; if he has broken into and entered into the place of safekeeping, but has not taken any-thing, then thirty; if he has broken in, but not entered it, then twenty; if he had begun to broken in or open a door, but did not complete the action, then ten; if he is found with a sharp instrument waiting to steal the property, he is given a few light lashes. Crimes other than these are treated in a similar fashion. Although this method appears to be of benefit, there are no proofs as to the validity of the method. The above discussion concerns one of the ways in which the discretionary punishment differs from the hadd;

Second, although no pardon or intercession is allowed with respect to the hadd, pardon is permitted regarding the discretionary punishment, and inter-cession is also allowed; if the discretionary punishment is solely to do with the government, and for the purpose of setting straight a misdemeanour, and if it is not connected with the private claim of an individual, then the person in authority may examine whether it is best to grant a pardon or to impose the discretionary punishment, just as it is permitted to intercede on behalf of someone who asks for pardon. It is narrated of the Prophet, may the peace and blessings of Allah be upon him, that he said: "Intercede before me, and Allah will decide on the tongue of His Prophet what He wishes." If the right of an individual is involved, such as the discretionary punishment for an insult or an assault, then the person insulted or the person attacked both have a right in the matter, and the right of the government is to set the affair straight, and to take corrective measures concerning the persons involved: thus the person in authority may not annul this right of those who have suffered insult or aggression by granting a pardon, but rather he must ensure that this right is fulfilled, by imposing the discretionary punishment on the person who made the insults or committed the assault. If the persons who suffered the aggres-sion or the insults grant a pardon, then the person in authority may still choose either to impose the punishment as a corrective measure, or to spare and pardon them. If the two parties have pardoned each other the insults or the aggression before bringing the matter to him, then the discretionary punish-ment with respect to an individual's right is annulled. There is a difference of opinion in two respects as to whether the right of the government to take corrective measures is also annulled: the first, and it is the opinion of Abu 'Abdallah az-Zubayri, is that it is annulled, and the person in authority may not impose a discretionary punishment – the hadd for slander is more severe, but is annulled if a pardon is granted and there is even less justification for a discretionary punishment made on behalf of the government; the second, and this is more plausible, is that the person in authority may impose the discretionary punishment even if a pardon has been granted before the matter is submitted to him, just as he may impose it when the pardon is made after it has been submitted to him – as opposed to the pardon granted for slander in both cases – since imposing corrective measures are a necessary part of the public interest.

If there are mutual insults or acts of aggression between father and son, the discretionary punishment is not imposed on the father with respect to what he has done to the son, but it is imposed on the son with respect to what he has done to his father – just as the father is not killed for the murder of his son, but the son is put to death for the murder of his father; the discretionary punishment which can be imposed on the father is a right solely of the government for the purpose of taking correctional measures, and the son has no right in the matter, and the person in authority may personally grant him pardon; the discretionary punishment which can be imposed on the son is a shared right, both of the father and of the government: thus the person in authority may not grant pardon on his own initiative if the father demands that this punishment be carried out. This then is the second way in which discretionary punishments differ from the hadd-punishments.

Third, if anything perishes because of the application of the hadd, then there is no liability, whereas there is liability for loss caused by the imposition of a discretionary punishment. 'Umar ibn al-Khattab intimidated a woman with the result that she aborted and had a stillborn baby; he then consulted 'Ali, may Allah ennoble his face, and the latter advised him to pay the diyah of the foetus. There is a difference of opinion as to who pays the diyah of the discretionary punishment: according to some, it is payable by the clan of the person responsible for the matter, and according to others, by the bait al-mal; as for the kaffarah-expiation, it is paid from the wealth of the person responsible, according to the first opinion; according to the second opinion, it is said that it is taken from his wealth or, according to others, from the bait al-mal. Likewise, if a teacher inflicts a blow in the customary manner as a corrective measure and this causes the person to perish, then his clan becomes liable for his diyah, and the kaffarah is from his wealth. The husband may hit his wife if she acts in a refractory way towards her husband; if she dies from his blow, her diyah is the liability of his clan as long as he did not mean to kill her – in which case the right of retaliation is exercised against him.

As for the nature of the blows used in the imposition of the discretionary punishment, it is permitted that they be made using a stick or a whip without any knots, as in the case of the hadd-punishment. There is a difference of opinion as to whether it is permitted to use a whip which has not been unknotted: az-Zubayri considers that it is permitted, even if this represents a more severe beating than the normal hadd-punishment, and that it is still permitted if blood is drawn; the majority of the followers of ash-Shafi'i, may Allah be pleased with him, are of the opinion that it is prohibited, as this would be an aggravated and more severe form of the hadd, and this is forbidden – thus there is all the more reason why it should be prohibited in the case of a discretionary punishment; moreover, it is not permitted for blood to be spilt in the case of discretionary punishments.

Blows inflicted for the hadd-punishment must be distributed over the whole of the body after the parts susceptible to fatal injury are covered – so that each member receives its portion of the hadd; the beating may not be made just on one part of the body. There is a difference of opinion regarding the beating for a discretionary punishment: the majority of the followers of ash-Shafi'i consider that it should also be distributed over the whole of the body, and that it is prohibited to inflict it solely on one place; az-Zubayri differs in that he permits it to be done on one single place, arguing that if it is permitted to leave off completely from the whole body, it must be permitted to leave out some of the body – as opposed to what is practised in the case of the hadd.

The live-crucifixion of a person may be imposed as a discretionary punishment: the Prophet, may the peace and blessings of Allah be upon him, had a man crucified on the mountain known as Abu Na'b; if a person is crucified he is not prevented from eating or drinking or making the ablutions for the prayer; he should pray by making indications, and should repeat them when he is taken down; he is not to be crucified for longer than three days. It is permitted, by way of discretionary punishment, to have him stripped of his clothes, except for those which cover his private parts, and for him to be paraded in public while a herald proclaims his wrongdoings, if he repeats them and does not turn in tawbah. It is permitted to shave his head but not his beard. There is a difference of opinion as to whether it is permitted to blacken his face – most permit it, while a few prohibit it.

Chapter 20
Public Order (*hisbah*)

The term "hisbah" refers to commanding what is good when it is being neglected, and to forbidding what is bad if it is being practised. Allah ta'ala says: **"And so there must be from amongst you a group who call to the best and command the good and forbid what is bad"** (Qur'an 3: 104). This applies, in effect, to every Muslim; the difference between someone who voluntarily undertakes this and a muhtasib are nine in number:

First, the obligation of the muhtasib is by way of his appointment decided by the authorities, whereas the obligation on others is a shared obligation incumbent on the community as a whole;

Second, the muhtasib's undertaking of the task is a necessary part of his appointment, which he is not allowed to transfer to another, whereas the undertaking of individuals is done voluntarily by way of a supererogatory action which they are permitted to pass on to others;

Third, the muhtasib's post is set up so that people may have recourse to him concerning matters which must be discouraged, whereas the one who does it voluntarily does not occupy a post set up for this;

Fourth, the muhtasib has to respond to people's complaints, whereas others do not;

Fifth, the muhtasib has to watch out for manifest incidents of evil, so that he may denounce them, and to investigate those acts of good behaviour which have been abandoned, so that he may command that they be renewed, whereas the ones who do it voluntarily do not have to search for or investigate these matters;

Sixth, the muhtasib has to have assistants to participate in denouncing evil, as he will be better able to do the task for which he has been appointed, if he is in a stronger and more powerful position, whereas the ones who do it voluntarily may not seek the assistance of helpers;

Seventh, he may impose discretionary punishments in matters of manifest evil, as long as they do not surpass the limits of the hadd-punishments, whereas the one who undertakes hisbah voluntarily may not do this;

Eighth, he may be paid for his hisbah from the bait al-mal, whereas the one who voluntarily undertakes hisbah may not be paid for denouncing evil;

Ninth, he may use his ijtihad-judgement concerning matters regarding customary practice – but not matters of the shari'ah- such as layouts in the markets, and setting up projecting sections; thus he affirms or rejects such matters in accordance with the results of his ijtihad, whereas the one who voluntarily undertakes the duty of hisbah may not do this.

This then concludes the nine differences between the person responsible for hisbah – that is, commanding to the good and forbidding evil – and the one who voluntarily undertakes this task, even though he may also command to the good and forbid evil. The conditions for the muhtasib are that he be a free man, just, of sound judgement, firm and severe in the deen, and clearly aware of what evil behaviour is. The fuqaha from among the followers of ash-Shafi'i differ in two ways as to whether he is to compel people to desist from an evil about which the fuqaha differ, based on his own ijtihad and opinion about it: the first, which is the opinion of Abu Sa'id al-Istakhri, is that he may compel others in conformity with his own ijtihad and judgement; based on this, then, the muhtasib must be an 'alim from amongst the people who make ijtihad concerning legal rulings in the deen – so that he may come to a decision regarding matters of controversy; and the second, is that he may not compel people to accept his ijtihad and judgement, because anyone may make his own ijtihad concerning matters which are disputed: based on this, then, it is permitted that the muhtasib is not among the people of ijtihad, as long as he is aware of the evil acts about which there is consensus.

✳
✳ ✳

It must be appreciated that hisbah lies half way between the activity of the judiciary and that of the investigation of complaints and abuse. It resembles the judiciary in two ways, it is more restricted than it in two ways, and it is more extensive than it in two ways.

As for the two ways in which it resembles the judiciary:

First, it is permitted to have recourse to the muhtasib, and it is permitted for the latter to listen to the complaint of someone against a third party in front of him – with respect to individual claims – whereas this is not permitted in cases of complaint in general, but rather in one of the following three: **i.** concerning cases of short measure and underweight; **ii.** concerning cheating and deceit regarding the object sold or the price; **iii.** concerning delay and prevarication in payment of a debt which is due, when the debtor is in a position to pay. His authority extends to these three kinds of complaint, but not to others, as they are connected with manifest evil: he is appointed to get rid of it; this ensures a clear benefit which he is appointed to establish: the sphere of hisbah is to make sure that claims are met, and to help others to fulfil them; the person responsible for this must not exceed this authority and make a final and irrevocable decision (concerning matters not in his sphere);

Second, the second matter in common is that the muhtasib may compel the defendant to fulfil any obligation towards him, whereas this is not the case in general for all obligations; rather, it is just for those claims which he is permitted to entertain; thus if a debt is due by the avowal and affirmation of the debtor himself, when he himself can pay and has ample means, then the latter must be made to fulfil his duty towards the claimant ,as any delay on his part is considered reprehensible – and the muhtasib's task is to put an end to this delay.

As for the two ways in which the hisbah is more restricted than the authority of the judiciary, they are the following:

First, he is not able to entertain complaints of a general nature, such as contracts, transactions and all other rights and claims which do not constitute reprehensible activities of a manifest kind; thus he may not even start to consider such complaints, or to offer a judgement concerning them, irrespective of whether the amount involved is great or small, even if it is a dirham or less – unless he has been given explicit authority over such matters which is over and above his nomination to the hisbah: if he has been given this extra authority, then he combines the roles of the judiciary and the hisbah, and in this case one must ensure that he is one of the people of ijtihad. If his appointment is restricted to hisbah, then the qadis and judges are more entitled to investigate matters involving both important and insignificant amounts;

Second, the muhtasib is limited to dealing with rights and claims which have been acknowledged; if, however, denials and disputes have arisen between two parties, he may not investigate such cases: it is rather the judge who has to listen to the testimonies, and to have the parties swear on oath – whereas the muhtasib may not hear witnesses in order to establish a claim, or compel someone to swear on oath in order to reject this claim; the qadis and the judges are thus more entitled to hear testimony and to have the litigants swear on oath.

As for the two ways in which the muhtasib's sphere of authority exceeds that of the judiciary, they are the following:

First, the muhtasib may investigate those matters in which he is commanding concerning the good or forbidding evil, even if the litigant seeking his help is not present – whereas the Qadi may not involve himself like this unless the litigant is present from whom he may then hear his claim; if, however, the Qadi does involve himself, then he excludes himself from the post to which he has been appointed, and infringes the basis of his authority;

Second, the muhtasib has to exercise the sovereignty of a government official, and so he may have recourse to the haughtiness and arrogance of the forces of order when dealing with reprehensible matters, whereas the judiciary may not: hisbah is involves enforcement and any excessive behaviour on behalf of the muhtasib when exercising his sovereignty and severity is not regarded as an injustice or undue harshness; the Qadi, however, is there to establish justice and should rather act with gentleness and gravity – and so any departure from this, such that he assumes the imperiousness of the hisbah, represents an outrage and an excess: thus the sphere of each is different, and when the authority of each is exceeded, the limits are infringed.

As for the comparison between hisbah and the investigation of complaints there is a resemblance which joins them, and a difference which separates them. As for the resemblance which joins them, it has two aspects: the first, is that its activity is based on intimidation applied with the force of authority and with cnergetic severity and the second, is that this activity may be concerned with matters of public interest and with seeing that manifest acts of wrong-doing are denounced. As for the difference between them it also has two aspects: the first, is that investigation in cases of complaint is instigated because of the incapacity of the qadis to deal with them, investigation in the realm of hisbah is instigated because the Qadi disdains to do it; for this reason, the rank of investigator of complaints is higher, and that of the hisbah is lower. The person in charge of grievances may make a signed order both to the Qadi and to the muhtasib, while the Qadi may not make one to the person responsible for resolving grievances, but he may to the muhtasib; the latter may not make one to either of them. This then is the first difference; and the second, is that the person responsible for grievances may pronounce judgements, while the person in charge of hisbah may not.

✳

✳ ✳

What we have described above concerning the activity of the hisbah – together with an explanation of the differences between the latter and both the judiciary and the court of grievances – having been completed, we shall now explain what it consists of, that is, the two spheres of commanding to the good, and forbidding what is bad.

1. Commanding to the good may be classed in three ways: that which concerns the rights of Allah, that which concerns the rights of individuals, and that which is common to both:

A. That concerned with the rights of Allah is of two types: the first is the obligation to command to this good a group of persons, rather than an individual, as in the case of the Friday-prayer when it is not established in an inhabited region: if there are sufficient numbers to warrant its establishment, such as forty or more, then they must be made to establish it; they are commanded to do it, and they are punished if they do not; if they are of a number about which there is a difference of opinion as to whether the jumu'ah-prayer should be established thereby, then both he and the people find themselves in one of four circumstances: **i.** both he and the people are of the opinion that the jumu'ah-prayer should be established by this number, and so he must command them to establish it, and they must make haste to obey this command; however, if they omit to do it, he punishes them in a milder fashion than if he were to punish them for not doing it in the situation where there is a consensus of opinion about it; **ii.** both parties agree that they are not sufficient in number to form the jumu'ah, and so he may not order them to do it: rather he is more entitled to prohibit it, if it is established; **iii.** the people consider that there are sufficient numbers to establish it, but the muhtasib does not, in which case he may not oppose them in this, nor even order them to establish it, as he himself is not of this opinion; he is also not allowed to prohibit them from doing it, or to prevent them from doing something which they consider is an obligation on them; **iv.** the muhtasib considers that it should be established, but the people do not: this may lead to a situation whereby its continued omission means that the jumu'ah is no longer practised at all for some time, even though a time might arrive when the numbers do indeed become sufficient; the question in this case is whether the muhtasib should command them to establish it, for fear that it might fall out of use. There are two aspects to the matter among the followers of ash-Shafi'i: the first, the opinion of Abu Sa'id al-Istakhri, is that he may command them to do it, considering thereby the public interest in the matter – lest the young child grow up without this practice, and so come to believe that it can be omitted when numbers increase, just as it can be omitted when they are insufficient. Ziyad takes a similar reasoning into account concerning the people's praying the jumu'ahs in Basra and Kufa: if they prayed in the courtyard, they would wipe the earth off their foreheads when they got up, and so he ordered that pebbles be thrown over the courtyard of the jumu'ah-mosque, saying: "I fear lest, with the passing of time, the young as they grow up will think that wiping one's forehead after the prostration is a sunnah of the prayer." The second opinion is that the muhtasib should not involve himself in their affair, as he is not these to compel the people to his way of thinking, and that he should not impose his opinion on them in matters of the deen, given that ijtihad is permitted when they are of the belief that lack of numbers prohibits them from legally fulfilling the jumu'ah.

As for ordering them to do the 'Eid-prayer, this he may do: there is a difference of opinion as to whether commanding them to do it is a binding duty on his part, or a right which he is permitted to exercise: there are two aspects to this matter amongst the followers of ash-Shafi'i, depending on whether they consider this prayer a sunnah, or an obligation on the community as a whole. For those who say that it is a sunnah, the order to establish it is recommended; for those who consider it an obligation on the community, then his ordering them to do it must necessarily take place.

As for the (five) daily prayers in the mosques, and calling the adhan for these prayers, these constitute the rites of Islam and the signs of worship by which the Messenger of Allah distinguished Dar al-Islam from Dar ash-Shirk: thus if the people of a region or a locality agree to abandon the group-prayers in their mosques, and the adhan at the time of the prayers, then the muhtasib is recommended to order them to call the adhan and to establish the group-prayers: as for whether this is an obligation on him – so that he commits a wrong action by not doing this – or a recommended action, for which he will be rewarded, the followers of ash-Shafi'i differ as to whether or not the Sultan is obliged to fight those in a country or locality who agree not to call the adhan and not to establish the prayer.

If an individual omits to pray the jumu'ah prayer, or to call the adhan and the iqamah for the prayer, the muhtasib should not raise any objections as long as he does not make a habit of this, as these practices are only recommended and may be omitted for a valid reason – unless any suspicion arises in the matter, or the person in question makes a habit of it, or one fears that his example might influence others; he then considers the public benefit to be served by preventing him from belittling these sunnahs of worship; any warnings given to him for abandoning the group-prayer should be made after considering his circumstances: it has been narrated that the Prophet, may the peace and blessings of Allah be upon him, said, "I thought on one occasion to order my Companions to gather wood, and then to order them to do the prayer – so that when the adhan had been called and the iqamah had been said, I would then go round to the houses (of those) who did not attend the prayer and set fire to them."

As for his warning a group of isolated persons or an individual who, for example, delay the prayer until its allotted time has passed, then he should remind them and order them to perform it, and pay attention to the person's reply; if he says: "I did not do it because I forgot," then he urges him to do it as soon as he remembers it, but he does not punish him; if he says: "I have omitted to do it out of disdain and scorn," then he is punished and reprimanded and compelled to do it; no objection is to be made against someone who delays it, but is still within the time, as there is a difference of opinion amongst the fuqaha as to the benefit in delaying it. If, in a region, the people have agreed to delay the group-prayer until the latest possible time, while the muhtasib considers that it is better to pray it earlier, then there are two opinions as to whether he should order them to do it earlier: if all the people consider it should be late, then the young will grow up thinking that this is in fact the time, and not the earlier time; if some of them do it earlier, he should leave those who delay it alone, and put his own opinion as to its delay aside. As for the adhan and the qunut supplication in the prayer, if such practices are contrary to the opinion of the muhtasib, the latter should not intervene, neither to command them nor to prohibit them, as long as they are allowed by the ijtihad (of the fuqaha) – as this would be outside the sphere of his competence, as we have explained above. This is likewise the case with purification: if a person undertakes it in a manner which is permitted, but which is contrary to the opinion of the muhtasib, for example, when he gets rid of major impurities with liquids (other than water), and performs wudu with water which has been adulterated with dust, albeit itself pure, or restricts the wiping of the head to the minimum part thereof, or if he overlooks an impure stain the size of a dirham, then in all these matters, he should not involve himself with the person in any way, either regarding an order or a prohibition; as for his getting involved, for example, when the person does wudu with date-wine when there is no water, then there are two opinions – because such a practice might result in its being regarded as permitted in all circumstances, and it may be that people might then become intoxicated from drinking it.

It is in the realm of examples such as these that his ordering to the good should be executed with respect to the rights of Allah.

B. As for commanding to the good with respect to the rights of individuals, they are of two kinds, the general and the particular:

i. As for the general, when for example the water-supply of a town fails, or a wall threatens to collapse, or travellers arrive at night in a state of need and the inhabitants avoid helping them – then as long as there is money in the bait al-mal which, if used, would not cause harm to these inhabitants, he should order the water-supply to be restored, the wall to be rebuilt and the travellers to be helped on their way, as these are claims incumbent on the bait al-mal and not on the inhabitants; the same should be done if their mosques and Friday-mosques are falling into disrepair; if there are no funds available in the bait al-mal, then the order to rebuild the walls, or to restore the water-supply, or to repair the mosques and the Friday-mosques, or to take care of the travellers, is directed to all those amongst the inhabitants who have the means, and no one of them is assigned this task alone; if those with means commence this work, and begin to take care of the travellers, and work towards the completion of these tasks, then the muhtasib is no longer entitled to order people to do these things, and they do not have to seek permission to take care of the travellers, or to rebuild what has fallen into disrepair; if, however, they wish to demolish what is in ruins or fallen into disrepair, in order to rebuild it completely, then they cannot proceed to demolish what is, for the people of the town, a public place, unless they first ask the permission of a person in authority – not the muhtasib – who will grant them permission after they have undertaken to rebuild it.

As for those mosques which belong to particular clans and tribes, they do not have to ask permission; it is up to the muhtasib to see that they rebuild what they have demolished, but he cannot compel them to finish what they have commenced. If those with means desist from rebuilding what is in ruins, or from repairing what is in a state of disrepair, the muhtasib should leave them and the town alone, if residence in it is still possible and if there is still sufficient water, however, small the supply. If residence in the town is too difficult because of the lack of water and the collapse of the walls, then an examination of the situation is made: if the town is on a frontier and abandoning it would be detrimental to Dar al-Islam, the person in authority may not allow the people to leave it: the ruling in this situation is the same as that in the case of disasters – that is, that all persons with means are obliged to contribute. In such disasters, it is up to the muhtasib to alert the Sultan as to the situation, and to encourage the people of means to undertake the work. If it is not a frontier town, and if abandoning it would not harm Dar al-Islam, then his affair is easier and his rule lighter: the muhtasib may not compel the inhabitants to rebuild the town, since the Sultan is more obliged to undertake this. If the latter lacks funds to do the rebuilding, then the muhtasib should say to them: "As long as the Sultan is unable to do this, you have the choice between leaving the town, or becoming liable for the expenses needed to rebuild it and make it inhabitable again;" if they agree to this obligation, then he charges the community with what its members are able to do, but he may not compel any individual in particular from amongst them to undertake any small or large task if they are not disposed to do it; rather, he says, "Each of you should expend what he is well able and disposed to spend." Those who are without funds should help in the work: when all that is needed is there or liability for it is forthcoming in a satisfactory manner from each of those with means, then the muhtasib starts the work of repair, and he holds each of the community who has promised help to their promises. Although such a liability is not binding in private transactions, the ruling governing liability in cases of public interest is more extensive, as the ruling in question is more general. As this is a work of public interest, the muhtasib is not to undertake it without first seeking the permission of the Sultan, lest he should infringe the latter's duty in the matter, and given that this work of public interest is not part of his customary responsibility; if, however, the work is of minor importance, and it is difficult to seek permission of the Sultan, or if an increase in the harm (resulting from the disrepair) is feared because of the delay involved in seeking permission, then he may begin without seeking permission.

ii. As for the particular responsibility of the muhtasib regarding the rights of individuals, this refers to delays in the fulfilment of rights and claims and debts which are overdue: it is up to the muhtasib to order that they are discharged if the persons in question are able to discharge them, and if those entitled to them are demanding that they be fulfilled; he may not imprison them for this, as imprisonment must result from a judicial judgement; he may, however, resort to surveillance, as the claimant may also resort to it. He may not impose payment of day to day living expenses for near relations, because to whom and by whom it is made is subject to ijtihad within the shari'ah – unless the judge has stipulated the amount, in which case he may see that payment is carried out. Likewise, guardianship of minors may only be undertaken after the judge has made a decision, in which case the muhtasib is permitted to order that it be undertaken in accordance with the stipulated conditions. As for the acceptance of the guardianship of inheritances and deposits, the muhtasib should not order anyone to undertake this, irrespective of whether they are important persons or anyone else, although he may command this in a general way, urging people to help each other in right action and to be persons of taqwa.

This then concludes the examples concerning which he is to order the good with respect to the rights of individuals.

C. As for his commanding the good regarding what is common both to the rights of Allah ta'ala and to the rights of individuals, these include seeing that those who have guardianship over women regarding their marriage ensure that their partner is found if they demand it, and seeing that the 'iddah-delay is completed if they are divorced; he must punish the woman who does not respect the 'iddah, but he may not punish those guardians who do not fulfil their duties. As for the man who denies being the parent of a child who is nevertheless his, he compels him to fulfil his rights as a father and imposes a discretionary punishment on him for his denial. He also sees that the rights of men and women slaves are respected by their masters, and that the latter do not impose tasks on them which are beyond their capabilities; likewise, he ensures that owners of beasts of burden are taken to account if they do not give them enough fodder, or if they use them for tasks beyond their capacities. Regarding someone who finds a child but fails to take care of it properly, he commands such a person either to fulfil the rights the foundling has over him, or to hand it over to someone who will and who does fulfil these rights. The same is true in the case of someone who finds stray animals, and who is negligent in their care: he orders that they be taken care of properly, or that they be handed over to those who can. He is liable for any harm which befalls such animals in his hands – although he is not in the case of the child he finds; moreover, he is still liable if he hands the stray animal over to another, although he is not if he hands over a foundling to another. These then are some examples of the kind of matters in which he is to order the good, regarding rights which are common to Allah and to man.

✻

✻ ✻

2. As for his forbidding reprehensible actions, they are of three types: those concerning the rights of Allah ta'ala, those concerning the rights of individuals, and those common to both.

A. As for the rights of Allah, they are also three kinds: those connected to acts of worship, those connected with prohibited acts, and those connected with transactions.

1. As for those connected with acts of worship, such as someone who wishes to deliberately contradict their legal form, or to intentionally change the nature of the sunnahs – for example, if someone wants to say the silent prayers aloud, or the prayers said aloud silently, or to make additions to the words of remembrance in the prayer, or to the adhan, which are not part of the sunnah – then it is up to the muhtasib to condemn this, and to punish the person responsible for this act of disobedience, as long as the person in question cannot say which imam he is taking as an example in the matter. Likewise, if a person omits to purify his body, his clothes or the place where he is praying, then the muhtasib should condemn his action if this is evident in his behaviour; he may not, however, punish him merely on the basis of accusation or suspicion – it is narrated that a muhtasib asked a man going into a mosque wearing his sandals whether he also used them when he went to the lavatory; when the man denied this, the muhtasib wanted him to swear on oath: this ignorance on his part, and an overstepping of the realm of hisbah – his bad opinion of the other had got the better of him. Likewise, if he thinks that a man is omitting to do a ghusl after being in a state of major impurity, or that a man is not doing the prayer or fasting, then he should not punish him on the basis of suspicion, nor subject him to reprimand; he may, however, on the basis of suspicion, admonish him and warn him of the torment of Allah for those who do not fulfil His rights. If he sees him eating during the month of Ramadan, he does not proceed to punish him until he has asked him why he is eating – if there is any cause for uncertainty in his situation: it may well be that he is sick, or on a journey; if he gives him a valid excuse in keeping with his circumstances, then he desists from reprimanding him, and he orders him to eat discreetly, so as not to expose himself to suspicion; it is not necessary to have him swear on oath if he is still suspicious of what he says, as he should trust his word. If he does not give him a valid excuse, then he reprimands him loudly as a warning, and punishes him as a deterrent; even if he understands his excuse, he reprimands him in a loud voice for having exposed himself to suspicion – lest the ignorant, unable to distinguish the situation in which he is excused from another situation, take his behaviour as an example.

As for someone who refuses to pay the zakah, if it is with respect to manifest wealth, then the zakah-official, in particular, is to take it from him by force and he is the one who is the most entitled to impose a discretionary punishment for fraud if he finds no valid excuse; if it regards hidden wealth, it is possible that the muhtasib is more particularly empowered to denounce him than the zakah-official, as the latter should not get involved in hidden wealth; it is also possible that the official is more particularly empowered to denounce the person owing the zakah, since if the latter does pay it to him, it will have been satisfactorily discharged. His punishment should be in accordance with the circumstances of the person refusing to pay the zakah; if the latter says that he has paid it privately, then his word is trusted.

When he sees a man engaged in begging people for zakah wealth, and is aware that he has means, either possessing wealth or being able to work, then he chastises him and punishes him – and it is the muhtasib rather than the zakah-official who is more suited to chastising him. 'Umar, may Allah have mercy on him, did this with respect to a group of those entitled to zakah. If he sees signs about him that suggest that he is a man of means, while he is asking people, then he informs him that such a practice is prohibited for someone who does not need to do it as though he does not reproach him, as it may be that in reality he is a poor person; if he engages in begging while full of vigour and with enough bodily strength to work, he restrains him and orders him to take up his profession; if he still insists on begging, then he is given a discretionary punishment until he stops doing it; if a person of means or capacity for work persists in begging – which is forbidden to him by his situation – then the person with wealth is compelled to spend it on himself, and someone capable of work is compelled to spend his wages on himself; it is not, however, up to the muhtasib to order this himself, as this requires a prior ruling: a judge is more entitled to carry this out; thus the matter is brought to the attention of the latter, so that he may take charge of it, or give permission for another to see to it.

If the muhtasib finds a person who engages in the science of the shari'ah, but who is not suited to be a faqih or a preacher, and he fears lest people will be deceived by false interpretation and incorrect answers, then he should denounce him for engaging in something for which he is not suited, and he makes this public so that people are not taken in by him; as for those persons whose situation is unclear to him he should not proceed with his denouncement until he has examined the matter. 'Ali ibn Abi Talib on one occasion passed Hasan al-Basri while he was talking to the people and he put him to a test, saying, "What is the pillar of the deen?" to which he replied, "Scrupulousness." Then he asked, "And what is it which blights it?" to which he replied, "Greed." 'Ali then responded, "Now you may talk to the people if you wish." If someone engaged in knowledge says something innovative, which contradicts the consensus and goes against textual evidence, and whose opinion is in opposition to the 'ulama of his time, then he should denounce and reprimand him; if he ceases and turns in tawbah, then all well and good, but if not, then the Sultan is more entitled to uphold the correct teaching of the deen; if one of the mufassirun proceeds to give an interpretation of the Book of Allah, in which he abandons the manifest meaning of the revelation in favour of an inner innovative sense to which he attaches the most obscure of meanings, or if one of the narrators of hadith reports in isolation hadiths whose meanings are abhorrent, or gives an incorrect interpretation of their import, then the muhtasib must denounce them, and prevent them from continuing. It is only correct that he should denounce them, provided that he can clearly distinguish between the valid and the invalid, and the right from the wrong – and this in one of two ways: either he is sufficiently able in his knowledge and his ijtihad for these matters to be clear to him, or the 'ulama of the time are agreed that such persons should be denounced and that they are being innovative – and so they have recourse to the muhtasib for his help, in which case the latter may rely on their opinion in order to denounce him, and on their consensus in order to prevent him from continuing.

2. As for prohibited acts, the muhtasib must prevent people from becoming involved in dubious situations and suspicious circumstances: the Prophet, may the peace and blessings of Allah be upon him, said: "Leave what causes you doubt for what does not cause you doubt." He should proceed to denounce such behaviour, and he should not impose any punishment before he has done this denouncing. Ibrahim an-Nakha'i relates that 'Umar ibn al-Khattab, may Allah be pleased with him, had forbidden men to do the tawaf of the Ka'bah with women; when he saw a man praying with the women, he hit him with his cord and the man said: "By Allah, if I have acted well, you have done me wrong, and if I have done wrong, you did not tell me;" then 'Umar said, "Were you not present (when I spoke of) my determination?" to which the other replied, "I was not present when you determined anything." Then 'Umar threw him the cord, saying, "Take your right of retaliation!" to which the other said, "I will not make the retaliation today!" 'Umar then said, "Pardon me!" to which the other said, "I do not pardon you!" They parted company at this; then 'Umar met him the following day and his colour changed; the man then said to him, "O Amir of the Believers, it looks as if what I did has made an impression on you?" to which 'Umar replied, "True." Then the man said: "I bear witness to Allah that I have pardoned you."

If the muhtasib sees a man standing with a woman in a busy street and there are no signs of any suspicious circumstances about them, then he should not get involved in reprimanding or rebuking them: in effect, people often have no alternative but to communicate thus. If, however, they are standing together in an empty street, then the very emptiness of the street is suspicious; he denounces this action, but without resorting immediately to chastising them more severely, lest they may be related to each other, saying, "If she is related to you, then do not expose her to dubious circumstances, and if she is not, then fear Allah lest this empty place lead you into disobeying Him." – then the chastisement should be in accordance with the indications of the affair. Abu'l-Azhar narrates that Ibn A'ishah saw a man talking to a woman in the street and said to him: "If she is your wife, then it is ill of you to speak to her in front of people, and if she is not, then it is even worse;" then he left them and began to speak with some people about hadith; then a note with the following written upon it was thrown into his lap:

As for the one you saw me with this morning, she was speaking to me as a messenger, who brought me a message which almost caused me to collapse, from a woman of languid glances, whose heavy hind parts draw her waist in; with the bow of youth hanging over her shoulder, she shoots – and she is without rival; if your ear had been between us, and if you had heard what we were saying, you would have seen that what you thought was evil in our affair was in fact good and beautiful.

Ibn A'ishah read it, and seeing the name Abu Nawas written at the top of it, he said: "What am I doing getting involved with Abu Nawas?" This degree of reproof by Ibn A'ishah is sufficient for a man of his like, but it would not be sufficient for those charged with hisbah and appointed to denounce such incidents; moreover, there is not an open declaration of corruption in the words of Abu Nawas: it might be that they indicate someone closely related to him even though both his situation and the obvious meaning of his words indicate his corruption and his dubious character; thus from the likes of Abu Nawa's it is reprehensible even though it may well not be reprehensible in others. Thus if the muhtasib sees something he disapproves in similar circumstances, then he should come and examine and take account of the situation, but he should not be hasty in denouncing anyone until he has sought to inform himself: Ibn Abi'z-Zinad, for example, reports of Hisham ibn 'Urwah, who said: "While 'Umar ibn al-Khattab, may Allah be pleased with him, was making tawaf of the House, he saw a man making the tawaf with a woman as fine and beautiful as a gazelle on his shoulders, and he was reciting:

I have become a submissive, obedient camel for her, crossing the plains;
I stop her from toppling forward, and take care lest she should fall and
perish, and I hope by this to receive a worthy reward,

'Umar, may Allah be pleased with him, then said to him: "O slave of Allah, who is this woman to whom you have given away your Hajj?" Then he replied: "My wife, O Amir of the Believers, and she is stupid, quarrelsome, a glutton, greedy and no longer has any parents." 'Umar then asked him, "Why do you not divorce her?" to which he replied, "She is beautiful, so I cannot hate her, and the mother of my children, so I cannot abandon her;" then 'Umar said: "So may your affair be with her." Abu Zayd says that the word "quarrelsome" (Arabic: *mirgham*) also means she talks nonsense (*mukhtalit*). Thus we see that 'Umar did not proceed immediately with reprobation, but rather informed himself – and when his doubts had been put to rest, then he treated him leniently.

If a man openly and blatantly drinks wine and he is a Muslim, then the wine is poured away and he is punished; if he is a dhimmi, he is punished for doing it openly, but the fuqaha differ as to whether it should be poured away: Abu Hanifah is of the opinion that it is not poured away, as it is treated as an article of wealth for which there is liability according to their rights; ash-Shafi'i says it is, as there is no liability for it, neither for a Muslim nor a nonbeliever. As for the person who openly displays date-wine, Abu Hanifah considers that it is treated as wealth attributable to Muslims and so he prohibits its being poured away, or the person who has displayed it from being punished; according to ash-Shafi'i, it is not an article of wealth and is like wine, and there is no liability on someone who pours it away. Thus the person in charge of hisbah should consider the situation, forbid that it be displayed openly, and take punitive measures if it was for drinking – although he may only pour it away if a judge from amongst those capable of ijtihad has given the order to do so, so as not to expose himself to a penalty if taken to court. As for the person who openly displays his drunkenness, and whose loss of intellect causes him to act stupidly, he is given a discretionary punishment for his uncontrolled drunkenness and manifest stupidity, but not the hadd-punishment.

As for the open display of forbidden musical instruments, the muhtasib must take them apart, so that they are (reduced to) mere pieces of wood and can no longer be regarded as instruments; the person is punished for displaying them, but they are not broken if the wood may be good for making something else.

As for dolls, they are not used in disobedience, but rather to accustom girls to bringing up children; there is, however, in this part of family custom an aspect which is akin to an act of disobedience, that is in the fashioning of figures and their being similar to idols: thus one aspect of them favours their use while another prohibits it, and so it is in accordance with the situation in which they are used that they are either disapproved or approved of. In effect, the Prophet, on whom be peace and blessings, came upon A'ishah, may Allah be pleased with her, while she was playing with dolls, and he allowed it and did not reprove her. It is narrated that Abu Sa'id al-Istakhri, one of the followers of ash-Shafi'i, took over the hisbah of Baghdad at the time of al-Muqtadir, and he put an end to the market for the small bitter grains known as *dadi* and prohibited their use, saying that they were only good for making prohibited date-wine – but he allowed the market for dolls and did not prohibit them, saying that A'ishah, may Allah be pleased with her, would play with dolls while the Messenger, may the peace and blessings of Allah be upon him, was watching, and he did not reprove her for that. As for what he said concerning playing with dolls, this is not an inconceivable ijtihad, but as for the market in dadi-grains, then it is true that they are mostly only used in nabidh – but they are also occasionally used as a medicine, and so his opinion is far-fetched: thus their sale for those who consider that nabidh is permitted is not disapproved of, and as for those who consider that it is not permitted, they must still be permitted, given that they may be used for other purposes: their sale is disapproved of, however, in light of the usual purpose to which they are put. The prohibition of Abu Sa'id in this, however, was not because its sale was forbidden in his opinion, but rather because it was being displayed openly for sale in a separate place in the market, but nevertheless next to other plants about which the fuqaha are of a consensus that they are allowed: thus he prohibited it so that ordinary people might appreciate the difference between this and other plants whose use is also permitted; moreover, there is nothing to prevent the denouncing of the open vaunting of certain permitted acts – thus boasting about permitted intercourse with wives and slaves may be denounced.

As for prohibited acts, the muhtasib should not try to spy them out as long as they are not being committed openly, and he should not uncover whatever may conceal such actions, lest he should expose someone who had deliberately sought secrecy: the Prophet, may the peace and blessings of Allah be upon him, said: "Whoever commits an ugly act, then let him veil himself with Allah's veil; whoever divulges such an action openly, then we impose the hadd-punishment of Allah ta'ala on him." If, however, there are overwhelming indications and signs that someone is committing such actions in secret, then they are to be treated in one of two ways:

A. In the case where a violation of a prohibition might occur before it can be found out, for example, when a trustworthy man informs the muhtasib that a man has gone to be alone with a woman to fornicate, or with a man in order to kill him, then in such circumstances he may spy on him and proceed to investigate and examine, lest some forbidden or prohibited act should occur which might have been avoided: likewise, if people voluntarily (make hisbah), they may proceed to investigate and examine the matter and denounce it, as happened in the case of Mughirah ibn Shu'bah: it is narrated that a woman of the Banu Hilal, known as Umm Jamil bint Mahjam ibn al-Afqam, who was married to a Thaqafi man called Jajjaj ibn 'Ubaid, used to visit him regularly. News of this reached Abu Bakrah ibn Masruh, Shibli ibn Ma'bad, Nafi' ibn al-Harith and Ziyad ibn 'Ubaid who then lay in hiding – and when the woman went in to him, they rushed in upon them: their bearing witness in front of 'Umar, may Allah be pleased with him, is a well-known event; 'Umar did not reprove them for having rushed in upon them – even though he gave them the hadd-punishment for slander for shortcomings in their evidence;

B. This concerns those acts which are not subject to this hadd and which fall short of this degree of gravity – in such cases it is not permitted to spy on the persons in question, nor to try to expose any attempt to conceal it. It is narrated that 'Umar, may Allah be pleased with him, went in amongst a group of people sitting together drinking wine in a place specially lit for the purpose, and said: "I have forbidden you to drink wine, and you sit and drink; I have forbidden you to light up these places, and you light them up;" to which they replied, "O Amir of the believers, Allah has forbidden you to spy, and you have spied; and He has forbidden you to enter a house without first asking permission, and you have entered;" then 'Umar, may Allah be pleased with him, said, "These two (reproaches of yours) for those two (of mine)," and he went away without getting involved any further. Thus anyone who hears the sound of forbidden instruments coming from a house, and the people are making their music clearly heard, then he should denounce them from outside the house: but he is not to impose upon them by entering, since what counts as abhorrent is what is manifest, and he is not to deliberately reveal anything else of the kind which is concealed.

3. As for forbidden transactions such as usury, invalid sales and whatever the shari'ah prohibits, when such transactions – about which there is a consensus as to their prohibition – are conducted with both contracting parties knowing that they are prohibited, then it is up to the muhtasib to denounce them, to prevent this occurring, and to take preventive measures; his order with respect to the punishment will vary in accordance with the circumstances and the gravity of what is prohibited. As for those transactions about which the fuqaha differ, as to whether they are prohibited or not, then the muhtasib should not get involved unless the arguments against their being prohibited are weak, and are only employed as a means to something which all are agreed is prohibited, like the usury involved in an inequitable cash for cash transaction made on the spot – the argument against its being prohibited is weak, and it is only a means to making a usurious transaction, which all are agreed is forbidden. As to whether denouncing such transactions is a part of his responsibility, there are two ways of considering them, as we have discussed above.

As for (underhand) dealings which may be included in the term transactions – excluding, however, illicit marriage contracts – the muhtasib should denounce them if the 'ulama agree that they are prohibited, but he should not get involved if there is a difference of opinion among the fuqaha – unless the difference is minor, and it is a means of attaining something forbidden about which there is a consensus, like temporary marriage, which is often used as a means of making fornication seem permitted. There are two aspects to his denouncing such contracts; instead of denouncing them, he should rather try to encourage contracts about which there is a consensus. As for transactions which consist of cheating with respect to articles of sale, or fraudulent practice regarding prices, the muhtasib should denounce them, prevent them occurring, and impose punishments in accordance with the situation. It has been narrated that the Prophet, may the peace and blessings of Allah be upon him, said: "Those who cheat are not with us." If such fraudulent practice involves cheating the buyer and concealing the irregularity from him, this is the more severely prohibited kind of cheating and the most criminal; the denunciation of such a practice is thus all the more severe, and the punishment all the more harsh; if however, the buyer is aware of the irregularity, then the wrongdoing is not so great, and the manner of denunciation is less harsh: in such cases, the buyer must be examined: if he bought the article to resell it, then the seller is denounced for his cheating, as is the buyer for intending to resell it, as he will be selling it to someone who is unaware that he is cheating; if, however, he buys it to use it, then the buyer is exempted from rebuke and only the seller is subject to this. The same is true in the case of fraudulent practice in prices. The muhtasib should also prevent people from milking cattle or letting milk collect in the udder at the time of sale – as these practices, being a form of cheating, are forbidden.

One of his most basic tasks is to prevent the practice of giving short amounts or weights by the use of deficient measures or balances: this is based on Allah ta'ala's threat which He makes when prohibiting such practices: the punishment should be all the more manifest and surveillance all the more frequent. The muhtasib may test and control the market weights and measures if he has doubts about them; if he has stamps for those instruments which he has tested, which are known amongst the people, and which are the only ones used, then this is safer and surer; if he does do this, and the people conduct transactions with each other using instruments which have not received this stamp, then they will be subject to rebuke in two ways if they make fraudulent dealings: the first, in their opposition to the muhtasib by not using his stamp and their denial of his rights from the Sultan; and the second, the fraud and short measure with regard to the customer, and his rejection of the laws of the shari'ah; however, if they use non-stamped weights and measures which are, free from defect and deficiency, then they are subject to rebuke only with respect to the right of the Sultan, in that they have opposed him; those who falsify this stamp are treated in the same way as counterfeiters of the stamp on dirhams and dinars: if this falsification is also accompanied by cheating, then they will be subject to rebuke and punishment in two ways: the falsification contravenes the right of the Sultan, and the cheating, the law of the shari'ah, and this latter is the graver of the two; if there is no cheating, only falsification, they will only be subject to the rebuke resulting from the Sultan's right, and this is the least serious of the two. If the town is extensive, so that its inhabitants need inspectors of weights, measures and currency, then the muhtasib should choose them, and take care only to appoint those whom he is satisfied are truthful and trustworthy; their wages are to be paid from the bait al-mal if there are sufficient funds for this; if not, he should fix their wages at an amount which is neither excessive, nor so deficient as to lead to favouritism or fraud in the assessment of weights and measures. Previously, the amirs used to choose them, arrange their duties and register their names in the diwans, so that no untrustworthy persons from outside might get involved. If any of these inspectors of weights and measures shows himself to be fraudulent by his increasing or decreasing of the amounts, then he is punished, expelled from the company of the inspectors, and prevented from getting involved in public works. This also applies to courtiers – that is, those who are trusted are allowed to do this task and those who are dishonest are not.

These then are the tasks undertaken by those in charge of the hisbah if the amirs decline to do them. As for the appointment of those responsible for apportioning inheritances and making assessments, the Qadi is more entitled to make these appointments than the muhtasibs, since responsibility for the wealth of orphans and those who are absent is assumed by representatives of the Qadi. As for the choice of guards connected to the tribes or the markets, this is made by the forces of order and government assistants.

If there is a dispute concerning short weight or measure, the muhtasib may investigate as long as the two parties are both contesting the matter – in which case the qadis are more entitled to investigate the matter than the muhtasibs, as they are more entitled to pronounce judgements, although the punishment is imposed by the muhtasib. If the governor takes up the case, this is permitted, as his powers are connected with those of the judges.

Among the things which the muhtasib may denounce in a general way, although not in a particular way or in the case of isolated individuals, are sales conducted using weights and measures not known by the people, even though they may be familiar to others elsewhere; if, however, two persons agree to use them, then he is not to oppose them in this by denouncing them or preventing them from using them; he should, however, prevent their use if people as a whole start to use them, since someone unfamiliar with them might use them and be deceived.

B. As for what he may denounce within the realm of purely individual rights, for example, when a man infringes the right of his neighbour in the restricted hareem-zone around his house, or by setting beams into his wall, then the muhtasib is not to get involved unless the neighbour seeks his assistance, because the right relates to the latter, and he may either pardon the infringement, or seek redress; if he does litigate against him, the muhtasib may investigate only if there is no dispute between them and no mutual denials, in which case he must put an end to the infringement and may impose a punishment in accordance with the circumstances; if they do dispute with each other, then the judge is more entitled to investigate. If one neighbour tolerates the infringement of the other, and does not seek at first to have what the other has unjustly erected demolished, but then later does seek redress, he may do this, and the muhtasib may have demolished what has been illegally constructed after having first been tolerated. If construction is commenced, and beams have been installed with the permission of the neighbour, and then the latter withdraws his permission the other neighbour is not obliged to demolish.

If the branches of a tree spread out over the house of a neighbour, the latter should seek the muhtasib's help in having the owner of the tree cut off the offending branches: but there is no punishment, as their spreading out into the other's domain is not of his making; if the roots of the tree spread beneath the ground, until they reach into the area of the neighbour, the owner of the tree does not have to uproot them, but the neighbour is not stopped from dealing with his land, even if it means cutting the roots. Likewise, if the owner of a house builds an oven in it, and its smoke molests the neighbour, then the muhtasib may not oppose him in this, and may not prevent him from doing so; likewise, if someone installs a mill, or a forge, or fuller's machinery, then he may not stop them, as people may deal with what they own as they wish, and people cannot prevent them from doing so.

If someone who has hired another acts incorrectly by either cutting his wage or increasing his work, then the muhtasib should stop the abuse and his

357

rebuke should be in proportion to the circumstances; if it is the hired person who is not fulfilling the right of the employer, by not working enough or by demanding more wages, then he should be prevented from doing so, and the muhtasib should denounce him if they both come before him to argue the case; if they are both of a different opinion and oppose each other with denials, a judge is more entitled to judge between them.

The muhtasibs are also responsible for overseeing three kinds of practitioners and artisans in the markets: those whom he must oversee to ensure that their work is up to standard and not defective, those whom he must ensure that they act in a trustworthy and not in a dishonest way, and those whose work he must inspect to ensure its quality or lack of it:

i. The first kind, in which he ensures the upholding of a standard is to do with doctors and teachers: the former, as they are dealing with people, and any negligence on their part would lead to death or sickness; the latter, by reason of the methods which they employ to bring up children, creating in them something which would be difficult to change once they become adult: thus the muhtasib should see that they have sufficient knowledge and good methods,   and he should prevent those with any deficiency or bad qualities which would lead to their causing illness in people, or corrupting of good behaviour.

ii. As for his ensuring that artisans are trustworthy and do not act dishonestly, as in the case of goldsmiths, weavers, fullers, or dyers – who might make off with people's property, he should see that only those who are trustworthy are allowed to stay; he makes those who show signs of dishonesty leave, and he makes this public, so that those who are unaware of their dishonesty are not deceived; it is also said, however, that the forces of law and order and government assistants are more qualified to investigate such persons rather than the muhtasibs, and this is more likely, as dishonesty is a form of theft.

iii. As for checking the quality or lack of it in work, this is the particular responsibility of the muhtasibs: they must denounce any bad or shoddy workmanship in general, even if there is no third party who has made a complaint to them. As for particular instances in which an artisan makes a habit of bad workmanship, or is guilty of fraudulent practice, then if someone seeks his help in the matter, he should respond by denouncing his work and taking punitive measures; if a penalty has to be paid, then he may take account of the penalty in question: if an assessment of value has to be made, the muhtasib should not get involved, as he lacks the capacity for making legal ijtihad, and a Qadi would be more entitled to investigate the matter; if there is no need for an assessment of worth, and the amount claimed is equivalent to the loss, and there is no ijtihad involved, and there is no counter claim, then the muhtasib should act by imposing the penalty and punish the wrong action, as he is responsible for establishing justice and taking punitive measures for violations of the law.

He may not fix the prices of foodstuffs or other goods for people, be it in times of low or high prices – although Malik permits this when the price of foodstuffs is high.

✳
✳   ✳

C. As for what the muhtasib may denounce with respect to those rights which are common both to Allah and to individuals, this includes, for example, stopping people from peering into their neighbours' houses; it is not necessary that someone who has a high building enclose his flat roof, but rather that he does not look down into other's houses. The dhimmis are prevented from constructing buildings higher than those of the Muslims; those who already own high buildings are allowed to stay in them, but they are prevented from looking down upon the Muslims or other dhimmis; he also makes sure that the conditions pertaining to their status with regard to wearing special clothes, to adopting a different outward form, and to their keeping silent on the subject of 'Uzayr and the Masih (Jesus), peace be upon them, are respected – and that he prevents the Muslims from insulting or injuring them, and imposes punishments on those who do this.

If there are imams of well-frequented mosques and Friday-mosques who prolong the prayer, so that weak persons are unable to follow them, and those who have things to do have to cease praying behind the imam, then the muhtasib should denounce this, just as the Messenger of Allah, may the peace and blessings of Allah be upon him, did to Mu'adh ibn Jabal when he used to prolong the prayer while leading the people, saying: "Are you a troublemaker O Mu'adh?" If the person insists on prolonging the prayer and refuses to stop he may not punish him for this, but rather he should replace him with someone who will recite shorter prayers.

If amongst the qadis there is someone who refuses to receive a litigant who comes to him and who refuses to decide between two parties if they have recourse to him, so that the ruling is suspended and the litigants suffer harm by this, then the muhtasib, if there is no valid excuse, must see to it that he fulfils the task of investigation between litigants and pronounces judgement between disputing parties: moreover, he must denounce any shortcoming, however high the rank of the Qadi in question. Ibrahim ibn Batha, the muhtasib for both sides of Baghdad, was passing the house of Abu 'Umar ibn Hammad, who at that time was the supreme judge, when he saw litigants sitting at his door, waiting for him to sit in judgement between them; the day was already well advanced, and the sun was hot; so he drew to a halt and called his assistant, saying: "Tell the supreme judge that there are litigants waiting at the door, and that the sun is up and they are suffering by waiting: either he should sit in judgement between them, or he should make his excuse known so that they may leave and return another time."

If an owner of a slave employs slaves for a task which they are unable to continue all the time, then his denouncing him and preventing him (from coercing them) is dependent on the slaves calling for his assistance, but it is only done as a reminder and admonition; if the slaves call for his assistance, he prevents the owner and takes punitive measures.

If an owner of animals employs them for tasks which they are not able to bear all the time, then the muhtasib should denounce him and prevent him from such practices, even if no one has complained to him; if the owner claims that the animals are capable of doing the task for which he is using them, then the muhtasib can investigate the case: even if the matter needs a degree of ijtihad, it is a question of customary practice, and so he can have recourse to people's habits and customs: thus it is not a legal ijtihad, but rather an ijtihad based on custom, from which the muhtasib cannot be excluded, even though he is excluded in the case of legal ijtihad.

If a slave complains to the muhtasib that his master is refusing to give him clothing and living expenses, then the muhtasib may order that they be given him, and may make sure that the master pays for them; if he complains that his master's payment for these two is not enough, the muhtasib is not to get involved, as the amount of the payment is subject to legal ijtihad, while the binding nature of the original ruling is not subject to legal ijtihad – because the amount is stipulated by a text, whereas its binding nature is not.

The muhtasib must prevent ship-owners from carrying a load which exceeds the capacity of the ship, lest it should lead to its sinking; likewise, he should stop them sailing when strong winds are blowing; if men and women are being carried, then he should also see that they are kept apart by a barrier, and if the ship is large enough, separate entrances to the lavatories should be installed for the women, lest they expose themselves when answering the call of nature.

If there is a market trader who is particularly accustomed to deal with women, the muhtasib should check his good behaviour and his trustworthiness; if he proves to have these two qualities, he is left to deal with the women, but if doubts arise, and there are clear signs of corrupt behaviour on his part, then he is stopped from dealing with them, and he is punished for getting involved with them. It has also been said that the forces of the law and the government inspectors should be the ones to denounce and prevent such behaviour, rather than the muhtasibs, as it should treated as an aspect of fornication.

The muhtasib must oversee the layout in the market, and allow people to stay where they are, as long as no harm is being done to passers-by – but he should prevent the occupation of places which causes harm to passers-by; this he may do without there being a previous complaint on the matter, although Abu Hanifah says that his action is dependent on such a complaint being made. If people erect a construction on a public highway, then they are stopped from doing so, even if the highway is broad: they should be made to demolish what they have built, even if it is a mosque, as the purpose of roadways is for travelling, and not for erecting buildings. If people put down their materials and building machinery in roadways and marketplaces temporarily, intending to move them after a while, then they may do so if no harm is caused to passers-by – but they are prevented from doing so if harm is caused to them; likewise, if there are projecting parts of a building, or arched passages, or water canals, or sewage drains: these are permitted if no harm is caused, but prohibited if harm is caused.

It is up to the muhtasib to make ijtihad as to what constitutes harm or not, as his judgement will be based on customary practice, rather than legal precedent. The difference between these two types of ijtihad is that legal ijtihad is that in which account is taken of the legal principle on which the ruling is based, whereas the ijtihad of customary practice is that whose ruling is based on what people habitually do in the circumstances: this difference will be made clear by distinguishing the cases in which the muhtasib may make ijtihad from those in which he may not make ijtihad.

It is up to the muhtasib to prevent corpses from being removed from their graves, whether owned privately or lying in common ground, unless they are taken from land which has been usurped, in which case the rightful owner may legally compel those who have buried a corpse there to transfer it elsewhere. There is a difference of opinion as to whether it is permitted to transfer corpses from land which has been flooded or subject to excessive damp: az-Zubayri permits it, while others prohibit it.

The muhtasib must prevent the castration of men and animals alike, and punish those responsible: if anyone is entitled to the right of retaliation or the blood-money, he should see that this claim is fulfilled to the satisfaction of the person entitled to it, as long as there is no dispute or counterclaim on behalf of the two parties. He must prevent older men from dyeing their hair black, unless they are making jihad in the way of Allah, and he should punish those who colour their hair for the sake of women; he should not, however, prevent the use of henna and katam dyes. He should stop any gain being made from fortune-telling and gaming, and should punish both those who receive payment and those who make it. This section could be enlarged as there are countless examples of wrongdoing: those we have mentioned will serve to illustrate those we have not.

The task of hisbah is one of the fundamental matters of the deen; the imams of the first generation would undertake it themselves, because of the general benefit involved and the great reward to be gained. When, however, the Sultan turned away from such business and appointed persons who commanded little respect, and it became a means of making money and receiving bribes, it became of little importance in people's eyes. However, just because an omission occurs in maintaining a fundamental principle, it does not mean that the ruling concerned has been annulled. The fuqaha have neglected to explain the rulings of hisbah to a degree which cannot be permitted: indeed the greater part of this book of ours treats of matters which the fuqaha have either neglected or discussed insufficiently; for this reason we have referred to what they have neglected, and we have treated in full what they have omitted. I ask Allah for success in for our purpose, and for help in what we have intended, by His favour and His wish, for He is enough for me and the Best of Guardians.

Glossary

A

'Abd al-Malik ibn Marwan: One of the fuqaha of Madinah who was later to hold the khilafah for a period during the first century of Islam. His judgements and rulings are constantly referred to by later scholars.

'Abdullah ibn 'Abbas: The cousin of the Prophet, may Allah bless him and grant him peace, and the Companion most gifted with tafseer of Qur'an; he also held office under the *Khulafa ar-Rashidun.*

'Abdullah ibn az-Zubayr: The first child born to the Muhajirun in Madinah, he later was sworn allegiance as Khalifah in the Hijaz for a short period.

Abu 'Abdallah az-Zubayri: An eminent Shafi'i scholar.

Abu Bakr as-Siddiq: The First of the *Khulafa ar-Rashidun.*

Imam Abu Hanifah: The faqih of Kufa in Iraq. Through the appointment of his main disciple Abu Yusuf as Chief Qadi of the Abbasids, his school became the dominant legal school of the khilafah, and so al-Mawardi, who was a Shafi'i, gives equal attention to Hanafi rulings.

Abu Hurairah: The Companion who was the foremost of their hadith narrators, and who was later put in authority over Bahrain.

Abu Yusuf: Chief Qadi of the Abbasids. His most famous work is *Kitabu'l-Kharaj* a subject which is also dealt with extensively in this work.

adhan: The call to prayer.

Al-Hajjaj ibn Yusuf: A general for 'Abd al-Malik ibn Marwan. He was noted for his severity and so 'Abd al-Malik placed him in authority over Iraq, which was at that time the source of every sedition and trial.

'alim plural **'ulama:** A person of knowledge, particularly of the deen.

Al-Quds: Jerusalem.

'Ali ibn Abi Talib: The fourth of the *Khulafa ar-Rashidun.* Known as the most capable in judgement of the Companions, the other Khulafa relied heavily on his expertise in this field.

amir: A commander of a province, or of an army, appointed by the Khalifah.

Amir al-Mumineen: The Commander of the Believers, i.e. the Khalifah.

amirate: The position and office of the amir.

Ansar: The "Helpers" of Madinah who took the Prophet, may Allah bless him and grant him peace, and the other emigrants from Makkah into their homes and their lives and defended him.

'Arafah: The plain on which the pilgrims stand during the central rite of the Hajj.

Imam ash-Shafi'i: A scholar who in his early years learnt from Imam Malik ibn Anas. He then travelled to Iraq and studied with Muhammad ibn al-Hasan ash-Shaybani, Imam Abu Hanifah's second main student, among others, and then on to Cairo where he met al-Layth ibn Sa'd and others.

Az-Zubayr ibn al-'Awwam: One of the ten Companions promised the Garden.

Az-Zuhri: An eminent scholar of fiqh and hadith among the generation of the Followers (people who had known the Companions).

B

Baghdad (Madinat as-Salam): With the accession of the Abbasids to the Khilafah they founded the city of Baghdad as their capital.

bait al-mal: Literally "The House of Property"; it is a term which designates the funds which the Khalifah controls. There does not have to be an actual house in which the property is kept.

Bakkah: Another name for Makkah.

booty (*anfal* or *ghaneemah*): The property of an enemy who have been beaten in fighting belongs to the Muslim warriors, once a khums (fifth) has been taken for Allah and his Messenger.

C

copper: It was used for minting coins which were known as *Flous.* Their value is symbolic as opposed to gold and silver whose values are by weight. Flous was used for small transactions less than the value of a dirham. Zakah is not paid on it even if it amounts to a very great deal, except by traders and businessmen who estimate it as a part of their stock in trade. Traders do not, however, pay their zakah with flous but must pay it in gold or silver. Flous is also the modern Arabic term for paper money, which to some extent is governed by the same fiqh ruling, i.e. when viewed as a symbolic currency rather than a real currency.

D

daniq: The weight of a sixth of a dirham.

Dar al-Harb: The "Abode of War"; it is all land where the inhabitants have not accepted Islam, nor agreed to live under Islamic governance with payment of the jizyah, nor made a peace treaty with the Muslims.

Dar al-Islam: The "Abode of Islam"; it is all land where the Muslims live and the shari'ah is enforced.

Dar ash-Shirk: The "Abode of Idol-worship"; it is synonymous with Dar al-Harb.

dead land (*mawat*): Either previously uncultivated land, or once cultivated but now abandoned land. It belongs to whoever revives it.

deen: It derives from the word for debt (*dayn*) and indicates the life-transaction of Islam with acknowledgement of the debt owed to the Creator, as well as the many social and economic debts that humans owe to each other.

dhimmah: The contract of protection made with the Christians and the Jews and all others who are judged to be People of the Book, upon their accepting to live under Islamic governance and to pay the jizyah.

dhimmi: One of the people of dhimmah.

dinar: A gold coin.

dirham: A silver coin. Its weight was established under Islam as six daniqs, and ten dirhams weighed seven mithqals.

discretionary punishment (*ta'zir*): Any punishment for an offence which is not actually covered by a hadd-punishment.

Diwan: The institution of public record keeping.

diyah: A compensatory payment for a wound, or for a killing, if the wounded person or the relatives of the dead person agree to waive retaliatory rights.

E

eclipse: There are optional prayers to be said during the eclipses of both the sun and the moon.

'Eid: The festivals to mark the conclusion of the fast of Ramadan and of the Hajj. They are celebrated with prayer and remembrance of Allah.

F

faqih (plural **fuqaha**): One who knows the science of fiqh.

fay: That gained in jihad without any fighting. It goes to Allah and His Messenger.

fiqh: Literally "understanding", it means to understand whether any matter is obligatory, recommended, permitted, frowned upon or forbidden.

G

ghaneemah: That gained by fighting the enemy. See *booty.*

ghazwah: A battle – or military expedition.

gold: One of a number of commodities that may fittingly be used as a currency due to their common acceptance by the great bulk of people throughout history. Silver, grains, pulses and cattle, for example, have also always served as currencies.

grants or concessions (*iqta'*): It is in the power of the Imam to grant property or revenues to those whom he deems worthy of them.

H

hadd (plural **hudud**) **punishments:** Literally "limits", these punishments are corporal or capital punishments for drunkenness, theft, brigandage, murder, adultery, fornication, rape and apostasy, etc. They are governed by strict rules of evidence.

hadith: A narration of an event in the life of the Prophet, may Allah bless him and grant him peace, or his words. Not to be confused with sunnah.

Hajj: The pilgrimage to Makkah.

Haram: "Sacred" or "inviolable." Makkah and Madinah are each a Haram. Not to be confused with *haraam,* from the same Arabic root, which means "forbidden."

hareem: A reserve land adjacent to cultivated land - used either as a means of access, or for the purposes of irrigation, or habitation - without which it would not be possible to work the cultivated land. Similarly, the area surrounding a spring or a well or a canal or a house, needed to gain access to them.

Hijaz: The western coastal area of the Arabian peninsula in which lie Makkah, Madinah and Ta'if.

hima: Land set aside by the Khalifah, for example, for grazing horses that have been dedicated for jihad, or camels, cattle and flocks that have been collected as zakah and not yet distributed, of for common pasturage open to all.

hisbah: The office of the man (*muhtasib*) appointed to undertake, on behalf of the Muslims, the practice of commanding the good and forbidding the evil.

I

ihlal: To become free of ihram, e.g. after the Hajj.

ihram: To enter into the condition of an act of worship such as the prayer or the Hajj which forbids certain other actions, e.g. the one praying may not eat, laugh or talk with people, and the one on Hajj must wear two plain sheets of material (also known as *ihram*), is not allowed to wear anything that is stitched, nor to hunt or to kill animals or lice, nor to wear perfume or have intercourse with his wife, etc.

ijma': Consensus, i.e. of the people of knowledge.

ijtihad: literally "struggle" – to exercise personal judgement in legal matters, particularly in the case of a faqih.

Imam: When capitalised, the word in this book is always used for the Khalifah; thus **Imamate:** the Khilafah.

imam: Without capitals, it refers to the one who leads the prayer, and thus **imamate:** the leadership of the prayer.

J

Jahiliyyah: The age of "ignorance" before the coming of Islam.

jareeb: A measure of land. It amounts to ten *qasabah* (fathoms) squared; the qasabah is six cubits. So the jareeb is 3,600 square cubits.

jihad: Struggle, particularly fighting in the way of Allah, to establish Islam.

jizyah: The annual poll-tax levied on the male adults of the People of the

Book who have come under the governance of Islam, either by treaty or through military defeat.

Jumu'ah: Friday, and particularly the prayer at noon on that day.

K

Ka'bah: The house in Makkah built by Ibrahim and Isma'il, peace be upon them, for the worship of Allah.

kafir (plurals, **kuffar** and **kafirun**): One who covers over the true nature of existence and rejects the truth.

Khalifah (plural **Khulafa**): Literally "Successor", or the one who stands in, in the absence of a king. The Khalifah stands in for the Messenger of Allah, may the peace and blessings of Allah be upon him, in his role as leader of the Muslims, thus **Khilafah**: The office of the Khalifah.

kharaj: A tax levied on land by the ijtihad of 'Umar, may Allah be pleased with him. He decided not to divide conquered lands up among the fighting men (see **booty** and **ghaneemah**), but rather to leave them to their inhabitants in return for the payment of a tax on the land.

khums: The "fifth" taken for Allah and His Messenger from the booty, after which the remains are divided among the warriors.

Khusroes (*Kisra*): A generic term for the emperor of Persia. Also a silver coin of that name which the Muslims used for a period before minting Islamic coins.

M

Madinah: City. Almost literally "the place of the deen." Most commonly used for the Madinah of the Prophet, may the peace and blessings of Allah be upon him.

Majus: Zoroastrians — they are dualists. By a known sunnah they are treated in the same manner as the People of the Book. This ruling was extended to followers of other religions, such as the Buddhists, who are not specifically named in the Book (the Qur'an) or the Sunnah.

Imam Malik ibn Anas: The imam, faqih and narrator of hadith of the city of Madinah. He taught Imam ash-Shafi'i and Muhammad ibn al-Hasan ash-Shaybani directly, as well as teaching the principle teachers of all the imams of hadith such as al-Bukhari, Muslim, at-Tirmidhi, an-Nasa'i, ibn Majah and Abu Dawud. His Muwatta is a record of the Sunnah of the Prophet, the peace and blessings of Allah be upon him, and of the Khulafa and the People of Madinah up until Malik's time.

Al-Ma'mun: Khalifah of the Abbasids. Most famously he was responsible for the translation into Arabic of the philosophical, scientific and medical works of the Greeks.

mimbar: Steps on which the imam stands to deliver the khutbah on the day of Jumu'ah.

mithqal: A weight.

mu'adhdhin: The one who calls people to the prayer with the adhan.

Mu'awiyyah ibn Abi Sufyan: The Companion of the Prophet, peace be upon him, and the Khalifah whom as-Suyuti affirmed had the longest khilafah undisturbed by divisions and dissensions.

Muhajirun: The emigrants, i.e. who emigrated from Makkah to escape persecution. The first two emigrations (*hijrah*) were to Abyssinia, and the last to Madinah.

Muhammad ibn al-Hasan (ash-Shaybani): often referred to merely as Muhammad, he is the second main pupil of Abu Hanifah. He had also studied fiqh with Malik ibn Anas for a number of years in Madinah and narrates a version of the Muwatta from him, although he added in judgements of Abu Hanifah. Along with Abu Yusuf he is held to be the real founder of the Hanafi madhhab.

Muhsan (Muhsanah, fem.): A person, male or female, who is or has been married, even if only one time and for a short period, if caught in adultery by four just witnesses or if he or she confesses, thus becomes liable for the full hadd-punishment of stoning. Otherwise men and women who are not Muhsan, if guilty of fornication, are liable only to the lesser hadd-punishment of flogging.

Muhtasib: The man charged with the office of hisbah.

mujtahid: The faqih who is qualified to make ijtihad.

mumin (plural **muminun**): A believer, someone with iman.

muqasamah: payment of the kharaj tax by means of paying a fixed proportion of the harvest, rather than monetary payment.

mushrik (plural **mushrikun**): A person who commits shirk, i.e. who associates others with Allah in worship.

Muzdalifah: A station on the Hajj. The pilgrims walk there from 'Arafah with the setting of the sun and pray the sunset and night prayers there; then, after sleeping, they pray the dawn prayer before proceeding to Mina.

N

naqeeb: Literally the chief of a tribe. Here, the head of a tribunal for settling disputes and legal matters within noble families, e.g. among the Talibun (the descendants of Abu Talib).

nisab: The minimum amount of zakatable wealth which when possessed untouched for a year requires its owner to pay the zakah on it.

O

Oaths: Oaths form a complementary role to evidence in Islamic law. If a person is accused of an offence without the evidence of sufficient witnesses of good standing, he or she may swear an oath as to his or her innocence to avert punishment. 'Umar ibn al-Khattab, may Allah be pleased with him, said: "It is up to the plaintiff to supply evidence, and it is up to the defendant to swear on oath."

Q

Qadi: The judge. He sits between contending parties and arrives at equitable decisions by means of the shari'ah.

qafeez: a measure of land of ten qasabah by one qasabah, i.e. 360 square cubits. Also a weight of eight pounds (of crops) having a value of three dirhams of the mithqal weight. It was used to assess and pay the kharaj.

qasabah: a measure of six cubits.

qiblah: The direction to which one turns oneself in prayer, i.e. for the Muslims, towards the Ka'bah in Makkah.

Quraysh: The Arabs descended from an-Nadr and thence from Isma'il ibn Ibrahim, peace be upon them.

R

rain-prayer : The prayer which is done when drought strikes. An essential part of it is self-examination and renunciation of all wrong actions.

ribat: A fortress on the frontiers of the Muslim community. Its people are Murabitun.

S

sadaqah (plural **sadaqat**): A synonym for zakah in the language of fiqh and in this book. It has come to mean a voluntary act of charity.

Sa'id ibn al-Musayyab: One of the eminent fuqaha of Madinah and a teacher of Malik ibn Anas.

salah: Prayer.

as-Sawad: The name for a huge area of agricultural land in Iraq. 'Umar ibn al-Khattab decided not to divide it among the warriors who had conquered it, but to levy the kharaj tax on it instead. It yielded enormous wealth.

shari'ah: The legal and social modality of a people based on the revelation of their Prophet. It derives from the root for a "road."

sikkah: The die with which coins were minted and thence the coins themselves.

Sultan: "Authority"; another term for Khalifah.

sunnah: The customary practice of a person or group of people. The Sunnah is the practice of the Prophet, may Allah bless him and grant him peace.

T

tafsir: Commentary and explanation of the Qur'an.

takbir: The pronunciation of Allahu Akbar (Allah is greater).

tawaf: A single circuit of the Ka'bah. It is customary to do seven tawafs at a time.

tawbah: Turning, i.e. away from shirk, kufr and disobedience to tawhid, iman and obedience.

tawhid: Affirmation of the Divine Unity.

U

'Umar ibn al-Khattab: The second of the *Khulafa ar-Rashidun,* many of whose judgements and rulings are the basis of much of the shari'ah in this book.

'Umar ibn 'Abd al-'Aziz: A Khalifah from the Umayyads who had been schooled in fiqh in Madinah, and who was responsible for a revival of much of the sunnah in his time. He also authorised the 'ulama to compile and record the sunnah for fear that it might vanish.

Ummah: The Islamic community as a global entity.

'Urwah ibn az-Zubayr: A son of az-Zubayr ibn al-'Awwam, and one of the important fuqaha of Madinah.

'ushr: A tenth. The zakah on agricultural produce is a tenth of the harvest. If it has been irrigated by human endeavour then the zakah is a twentieth.

usury (*riba*): Usury is one of the great wrong actions and is second only to shirk (associating others with Allah) in gravity. There are two types: *riba al-fadl* and *riba an-nasi'ah*. The first involves any discrepancy in quantity in an exchange of, for example, gold for gold, silver for silver, or wheat for wheat. The second, is that there should be a gap in time in the exchange of two quantities even if they match in quantity and quality. Most modern transactions involve both types of usury, e.g. interest charges from banks and building societies. The use of paper money is forbidden because it is an I.O.U. (originally for gold or silver deposited in the bank) and I.O.U's may not be traded, as they count as the usurious trade of a debt for a debt.

'Uthman ibn 'Affan: The third of the *Khulafa ar-Rashidun.*

W

waqf (plural **awqaf**)**:** An endowment of money or property that yields an income dedicated to a certain end, e.g. to the maintenance of very poor people, or of a specific family, or of seekers of knowledge. It is permitted to bequeath up to a third of one's property in this way. Someone may be appointed to administer the waqf and may have a salary for doing so. It was the ijtihad of 'Umar ibn al-Khattab that made the lands conquered in his age a permanent waqf for the benefit of the Muslims.

wazirs: A minister, either delegatory or executive. It must be noted that once wazirate had become institutionalised, it produced wazirs with more effective power than that of the khulafa whose power became largely titular. The Abbasid Harun ar-Rashid grasped what had happened, and in a very famous instance destroyed the houses of the Barmecides, whose power was destabilising the khilafah itself.

Z

zakah: The third pillar of Islam which is almost invariably paired in the Qur'an with the salah. As is evident from this work, the Khalifah must appoint assessors who both collect the zakah and distribute it. It is not a voluntary charity.

Index

D

daniq 117, 122, 176, 222-3

Dar al-'Ahd 202

Dar al-Harb 6, 60, 76, 85-7, 94, 199, 201-3, 205, 206, 209, 212, 272, 295

Dar al-Islam 6, 8, 77, 85-7, 91, 94, 201-3, 208-9, 212, 272, 295, 342, 345

Dar ash-Shirk 342

dates 32, 79-80, 88, 91, 122, 173, 201, 216, 243, 247, 250, 257, 260, 264, 274, 321, 344, 351-2

dead land (*mawat*) 220, 252-5, 259, 262-7, 270-2, 281

deen 5, 7-8, 10, 27-9, 34, 38, 48, 51, 53-4, 57, 59-60, 63, 66, 68-70, 73-5, 83, 99-100, 117, 127-128, 142, 145, 153, 206-9, 211-12, 234, 240, 286, 290, 309, 326, 338, 342, 349, 362

dhimmah 44, 201

dhimmi 28, 44, 91, 172, 176, 178, 183, 191, 200, 202, 204, 208, 211-2, 214-5, 239-240, 243, 246, 264, 272, 288, 294, 351, 359

dinar 111, 121, 172, 177, 181, 210, 224, 244, 246, 264, 286, 288, 319-20, 327, 353, 355

dirham 71, 111, 122, 124-5, 137, 176-7, 181, 196, 210, 215-7, 221-5, 243, 245, 248-9, 251, 255, 264, 273-4, 282, 284-5, 287, 319, 328, 339, 344, 355

discretionary punishment 86, 89, 93, 96, 133, 145, 161, 166, 179, 225, 239-41, 251, 309, 311-2, 314, 318, 323-4, 328, 332-6, 338, 346, 348, 352

diwan 9, 58, 121-5, 145, 211, 215, 220, 274, 276, 279, 282-4, 286-95, 298, 304-8

diyah 326, 328-31, 335-6

E

eclipse 156-8, 237

'Eid 52, 110, 125, 150, 156-8, 342

F

faqih, pl. fuqaha 7, 10, 13-7, 24-5, 27, 33, 38, 51, 65, 84, 93, 100, 102, 120, 131-3, 140, 142, 150, 152-5, 157, 165, 167, 170, 172-3, 176-7, 191-2, 200, 209, 220, 223-5, 235, 238-9, 241, 246, 248, 256, 260, 268-9, 271, 274, 277, 284, 291-2, 294, 298-9, 301, 304-5, 311, 313, 315, 319, 325, 338, 343, 349, 351, 353-4, 362

fay 28, 58, 76-7, 84-5, 87-8, 91, 146, 182, 186-92, 204, 207, 210, 217-8, 241-3, 246, 248, 274-9, 302

fiqh 153

G

ghaneemah 186, 192, 203-4, 302
ghazwah 205
gold 5, 116, 120-1, 125-6, 168, 176-7, 181, 223-4, 232-3, 280, 320, 327-8, 358
grants 8, 53, 270, 274, 276, 288

H

hadd-punishments 28, 48, 51, 54, 68, 81-2, 89, 93-7, 108-10, 144, 146, 161, 166-7, 212, 239, 309-18, 321-5, 332-6, 338, 352-3
hadith 5, 12, 99, 101, 179, 225, 241, 247, 268, 305, 322, 349-50
Hajj 8, 48, 52, 84, 88, 125, 139, 160-7, 229-30, 235, 238, 245, 314, 351
Haram 227-8, 230, 233-4, 236-41, 246, 328
hareem 252, 254-5, 259-62, 265, 267, 357
Harun ar-Rashid 221
hashimiyyah 221-2, 247
Hijaz 154, 206, 227, 240-1, 243, 246
Hijrah 188, 206, 235, 245, 285
hima 8, 263
hiqqah 170
hisbah 6, 9, 337-41, 347, 350, 352-3, 356, 362

I

Ibn 'Abbas 21-2, 32, 72-3, 93-4, 178, 204, 231-2, 251
ibn laboun 169
ibnat laboun 169, 170
Ibrahim an-Nakha'i 93, 228, 319, 349
ihlal 165, 167, 229, 238-9
ihram 157, 161-7, 229, 238-9
ijma' 101
ijtihad 12, 14, 37, 51, 100-4, 107, 110, 112-3, 118-20, 134-5, 147, 152, 157, 161, 172-3, 180, 186, 191, 193, 207, 210, 213, 220, 251, 269, 294-6, 302, 307, 310, 338-9, 342-3, 346, 349, 352, 359-61
'Ikrimah ibn Abi Jahl 195, 206
Imam (Khalifah) 10-2, 14, 16, 18-20, 22, 26-7, 29-35, 37, 41-2, 48, 53, 78, 87-90, 93-5, 99, 115, 121-2, 128, 165, 169, 172, 178, 184, 187-90, 192-4, 197, 201, 203-5, 210-1, 213-4, 217-8, 241, 251-2, 270-3, 275, 279, 302-3, 310, 317
imams (of salah) 150-7, 159, 163-4, 166-7, 268, 347, 359
Imamate (Khilafah) 8, 10, 48, 117, 120, 142, 150
imamate (of prayer) 8, 10-20, 22-3, 29-37, 41, 54, 100, 110, 150-4, 156

Z

Notes

Notes

Notes